Topic relevant selected content from the highest rated entries, typeset, printed and shipped.

Combine the advantages of up-to-date and in-depth knowledge with the convenience of printed books.

A portion of the proceeds of each book will be donated to the Wikimedia Foundation to support their mission: to empower and engage people around the world to collect and develop educational content under a free license or in the public domain, and to disseminate it effectively and globally.

The content within this book was generated collaboratively by volunteers. Please be advised that nothing found here has necessarily been reviewed by people with the expertise required to provide you with complete, accurate or reliable information. Some information in this book maybe misleading or simply wrong. The publisher does not guarantee the validity of the information found here. If you need specific advice (for example, medical, legal, financial, or risk management) please seek a professional who is licensed or knowledgeable in that area.

Sources, licenses and contributors of the articles and images are listed in the section entitled "References". Parts of the books may be licensed under the GNU Free Documentation License. A copy of this license is included in the section entitled "GNU Free Documentation License"

All used third-party trademarks belong to their respective owners.

Contents

Articles

Nathan Fillion	1
Saving Private Ryan	6
Blast from the Past (film)	16
Dracula 2000	19
Outing Riley	23
Serenity (film)	25
Slither (2006 film)	39
Trucker (film)	44
Waitress (film)	46
White Noise: The Light	49
Super (2010 American film)	51
Much Ado About Nothing (2012 film)	57
Two Guys and a Girl	59
Star Crossed (The Outer Limits)	68
Firefly (TV series)	70
Buffy the Vampire Slayer (TV series)	90
Miss Match	109
I Do (Lost)	112
Drive (TV series)	116
Robot Chicken	121
List of *Desperate Housewives* characters	126
Dr. Horrible's Sing-Along Blog	146
James Gunn's PG Porn	156
Wonder Woman (film)	159
Castle (TV series)	165
Green Lantern: Emerald Knights	171

References

Article Sources and Contributors	175
Image Sources, Licenses and Contributors	180

Article Licenses

License	181

Nathan Fillion

Nathan Fillion	
Born	March 27, 1971 Edmonton, Alberta, Canada
Occupation	Actor
Years active	1993–present

Fillion at the 2005 premiere of *Serenity*

Nathan Fillion (pronounced /ˈfɪljən/, as in *million*, born March 27, 1971) is a Canadian actor, currently starring as Richard Castle on the ABC series *Castle*. He is also known for his portrayal of the lead role of Captain Malcolm Reynolds in the television series *Firefly* and its feature film continuation, *Serenity*.

He has acted in traditionally distributed films like *Slither* and *Trucker*, Internet-distributed films like *Dr. Horrible's Sing-Along Blog*, voice-over work like the video games *Halo 3: ODST* and *Halo: Reach*, television soap operas and sitcoms, and in the theatre.

Early life

Fillion was born in Edmonton, Alberta, the younger son of Cookie and Bob Fillion, both of whom are retired English teachers.[1] He has an older brother, Jeff,[2] and attended Holy Trinity Catholic High School, Concordia University College of Alberta, and the University of Alberta, where he was a member of the Kappa Alpha Society. According to Fillion, he is descended from Confederate Lieutenant General Jubal Anderson Early.[3]

Career

1994-2009

After working in several theatre, television and film productions, including Theatresports with Rapid Fire Theatre and the improvised soap opera *Die-Nasty*, Fillion moved to New York City in 1994 where he acted in the soap opera *One Life to Live* as Joey Buchanan, for which he was nominated in 1996 for a Daytime Emmy Award for Outstanding Younger Actor in a Drama Series. In 1997, he left the series to pursue other projects (but would return for a brief guest appearance in 2007).[4]

After moving to Los Angeles, he played a supporting role in the sitcom *Two Guys, a Girl, and a Pizza Place*, and was cast as James Frederick "The Minnesota" Ryan in Steven Spielberg's *Saving Private Ryan*. Fillion had a recurring role as Caleb in the final season of Joss Whedon's series *Buffy the Vampire Slayer* and auditioned for the role of Angel in early 1996.

In 2002, Fillion starred as Captain Malcolm Reynolds in the Joss Whedon science fiction television series *Firefly*, for which he won the 'Cinescape Genre Face of the Future — Male' award by the Academy of Science Fiction, Fantasy & Horror Films, USA. Fillion also won the Syfy Genre Awards in 2006 for 'Best Actor/Television' and was runner-up for 'Best Actor/Movie'.[5] Fillion has claimed his time on *Firefly* to be the best acting job he ever had.[6] Although the show was cancelled, it was adapted to the big screen; he reprised his role as Mal in Whedon's movie *Serenity* (2005).

Fillion lent his voice to the animated series *King of the Hill* in 2001, the video game *Jade Empire* (as the voice of Gao the Lesser), and the animated series *Justice League Unlimited* (as Vigilante in the episodes "Hunter's Moon" and "Patriot Act") in 2005 and 2006. Fillion starred in James Gunn's 2006 horror film *Slither*. For his starring role as Bill Pardy, he garnered a 2006 *Fangoria* Chainsaw Awards nomination in the category of *Dude You Don't Wanna Mess With*.[7]

Fillion starred in the romantic comedy film *Waitress*, written and directed by the late Adrienne Shelly, which premiered at the Sundance Film Festival January 21, 2007 and opened in theaters on May 2, 2007. According to Box Office Mojo, *Waitress* grossed $22,125,001 in worldwide sales as of May 13, 2008, and $29.22 million in rentals as of January 28, 2008.[8] [9] Fillion starred in *White Noise 2: The Light*. He made one appearance in the 2006–2007 season of the television show *Lost*, as Kevin, Kate's ex-husband.

In October 2006, Fillion signed a talent holding contract with the Fox Broadcasting Company, and in December 2006, *The Hollywood Reporter*[10] confirmed that Fillion was cast as Alex Tully in the series *Drive*, which debuted on Fox in the spring of 2007. *Drive* was created by Fillion's longtime friend and former *Angel* and *Firefly* writer Tim Minear. Ivan Sergei played Alex Tully in the original pilot episode of *Drive*. The first two *Drive* episodes premiered on April 13, 2007 in Canada (April 15, 2007 in the United States). However, the show did not deliver the ratings Fox desired, and on April 25, 2007, the network announced that the series was cancelled.[11] [12] The final two produced episodes were supposed to air back-to-back on Fox in July 2007, but did not actually become available until July 15 when they were posted on the *Drive* MySpace page.[13]

He reprised his 1990s role as *One Life to Live*'s Joey for the series' 9,999th and 10,000th episodes, aired August 16, 2007 and August 17, 2007.[14] [15] [16]

Fillion joined the cast of ABC's *Desperate Housewives* at the beginning of the Fall 2007 season as Dr. Adam Mayfair. His first appearance was in the episode "Now You Know", which aired on September 30, 2007.

He voiced the role of a Marine Sergeant in the Xbox 360 game *Halo 3*, alongside fellow *Firefly* stars Alan Tudyk and Adam Baldwin. At one point early in the first mission, he identifies himself as "[Sergeant] Reynolds" over the radio, referring to his character's name from the TV series *Firefly*. All three actors are given personalities in the game that match those of their characters from *Firefly*. He provides the voice and portrayed likeness for Gunnery Sergeant Edward Buck in the *Halo 3* expansion, *Halo 3: ODST*,[17] a role he briefly reprised in *Halo: Reach*.

2009-present

In March 2009, the first episode of the ABC television series *Castle* aired, in which Fillion stars as the title character Richard Castle, a mystery novelist who helps the NYPD solve crimes. In May 2009, ABC green-lit the production of the series for a second season.[18] In 2009, Fillion was nominated for Satellite Award for Best Actor – Television Series Drama for his performance in *Castle*. On March 30, 2010, ABC announced that *Castle* had been renewed for its third season with a 22-episode full-season order.[19] ABC is promoting the series by releasing the Richard Castle novels *Heat Wave* (Hard Back ISBN 978-1-4013-2382-0, Paperback ISBN 9781401310400) and *Naked Heat* (Hard Back ISBN 978-1-4013-2402-5; Paperback ISBN 9780786891368) online and worldwide in hardback and in paperback.[20] *Castle* was renewed for a fourth season on January 10, 2011.[21]

Fillion was featured in a spoof porn web video on Spike called "Nailing Your Wife", part of the *PG Porn* series.[22]

In late September 2011, Fillion guest starred as the Action Sports 1 anchor in the comedy web series *Husbands*.[23]

He will be playing Dogberry in the upcoming independent film *Much Ado About Nothing*, based on the Shakespeare play of the same name, written and produced by Joss Whedon.[24] [25]

Charity work

Fillion co-founded the non-profit organization Kids Need to Read with author PJ Haarsma in 2007 to help inspire kids' imaginations by getting more books into underfunded libraries.[26] While speaking at schools around the country, Haarsma discovered that many libraries cannot afford to purchase new books and children pleaded with him to get a copy of his book.

Filmography

Film

Year	Title	Role	Notes
1994	*Strange and Rich*	Walter Hoade	
1998	*Saving Private Ryan*	Pvt. James Frederick 'Minnesota' Ryan	
1999	*Blast from the Past*	Cliff	
2000	*Dracula 2000*	Father David	
2003	*Water's Edge*	Robert Graves	
2004	*Outing Riley*	Luke Riley	
2005	*Serenity*	Malcolm Reynolds	
2006	*Slither*	Bill Pardy	
2007	*White Noise: The Light*	Abe Dale	
2007	*Waitress*	Dr. Jim Pomatter	
2008	*Trucker*	Runner	
2010	*SUPER*	The Holy Avenger	
2012	*Much Ado About Nothing*	Dogberry	Post-production

Television

Year	Title	Role	Notes
1993	*Ordeal in the Arctic*	Master Warrant Officer Tom Jardine	TV movie
1996	*Spin City*	Guy (uncredited)	Episode: "A Star Is Born"
1997	*Total Security*	Troy Larson	Episode: "Das Bootie"
1998	*Maggie Winters*	Ronald	Episode: "Mama's Got a Brand New Bag"
1998-2001	*Two Guys and a Girl*	Johnny Donnelly	60 episodes
1999	*The Outer Limits*	Michael Ryan	Episode: "Star Crossed"
2001	*King of the Hill*	Frisbee Guy (voice)	Episode: "Luanne Virgin 2.0"
2002	*Pasadena*	Rev. Glenn Collins	3 episodes

2002-2003	*Firefly*	Malcolm 'Mal' Reynolds	14 episodes
2003	*Alligator Point*	Bill	TV movie
2003	*Buffy the Vampire Slayer*	Caleb	5 episodes
2003	*Miss Match*	Adam Logan	6 episodes
2004	*Hollywood Division*	Det. Tommy Garrett	TV movie
2005	*Justice League*	Various (voice)	Episode: "Hunter's Moon"
2006	*Justice League*	Various (voice)	Episode: "Patriot Act"
2006	*Lost*	Kevin Callis	Episode: "I Do"
2007	*Drive*	Alex Tully	6 episodes
2007	*One Life to Live*	Joey Buchanan	TV series
2007	*Robot Chicken*	Various (voice)	Episode: "Losin' the Wobble"
2007-2008	*Desperate Housewives*	Dr. Adam Mayfair	11 episodes
2008	*Dr. Horrible's Sing-Along Blog*	Captain Hammer	TV miniseries
2008	*James Gunn's PG Porn*	Chris	Episode: "Nailing Your Wife"
2009	*Wonder Woman*	Steve Trevor (voice)	Video
2009	*Robot Chicken*	Various (voice)	Episode: "We Are a Humble Factory"
2009-present	*Castle*	Richard Castle	Main character
2010	*The Venture Bros.*	Brown Widow (voice)	Episode: "Bright Lights, Dean City"
2011	*Green Lantern: Emerald Knights*	Hal Jordan (voice)	Video
2011	*The Morning After*		Episode: "1.173"
2011	*Robot Chicken*	Various	Episode: "Some Like It Hitman"
2012	*Justice League: Doom*	Hal Jordan (voice)	Video, completed

Video games

Year	Title	Role
2005	*Jade Empire*	Gao the Lesser (voice)
2007	*Halo 3*	Sergeants (voice)
2009	*Halo 3: ODST*	Buck (voice)
2010	*Halo: Reach*	Gunnery Sgt. Buck (voice)

References

[1] "Serenity star was 'a geeky kid'" (http://www.canada.com/edmontonjournal/news/cityplus/story.html?id=a995c60a-4eba-425e-bc46-8ff015781340&k=35179). Canada.com. 2005-12-30. . Retrieved 2010-08-04.

[2] "Nathan Fillion Biography — Yahoo! Movies" (http://movies.yahoo.com/movie/contributor/1804371996/bio). Movies.yahoo.com. 1971-03-27. . Retrieved 2010-08-04.

[3] "Hour long Podcast interview with Nathan Fillion June 2008 Nathan talks about Early, Firefly, Serenity, Dr. Horrible, Casle pilot filming...just about everything. Recently he announced that he is an avid reader of Popular Science and Dwell magazines" (http://jimmyaquino.typepad.com/comicnewsinsider/2008/06/cni-one-shot-na.html). Jimmyaquino.typepad.com. 2008-06-14. . Retrieved 2010-08-04.

[4] Rancilio, Alicia (March 16, 2009). "Nathan Fillion proud of his soap opera roots" (http://news.yahoo.com/s/ap/20090316/ap_en_tv/tv_people_nathan_fillion_4). *Yahoo! News*. Associated Press. .

[5] "Syfy Portal Awards" (http://web.archive.org/web/20061107100529/http://www.syfyportal.com/news.php?id=2895). Archived from the original (http://syfyportal.com/news.php?id=2895) on 2006-11-07. . Retrieved 2006-10-08.
[6] Fillion, Nathan. *Here's How It Was: The Making of Firefly* (Firefly: The Complete Series (DVD)).
[7] "Nathan Fillion nominated at Fango Chainsaw Awards 2006" (http://www.whedon.info/article.php3?id_article=17655). *Fangoria*. August 28, 2006. . Retrieved 2008-05-13.
[8] "'Waitress': Summary" (http://www.boxofficemojo.com/movies/?page=main&id=waitress.htm). *Box Office Mojo*. . Retrieved 2008-05-13.
[9] "'Waitress': DVD/Home Video" (http://www.boxofficemojo.com/movies/?page=homevideo&id=waitress.htm). *Box Office Mojo*. . Retrieved 2008-05-13.
[10] Andreeva, Nellie (2006-12-15). "'Drive' time for Fillion at Fox" (http://www.hollywoodreporter.com/hr/content_display/television/news/e3i0123c6f82e9d75a960daf0920816a410). *The Hollywood Reporter*. .
[11] Schneider, Michael (April 25, 2007). "*Drive* runs out of gas" (http://www.variety.com/article/VR1117963779.html?categoryid=14&cs=1). *Variety*. . Retrieved 2008-05-13.
[12] Ausiello, Michael (April 25, 2007). "Fox cancels *Drive*" (http://community.tvguide.com/blog-entry/TVGuide-Editors-Blog/Ausiello-Report/Exclusive-Fox-Cancels/800013604#comments). *TV Guide*. . Retrieved 2008-05-13.
[13] Posted on July 16, 2007 (2007-07-16). "5.0" (http://www.timminear.net/archives/drive/000147.html). Timminear.net. . Retrieved 2010-08-04.
[14] "Fillion back to *OLTL*", *Soap Opera Digest*, Vol. 32, No. 31, July 31, 2007, page 5.
[15] "*One Life to Live* recap (8/16/07)" (http://web.archive.org/web/20080423053654/http://abc.go.com/daytime/onelifetolive/episodes/2007/20070816.html). ABC.com (Internet Archive). August 16, 2007. Archived from the original (http://abc.go.com/daytime/onelifetolive/episodes/2007/20070816.html) on 2008-04-23. . Retrieved April 23, 2008.
[16] "*One Life to Live* recap (8/17/07)" (http://web.archive.org/web/20080423053649/http://abc.go.com/daytime/onelifetolive/episodes/2007/20070817.html). ABC.com (Internet Archive). August 17, 2007. Archived from the original (http://abc.go.com/daytime/onelifetolive/episodes/2007/20070817.html) on 2008-04-23. . Retrieved April 23, 2008.
[17] Robinson, Andy (2008-11-17). "Halo 3 Recon goes open-world" (http://www.computerandvideogames.com/article.php?id=201842). Computer and Video Games. . Retrieved 2008-12-05.
[18] Littleton, Cynthia (May 15, 2009). "ABC's pilot pickup spree" (http://www.variety.com/article/VR1118003771.html?categoryid=14&cs=1). *Variety*. .
[19] "Castle Renewed for Third Season" (http://www.tvguide.com/News/Castle-Renewed-Season-1016784.aspx). *tvguide.com*. March 30, 2010. . Retrieved March 30, 2010.
[20] "Richard Castle novel 'Heat Wave'" (http://castletv.net/pre-order-heat-wave-novel). Castletv.net. . Retrieved 2010-08-04.
[21] "'Modern Family', 'Grey's Anatomy', 'Castle', get early pickups; so do 3 other shows" (http://blog.zap2it.com/frominsidethebox/2011/01/modern-family-greys-anatomy-castle-get-early-pickups-so-do-3-other-shows.html). Zap2It. . Retrieved January 10, 2011.
[22] "Nailing Your Wife" (http://www.spike.com/video/pg-porn-pg-porn/3041858). Spike.com. . Retrieved 2010-08-04.
[23] "HUSBANDS 3: Being Britney!" (http://blip.tv/husbands-the-series/husbands-3-being-britney-5570984). Blip. . Retrieved September 20, 2011.
[24] "MUCH ADO ABOUT NOTHING" (http://muchadothemovie.com/documents/MuchAdoPressRelease.pdf). MuchAdoTheMovie.com. . Retrieved November 6, 2011.
[25] "Joss Whedon on his secret film of 'Much Ado About Nothing': 'This is the best vacation I've ever taken' -- EXCLUSIVE" (http://insidemovies.ew.com/2011/10/24/joss-whedon-sean-maher-amy-acker-much-ado-exclusive). Ew.com. . Retrieved November 6, 2011.
[26] Horn, Steven (2007-08-16). "Nathan Fillion Interviews PJ Haarsma" (http://comics.ign.com/articles/813/813133p1.html). Comics.ign.com. . Retrieved 2010-08-04.

External links

- Nathan Fillion (http://www.imdb.com/name/nm0277213/) at the Internet Movie Database

Saving Private Ryan

Saving Private Ryan	
Theatrical release poster	
Directed by	Steven Spielberg
Produced by	Ian Bryce Mark Gordon Gary Levinsohn Steven Spielberg
Written by	Robert Rodat
Starring	Tom Hanks Edward Burns Matt Damon Tom Sizemore
Music by	John Williams
Cinematography	Janusz Kamiński
Editing by	Michael Kahn
Studio	Amblin Entertainment DreamWorks Mark Gordon Productions Mutual Film Company Paramount Pictures
Distributed by	DreamWorks Paramount Pictures
Release date(s)	July 24, 1998
Running time	169 minutes
Country	United States
Language	English
Budget	$70 million[1]
Box office	$481,840,909[2]

Saving Private Ryan is a 1998 American war film set during the invasion of Normandy in World War II. It was directed by Steven Spielberg, written by Robert Rodat. The film is notable for the intensity of its opening 27 minutes, which depicts the Omaha Beach assault of June 6, 1944. Afterwards, it follows Tom Hanks as U.S. Army Captain John H. Miller and seven men (Tom Sizemore, Edward Burns, Barry Pepper, Vin Diesel, Giovanni Ribisi, Adam Goldberg, and Jeremy Davies), as they search for a paratrooper, Private First Class James Francis Ryan (Matt Damon), who is the last surviving brother of four servicemen.

Rodat conceived the film's story in 1994 when he saw a monument dedicated to eight siblings killed in the American Civil War. Rodat imagined a similar sibling narrative set in World War II. The script was submitted to producer Mark Gordon, who handed it to Hanks. It was finally given to Spielberg, who decided to direct. The film's premise is loosely based on the real-life case of the Niland brothers.

Saving Private Ryan was well received by audiences and garnered considerable critical acclaim, winning several awards for film, cast, and crew as well as earning significant returns at the box office. The film grossed US$481.8

million worldwide, making it the highest-grossing domestic film of the year. The Academy of Motion Picture Arts and Sciences nominated the film for eleven Academy Awards; Spielberg's direction won him a second Academy Award for Best Director. *Saving Private Ryan* was released on home video in May 1999, earning $44 million from sales.

Plot

The film opens as an elderly World War II veteran and his family visit the Normandy American Cemetery and Memorial at Colleville-sur-mer, Normandy, France. The scene cuts to the morning of June 6, 1944, the beginning of the Normandy invasion, as American soldiers prepare to land on Omaha Beach. They struggle against dug-in German infantry, machine gun nests, and artillery fire, which cut down many of the men. Captain John H. Miller, the company commander of Charlie Company, 2nd Ranger Battalion, survives the initial landing and assembles a group of soldiers to penetrate the German defenses, leading to a breakout from the beach.

The scene then shifts to the United States where General George Marshall is informed that three of four brothers in the Ryan family have all died within days of each other and that their mother will receive all three notices on the same day. He learns that the fourth son, Private First Class James Francis Ryan of Baker Company, 506th Parachute Infantry Regiment, 101st Airborne Division is missing in action somewhere in Normandy. After reading to his staff Abraham Lincoln's letter to Mrs. Bixby, Marshall orders that Ryan be found and sent home immediately because of the Sole Survivor Policy.

Back in France, three days after D-Day, Miller receives orders to find Ryan. He assembles six men from his company (Horvath, Mellish, Reiben, Jackson, Wade, and Caparzo), plus one detailed from the 29th Infantry Division (Upham), a clerk who speaks fluent French and German, to accomplish the task. With no information about Ryan's whereabouts, Miller and his men move out to Neuville. On the outskirts of Neuville they meet a platoon from the 101st. After entering the town, Caparzo is wounded by a sniper in the chest, and slowly bleeds to death, since nobody can go out into the open without getting hit. Jackson is able to kill the sniper after Caparzo dies. They locate a Private James Frederick Ryan from Minnesota, but soon realize that he's not their man. They find a member of Charlie Company, 506th, who informs them that his drop zone was at Vierville and that Baker and Charlie companies had the same rally point. Once they reach it, Miller locates a friend of Ryan's, who reveals that Ryan is defending a strategically important bridge over the Merderet River in the town of Ramelle.

On the way to Ramelle, Miller decides to take the opportunity to neutralize a small German machine gun position close to an abandoned radar station, despite the misgivings of his men. Wade, their medic, is fatally wounded in the ensuing skirmish. The last surviving German, known only as "Steamboat Willie", incurs the wrath of all the squad members except Upham, who protests to Miller about letting the squad shoot the German soldier. The German pleads for his life and Miller decides to let him walk away, blindfolded, and surrender himself to the next Allied patrol. Viewing Miller's decision as letting the enemy go free, and no longer confident in Miller's leadership, Reiben declares his intention to desert the squad and the mission, prompting a confrontation with Horvath. The argument heats up, until Miller defuses the situation by revealing his pre-war occupation as an English teacher, a question upon which the squad had set up a betting pool. Reiben then reluctantly decides to stay.

The squad finally arrives on the outskirts of Ramelle, where they come upon three paratroopers ambushing a German half-track. Among the paratroopers is Ryan. After entering Ramelle, Ryan is told of his brothers' deaths, and their mission to bring him home, and that two lives had been lost in the quest to find him. He is distressed at the loss of his brothers, but does not feel it is fair to go home, asking Miller to tell his mother "when you found me I was here, and I was with the only brothers I have left," looking at the small band whose duty it was to defend a bridge and destroy an approaching German mechanized unit. Miller decides to take command and defend the bridge with what little manpower and resources are available.

The Germans arrive in force with more than 50 men supported by armor. In spite of inflicting heavy German casualties and even destroying two tanks with stiky bombs, most of the men—including Jackson, Mellish, and

Horvath—are killed. While attempting to blow the bridge, Miller is shot and mortally wounded. Just before a Tiger I reaches the bridge, an American P-51 Mustang flies over and destroys it, followed by more Mustangs and advancing American infantry and M4 Sherman tanks who rout the remaining Germans. Upham, who was cut off from the Americans and hid in a ditch positioned next to German soldiers, executes "Steamboat Willie" upon finding him with a group of surrendering Germans and after witnessing him being the one who shot Miller. Ryan, Reiben, and Upham are the only survivors of the battle. Ryan is with Miller as he dies and says his last words, "James... earn this. Earn it."

Back in the present, the elderly veteran is revealed to be Ryan at Miller's grave. He asks his wife to confirm that he has led a good life and that he is a "good man" and thus worthy of the sacrifice of Miller and the others. He then salutes Miller's grave as the camera pans down the gravestones to a placid American flag.

Cast

- Tom Hanks as Captain John H. Miller
- Tom Sizemore as Technical Sergeant Mike Horvath
- Edward Burns as Private First Class Richard Reiben, an automatic rifleman
- Barry Pepper as Private Daniel Jackson, a marksman
- Adam Goldberg as Private Stanley "Fish" Mellish, a rifleman
- Vin Diesel as Private First Class Adrian Caparzo, a rifleman
- Giovanni Ribisi as Technician Fourth Grade Irwin Wade, a medic
- Jeremy Davies as Technician Fifth Grade Timothy E. Upham, a cartographer
- Matt Damon as Private First Class James Francis Ryan, a paratrooper
- Ted Danson as Captain Fred Hamill, a pathfinder
- Paul Giamatti as Staff Sergeant William Hill, a paratrooper
- Dennis Farina as Lieutenant Colonel Walter Anderson
- Harrison Young as James Francis Ryan, present day
- Harve Presnell as General George C. Marshall, Chief of Staff of the United States Army
- Leland Orser as Second Lieutenant DeWindt, pilot of a crashed glider
- Bryan Cranston as Colonel I. W. Bryce, an officer at the War Department
- Dale Dye as an officer at the War Department.
- Nathan Fillion as Private James Frederick Ryan
- Max Martini as Corporal Fred Henderson, ranking NCO paratrooper at Ramelle
- Demetri Goritsas as Private Parker, a paratrooper

Production

Development

In 1994, Robert Rodat saw a monument in Putney Corners, New Hampshire, memorializing those who had died fighting from the Civil War to Vietnam. He noticed the names of eight siblings who died during the American Civil War. Inspired by the story, Rodat did some research and decided to write a similar story set in World War II. Rodat's script was submitted to producer Mark Gordon, who liked the story but only accepted the text after 11 redrafts. Gordon shared the finished script with Hanks, who liked it and in turn passed it along to Spielberg to direct. A shooting date was set for June 27, 1997.[3] Before filming began, several of the film's stars, including Edward Burns, Barry Pepper, Vin Diesel, Adam Goldberg, Giovanni Ribisi, and Tom Hanks, endured ten days of "boot camp" training and work on the film set to prepare for their roles. Matt Damon was not brought into the camp intentionally, to make the rest of the group feel resentment towards the character.[4]

Spielberg had already demonstrated his interest in World War II themes with the films *1941*, *Empire of the Sun*, *Schindler's List*, and the *Indiana Jones* series. Spielberg later co-produced the World War II themed television miniseries *Band of Brothers* and its counterpart *The Pacific* with Tom Hanks. When asked about this by *American Cinematographer*, Spielberg said, "I think that World War II is the most significant event of the last 100 years; the fate of the Baby Boomers and even Generation X was linked to the outcome. Beyond that, I've just always been interested in World War II. My earliest films, which I made when I was about 14 years old, were combat pictures that were set both on the ground and in the air. For years now, I've been looking for the right World War II story to shoot, and when Robert Rodat wrote *Saving Private Ryan*, I found it."[5]

The D-Day scenes were shot in Ballinesker Beach, Curracloe Strand, Ballinesker, just east of Curracloe, Wexford, Ireland.[6] [7] [8] Filming began June 27, 1997, and lasted for two months.[9] [10] [11] Some shooting was done in Normandy, for the Normandy American Cemetery and Memorial in Colleville-sur-Mer and Calvados. Other scenes were filmed in English locations such as a former British Aerospace factory in Hatfield, Hertfordshire, London, Thame Park, Oxfordshire, and Wiltshire. Production was due to also take place in Seaham, County Durham, but government restrictions disallowed this.[12]

Portraying history

Saving Private Ryan has been critically noted for its realistic portrayal of World War II combat. In particular, the sequence depicting the Omaha landings was voted the "best battle scene of all time" by *Empire* magazine and was ranked number one on *TV Guide's* list of the "50 Greatest Movie Moments".[13] The scene cost US$12 million and involved up to 1,500 extras, some of whom were members of the Irish Reserve Defence Forces. Members of local reenactment groups such as the Second Battle Group were cast as extras to play German soldiers.[14] In addition, twenty to thirty actual amputees were used to portray US soldiers maimed during the landing.[15] Spielberg did not storyboard the sequence, as he wanted spontaneous reactions and for "the action to inspire me as to where to put the camera".[16]

The historical representation of Charlie Company's actions, led by its commander, Captain Ralph E. Goranson, was well maintained in the opening sequence. The sequence and details of the events are very close to the historical record, including the seasickness experienced by many of the soldiers as the landing craft moved toward the shoreline, significant casualties among the men as they disembarked from the boats, and difficulty linking up with adjacent units on the shore. The contextual details of the Company's actions were well maintained, for instance, the correct code names for the sector Charlie Company assaulted, and adjacent sectors were used. Included in the cinematic depiction of the landing was a follow on mission of clearing a bunker and trench system at the top of the cliffs which was not part of the original mission objectives for Charlie Company, but which they did undertake after climbing the cliffs at Pointe du Hoc.[17]

The landing craft used included twelve actual World War II examples, 10 LCVPs and 2 LCMs, standing in for the British LCAs that the Ranger Companies rode in to the beach during Operation Overlord.[17] [18] The film-makers used underwater cameras to better depict soldiers being hit by bullets in the water. Forty barrels of fake blood were used to simulate the effect of blood in the seawater.[15] This degree of realism was more difficult to achieve when depicting World War II German armored vehicles, as few examples survive in operating condition. The Tiger I tanks in the film were copies built on the chassis of old, but functional Soviet T-34 tanks.[19] The two vehicles described in the film as Panzers were meant to portray Marder III tank destroyers. One was created for the film using the chassis of a Czech-built Panzer 38(t) tank[20] similar to the construction of the original Marder III; the other was a cosmetically modified Swedish SAV m/43 assault gun, which also used the 38(t) chassis.[21]

Inevitably, some artistic license was taken by the filmmakers for the sake of drama. One of the most notable is the depiction of the 2nd SS Panzer Division Das Reich, as the adversary during the fictional Battle of Ramelle. The 2nd SS was not engaged in Normandy until July, and then at Caen against the British and Canadians, one hundred miles east.[22] Furthermore, the Merderet River bridges were not an objective of the 101st Airborne Division but of the

82nd Airborne Division, part of Mission Boston.[23] Much has been said about various "tactical errors" made by both the German and American forces in the film's climactic battle. Spielberg responded, saying that in many scenes he opted to replace sound military tactics and strict historical accuracy for dramatic effect.[24]

To achieve a tone and quality that was true to the story as well as reflected the period in which it is set, Spielberg once again collaborated with cinematographer Janusz Kamiński, saying, "Early on, we both knew that we did not want this to look like a Technicolor extravaganza about World War II, but more like color newsreel footage from the 1940s, which is very desaturated and low-tech." Kamiński had the protective coating stripped from the camera lenses, making them closer to those used in the 1940s. He explains that "without the protective coating, the light goes in and starts bouncing around, which makes it slightly more diffused and a bit softer without being out of focus." The cinematographer completed the overall effect by putting the negative through bleach bypass, a process that reduces brightness and color saturation. The shutter timing was set to 90 or 45 degrees for many of the battle sequences, as opposed to the standard of 180 degree timing. Kamiński clarifies, "In this way, we attained a certain staccato in the actors' movements and a certain crispness in the explosions, which makes them slightly more realistic."[25]

Release

The film was distributed by DreamWorks in North America and by Paramount Pictures internationally. As a result of Paramount's 2005 acquisition of DreamWorks, Paramount has gained North America distribution rights as well (though still through the DreamWorks division). *Saving Private Ryan* was a critical and commercial success and is credited with contributing to a resurgence in America's interest in World War II. Old and new films, video games, and novels about the war enjoyed renewed popularity after its release.[26] The film's use of desaturated colors, hand-held cameras, and tight angles has profoundly influenced subsequent films and video games.[27] [28] *Saving Private Ryan* was released in 2,463 theatres on July 28, 1998, and grossed $30.5 million on its opening weekend. The film grossed $216.5 million in North America and $265.3 million on other territories, bringing its worldwide total to $481.8 million and making it the highest grossing domestic film of the year.[1]

Reception

Critical reception for the film was generally positive, with much praise for the realistic battle scenes[29] and the actors' performances,[30] but earning some criticism for the script and for ignoring the contributions of several other countries to the D-Day landings in general and at Omaha Beach specifically.[31] The most direct example of the latter is that during the actual landing the 2nd Rangers disembarked from British ships and were taken to Omaha Beach by Royal Navy landing craft (LCAs). The film depicts them as being United States Coast Guard-crewed craft (LCVPs and LCMs) from an American ship, the USS Thomas Jefferson (APA-30).[17] [32] [33] This criticism was far from universal with other critics recognizing the director's intent to make an "American" film.[34] The film was not released in Malaysia after Spielberg refused to cut the violent scenes;[35] however, the film was finally released there on DVD with an 18SG certificate much later in 2005. It currently scores 93% "Certified Fresh" on Rotten Tomatoes[36] and 90% on Metacritic,[37] two film review aggregate sites. Many critics associations, such as New York Critics Circle and Los Angeles Film Critics Association, chose *Saving Private Ryan* as Film of the Year.[38] Roger Ebert gave it four stars out of four and called it "a powerful experience".[30]

Filmmaker Quentin Tarantino has expressed admiration for the film and has cited it as an influence on his 2009 war epic, *Inglourious Basterds*.[39] In an interview, Tarantino told interviewer Samuel Blumenfeld, "Spielberg is doing something unheard of with the opening of this movie. When you watch the sequence of the landing, it's no longer possible to look the same way at *The Longest Day*, or even Samuel Fuller's *The Big Red One*... *Saving Private Ryan* made me aware of some issues raised by the cinema of war that I was unable to ask on my own. The idea that forty men on a boat are exterminated in seconds by a volley of machine gun fire is terrifying. Can you imagine the most atrocious carnage? Obviously, yes. Except that throughout the scene, you are persuaded to attend the worst slaughter in history. The sequence of the knife fight between a U.S. soldier and a Nazi at the end of the film is also as notable as the landing. I hate war movies where they show a soldier killing his opponents without sweating, as if it were insignificant. If I was fighting to save my skin, I think it would be a little more difficult. It's hard to kill someone, it takes sweat, and even with this, you have no guarantee of reaching your goals. Spielberg managed admirably to stage this scene with that dimension." [40]

The actor Richard Todd, who performed in *The Longest Day* and was amongst the first of the Allied soldiers to land in Normandy, said the film was "Rubbish. Overdone." [41] Other WWII veterans, however, stated that the film was the most realistic depiction of combat they had ever seen.[42] The film was so realistic that combat veterans of D-Day and Vietnam left theaters rather than finish watching the opening scene depicting the Normandy invasion. Their visits to posttraumatic stress disorder counselors rose in number after the film's release, and many counselors advised "'more psychologically vulnerable'" veterans to avoid watching it.[43]

The film was later nominated for eleven Academy Awards, with wins for Best Cinematography, Best Sound, Best Sound Effects Editing, Best Film Editing, and Best Director for Spielberg, but lost the Best Picture award to *Shakespeare in Love*, being one of a few that have won the Best Director award without also winning Best Picture.[44] The film also won the Golden Globes for Best Picture – Drama and Director, the BAFTA Award for Special Effects and Sound, the Directors Guild of America Award, a Grammy Award for Best Film Soundtrack, the Producers Guild of America Golden Laurel Award, and the Saturn Award for Best Action/Adventure/Thriller Film.[38] In June 2008, the American Film Institute revealed its "Ten Top Ten"—the best ten films in ten "classic" American film genres—after polling over 1,500 people from the creative community. *Saving Private Ryan* was listed as the eighth best film in the "epic films" genre.[45]

American Film Institute Lists

- AFI's 100 Years... 100 Thrills – #45
- AFI's 100 Years... 100 Cheers – #10
- AFI's 100 Years... 100 Movies (10th Anniversary Edition) – #71
- AFI's 10 Top 10 – #8 Epic film

Awards and nominations

Academy Awards

Award[46]	Person
Awarded	
Best Director	Steven Spielberg
Best Cinematography	Janusz Kamiński
Best Film Editing	Michael Kahn
Best Sound Effects Editing	Gary Rydstrom Richard Hymns
Best Sound	Gary Rydstrom Gary Summers Andy Nelson Ron Judkins
Nominated	
Best Picture	Steven Spielberg
Best Actor in a Leading Role	Tom Hanks
Best Original Screenplay	Robert Rodat

Best Art Direction	Tom Sanders
	Lisa Dean Kavanaugh
Best Makeup	Lois Burwell
	Conor O'Sullivan
	Daniel Striepeke
Best Original Dramatic Score	John Williams

Home media

The film debuted on home video in May 1999 with a VHS release that earned over $44 million. A later special edition, the D-Day 60th Anniversary Commemorative Edition, was released featuring an extra tape with documentary footage of the actual D-Day landings as well as the making of the film.[47] The DVD was released in November of the same year,[48] and was one of the best-selling titles of the year, with over 1.5 million units sold.[49] The original DVD was released in two separate versions: one with Dolby Digital and the other with DTS 5.1 surround sound. Besides the different 5.1 tracks, the two DVDs are identical. The film was also issued in a very limited 2-disc Laserdisc release in November 1999, making it one of the very last feature films to ever be issued in this format, as Laserdiscs ceased manufacturing and distribution by the year's end, due in part to the growing popularity of DVDs.[50] In 2004, a *Saving Private Ryan* special edition DVD was released to commemorate the 60th anniversary of D-Day. This two-disc edition was also included in a box set titled *World War II Collection*, along with two documentaries produced by Spielberg, *Price For Peace* (about the Pacific War) and *Shooting War* (about war photographers, narrated by Tom Hanks).[51] The film was released on Blu-ray Disc on April 26, 2010 in the UK and on May 4, 2010 in the US, as part of Paramount Home Video's premium Sapphire Series.[52] However, only weeks after its release, Paramount issued a recall due to audio synchronization problems.[53] The studio issued an official statement acknowledging the problem, which they attributed to an authoring error by Technicolor that escaped the quality control process, and that they had already begun the process of replacing the defective discs.[54] The remastered discs were released to the public on May 18, 2010.

Television broadcasts

On Veterans Day from 2001 through 2004, the American Broadcasting Company aired the film uncut and with limited commercial interruption. The network airings were given a TV-MA rating, as the violent battle scenes and the profanity were left intact. The 2004 airing was marred by pre-emptions in many markets because of the language, in the backlash of Super Bowl XXXVIII's halftime show controversy.[55] However, critics and veterans' groups such as the American Legion and the Veterans of Foreign Wars assailed those stations and their owners, including Hearst-Argyle Television (owner of 14 ABC affiliates); Scripps Howard Broadcasting (owner of eight); and Belo (the owner of four) for putting profits ahead of programming and honoring those who gave their lives at wartime, saying the stations made more money running their own programming instead of being paid by the network to carry the film, especially during a sweeps period. A total of 65 ABC affiliates—28% of the network—did not clear the available timeslot for the film, even with the offer of The Walt Disney Company, ABC's parent, to pay all fines for language to the Federal Communications Commission.[56] In the end, however, no complaints were lodged against ABC affiliates who showed *Ryan*, perhaps because even conservative watchdogs like the Parents Television Council supported the unedited rebroadcast of the film.[57]

From 2005 through 2008, TNT acquired the rights to air the film, usually airing it as ABC did on Veterans Day, complete and uncut. Currently, the film can be seen (as of 2010) in syndication and also on Turner Classic Movies.

References

Notes

[1] "Saving Private Ryan" (http://boxofficemojo.com/movies/?id=savingprivateryan.htm). Box Office Mojo. . Retrieved September 5, 2008.
[2] "Saving Private Ryan" (http://boxofficemojo.com/movies/?id=savingprivateryan.htm). Box Office Mojo. . Retrieved April 8, 2010.
[3] "Message in a Battle" (http://www.ew.com/ew/article/0,,284082,00.html). Entertainment Weekly. July 24, 1998. . Retrieved September 5, 2008.
[4] "Boot Camp" (http://www.rzm.com/pvt.ryan/production/scenes/bootcamp.html). Behind the Scenes. . Retrieved September 5, 2008.
[5] "Five Star General" (http://www.theasc.com/magazine/aug98/five/index.htm). American Cinematographer Online Magazine. August 1998. . Retrieved September 5, 2008.
[6] "Omaha Beach" (http://www.sproe.com/o/omaha-beach.html). Saving Private Ryan Online Encyclopedia. . Retrieved September 5, 2008.
[7] "Dog One" (http://www.sproe.com/d/dog-one.html). Saving Private Ryan Online Encyclopedia. . Retrieved September 5, 2008.
[8] "Saving Private Ryan" (http://www.iftn.ie/locations/sublinks_static/wexford/?act1=record&aid=70&rid=1493&tpl=filmography_dets&only=1&force=1). The Irish Film & Television Network. . Retrieved September 5, 2008.
[9] "Private Ryan' expo" (http://www.wexfordpeople.ie/news/private--ryan-expo-697670.html). *Wexford People*. June 6, 2007. . Retrieved September 5, 2008.
[10] "Ryan's slaughter" (http://www.independent.ie/national-news/ryans-slaughter-434700.html). *Independent*. August 3, 1998. . Retrieved September 5, 2008.
[11] "Saving Private Ryan" (http://www.britannia.org/film/filmdetails.php?FilmID=00000506). Britannia Film Archives. . Retrieved September 5, 2008.
[12] "Saving Private Ryan". *Sunderland Echo*. November 2, 1999.
[13] "50 Greatest Movie Moments" (http://www.filmsite.org/tvguidemoments4.html). *TV Guide*. March 24, 2001. . Retrieved September 5, 2008.
[14] "Roaring back to the forties" (http://www.matlockmercury.co.uk/news/Roaring-back-to-the-forties.4362770.jp). Matlock Mercury. August 6, 2008. . Retrieved September 5, 2008.
[15] "How we made the best movie battle scene ever" (http://www.independent.ie/unsorted/features/how-we-made-the-best-movie-battle-scene-ever-91583.html). *Independent*. June 7, 2006. . Retrieved September 5, 2008.
[16] "Steven Spielberg Goes To War" (http://www.empireonline.com/interviews/interview.asp?IID=239). *Empire*. . Retrieved January 17, 2010.
[17] Saving Private Ryan: Company C, 2nd Ranger Battalion (http://www.sproe.com/c/company-c.html). Sproe.com. Retrieved on 2011-09-08.
[18] Saving Private Ryan: LCM (3) (http://www.sproe.com/l/lcm.html). Sproe.com (2009-04-11). Retrieved on 2011-09-08.
[19] "Ryan Tigers" (http://www.sbg1.mistral.co.uk/spr1.htm). Second Battle Group. . Retrieved September 5, 2008.
[20] "Marders" (http://www.sbg1.mistral.co.uk/spr2.htm). Second Battle Group. . Retrieved September 5, 2008.
[21] Reproductions of Panzers based on modern Tanks (http://the.shadock.free.fr/Repros.pdf).shadock.free.fr. Last update: March 9th, 2010]
[22] "Normandy and Falaise—April to August 1944" (http://www.dasreich.ca/normandy.html). Das Reich. . Retrieved September 5, 2008.
[23] "U.S. Airborne in Cotentin Peninsula" (http://www.6juin1944.com/assaut/aeropus/en_index.php). D-Day: Etats des Lieux. . Retrieved September 5, 2008.
[24] Sunshine, Linda (July 24, 1998). *Saving Private Ryan, The Men, The Mission, The Movie: A Steven Spielberg Movie*. Newmarket Press. ISBN 155704371X.
[25] "Combat Footage" (http://www.sproe.com/s/spr.html). Saving Private Ryan Online Encyclopedia. . Retrieved September 8, 2008.
[26] Desowitz, Bill (May 20, 2001). "COVER STORY; It's the Invasion of the WWII Movies". *Los Angeles Times*.
[27] Nix (May 25, 2002). "Saving Private Ryan (1998) Movie Review" (http://www.beyondhollywood.com/saving-private-ryan-1998-movie-review/). Beyond Hollywood. . Retrieved September 5, 2008.
[28] Tom Chick (December 8, 2008). "A Close Encounter with Steven Spielberg" (http://videogames.yahoo.com/celebrity-byte/steven-spielberg/1271249). *Yahoo!*. . Retrieved December 11, 2008.
[29] Turan, Kenneth (July 24, 1998). "Saving Private Ryan review" (http://www.calendarlive.com/movies/reviews/cl-movie980723-5,0,6595970.story). *Los Angeles Times*. .
[30] "Saving Private Ryan" (http://rogerebert.suntimes.com/apps/pbcs.dll/article?AID=/19980724/REVIEWS/807240304/1023). Roger Ebert. . Retrieved September 5, 2008.
[31] "Saving Private Ryan — Film Review" (http://www.totalfilm.com/cinema_reviews/saving_private_ryan). Total Film. . Retrieved September 5, 2008.
[32] "Veterans riled by Ryan" (http://news.bbc.co.uk/2/hi/entertainment/299784.stm). BBC. March 19, 1999. . Retrieved September 5, 2008.
[33] "LCM" (http://www.sproe.com/l/lcm.html). Saving Private Ryan Online Encyclopedia. . Retrieved September 5, 2008.
[34] Reynolds, Matthew. "Saving Private Ryan" (http://www.channel4.com/history/microsites/H/history/e-h/film-saving.html). Channel 4. . Retrieved September 6, 2008.

[35] "Malaysia bans Spielberg's Prince" (http://news.bbc.co.uk/1/hi/entertainment/263905.stm). BBC. January 27, 1999. . Retrieved September 5, 2008.
[36] "Saving Private Ryan (1998)" (http://www.rottentomatoes.com/m/saving_private_ryan/). Rotten Tomatoes. . Retrieved April 17, 2010.
[37] "Saving Private Ryan reviews" (http://www.metacritic.com/video/titles/savingprivateryan). Metacritic. . Retrieved April 17, 2010.
[38] "Awards for Saving Private Ryan" (http://www.imdb.com/title/tt0120815/awards). Internet Movie Database. . Retrieved September 6, 2008.
[39] Quentin Tarantino's favorite WWII movies – Film – Time Out New York (http://newyork.timeout.com/arts-culture/film/46594/quentin-tarantinos-favorite-wwii-movies). Newyork.timeout.com (2009-08-18). Retrieved on 2011-09-08.
[40] De Palma a la Mod (http://www.angelfire.com/de/palma/blog/index.blog/1378661/tarantino-on-icasualties-of-wari/). Angelfire.com (2009-08-29). Retrieved on 2011-09-08.
[41] Meeke, Kieran. "60 seconds interview: Richard Todd" (http://www.metro.co.uk/showbiz/interviews/987-richard-todd). Metro (British newspaper). . Retrieved April 24, 2011.
[42] Basinger, Jeanine (October 1998). "Translating War: The Combat Film Genre and Saving Private Ryan" (http://ics.leeds.ac.uk/papers/vp01.cfm?outfit=pmt&folder=933&paper=940). *Perspectives, the Newsmagazine of the American Historical Association*. .
[43] Halton, Beau (August 15, 1998). "'Saving Private Ryan' is too real for some" (http://jacksonville.com/tu-online/stories/081598/met_2a1priva.html). *The Florida Times-Union* (Jacksonville, Florida). . Retrieved June 12, 2011.
[44] "Academy Awards, USA: 1999" (http://us.imdb.com/Sections/Awards/Academy_Awards_USA/1999). IMDB. . Retrieved September 5, 2008.
[45] "AFI's 10 Top 10" (http://www.afi.com/10top10/epic.html). American Film Institute. June 17, 2008. . Retrieved June 18, 2008.
[46] "The 71st Academy Awards (1999) Nominees and Winners" (http://www.oscars.org/awards/academyawards/legacy/ceremony/71st-winners.html). *oscars.org*. . Retrieved 2011-11-19.
[47] Graser, Marc (July 29, 1999). "'Ryan's' next attack: sell-through market" (http://www.variety.com/article/VR1117744320.html?categoryid=13&cs=1). *Variety*. . Retrieved September 6, 2008.
[48] "Dreamworks' *Saving Private Ryan* DVD press release" (http://www.thedigitalbits.com/articles/ryanpress.html). September 13, 1999. . Retrieved September 6, 2008.
[49] "The Matrix disc soars beyond 3 million mark" (http://www.videobusiness.com/article/CA621040.html). January 8, 2000. . Retrieved September 6, 2008.
[50] Kelley III, Bill (July 22, 1999). "'Private Ryan' Is A No-Show On DVD Format". *Virginian-Pilot*.
[51] "Saving Private Ryan: D-Day 60th Anniversary Commemorative Edition review" (http://dvd.ign.com/articles/519/519108p1.html). IGN. May 26, 2004. . Retrieved September 6, 2008.
[52] "Saving Private Ryan Blu-ray Announced" (http://www.blu-ray.com/news/?id=4138). Blu-ray.com. February 8, 2010. . Retrieved February 10, 2010.
[53] http://www.highdefdigest.com/news/show/Recall/Paramount_Issues_RECALL_of_Saving_Private_Ryan/4714
[54] http://www.thedigitalbits.com/mytwocentsa179.html
[55] Oldenburg, Ann (November 11, 2004). "Some stations shelved 'Private Ryan' amid FCC fears" (http://www.usatoday.com/life/television/news/2004-11-11-private-ryan_x.htm). *USA Today*. . Retrieved September 5, 2008.
[56] Martin, Ed (November 17, 2004). "Return of Janet Jackson's Breast; "Saving Private Ryan" Controversy" (http://web.archive.org/web/20080326190024/http://www.mediavillage.com/jmentr/2004/11/17/jmer-11-17-04/). mediaVillage. Archived from the original (http://www.mediavillage.com/jmentr/2004/11/17/jmer-11-17-04/) on March 26, 2008. . Retrieved April 17, 2010.
[57] Sussman, Gary (November 11, 2004). "War of Attrition" (http://www.ew.com/ew/article/0,,780972,00.html). EW.com. . Retrieved June 7, 2009.

Further reading

- Kershaw, Alex (May 11, 2004). *The Bedford Boys: One American Town's Ultimate D-day Sacrifice*. Da Capo Press. ISBN 0306813556.
- Lefebvre, Laurent (September 2008). *29th Division ... a division of heroes* (http://www.americandday.org/). American d-Day. ISBN 295199639X.
- Lefebvre, Laurent (June 1, 2004). *They Were on Omaha Beach* (http://www.americandday.org/). American d-Day. ISBN 2951996357.

External links

- *Saving Private Ryan* (http://www.imdb.com/title/tt0120815/) at the Internet Movie Database
- *Saving Private Ryan* (http://www.allrovi.com/movies/movie/v163037) at AllRovi
- *Saving Private Ryan* (http://www.boxofficemojo.com/movies/?id=savingprivateryan.htm) at Box Office Mojo
- *Saving Private Ryan* (http://www.rottentomatoes.com/m/saving_private_ryan/) at Rotten Tomatoes
- American D-day (http://www.americandday.org/)
- 29th Infantry Division Historical Society (http://www.29infantrydivision.org/)
- Omaha Beach (http://www.britannica.com/dday/article-236190) at Encyclopædia Britannica

Blast from the Past (film)

Blast from the Past	
Theatrical release poster	
Directed by	Hugh Wilson
Produced by	Amanda Stern Hugh Wilson Renny Harlin
Screenplay by	Hugh Wilson Bill Kelly
Story by	Hugh Wilson
Starring	Brendan Fraser Alicia Silverstone Christopher Walken Sissy Spacek Dave Foley
Music by	Steve Dorff
Cinematography	Jose Luis Alcaine
Editing by	Don Brochu
Distributed by	New Line Cinema
Release date(s)	February 12, 1999
Running time	112 minutes
Country	United States
Language	English
Budget	$35 million
Box office	$40,263,020

Blast from the Past is a 1999 romantic comedy film based on a story and directed by Hugh Wilson and starring Brendan Fraser, Alicia Silverstone, Christopher Walken, Sissy Spacek, and Dave Foley.

Plot

Calvin Webber (Christopher Walken) is a brilliant and eccentric Caltech nuclear physicist, living during the Cold War. His extreme fear of a nuclear holocaust leads him to build an enormous self-sustaining fallout shelter beneath his suburban home. One night, while he and his pregnant wife, Helen (Sissy Spacek), are entertaining guests, a family friend comes to inform him that John F. Kennedy and Nikita Khrushchev are getting into a debate. The family turns on their television, and watch in horror. When the Cuban Missile Crisis begins, they ask their guests to leave, and they head down into the shelter. Meanwhile, a pilot is having problems with his plane; he is ordered to eject, believing his jet will crash into the Pacific Ocean. Just as the Webbers descend into the shelter, the plane veers off and crashes into the Webber home, leaving their friends and family to believe the family has died. The family, having seen the resulting fireball just as they lock themselves in their shelter, believe that the unthinkable has happened and that they are the sole survivors of a nuclear war. The locks on the shelter are set for 35 years and cannot be overridden by anyone inside or outside the shelter — for "their own protection" according to Calvin

Webber.

A few days after the locks have been engaged, Mrs. Webber goes into labor and gives birth to a baby boy, whom they name Adam. During the roughly 35 years they are down in the shelter, the world above drastically changes, while the Webbers' life remains frozen in 1962. Adam is taught in several languages, all school subjects, dance, boxing, and many other things. The family passes time watching black and white films and kinescopes of television programs via a projector rigged to a television. Adam is given his father's baseball card collection and shares in various companies. In the present, the timer on the locks releases, and Calvin decides to check out the surroundings above the shelter (in full protective gear), which has turned into a ghetto. He mistakes this for a post-apocalyptic world and wants his wife and grown son (Brendan Fraser) to stay in hiding, but suffers from chest pain. Adam, who is naïve but well-educated, is sent for supplies and help, thus beginning his adventures.

Much of the humor in the film is derived from his being unaccustomed to the lifestyle of the present (such as using the term negro, and believing "shit" is a French compliment), believing "gay" means happy, and finding awe in simple things of modernity. Early on, he meets Eve Vrustikoff (Alicia Silverstone) at a card store, where she works, and where he went to sell his father's classic baseball cards. She stops the store owner from ripping Adam off and is immediately fired. Adam asks Eve to take him to the Holiday Inn, in exchange for a baseball card, worth $4,000. The next morning, at the Holiday Inn, Eve comes to give back the card to Adam, and after a brief conversation, Eve informs Adam that she has to look for a new job. In exchange for $1,000 a week, Adam asks Eve to work for him, she agrees to help him buy the supplies and his search for a "non-mutant wife from Pasadena". Meanwhile, Adam meets Eve's gay housemate and best friend, Troy (Dave Foley), who offers advice and commentary as Adam and Eve fall in love.

Adam continually impresses both Eve and Troy with his array of talents including an energetic swing dance that garners the attention of Eve's rival, Sophie (Carmen Moré), who starts flirting with the naive Adam, spurning Eve when he goes home with her. Adam returns later, having admitted to rejecting Sophie's advances and tells Eve about his past. The sheer notion of the story scares Eve into thinking he is a sociopath or psychotic and delusional and she contacts a medical institution to have him committed, which he escapes. After Adam is gone, Troy and Eve find that he has "millions upon millions, upon millions of dollars" worth of stocks, and the lifestyle they find he has been living seems straight out of the 1960s. Eventually, Eve finds Adam and the two make up, Adam finally introducing Eve to his sheltered parents.

At the conclusion of the film, Calvin and Helen move into a home at the surface that their son has had constructed with the wealth he has acquired from selling stocks, which acquired great value from splits over the years. Only Calvin is informed that the catastrophe they went into seclusion for was in fact a plane crash, for fear Helen would be incredibly angry at her husband for her years of mistaken confinement. The film ends with Helen at peace with her newfound freedom from the shelter, Adam and Eve engaged to be married, while Calvin, certain that the "Commies" have faked the collapse of the Soviet Union, starts pacing out measurements for a new fallout shelter.

Cast

- Brendan Fraser as Adam Webber
- Alicia Silverstone as Eve Vrustikoff
- Christopher Walken as Calvin Webber
- Sissy Spacek as Helen Webber
- Dave Foley as Troy
- Joey Slotnick as Soda Jerk/"Archbishop" Melker
- Dale Raoul as Mom
- Rex Linn as Dave
- Cynthia Mace as Betty
- Harry S. Murphy as Bob

- Hugh Wilson as Levy
- Carmen Moré as Sophie
- Nathan Fillion as Cliff
- Jenifer Lewis as Dr. Nina Aron
- John F. Kennedy (*uncredited, archive footage*) as himself (reveals existence of Cuban missiles)
- Fidel Castro (*uncredited, archive footage*) as himself
- Nikita Khrushchev (*uncredited, archive footage*) as himself (shakes fist at the U.N.)

Reception

Critical reception

The film received mixed to positive reviews from critics. On Rotten Tomatoes, the film had an overall score of 59% of the comments positive.[1] On Metacritic had a score of 48% with a 9.0/10 "Mixed or average reviews". Roger Ebert gave the film 3 out of 4 stars saying "the movie is funny and entertaining in all the usual ways, yes, but I was grateful that it tried for more: that it was actually about something, that it had an original premise, that it used satire and irony and had sly undercurrents."[2]

Box office

Blast from the Past opened in North American theaters on February 12, 1999 and took in $7,771,066 earning it 5th place at the box office for the weekend.

References

[1] *Blast from the Past* (http://www.rottentomatoes.com/m/blast_from_the_past/) at Rotten Tomatoes
[2] http://rogerebert.suntimes.com/apps/pbcs.dll/article?AID=/19990212/REVIEWS/902120301/1023

External links

- *Blast from the Past* (http://www.imdb.com/title/tt0124298/) at the Internet Movie Database
- *Blast from the Past* (http://www.allrovi.com/movies/movie/v176002) at AllRovi
- *Blast from the Past* (http://www.boxofficemojo.com/movies/?id=blastfromthepast.htm) at Box Office Mojo
- *Blast from the Past* (http://www.rottentomatoes.com/m/blast_from_the_past/) at Rotten Tomatoes

Dracula 2000

Dracula 2000	
Theatricla release poster	
Directed by	Patrick Lussier
Produced by	W.K. Border Joel Soisson Wes Craven
Written by	Joel Soisson Patrick Lussier
Based on	*Dracula* by Bram Stoker
Starring	Jonny Lee Miller Justine Waddell Gerard Butler Colleen Ann Fitzpatrick Jennifer Esposito Danny Masterson Jeri Ryan Lochlyn Munro Sean Patrick Thomas Omar Epps Christopher Plummer
Music by	Marco Beltrami
Cinematography	Peter Pau
Editing by	Peter Devaney Flanagan Patrick Lussier
Distributed by	Dimension Films
Release date(s)	December 22, 2000
Running time	99 minutes
Country	United States
Language	English
Budget	$28 million
Box office	$47,053,625[1]

Dracula 2000, also known internationally as *Dracula 2001*,[2] is a 2000 horror film written and directed by Patrick Lussier. The film stars Gerard Butler, Christopher Plummer, Jonny Lee Miller, Justine Waddell, Omar Epps, Colleen Fitzpatrick, Jeri Ryan, and Jennifer Esposito.

Dracula 2000, the promotional title of which is *Wes Craven Presents: Dracula 2000,* builds upon Bram Stoker's 1897 novel *Dracula*, with Count Dracula resurrected in the year 2000. The movie was a critical and commercial disappointment, though it gained a cult following which resulted in two direct-to-video sequels.

Plot

Matthew Van Helsing (Plummer), the alleged descendant of the famed 19th century Dutch medical doctor, Abraham Van Helsing, owns an antique shop in early 21st century London. One night with Van Helsing upstairs, his secretary, Solina (Jennifer Esposito), allows a group of thieves, led by her boyfriend, Marcus (Omar Epps), into the shop. The thieves infiltrate the shop's underground high-security vault and find a sealed silver coffin protected by a deadly defense system. Based on the level of security surrounding the coffin, Solina and Marcus decide that the coffin's contents must be valuable, so they escape with it and flee to New Orleans, Louisiana. When Van Helsing discovers that the coffin has been stolen, he boards a plane to America, telling his apprentice, Simon Sheppard (Jonny Lee Miller), to remain in London. Simon does not follow his mentor's orders and travels to Louisiana as well.

Aboard the plane, one of the thieves manages to open the coffin, revealing the dormant body of Count Dracula (Butler). Dracula awakens and attacks the thieves, causing the plane to crash in the Louisiana swamps. Dracula survives the crash and travels to New Orleans where college students Mary Heller (Waddell) and Lucy Westerman (Fitzpatrick) are living. Mary is estranged from her family and has recently been plagued by dreams of a strange, terrifying man.

Van Helsing and Simon arrive in New Orleans and destroy the newly turned vampires left in Dracula's wake. After the battle, Van Helsing reveals to Simon that he is in fact the original Abraham Van Helsing who defeated Dracula in 1897. Because he was unable to destroy Dracula permanently, Van Helsing hid Dracula's body and prolonged his own life with regular injections of Dracula's blood until, one day, he could discover a way to kill Dracula for good. Simon is intrigued by Dracula's hatred of all things Christian and wonders why Dracula is also particularly vulnerable to silver.

Van Helsing also tells Simon about his daughter, Mary, who was taken from England by her mother after the truth about his identity came to light. Since Mary was conceived after Van Helsing began his injections, she shares blood and a telepathic link with Dracula. Van Helsing knows that Dracula senses Mary's existence and is in New Orleans to find her.

Van Helsing and Simon try to reach Mary before Dracula does, but fail to do so before Dracula turns Lucy into a vampire. Dracula and his three new brides, Solina, Lucy, and Valerie, corner Van Helsing and kill him. Simon and Mary escape, only to be captured by Dracula shortly thereafter.

Dracula takes Mary to a rooftop and reveals his secret: He is none other than Judas Iscariot, the one who betrayed Jesus for a bribe of thirty pieces of silver. As he went to hang himself, the rope snapped and as punishment he was cursed and had to live for two thousand years as a vampire. The three brides appear with Simon, and Dracula tells Mary to bite him. She fakes the bite and together Mary and Simon kill the three brides. Angered, Dracula tried to throw her from the rooftop. Mary wraps some cable from a large crucifix around Dracula's neck and they both fall from the roof. Dracula hangs as he attempted to do two thousand years before, but this time the rope does not break, and he burns in the first sunlight.

Cast

- Gerard Butler as Count Dracula (Judas Iscariot)
- Christopher Plummer as Matthew/Abraham Van Helsing
- Jonny Lee Miller as Simon Sheppard
- Justine Waddell as Mary Heller
- Danny Masterson as Nightshade
- Jeri Ryan as Valerie Sharpe
- Colleen Fitzpatrick as Lucy Westerman
- Jennifer Esposito as Solina
- Lochlyn Munro as Eddie

- Sean Patrick Thomas as Trick
- Omar Epps as Marcus
- Tig Fong as Dax
- Tony Munch as Charlie
- Shane West as J.T.
- Tom Kane as The Newscaster
- Nathan Fillion as Father David
- David J. Francis as Jesus of Nazareth

Box office and reception

Dracula 2000 opened at #7 in its first week at the box office with $8.6 million. In its second week, the film had a 56.5% drop-off, but hung onto the #8 spot. The film grossed $33 million domestically and $47 million worldwide, on a $28 million budget. On its initial video release, it grossed an additional $32 million in the US and Canada and is still making money worldwide. *Dracula 2000* was the sixth highest grossing film for Miramax/Dimension Films in 2000, exceeding the box office takes of such expensive Dimension Films releases like *Reindeer Games* and *Impostor*, as well as the Miramax Film December opener for that year, *All the Pretty Horses*.[3]

Critically, *Dracula 2000* has earned a rating of 15% on Rotten Tomatoes[4] and 26 out of a 100 on Metacritic.[5] Berge Garabedian of *JoBlo* offered a positive review, calling it "A fun vampire movie", "a novel adaptation of an old time legend", and "[good] for pretty much anyone looking for some enjoyable bloody fun."[6] *BeyondHollywood.com* wrote, "*Dracula 2000* is not the worst vampire movie I've seen, but it's definitely not the best either. There are some very good moments, most of them featuring the frail Van Helsing as he attempts to battle the fast and deadly vampires. Also, I appreciated the background given to Dracula's aversion to silver, crosses, and God, as well as Dracula's 'true' origins. Not bad work, but it could have been much better."[7]

Owen Gleiberman of *Entertainment Weekly* gave the film a "C-" score,[8] while James Berardinelli of *ReelViews* panned the film, writing: "Of all the indignities to have been visited upon Dracula during the past century (including being the "inspiration" for a cereal and a *Sesame Street* character, and being lampooned by Mel Brooks), none is more unsettling than what has happened to the world's most famous vampire in *Dracula 2000*."[9]

Soundtrack

The film's rock soundtrack includes Linkin Park's song "One Step Closer", System of a Down's cover of Berlin's "The Metro", Slayer's song "Bloodline" and Disturbed's song "A Welcome Burden". The original music score is composed by future Academy Award-nominee Marco Beltrami.

Sequels

Dracula 2000 was followed by two direct-to-video sequels, *Dracula II: Ascension* in 2003 and *Dracula III: Legacy* in 2005. Patrick Lussier and Joel Soisson, who directed and wrote all three films, created a plot for a fourth film and discussed releasing it theatrically, but no film has yet been produced.[10]

References

[1] "Box Office" (http://www.boxofficemojo.com/movies/?id=dracula2000.htm). .
[2] http://www.imdb.com/title/tt0219653/
[3] *Dracula 2000* (http://www.boxofficemojo.com/movies/?id=dracula2000.htm) at Box Office Mojo
[4] "*Dracula 2000* Movie Reviews, Pictures" (http://www.rottentomatoes.com/m/dracula_2000/). Rotten Tomatoes. . Retrieved 2009-07-08.
[5] "Wes Craven Presents: Dracula 2000 (2000): Reviews" (http://www.metacritic.com/film/titles/dracula2000). Metacritic. . Retrieved 2009-07-08.
[6] JoBlo's movie review of Dracula 2000: Justine Waddell, Christopher Plummer, Gerard Butler Berge Garabedian, *JoBlo*, 2009 (http://www.joblo.com/reviews.php?mode=joblo_movies&id=776)
[7] Dracula 2000 (2000) Movie Review | BeyondHollywood.com | Movie News, Reviews, and Opinions (http://www.beyondhollywood.com/dracula-2000-2000-movie-review/)
[8] Wes Craven Presents: *Dracula 2000* | Movie Review (http://www.ew.com/ew/article/0,,93618~1~~,00.html) Owen Gleiberman, *Entertainment Weekly*, 3 January 2001.
[9] Berardinelli, James. *Dracula 2000* review (http://www.reelviews.net/movies/d/dracula2000.html), *ReelViews*, 2000.
[10] BD Horror News - Patrick Lussier Talks Fourth 'Dracula' Film (http://www.bloody-disgusting.com/news/16438), BloodyDisgusting.com, 10 June 2009.

External links

- *Dracula 2000* (http://www.imdb.com/title/tt0219653/) at the Internet Movie Database
- *Dracula 2000* (http://www.allrovi.com/movies/movie/v229538) at AllRovi
- *Dracula 2000* (http://www.rottentomatoes.com/m/dracula_2000/) at Rotten Tomatoes
- *Dracula 2000* (http://www.boxofficemojo.com/movies/?id=dracula2000.htm) at Box Office Mojo
- *Dracula 2000* (http://www.metacritic.com/movie/dracula2000) at Metacritic

Outing Riley

Outing Riley	
Theatrical release poster	
Directed by	Pete Jones
Produced by	Judd Nissen Patrick Peach Bruce Terris
Written by	Pete Jones
Starring	Pete Jones Nathan Fillion Stoney Westmoreland Dev Kennedy Michael McDonald
Music by	Rick Butler Fred Rapaport
Cinematography	Peter Biagi
Editing by	Gregg Featherman
Distributed by	Wolfe Releasing
Release date(s)	October 10, 2004
Running time	99 min.
Country	United States
Language	English
Budget	$700,000

Outing Riley is a 2004 comedy film written, directed, and starring Pete Jones, about a gay man coming out to his three brothers.[1][2] It was screened at the 2004 Chicago International Film Festival and released on video in 2007.[3]

Plot

Bobby Riley (Pete Jones) is a gay man in the closet, afraid to come out to his three older brothers, even though he's over 30, makes his own money, lives on his own, and is being pressed by his more liberal sister, his boyfriend, and his lesbian beard to tell them. The death of his father and a fishing trip with his brothers provide occasions when he could tell them, but he fails. The expectations of a close-knit Irish Catholic family in Chicago are hard for him to overcome. Eventually all the family's secrets are revealed, his brothers' as well as Bobby's, and the siblings all grow closer in the process.[2]

Cast
- Pete Jones as Bobby Riley
- Nathan Fillion as Luke Riley
- Stoney Westmoreland as Connor Riley
- Dev Kennedy as Jack Riley
- Michael McDonald as Andy
- Julie Pearl as Maggie Riley
- Bob Riley as Mr. Riley
- Wendy Snyder as Smoking Woman

References
[1] LISA NESSELSON (2004-11-10). "Outing Riley" (http://www.variety.com/review/VE1117925516.html?categoryid=31&cs=1&p=0). *Variety.* . Retrieved 2008-04-07.
[2] Don Willmott. "Outing Riley" (http://www.filmcritic.com/misc/emporium.nsf/reviews/Outing-Riley). Filmcritic.com. . Retrieved 2008-04-07.
[3] Erik Childress. "Outing Riley" (http://efilmcritic.com/review.php?movie=10922). efilmcritic.com. . Retrieved 2008-04-07.

External links
- *Outing Riley* (http://www.imdb.com/title/tt0379265/) at the Internet Movie Database
- *Outing Riley* (http://www.allrovi.com/movies/movie/v317802) at AllRovi

Serenity (film)

Serenity	
Film poster	
Directed by	Joss Whedon
Produced by	• Christopher Buchanan • David V. Lester • Barry Mendel • Alisa Tager
Written by	Joss Whedon
Starring	• Nathan Fillion • Gina Torres • Alan Tudyk • Morena Baccarin • Adam Baldwin • Jewel Staite • Sean Maher • Summer Glau • Ron Glass • Chiwetel Ejiofor • David Krumholtz
Music by	David Newman
Cinematography	Jack N. Green
Editing by	Lisa Lassek
Distributed by	Universal Pictures
Release date(s)	• August 22, 2005 (EIFF) • September 30, 2005
Running time	119 minutes
Country	United States
Language	English
Budget	$39 million
Box office	$38,869,464[1]

Serenity is a 2005 space western film written and directed by Joss Whedon. It is a continuation of the short-lived 2002 Fox science fiction television series *Firefly*, taking place after the events of the final episode. Set in 2518, *Serenity* is the story of the captain and crew of a cargo ship. The captain and first mate are veterans of the Unification War, having fought on the losing side. Their lives of petty crime are interrupted by a psychic passenger who harbors a dangerous secret.

The film was released in North America on September 30, 2005 by Universal Pictures. It received generally positive reviews and was number two its opening weekend, taking in $10.1 million its first weekend. The movie spent two weeks in the top ten, and its total domestic box office gross was $25.5 million with a foreign box office gross of $13.3 million.[1] However, it did not make back its budget until its release on DVD. *Serenity* won film of the year awards from *Film 2005*[2] and *FilmFocus*.[3] It also won IGN Film's Best Sci-Fi, Best Story and Best Trailer awards and was runner up for the Overall Best Movie.[4] It also won the Nebula Award for Best Script for 2005, the 7th annual 'User Tomato Awards' for best Sci-Fi movie of 2005 at Rotten Tomatoes, the 2006 viewers choice Spacey

Award for favorite movie, the 2006 Hugo Award for Best Dramatic Presentation, Long Form[5] and the 2006 Prometheus Special Award.[6]

Plot

In 2518, humanity has moved to another star system. The inner planets are controlled by the Alliance with frontier justice among the outer planets. A young girl, River Tam, is being mentally and physically conditioned by Alliance scientists. She is rescued from them by her brother, Simon and the two seek refuge aboard the *Firefly*-class transport ship *Serenity* captained by Malcolm "Mal" Reynolds. An Alliance agent, the Operative, is tasked with eliminating River as she has been observed by Alliance politicians and may have learned certain secrets due to her psychic abilities.

Aboard *Serenity*, Mal brings River on a bank raid against her brother's wishes. They are attacked by Reavers, animalistic humans who savagely mutilate, rape, and murder their victims. They escape, but Simon decides to leave *Serenity* at the next port. While Mal meets fences Fanty and Mingo, River becomes entranced by a TV commercial and begins attacking everyone. Before she can attack Mal, Simon arrives and shouts a "safe word" which causes her to fall asleep. Mal then picks River up and carries her back to *Serenity*. The crew contacts a reclusive hacker known as Mr. Universe who analyzes the commercial and discovers a subliminal message being broadcast across the Alliance designed to trigger River. He notes that River whispered the name "Miranda" before attacking.

Mal receives a call from Inara, a former passenger. Suspecting a trap but realizing that she is in danger, Mal visits Inara and is confronted by the Operative. The Operative offers to let Mal go free if he turns River over, but thanks to Inara's quick thinking she and Mal escape. After another of River's outbursts, the crew learns about Miranda, an outer rim planet thought to have been rendered uninhabitable as the result of a terraforming accident. *Serenity* travels to Haven, a mining colony and home of Shepherd Book, a former passenger and friend of the crew. They discover the outpost has been destroyed by Alliance forces. The Operative has ordered the deaths of all of Mal's contacts to deny him a safe haven and promises that he will continue to pursue them until River is turned over.

Mal orders *Serenity* modified to resemble a Reaver ship so they can reach Miranda. After sailing through a fleet of Reaver vessels, the crew discovers a normal planet, with its cities empty and laden with corpses. They discover a log recorded by an Alliance survey team explaining that the Alliance administered a chemical designed to suppress aggression, which killed off the populace. However, one tenth of the population instead became hyper-aggressive and unstable. The Alliance is responsible for the creation of the Reavers.

Mal contacts Mr. Universe's transmitter to arrange to have the log transmitted throughout the *verse*, but the Operative is already there. *Serenity* departs Miranda, but as they leave Reaver territory, they open fire on one of the ships. The Reavers pursue *Serenity* to Mr. Universe's planet where they engage the waiting Alliance fleet. The Operative's ship is destroyed but he survives in an escape pod. In the confusion, *Serenity* manages to crash land, but pilot Wash is killed by a pursuing Reaver ship. Finding Mr. Universe dead, Mal learns from a recorded message of a second transmitter. The crew sets up a last stand against the pursuing Reavers, buying Mal the time he needs to send the message. The crew find themselves overwhelmed by the Reavers and retreat behind a set of blast doors, but find they will not close. Zoe and Kaylee are injured, but Simon discovers he has left his medical kit at their prior position. As he rises to retrieve it, he is shot. He apologizes to River for failing her, but she announces that it is her turn to take care of Simon. She charges through the blast doors, triggering the closing mechanism and throws the medical kit to Simon before being dragged away by Reavers.

Mal finds the transmitter, but The Operative reveals himself and the two begin fighting. Mal disables The Operative and restrains him next to a railing, forcing him to watch the recording from Miranda. Mal returns to his crew finding them safe. The blast doors open to reveal River has single-handedly defeated the Reavers. The wall behind her explodes and they are surrounded by Alliance troops. The Operative, realizing he has been lied to by the government, gives the order for Alliance operatives to stand down from executing the *Serenity* crew.

After the crew buries their dead friends on Haven, they patch up *Serenity* in a repair yard on Persephone. Kaylee and Simon consummate their relationship. The Operative tells Mal that the Alliance has been weakened and that Mal and his crew are safe for the moment. *Serenity* returns to space with Mal at the helm and River acting as copilot.

Cast

- Nathan Fillion as Malcolm "Mal" Reynolds: A former sergeant on the losing side of the Unification War, he struggles to survive free and independent of the Alliance. Captain Malcolm Reynolds was named #18 in *TV Guide*'s "25 Greatest Sci-fi Legends" list in 2004.[7]
- Gina Torres as Zoe Washburne (née Alleyne): A former corporal who fought under Mal in the war, and Wash's wife. She is fiercely loyal to Mal, whom she addresses as "sir".
- Alan Tudyk as Hoban "Wash" Washburne: The pilot of the ship, and Zoe's husband. He often acts as a voice of reason on the ship.
- Sean Maher as Simon Tam: Simon is River's loving older brother who helped rescue her from the Alliance. He and River are taken in by the crew of *Serenity*. A trauma surgeon before the rescue, he serves as a doctor to the crew. His life is defined by his sister's needs.[8]
- Summer Glau as River Tam: River is a seventeen-year old psychic genius. She and her brother are taken in by the crew of *Serenity* after he rescues her from an Alliance Academy where she was subjected to medical experimentation and brainwashing. The Alliance's pursuit of River acts as the film's motive. However, more abstractly the film is the "story of Mal as told by River".[9]
- Morena Baccarin as Inara Serra: A Companion who formerly rented one of *Serenity*'s shuttles. In one of the Operative's traps, Mal is reunited with Inara at her training house, and the two escape back to *Serenity*.
- Adam Baldwin as Jayne Cobb: A mercenary skilled with weapons, Jayne is often the "main gun" for jobs and is someone who can be depended on in a fight.[10] Jayne acts and seems dumb most of the time, but may be smarter than he lets on.[8] As Whedon states several times, he is the person that will ask the questions that no one else wants to.[11]
- Jewel Staite as Kaywinnit Lee "Kaylee" Frye:[12] [13] the ship's mechanic, has an intuitive, almost symbiotic, relationship with machines and is, consequently, something of a mechanical wizard. She is also notable for a persistently bright and sunny disposition, and her crush on Simon Tam.
- Ron Glass as Shepherd Derrial Book: A *shepherd*, or preacher, with a mysterious past, Book was once a passenger on *Serenity*, but now resides on the planet Haven. Mal and the crew look to him for help.
- Chiwetel Ejiofor as The Operative: A ruthless, intelligent agent of the Alliance assigned to track down River and Simon. Although Ejiofor was on the top of the casting director's list for the role, the studio wanted someone better known. Whedon, however, was eventually able to cast Ejiofor.[14]
- David Krumholtz as Mr. Universe: A "techno-geek" with good relations with the crew of *Serenity*, especially Wash, Mr. Universe lives with his "love-bot" wife and monitors incoming signals from around the universe.

Production

Development

The film is based on *Firefly*, a television series canceled by Fox television in December 2002, after 11 of its 14 produced episodes had aired.[15] When attempts to have another network acquire the show failed, creator Joss Whedon attempted to sell it as a film. Through a business connection, he was introduced to Mary Parent with Universal Pictures, who immediately signed on after watching the episodes on DVD.[15] By June 2003, actors Nathan Fillion and Adam Baldwin confirmed the deal on the official *Firefly* forum, as did Whedon in several interviews.[16] [17] [18]

Writing

After Universal Studios acquired the movie rights to *Firefly* from Fox, Whedon began writing the screenplay. His task was to explain the premise of a television series that few had seen without boring new viewers or longtime fans. He based his story on original story ideas for *Firefly*'s unfilmed second season.[19] Whedon's original script was 190 pages, and attempted to address all major plot points introduced in the series. After presenting the script to Universal under the title "The Kitchen Sink", Whedon was asked to cut down the script to a size filmable under his budget constraints.[19] Universal planned to begin shooting in October 2003, but delays in finishing the script postponed the start of shooting to June 2004.[15]

The opening sequence shifts perspectives several times, from a traditional narrative to that of a schoolroom which is later revealed to be River's disjointed memories. Whedon said in the DVD commentary that the approach works thematically as well, since it depicts River's fractured state of mind. Once the narrative reaches *Serenity* herself, Whedon uses a long tracking shot of several minutes to establish "safety",[9] as well as (re-)introduce every character aboard ship and touch on their personality and motivations.

Filming

Universal, while on board with the movie, was not willing to spend the typical $100 million for a story set in space. Whedon convinced them he could do it for less money, and do it in 50 days, instead of the usual 80.[20] On March 3, 2004 the movie was officially given the greenlight to enter production and was revealed to have a budget of under $40 million.[21] Typically, production of a movie would try to save money by not filming in Los Angeles, but Whedon insisted on staying local.

Principal photography began on June 3, 2004. Joss Whedon said that the film would be titled *Serenity*, in order to differentiate it from the TV series. (Whedon also mentions in the *Serenity* DVD commentary that Fox still owned the rights to the name 'Firefly').[22] All nine principal cast members from the television series (Adam Baldwin, Alan Tudyk, Gina Torres, Jewel Staite, Morena Baccarin, Nathan Fillion, Ron Glass, Sean Maher, and Summer Glau) returned for the movie. Stunt coordinator Chad Stahelski, a student of Jeet Kune Do under Dan Inosanto, created a customized fighting style for Summer Glau to use in the film's fight scenes. It was a hybrid of Kung Fu, kickboxing and elements of ballet, all combined to create a "balletic" martial art.[23]

One cost-cutting item that could not be reused from the television show was the original set of the interior of the spaceship *Serenity*, which had to be entirely rebuilt using frozen images from the *Firefly* DVD set.[20] The set for the failed colony, Miranda, was filmed on location at Diamond Ranch High School in Pomona, California.[24]

On September 17, 2004, Whedon announced on the movie's official website that shooting had been completed.

Design

Renowned comic book artist Bernie Wrightson, co-creator of *Swamp Thing*, contributed concept drawings for the Reavers.[25] Other comic book artists who contributed to the production design include Joshua Middleton and Leinil Francis Yu (*Visual Companion*).

Serenity costumes are influenced by Wild West style: natural materials such as wool, cotton, and leather in drab earth tones predominate. Some clothing also reflects an east, south, and southeast Asian and Indian fusion of color and beauty[26] as well as influences from the American Civil War, late 19th century as well as the 1930s depression era. Mal's suspenders are strongly influenced by a World War II design.[27] The clothing of the Alliance organization within the series (in reality, reused uniforms from *Starship Troopers*[28]) is monolithically monochromatic, similar to the uniforms of the Galactic Empire in the *Star Wars* films. *Serenity* appears to be influenced by Western genre set design, in particular, entertainment programs set in the West during the 1970s and 1980s such as *Little House on the Prairie*. The cramped interior of the *Serenity* ship itself appears to be strongly influenced by the "worn future" precedent set by the famous fictional *Star Wars* spaceship the *Millennium Falcon*[29] but devolved even further. In a similar vein to the film *Star Wars Episode IV: A New Hope*, *Serenity* goes for an occasional underdone look, or "used future", as *Star Wars* creator George Lucas refers to it.[30]

> "Serenity" was clearly written by someone who grew up worshiping at the altar of Han Solo and the space marines in Aliens, but this genre picture is still a thrillingly original science fiction creation. The writing is as good as in the best "Star Trek" episodes, while offering a thoughtfully bleak vision of the future that brings to mind Blade Runner."[31]
>
> —Peter Hartlaub, San Francisco Chronicle

This future envisioned in *Serenity* has two political and cultural centers: Anglo-American and Chinese. Characters all speak English and Mandarin, with the latter language reserved for the strongest curse words.[32] While these two are the dominant languages of the film, other languages are also spoken in the *Firefly / Serenity* universe, including Russian (spoken by Simon during the movie). The safeword phrase that Simon uses to shut River down, "Eta kuram na smekh", is a Russian expression ("Это курам на смех"). Literally, it means, "That's for chickens to laugh at" — a Russian idiom for "That's ridiculous".[33] The Japanese Katakana characters are also present around the universe, most obviously seen in the flowing script on River's desk screen at her school. A sticker with the Arabic word "الدحار" (ad-dHār) appears behind Jayne's head on a wall inside Serenity's bridge when the crew is discussing whether or not they should go to Miranda.

Visual effects

As the budget for the film was considerably smaller than for other films, practical special effects were used as much as possible: if a CGI composite was required, as many tangible sets and props as possible were constructed to minimize the use of CGI effects.[34] The most technically challenging scene was the mule skiff chase.[34] For budgetary reasons, a gimbal and CGI, much like those used in the pod race in *Star Wars Episode I: The Phantom Menace*, were quickly ruled out, creating a challenge for the production team to find an alternative.[20] Instead, the crew fashioned a trailer with a cantilevered arm attached to the "hovercraft" and shot the scene while riding up Templin Highway north of Santa Clarita.[20] *Serenity* visual effects supervisor Loni Peristere stated in a Los Angeles Times article, "Traditionally this would have been, like, a 30-day shoot. I think we did it in five."[20] Zoic Studios, the CG-rendering company that produced the graphics for the series, had to perform a complete overhaul of their computer model of *Serenity*, as the television model would not stand up to the high-definition scrutiny of cinema screens (and High-definition video resolution).[35] [36]

Musical score

The film's musical score was composed by David Newman, and performed by the Hollywood Studio Symphony under Newman's direction. According to director Joss Whedon's sleeve notes for the album, Newman was recommended by Universal's music executives when he requested a musician capable of "everything". Whedon's directions to Newman for the *Serenity* theme were that he wanted something homemade and mournful that would let viewers know that they were now "home" and evoke the idea of the pioneer, when everyone only had what they could carry.[37] The official soundtrack was released on CD on September 27, 2005.

It is of note that the acoustic guitar version of the "Ballad of Serenity" (from *Firefly*), which was used at the end of the film's credits, is absent from the soundtrack.

Release

Hoping to generate buzz through early word-of-mouth, Universal launched an unprecedented 3-stage campaign to sneak preview the then unfinished movie in 35 US cities where the series had earned high Nielsen ratings. The first stage of screenings was held in 10 cities on May 5, 2005. The second stage, held on May 26, 2005, added 10 more cities and was also the source of controversy when theaters began selling tickets before the official announcement was made, leading some shows to be immediately sold out. The third round, with an additional 15 cities, was held on June 23, 2005. The screenings proved successful, with all three stages selling out in less than 24 hours, the screening in Washington, D.C. sold out in a mere 22 minutes and the screening in Phoenix in only eight minutes.[38][39]

Australian audiences were the first outside North America to get preview screenings. After an exclusive Sydney test screening, Melbourne held a public screening on July 21, 2005. This was followed by a film festival screening on the Gold Coast on July 22, 2005. Public preview screenings were held in Adelaide and Sydney on August 1, 2005, and Perth on August 4, 2005. Further screenings were held in Victoria, Tasmania, and Queensland in late August. There had been a screening of the unfinished film in February 2005 at the British Film Institute in London. This version of the film had a temporary score, including movements from Braveheart, as well as some unrendered effects and scenes which were later deleted. The audience comprised industry professionals and fans.

A showing of the finished film billed as the "Gala Premiere" was held at the Edinburgh International Film Festival on August 22, 2005,[40] followed by an interview with Whedon the next day,[41] and preview screenings across the United Kingdom and Ireland on August 24, 2005, in London, Birmingham, Manchester and Dublin. Several of the screenings in all the countries featured the attendance of Joss Whedon and the film's cast, followed by a Q&A session with the audience. Whedon also attended two Q&A sessions after sold-out screenings of the finished film in Melbourne and Sydney on September 12, 2005 and September 13, 2005.

The trailer also generated considerable buzz on the internet. It was uploaded on April 26, 2005 and by April 28, 2005, it topped the Yahoo Buzz Index.[42][43] On October 5, 2005, Universal made the first nine minutes of *Serenity* available online.[44] A browser plug-in allowed the viewer to see the opening of the film in full-screen broadcast quality (bandwidth permitting). The clip was removed a few weeks later.

Serenity was also the first motion picture to be screened digitally, fully DCI-compliant.[45]

Marketing

Several tie-in products were released to promote the film; The novelization of the film was written by Keith R. A. DeCandido, and published by Simon & Schuster imprint Pocket Star Books on 2005-09-01.[46] *Serenity: The Official Visual Companion* was written by Joss Whedon, published by Titan Books, and released on September 1, 2005 in paperback. It contained the film's screenplay, along with other supplemental features such as concept art, film images, and a map of the universe. A role-playing game titled *Serenity*, published by Margaret Weis Productions, Ltd, was released in 2005. This was followed by *Serenity: Out in the Black* by Tracy and Laura Hickman.

A three-issue comic book series titled *Serenity: Those Left Behind* was released from July through September 2005.[47] It was intended to bridge the gap between the end of the television series and the beginning of the film. The comic was written by Joss Whedon and Brett Matthews, illustrated by Will Conrad and Laura Martin, and published by Dark Horse Comics. The story focuses on the crew of *Serenity* taking a salvage job from Badger following a botched theft on a backwater planet, and the pursuit of River by the ominous blue-gloved men seen in the television series. In March through May 2008, a new *Serenity* miniseries, titled *Serenity: Better Days*,[48] was released, relating a heist where everything goes right and the crew finds themselves in a rare place: on easy street. The adventure takes place "before the movie and before certain people were iced"; i.e., in the timeframe of *Firefly*.

R. Tam sessions

Universal also employed a viral marketing campaign, producing five short videos that were released on the internet between August 16, 2005 and September 5, 2005. These short films, known as the "R. Tam sessions", depicted excerpts of counseling sessions with the character River Tam while she was being held at a "learning facility" known only as "The Academy". The counselor in these sessions is played by Joss Whedon himself. Taking place before the events of the film or the television series, the videos shed some light on the experiments and torture "The Academy" conducted on River. They "document" her transformation from a shy child prodigy to the mentally unstable character of the television series.[49]

Home video

Serenity was initially released on home video in North America on December 20, 2005. It was released on Region 1 DVD, UMD, and VHS, and the DVD quickly went to #1 in sales on Amazon.com.[50] It also spent two weeks in the top ten on *Billboard*'s Top DVD Sales charts, peaking at #3. As of January 15, 2006, the DVD/VHS rentals of the film had grossed around $9,190,000.[51] Included as extras on the DVD are an audio commentary by Joss Whedon, deleted scenes and outtakes, and several short documentaries. These documentaries include "Future History: The Story of Earth That Was", "What's in a Firefly", and "Re-Lighting the Firefly". Also included is a short introduction to the film by Joss Whedon, and an easter egg[52] that features a small featurette on the "Fruity Oaty Bar" commercial.[53] NASA astronaut Steven Swanson, a fan of the show,[54] took the Region 1 *Firefly* and *Serenity* DVDs with him on Space Shuttle Atlantis' STS-117 mission, which lifted off on Friday June 8, 2007. The DVDs will permanently reside on the International Space Station as a form of entertainment for the station's crews.[55]

The film was released as a two-disc set in Australia (Region 4) and parts of Europe (Region 2) on February 8, 2006. This version included new features, in addition to the supplemental material found on the North American (Region 1) release. At present, disc 2 is exclusive *only* to Australia and Benelux — Belgium, The Netherlands, Luxembourg and New Zealand. It was released in Germany as part of the special edition[56] However, other international territories may decide to release the 2nd disc as well. Added material for disc 1 includes "A Filmmaker's Journey: Journey with Joss from Script to Screen", which is available on all international DVDs, but not the US version. Added material for disc 2 includes a Joss Whedon Q&A session filmed at Fox Studios in Sydney, extended scenes, and two documentaries titled "Take a Walk on Serenity" and "The Green Clan". An "exclusive collector's tin" version of *Serenity* was released for the two disk edition by the EzyDVD chain of stores in Australia.[57]

Serenity was released on HD DVD on April 18, 2006, and was one of the first films to be released on the format. It ranked in the later 100s on Amazon.com in top selling DVDs. Given the low demand for HD DVDs at that point, this is quite notable. The disc included all of the bonus features found on the original Region 1 disc. As of November 29, 2006 *Serenity* was the fifteenth highest-selling HD DVD. After the title key for *Serenity* was copied from a software player (as documented in Muslix64's doom9 forum thread [58]) and posted on the internet as a riddle,[59] the film soon became the first HD DVD release to be released on the BitTorrent network on January 12, 2007.[60] The pirated release was a 19.6 GB 1080p VC-1 .EVO file with 5.1 DDPlus encoded sound. Although many other releases soon followed after the discoveries in muslix64's thread, *Serenity*'s marked the beginning of widespread HD DVD pirating.

A two-disc Collector's Edition DVD of the film was released for Region 1 on August 21, 2007. According to Whedon, the excellent sales figures for the "Normal Edition" DVD allowed this release.[61] The DVD included all of the once-Australian-exclusive bonus features, sans the Joss Whedon Q&A session filmed at Fox Studios in Sydney, and with new content including a DTS 5.1 surround track, a second commentary with Whedon, Nathan Fillion, Adam Baldwin, Summer Glau and Ron Glass, the R. Tam sessions (dubbed "Session 416"), and the *Sci-Fi Inside: Serenity* documentary.[62] [63] Universal Pictures redesigned the film's official website to reflect the new DVD set.[64]

On Tuesday, December 30, 2008, Serenity was released on Blu-ray Disc.

Charity screenings

Beginning in January 2006, fans (with Universal's blessing) began organizing charity screenings of *Serenity* to benefit Equality Now, a human rights organization supported by Joss Whedon. By mid-June, 41 such screenings had been confirmed for cities in Australia, Canada, England, New Zealand, and the United States, and as of June 19, 2006, there were 47 scheduled screenings. The project was referred to as "Serenity Now/Equality Now" on the official website, is often referred to in shortened form as "Serenity Now", and was coordinated through "Can't Stop The Serenity".[65], [66]

This has become a multi-venue event held each calendar year in various countries and cities and on various dates throughout the year. Funds raised by the events go to Equality Now (and other charities[67]). The following are results from past and ongoing events (in USD):[68]

- 2006: $65,000
- 2007: $106,000
- 2008: $107,219
- 2009: $137,331
- 2010: $127,000
- 2011: $44,017 (as of August 23, 2011)

Reception

Box office performance

Despite critical acclaim and high anticipation, *Serenity* performed poorly at the box office. Although several pundits predicted a #1 opening,[69] [70] [71] the film opened at #2 in the United States, taking in $10.1 million its first weekend, spending two weeks in the top ten, and closed on November 17, 2005 with a domestic box office gross of $25.5 million.[1] Movie industry analyst Brandon Gray described *Serenity*'s box office performance as "like a below average genre picture".[72]

Serenity's international box office results were mixed, with strong openings in the UK, Portugal and Russia, but poor results in Spain, Australia, France and Italy. United International Pictures canceled the film's theatrical release in at least seven countries, planning to release it directly to DVD instead. The box office income outside the United States was $13.3 million, with a worldwide total of $38.9 million,[73] slightly less than the film's $39 million budget, which does not include the promotion and advertising costs.

Critical reception

Serenity received mostly positive reviews from film critics, with 81% positive ratings at the movie review website Rotten Tomatoes.[74] Ebert and Roeper gave the film a "Two Thumbs Up" rating,[75] and *The San Francisco Chronicle* called it "a triumph",[31] while *The New York Times* described it as a modest but superior science fiction film.[76] Science fiction author Orson Scott Card called *Serenity* "the best science fiction film ever", further stating "If *Ender's Game* can't be this kind of movie, and this good a movie, then I want it never to be made. I'd rather just watch *Serenity* again."[77]

However, some reviewers felt the film was unable to overcome its television origins, and did not successfully accomplish the transition to the big screen. *USA Today* wrote that "the characters are generally uninteresting and one-dimensional, and the futuristic Western-style plot grows tedious" while *Variety* declared that the film "bounces around to sometimes memorable effect but rarely soars".

Awards

- Film of the year awards from Film 2005[2] and FilmFocus.[3]
- IGN Film's Best Sci-Fi, Best Story and Best Trailer awards and runner up to *Batman Begins* for the Overall Best Movie[4]
- Won the 7th annual 'User Tomato Awards' for best Sci-Fi movie of 2005 at Rotten Tomatoes.
- Won Nebula Award for Best Script for 2005.
- 2006 viewers choice Spacey Award for favorite movie.
- Voted as the best film of 2006 by the writers for the website Box Office Prophets and it came 12th Best film of 2006 in the website's readers poll.
- Won Best Dramatic Presentation, Long Form at the 2006 Hugo Awards.[5]
- SyFy Genre Awards 2006:[78]
    - Best Movie Runner-Up
    - Best Actor/Movie Runner-Up: Nathan Fillion
    - Best Actress/Movie Runner-Up: Summer Glau
- *SFX magazine*'s best sci-fi movie of all time.[79] [80] [81]

In other media

On February 20, 2009 NASA announced an online poll to name Node 3 of the International Space Station, and NASA-suggested options included Earthrise, Legacy, Serenity, and Venture.[82] At the March 20, 2009 poll close, 'Serenity', led those four choices with 70% of the vote, though the winner of the poll was 'Colbert', a reference to late night comedy show host Stephen Colbert (In the end, the poll was discarded and the node was eventually named 'Tranquility').[83] Multiple internet sites have asserted that that name is a nod to the Whedon-created fictional spacecraft,[84] [85] while Fox News observed simply that it "shares the name of a spaceship in the cult favorite television series 'Firefly'".[86]

Themes and cultural allusions

While the film depicts the Alliance as an all-powerful, authoritarian-style regime, Whedon is careful to point out that it is not so simple as that. "The Alliance isn't some evil empire," he explains, but rather a largely benevolent bureaucratic force. The Alliance's main problem is that it seeks to govern everyone, regardless of whether they desire to belong to the central government or not.[87] What the crew of Serenity, and specifically Mal and his lifestyle, represent is the idea that people should have the right to make their own decisions, even if those decisions are bad.[88]

The Operative embodies the Alliance and is, as Whedon described, the "perfect product of what's wrong with the Alliance". He is someone whose motives are to achieve a good end, a "world without sin". The Operative believes so strongly in this idea that he willingly compromises his humanity in furtherance of it - as he himself admits, he would have no place in this world. In contrast, Mal is, at the movie's beginning, a man who has lost all faith.[89] By the end of the movie, however, Mal has finally come to believe in something — individual liberty — so strongly that he becomes willing to lay down his life to preserve it.[88] [90] Whedon has said that the most important line in the film is Mal's contented promise to the Operative at its climax: "I'm going to show you a world without sin", as he shows him the Miranda footage. Whedon's point is that a world without sin is a world without choice, and that choice is ultimately what defines humanity.[88]

Joss Whedon said in the DVD commentary track that the planet "Miranda" was named for Shakespeare's Miranda in *The Tempest*, who says in Act V, scene I: "O brave new world, / That has such people in't!"[90] The Alliance had hoped that Miranda would be a new kind of world, filled with peaceful, happy people, and represents the "inane optimism of the Alliance".[91]

Malcolm Reynolds, the main character in this film, shoots at least three unarmed people, even one that was surrendering. On the DVD director's commentary, director Joss Whedon stated that he included this scene as "a reaction to the Greedo incident in *Star Wars*."

The Fruity Oaty Bar commercial is partially inspired by Mr. Sparkle, the mascot of a fictional brand of dish-washing detergent, who was featured in *The Simpsons* episode "In Marge We Trust".[92] Whedon also mentions, in a feature on the *Serenity* DVD, that when the Fruity Oaty Bar commercial was being designed, he constantly asked the animators to redesign it and make it even *more* bizarre than the previous design, until it arrived at the version presented on screen.

Sequel possibilities

Fans of *Firefly* had hoped that if *Serenity* had been successful, it might lead either to a revival of the television series or a film franchise (colloquially referred to as the "Big Damn Trilogy", or BDT).[93] [94] The former was always unlikely, since Fox still owns the *Firefly* television rights and Joss Whedon reportedly refused to work for Fox again[95] (though he has since written and produced the television series *Dollhouse* for the network). Fans' hopes for further theatrical films appear to have been partially dashed by *Serenity*'s mediocre box office showing. Whedon has stated that if a sequel is made, he hopes to address the character Book's backstory and deal with Jubal Early, a bounty hunter character in *Firefly*.[96] The first major sequel rumor began on December 1, 2005, when IGN Filmforce reported that Universal had expressed an interest in making a *Serenity* TV movie for broadcast on the Sci-Fi Channel (which is owned by Universal), and eventual DVD sale. It was expected that commissioning of a television sequel would be contingent on strong DVD sales of *Serenity*.[97] In a January 2006 interview, Whedon doubted the chances of a sequel.[98] On June 23, 2006 a number of fans organized and spread word of "Serenity Day", on which all fans were proposed to purchase a copy of *Serenity* in an attempt to convince Universal that a sequel would be profitable. The significance of this day was that June 23, 2006 was the one-year anniversary of the third and final advance screening of *Serenity* prior to its release, as well as Joss Whedon's birthday. The impact of the event could be seen from *Serenity* reaching #2 in the Amazon DVD Charts,[99] the highest ranking the DVD had reached since January 16, 2006.[100]

On October 1, 2006, Whedon posted a comment to the Whedonesque.com website, responding to a rumor that he was currently working on a sequel to *Serenity*. He wrote,

> There's no sequel, no secret project regarding *Serenity* or somesuch and I'm not even sure how anyone thought there was talk there. I've seen Nathan and Tim (and Summer and Alan) recently because they're my friends because I'm so, yeah, awesome. So let's put that to bed and smother it with a pillow.[101]

Whedon's response to the rumor consequently sparked many websites to publish articles stating that he would never work on a sequel to *Serenity*. Whedon again returned to Whedonesque.com to respond to the new stories and wrote,

> Holy Mother of Oats! I turn my back for five minutes (that's how long it takes to admire my lovely back) and the interweb goes banoonoos! Isn't there any ACTUAL news to get wrong? Sorry about all this; it might be best if I just stay off the computer for a while.... Here's a thing: when *Firefly* was cancelled, my heart got broke. Sounds a bit much, but it changed me. Not even *Serenity* could patch that wound. I'm wearier, warier — after all those years as a movie writer, you'd think I'd be prepared for another lesson on my unimportance in the scheme of things, but I wasn't.... All these rumor of projects or the death of projects... When the two worlds align and something actually happens, whatever it is, you guys know I'll be on this site as soon as I'm allowed to be. And I'll be very very clear. There is no news. Not never, just now.[102]

In an interview at the 2007 Comic-Con, Whedon stated that he believes hope for a sequel rests in the sales of the Collector's Edition DVD.[103] [104] In an August 2007 interview with Amazon.com prior to the Collector's Edition DVD release, Whedon stated, "It's still on my mind, I mean, but I don't know if mine is the only mind that it's on." He later said, "You know, whether or not *anybody* who's involved would be available at that point — everybody's working, I'm happy to say — is a question, but whether I would want to do another one is not a question."[105] On

October 4, 2007, Alan Tudyk suggested in an interview that Universal was considering another film due to DVD sales,[106] although Joss Whedon later discounted Tudyk's statement as being "wishful thinking."[107]

References

[1] "Serenity (2005) - Daily Box Office" (http://www.boxofficemojo.com/movies/?page=daily&id=serenity.htm). Box Office Mojo. . Retrieved 2006-08-27.
[2] "Films Of The Year" (http://web.archive.org/web/20060709160630/http://www.bbc.co.uk/films/film2005/filmofyear_2005.shtml). BBC. Archived from the original (http://www.bbc.co.uk/films/film2005/filmofyear_2005.shtml) on 2006-07-09. . Retrieved 2006-08-27.
[3] "Serenity" (http://www.filmfocus.co.uk/specials/review2005-1.asp). FilmFocus. . Retrieved 2006-08-27.
[4] "The Best of 2005" (http://bestof.ign.com/2005/movies/). IGN Film. . Retrieved 2006-08-27.
[5] "Hugo and Campbell Awards Winners" (http://www.locusmag.com/2006/News/08_HugoCampbellWinners.html). *Locus Online*. 2006-08-26. . Retrieved 2006-08-27.
[6] Russell, M.E. (2006-06-24). "The Browncoats Rise Again" (http://www.weeklystandard.com/Content/Public/Articles/000/000/005/757fhfxg.asp). The Daily Standard. . Retrieved 2006-07-16.
[7] July 26, 2004 TV Guide, p. 34
[8] Whedon, *Firefly: the complete series: "Serenity" commentary*
[9] Whedon, *Serenity: Director's Commentary*, track 1 "Living Weapon"
[10] Whedon, *Firefly: the complete series: "Train Job" commentary*, track 10
[11] Whedon, *Serenity: Director's Commentary*, track 7 "Mr. Universe"
[12] Staite, Jewel (2004). "Kaylee speaks: Jewel Staite on Firefly". In Jane Espenson, Glenn Yeffeth. *Finding Serenity, anti-heroes, lost shepherds and space hookers in Joss Whedon's Firefly*. Dallas: BenBella books. pp. 227. ISBN 1-932100-43-1. PN1992.77.F54F56 2005. "Aside from playing Kaywinnit Lee "Kaylee" Frye in Firefly and Serenity"
[13] "The shooting script" (http://www.titanbooks.com/products/uk/9568-serenity_the_official_visual_companion/). *Serenity, the official visual companion* (paperback ed.). London: Titan books. 09 2005. pp. 78. ISBN 9781845760823. . "Kaywinnit Lee Frye, as sweet and cheerful as she is mechanical [...] Kaylee is opening the doors"
[14] Whedon, *Serenity: The Official Visual Companion*, pp.21, 24.
[15] Whedon, *Serenity: The Official Visual Companion*, p.17
[16] "Captain on Deck! hello to all" (http://forums.prospero.com/foxfirefly/messages?msg=8664.1). Official Firefly Forum. 2003-06-13. . Retrieved 2006-07-06.
[17] ""Serenity Saloon" is open fer bidness" (http://forums.prospero.com/foxfirefly/messages?msg=4235.193900). Official Firefly Forum. 2003-06-06. . Retrieved 2006-07-06.
[18] ""Serenity Saloon" is open fer bidness" (http://forums.prospero.com/foxfirefly/messages?msg=4235.194037). Official Firefly Forum. 2003-06-06. . Retrieved 2006-07-06.
[19] *Serenity Collector's Edition DVD cast commentary*
[20] McNamara, Mary (October 9, 2005). "Hollyworld: Down-home directing" (http://www.calendarlive.com/printedition/calendar/cl-ca-homefront9oct09,0,2503431.htmlstory). *Los Angeles Times*. . Retrieved 2008-03-09.
[21] Snyder, Gabriel (2004-03-21). "'Firefly' feature alights" (http://www.variety.com/article/VR1117901954.html?categoryid=13&cs=1). Variety. . Retrieved 2006-07-02.
[22] Snyder, Gabriel (2004-03-03). "Whedon's 'Serenity' greenlit" (http://www.variety.com/article/VR1117901089?categoryid=13&cs=1&query=firefly&display=firefly). Variety. . Retrieved 2006-07-02.
[23] stated by Summer Glau in several interviews ((http://sci-fi-online.50megs.com/2006_Interviews/06-01-30_SummerGlau.htm), (http://movies.about.com/od/serenity/a/serentysg120604.htm))
[24] "Dead city of Miranda/modern American high school" (http://whedonesque.com/comments/10109). Whedonesque.com. 2006-04-19. . Retrieved 2006-07-02.
[25] Epstein, Daniel Robert (c. 2005-09-30). "Interview with Joss Whedon" (http://suicidegirls.com/words/Joss+Whedon/). *Suicide Girls*. . Retrieved 2006-05-19.
[26] None, Radegund (2006-08-29). "Official Costumes" (http://browncoats.com/index.php?ContentID=42ea915100af6). browncoats.com. . Retrieved 2006-09-26.
[27] Skaro, Jo (2005-07-00). "Even Space Cowboys Hanker to Look Shiny" (http://www.skaro.com/firefly_cos.html). skaros.com. . Retrieved 2006-09-26.
[28] Koukoulas, Steve. "Firefly the Complete Series" (http://www.dvd.net.au/review.cgi?review_id=4273). dvd.net.au. . Retrieved 2006-09-26.
[29] Tyler, Joshua (2005-09-29). "Movie Review" (http://www.cinemablend.com/reviews/Serenity-1157.html). cinemablend.com. . Retrieved 2006-09-26.
[30] Gibner, Jason. "Genius in the Shadows" (http://web.archive.org/web/20061206155205/http://www.annarborpaper.com/content/issue24/murch_24.html). annarborpaper.com. Archived from the original (http://www.annarborpaper.com/content/issue24/murch_24.html) on 2006-12-06. . Retrieved 2007-01-07.

[31] Hartlaub, Peter (2005-09-30). "'Serenity' earns director Whedon spot on sci-fi's Mount Rushmore" (http://sfgate.com/cgi-bin/article.cgi?file=/c/a/2005/09/30/DDGP7EVFH91.DTL). San Francisco Chronicle. .

[32] Espenson, Jane (2005-09). "Finding Serenity - Anti-Heroes, Lost Shepherd and Space Hookers in Joss Whedon's Firefly" (http://www.troynovant.com/Franson/Espenson/Finding-Serenity.html). . Retrieved 2006-10-13.

[33] eyeofhorus (2005-09-13). "Having a beer with Joss" (http://web.archive.org/web/20051224181843/http://serenitymovie.com.au/viewtopic.php?t=718). *Serenity Oz (serenitymovie.com.au)*. Archived from the original (http://serenitymovie.com.au/viewtopic.php?t=718) on 2005-12-24. . Retrieved 2006-05-19.

[34] Whedon, *Serenity: Director's Commentary*, "What's In A Firefly"

[35] Miller, Gerri. "Inside 'Serenity'" (http://entertainment.howstuffworks.com/serenity2.htm). . Retrieved 2006-07-09.

[36] "Interview with Zoic Studios' Visual Effects for Serenity" (http://web.archive.org/web/20060318164830/http://www.newtek.com/lightwave/profiles/Serenity/index.php). NewTek.com. 2006-01-24. Archived from the original (http://www.newtek.com/lightwave/profiles/Serenity/index.php) on 2006-03-18. . Retrieved 2006-07-09.

[37] Whedon, *Serenity: Director's Commentary*, Track 3 "Aboard Serenity".

[38] "More Serenity Screenings Announced, Sell Out Immediately" (http://www.rottentomatoes.com/news/comments/?entryid=194977). rottentomatoes.com. 2005-05-12. . Retrieved 2006-07-11.

[39] "Serenity Screenings Sell Out" (http://slashdot.org/articles/05/05/01/1319212.shtml?tid=214&tid=97). slashdot. 2005-05-01. . Retrieved 2006-07-11.

[40] Serenity (http://www.edfilmfest.org.uk/movies/show/serenity/) at the Edinburgh International Film Festival

[41] Reel Life: Joss Whedon Live Onstage Interview (http://www.edfilmfest.org.uk/movies/show/reel_life__joss_whedon/) at the Edinburgh International Film Festival

[42] "Serenity Trailer Now Online!" (http://whedonesque.com/comments/6566). Whedonesque.com. 2005-04-26. . Retrieved 2006-07-11.

[43] "Serene on the Screen" (http://web.archive.org/web/20061028210018/http://buzz.yahoo.com/buzz_log/entry/2005/04/28/1300/). Yahoo Buzz Index. 2005-04-28. Archived from the original (http://buzz.yahoo.com/buzz_log/entry/2005/04/28/1300/) on 2006-10-28. . Retrieved 2006-07-11.

[44] Serenity preview now closed (http://video.vividas.com/CDN1/3929_Serenity/web/index.html)

[45] "Free Screening of "Serenity" at ETC on Nov. 7, 2005; First Screening of Fully Compliant DCI Feature" (http://www.2-pop.com/articles/article_13775.shtml). 2-pop.com. 2005-10-28. . Retrieved 2008-07-15.

[46] "Serenity (Mass Market Paperback)" (http://www.simonsays.com/content/book.cfm?sid=33&pid=505351). Simon & Schuster. . Retrieved 2008-02-09.

[47] http://comicbookdb.com/title.php?ID=468

[48] http://comicbookdb.com/title.php?ID=17336

[49] R_Tam_Sessions_Full.mov (http://ia300116.us.archive.org/1/items/R._Tam_Sessions_Complete_4/R_Tam_Sessions_Full.mov) (The site's FAQ states that it was not involved with the making of these videos in any way.)

[50] "Serenity DVD Amazon sales rank tracker" (http://www.fireflyfans.net/amazonserenity.asp). Fireflyfans.net. .

[51] "Top Renters for Week Ended January 15, 2006" (http://www.videobusiness.com/index.asp?layout=marketData&content=topvideorenters&weekending=1/15/2006&Submit=Go). VideoBusiness.com. . Retrieved 2006-03-12.

[52] The easter egg is included on the U.S., European and Canadian editions.

[53] Titled "We'll Have A Fruity Oaty Good Time", it can be found by going to the main menu, selecting but not activating "play movie", then pressing the left button. A design on the right will highlight. Press play. DVD Easter Egg found on Serenity (Widescreen) (http://www.dvdtown.com/easteregg/serenitywidescreen/17341/614)

[54] BREAKING ATMO - Meet Your Browncoat Astronaut (http://www.breakingatmo.com/status/2007/06/meet-your-browncoat-astronaut)

[55] LiveScience.com Blogs » Blog Archive » Board Game, Sci-Fi to Ride Shuttle Atlantis to ISS (http://www.livescience.com/blogs/2007/06/07/board-game-sci-fi-to-ride-shuttle-atlantis-to-iss)

[56] "German Special Edition on Amazon.de" (http://www.amazon.de/exec/obidos/ASIN/B000E6UUO6). .

[57] Serenity (EXCLUSIVE Collector's Tin) (2 Discs) @ EzyDVD (http://www.ezydvd.com.au/item.zml/784707)

[58] http://forum.doom9.org/showthread.php?t=119871

[59] welcome slashdot (http://pastebin.com/853659)

[60] www.hdtvblogger.com Coming Soon! (http://www.hdtvblogger.com/2007/01/12/and-so-it-starts-first-real-hd-dvd-rip-up-on-torrent-sites)

[61] Whedon, Joss (2007-03-01). "Serenity: Special Edition DVD to be released in July" (http://whedonesque.com/comments/12606#164745). Whedonesque.com. . Retrieved 2008-05-26.

[62] Serenity (US - DVD R1) in News > Releases at DVDActive (http://www.dvdactive.com/news/releases/serenity5.html)

[63] Universal Studios Home Entertainment :: From Universal Home Entertainment: Serenity Collector's Edition on DVD August 21, 2007 (http://sev.prnewswire.com/entertainment/20070731/LATU15431072007-1.html)

[64] Serenity DVD — Serenity movie - firefly serenity movie (http://www.serenitymovie.com/)

[65] http://www.cantstoptheserenity.com/

[66] "Can't Stop The Serenity" (http://www.cantstoptheserenity.com/). .

[67] "Can't Stop the Serenity website (The Cause – Equality Now). (http://www.cantstoptheserenity.com/about/cause/) "Other Worthy Causes: While the majority of profits from a screening go to Equality Now, organizers can choose to donate up to 25% to other charities of their choice."
[68] "Can't Stop the Serenity website (History). (http://www.cantstoptheserenity.com/about/history-2/) *Retrieved September 27, 2011*
[69] Karger, Dave (2005-09-29). "Back in Commission" (http://www.ew.com/ew/report/0,6115,1111625_1_0_,00.html). Entertainment Weekly. .
[70] Gray, Brandon (2005-09-29). "BOX OFFICE FORECAST" (http://boxofficemojo.com/forecast/2005/3.htm). Box Office Mojo. .
[71] "Box Office Forecast" (http://www.boxofficereport.com/wbon/old/093005.shtml). Box Office Report. .
[72] Gray, Brandon (2005-10-17). "'Fog' Tops Soggy Weekend" (http://www.boxofficemojo.com/news/?id=1919&p=.htm). Box Office Mojo. .
[73] "Serenity (2005) - International Box Office" (http://www.boxofficemojo.com/movies/?page=intl&id=serenity.htm). Box Office Mojo. .
[74] Serenity (2005) (http://www.rottentomatoes.com/m/serenity/) at Rotten Tomatoes
[75] Ebert & Roeper, Reviews for the Weekend of October 1 - 2, 2005 (http://tvplex.go.com/buenavista/ebertandroeper/051003.html)
[76] Dargis, Manohla (2005-09-30). "Scruffy Space Cowboys Fighting Their Failings" (http://www.nytimes.com/2005/09/30/movies/30sere.html/partner/rssnyt?ex=1129262400&en=c8b757b751be776f&ei=5070). New York Times. .
[77] Card, Orson Scott (2005-09-30). "Uncle Orson Reviews Everything" (http://www.hatrack.com/osc/reviews/everything/2005-09-30-extra.shtml). *Hatrack.com*. . Retrieved 2006-05-19.
[78] "SyfyPortal Awards" (http://web.archive.org/web/20061107100529/http://www.syfyportal.com/news.php?id=2895). Archived from the original (http://syfyportal.com/news.php?id=2895) on 2006-11-07. . Retrieved 2006-10-08.
[79] "'Serenity' Beats 'Star Wars' in Best Sci-Fi Film Poll" (http://www.b.cinematical.com/2007/04/02/serenity-beats-star-wars-in-best-sci-fi-film-poll/). . Retrieved 2007-04-03.
[80] "Serenity named top sci-fi movie" (http://news.bbc.co.uk/1/hi/entertainment/6517155.stm). *BBC News*. 2007-04-02. . Retrieved 2007-04-03.
[81] "Serenity crowned top sci-fi movie" (http://www.999today.com/mediaandentertainment/news/story/10222.html). . Retrieved 2007-04-03.
[82] Yembrick, John (2009-02-20). "Be Part Of History -- Help NASA Name The Next Space Station Module" (http://www.nasa.gov/home/hqnews/2009/feb/HQ_09034_Name_Node3_prt.htm). NASA. . Retrieved 2009-03-23.
[83] "Help NASA Name Node 3" (http://www.nasa.gov/externalflash/name_ISS/index.html). 2009-03-20. . Retrieved 2009-03-23.
[84] "Help NASA Name a Node" (http://www.sfuniverse.com/2009/03/02/help-nasa-name-a-node/). SFUniverse.com. 2009-03-02. . Retrieved 2009-03-23.
[85] Newitz, Annalee (2009-03-05). "Vote to Make Serenity Into a Real Space Vessel!" (http://io9.com/5164695/vote-to-make-serenity-into-a-real-space-vessel/). io9.com. . Retrieved 2009-03-23.
[86] "Stephen Colbert Tries to Take Over Space Station" (http://www.foxnews.com/story/0,2933,506126,00.html). Fox News. 2009-03-06. . Retrieved 2009-03-23.
[87] Whedon, *Serenity: Director's Commentary*, track 11 "Miranda"
[88] Whedon, *Serenity: Director's Commentary*, track 17 "Fighting for Belief"
[89] Whedon, *Serenity: Director's Commentary*, track 2 "A Better World"; Whedon, Serenity: The Official Visual Companion, p. 21.
[90] Whedon, *Serenity: Director's Commentary*, track 10 "Posing a Threat".
[91] Whedon, *Serenity: Director's Commentary*, Track 14, "Learning the Secret"
[92] Whedon, *Serenity: Making of Fruity Oaty Bar on Serenity DVD*
[93] Daniel Terdiman (2007-08-03). "Fans of sci-fi 'Serenity' follow their bliss" (http://web.archive.org/web/20060621222119/http://news.zdnet.com/2100-1040_22-6085564.html). News.com. Archived from the original (http://news.zdnet.com/2100-1040_22-6085564.html) on 2006-06-21. . Retrieved 2006-06-20.
[94] Rebecca Murray (2004-12-06). "Nathan Fillion Talks About "Serenity": On Working with Joss Whedon and "Firefly's" Cancellation" (http://movies.about.com/od/serenity/a/serentynf120604.htm). About.com. . Retrieved 2008-01-30.
[95] "Completely completed SERENITY screens at Comic-Con! And..." (http://www.aintitcool.com/display.cgi?id=20781). Ain't It Cool News. 2005-07-25. . Retrieved 2006-06-24.
[96] "Interview : Joss Whedon" (http://www.moviesonline.ca/movienews_6536.html). Moviesonline.ca. . Retrieved 2008-02-07.
[97] "Exclusive: A Serenity Sequel?" (http://filmforce.ign.com/articles/673/673102p1.html). IGN.com. . Retrieved 2006-07-01.
[98] *Empire* (2006-01-09). "Serenity And Beyond - Exclusive: Whedon on Firefly's future" (http://www.empireonline.com/news/story.asp?NID=17800). Empire.com (http://www.empire.com/). . Retrieved 2008-01-30.
[99] "Serenity DVD Amazon Info Tracker" (http://www.fireflyfans.net/amazonserenity.asp). Fireflyfans.net. . Retrieved 2006-07-01.
[100] "Serenity Day website" (http://www.fireflyday.com). . Retrieved 2006-06-06.
[101] "Whedon Responds to sequel rumors @ Whedonesque" (http://whedonesque.com/comments/11487#143843). Whedonesque.com. . Retrieved 2006-10-04.
[102] "Whedon Responds to Rumors of Serenity Sequel Death" (http://www.whedonesque.com/comments/11513#144407). Whedonesque.com. . Retrieved 2006-10-06.
[103] Laremy Legel (2007-08-03). "COMIC CON: Exclusive Interview with Joss Whedon" (http://www.ropeofsilicon.com/news.php?id=6846). ropeofsilicon.com. . Retrieved 2007-08-03.

[104] Emily Christianson. "Comic-Con 07's Fantatsic Filmmakers: Joss Whedon Goes into 'Sugar Shock'" (http://www.hollywood.com/feature/Comic_Con_07s_Fantatsic_Filmmakers_Joss_Whedon_Goes_into_Sugar_Shock/4512280). Hollywood.com. . Retrieved 2007-08-06.
[105] Whedon's August 2007 interview with Amazon (http://anon.amazon.speedera.net/anon.amazon/upload/Universal-josswhedon/JossWhedon_Serenity.wma) (audio file)
[106] Clint Morris (2007-10-04). "Serenity 2 A New Hope?" (http://web.archive.org/web/20071007180847/http://www.moviehole.net/news/20071004_serenity_2_a_new_hope.html). www.moviehole.net. Archived from the original (http://www.moviehole.net/news/20071004_serenity_2_a_new_hope.html) on 2007-10-07. . Retrieved 2007-10-04.
[107] "What's in Your DVD Player, Joss Whedon?" (http://tv.msn.com/new-on-dvd/feature-article/default.aspx?news=281562). msn.com. 2007-11-04. . Retrieved 2007-11-06.

- DeCandido, Keith R.A. (August 30, 2005). *Serenity*. ISBN 1-4165-0755-8.
- Whedon, Joss (September 1, 2005). *Serenity: The Visual Companion*. ISBN 1-84576-082-4.
- Joss Whedon (December 9, 2003). *The Complete Series: Commentary for "Serenity"* (DVD). 20th Century Fox.

External links

- Official website (http://www.serenitymovie.com/)
- Official Australian website (http://www.serenitymovie.com.au/)
- *Serenity* (http://www.imdb.com/title/tt0379786/) at the Internet Movie Database
- *Serenity* (http://www.allrovi.com/movies/movie/v312564) at AllRovi
- *Serenity* (http://www.rottentomatoes.com/m/serenity/) at Rotten Tomatoes
- *Firefly* and *Serenity* (http://firefly.wikia.com/wiki/Main_Page) at Wikia
- Interview with *Serenity* visual effects supervisor (http://web.archive.org/web/20060101071608/http://www.vfxblog.com/vfx/2005/09/zoics_loni_peri.html)
- IGN visits the set of the film (http://movies.ign.com/articles/564/564677p1.html)
- Translations of Chinese used (http://fireflychinese.kevinsullivansite.net/index.html)

Slither (2006 film)

Slither	
Official poster for *Slither*	
Directed by	James Gunn
Produced by	Paul Brooks Eric Newman Thomas Bliss
Written by	James Gunn
Starring	Elizabeth Banks Nathan Fillion Michael Rooker Tania Saulnier Gregg Henry
Music by	Tyler Bates
Cinematography	Gregory Middleton
Editing by	John Axelrad
Studio	Gold Circle Films Strike Entertainment
Distributed by	Universal Pictures
Release date(s)	March 31, 2006
Running time	95 minutes
Country	United States
Language	English
Budget	$15 million[1]
Box office	$12,834,936[1]

Slither is a 2006 science fiction-horror-comedy film produced by Gold Circle Films and Strike Entertainment, released by Universal, written and directed by James Gunn, and starring Nathan Fillion, Elizabeth Banks, Michael Rooker, Gregg Henry, Tania Saulnier and Jenna Fischer, and is produced by Paul Brooks and Eric Newman. *Slither* is James Gunn's directorial debut.

Plot

A meteor housing a malevolent alien parasite called the Long One crashes into the town of Woodsville. While frolicking in the woods with Brenda (James), local big shot car dealer Grant Grant (Rooker) is subsequently infected and killed by the parasite. The parasite takes over his body and absorbs his consciousness and memories.[2] With the alien now in control of his body, 'Grant' begins to slowly change into a hideous sluglike monster.

No one suspects Grant of the serial pet murders that have occurred around town, however his wife Starla (Banks) begins to question his health. He avoids doctors appointments and crafts lies to keep her in the dark. Sensing her distance from her husband, her childhood crush, town sheriff Bill Pardy (Fillion), attempts to reassure and comfort her while not acting on his own feelings.

Grant infects the lonely and neglected Brenda with hundreds of his "offspring." He secrets her in an isolated barn where she in turn becomes massively obese as baby alien slugs grow inside her. Sheriff Bill Pardy leads a small group of officers on a hunt for Grant only to be lured into a trap where Brenda explodes releasing hundreds of the alien slugs. Most of Pardy's group become infected, zombie-like creatures. Strangely, the infected begin to want Starla and talk to her as if they are Grant.

Before long, the rest of the town become infected by the Long One's parasites and change into zombies controlled via a hive mind connection with 'Grant', who plans to infect the rest of the world until he is 'all that is' as shown during a failed bonding attempt with Kylie (Saulnier). Its consciousness, however, is tampered with by the real Grant's memories and his love for his wife, Starla. Sheriff Bill Pardy, Starla, Kylie, and Mayor MacReady (Henry) try to escape detection and to kill the Long One. The townspeople attack their vehicle, capturing Starla in the process.

The survivors, Sheriff Pardy and Kylie, track Starla, only to discover the infected are melding into one giant creature. They must risk their lives to stop the infestation from spreading any further. Starla charms the monster by calling him "Grant" and telling him they can be together, but as they get close to each other, she pulls a hairbrush handle from her underwear and stabs him in the chest. He slaps her with a tentacle and knocks her across the room. Meanwhile, Sheriff Pardy bursts in and tries to kill the monster with a grenade, but another tentacle knocks the grenade into the pool, where it detonates. The monster sends two sharp tentacles to stab Sheriff Pardy and infect him, and one is lodged in his stomach, but Pardy attaches the other to a small tank filling the Grant with gas, and Starla shoots the monster, causing it to explode.

All the infected suddenly turn into regular dead bodies, and the three survivors begin their slow walk to a hospital to see about the sheriff's wounds.

Cast

- Elizabeth Banks as Starla Grant
- Nathan Fillion as Bill Pardy
- Michael Rooker as Grant Grant
- Tania Saulnier as Kylie Strutemyer
- Gregg Henry as Jack MacReady
- Lorena Gale as Janene
- Jenna Fischer as Shelby Cunningham
- Jennifer Copping as Margaret
- Haig Sutherland as Trevor Carpenter
- Brenda James as Brenda Gutierrez
- Don Thompson as Wally Whale
- Patrick McAreavy as McGregor

Background and production

Gunn was said to be influenced by the wave of graphically violent horror B movies of the late 1970s and early 1980s, largely created by such directors as John Carpenter, Lloyd Kaufman, David Cronenberg, Stuart Gordon and Fred Dekker; it has close similarities to older staples like *Invasion of the Body Snatchers*, *Tremors*, *Night of the Living Dead*, and in particular *Night of the Creeps*. The film's similarities to other films triggered protests from filmgoers, according to journalist Steve Palopoli:

> "When the trailer for *Slither* came out, Internet boards about the movie suddenly lit up with protests from a legion of fans of the 1986 film *Night of the Creeps*. 'Alien slugs that turn people into zombies!' they cried. 'What a rip-off!' I bring this up not because I think *Slither*--which is a tongue-in-cheek pastiche of at least a

dozen '80s horror films--could really be considered a rip-off of any one of them except the first one, the second one and the fifth one."[3]

However, Gunn has stated that David Cronenberg's *Shivers* and *The Brood* were the two biggest influences on the story in *Slither*, along with the manga *Uzumaki* by Junji Ito.[4] [5] [6] [7] [8] *Slither* also pays homage to the studio Troma Films, where Gunn began his career. Troma co-founder Lloyd Kaufman has a cameo as a "Sad Drunk", and one scene includes a clip from the Troma film *The Toxic Avenger*.

Distribution

Slither was released on regular DVD and on HD DVD/DVD hybrid disc on October 24, 2006.[9] The HD version is presented in 1.85:1 widescreen encoded at 1080p and Dolby Digital-Plus 5.1 surround. In addition to the film, the DVD contains two making-of documentaries, one being solely dedicated to the visual effects. The DVD also contains deleted and extended scenes, a blooper reel, visual effects progressions, a set tour with Nathan Fillion, and audio commentary by James Gunn and Nathan Fillion. Also included are featurettes outlining how to make edible blood, and Lloyd Kaufman's documentary discussing his day on set, and the shooting of his one line (which was eventually cut from the film). Finally, there is an added bonus entitled "Who Is Bill Pardy?" which is a joke feature made by Gunn with the sole purpose of roasting Nathan Fillion, and was shown at the film's wrap party.[10]

Reception

Box office performance

Slither debuted in the United States and Canada on March 31, 2006 in 1,945 theaters. In its opening weekend, the film grossed $3,880,270 and ranked #8 at the U.S. and Canadian box office.[11] *Slither* grossed $7,802,450 in its theatrical run in the United States and Canada.[12] *Slither* also underperformed in France, grossing $236,261 from 150 screens.[13] The film grossed $5,032,486 as of February 6, 2008 in territories outside the United States and Canada for a worldwide gross of $12,834,936.[12] Its box office performance was substantially less than its total budget of $29.5 million, including marketing costs;[11] the production budget taking up about $15 million of the total.[14] Paul Brooks, president of *Slither*'s production company, Gold Circle Films, said the company was "crushingly disappointed" by the gross.[11] Universal Pictures distanced itself from *Slither*'s poor box office performance, citing their distribution of the film as merely part of a deal with Gold Circle Films.[15] *The Hollywood Reporter* speculated that *Slither*'s performance "might have killed off the horror-comedy genre for the near future."[11] Producer Paul Brooks offered this explanation about why *Slither* failed to catch on with movie-goers:

> "I think that because it was comedy-horror instead of pure horror is where the problem lay. It's the first comedy-horror in a long time, and maybe the marketplace just isn't ready for comedy-horror yet. It's difficult to think of other explanations."[11]

DVD performance

The DVD opened at #8 in sales and #15 in rentals, grossing $3,389,405[16] in sales and $2.08 million[17] in rentals in its opening week. The DVD total rental gross reached $11.1 million[18] and total DVD sales were $4,541,528 as of 2006.[19]

Critical reception

Slither received mostly positive reviews. Film review website Rotten Tomatoes, which calculates the consensus of critics across the United States, found that *Slither* was generally embraced favorably by critics,[20] with a rating of "85% fresh".[21] The movie was also featured in the April 14, 2006 issue of *Entertainment Weekly* as #1 on "The Must List"; "Ten Things We Love This Week".[22] *Slither* picked up the 2006 *Fangoria* "Chainsaw Award" for the

Highest Body Count, and garnered nominations in the categories of *Relationship From Hell, Dude You Don't Wanna Mess With*, and *Looks That Kill*.[23] Additionally, the horror magazine *Rue Morgue* named *Slither* the "Best Feature Film of the Year".[24] Among the critics who did not like the film, Roger Ebert and Richard Roeper gave *Slither* a "two thumbs down" rating on their television show, with Richard Roeper saying he was "all zombied out" after reviewing a wave of zombie-themed movies from the year before.[25] Guest critic Michael Phillips named *Slither* his DVD pick of the week on the television show *Ebert & Roeper*. *Slither* was listed as one of the "Top 25 DVDs of the Year" by Peter Travers in *Rolling Stone* magazine.[26]

References

[1] "Slither at Box Office Mojo" (http://boxofficemojo.com/movies/?id=slither.htm). boxofficemojo.com. 2010-01-21. . Retrieved 2010-01-21.

[2] James Gunn's Formspring (http://www.formspring.me/VonSpears/q/169616536925928950)

[3] Steve Palopoli (2006-04-05). "Film Reviews & Movie Showtimes 'Slither'" (http://www.metroactive.com/bohemian/04.05.06/slither-0614.html). Metro Active. . Retrieved 2009-01-03.

[4] Elaine Lamkin (September 2005). "Slither: Writer/Director James Gunn Gets Sticky" (http://www.bloody-disgusting.com/interview/135). Bloody-Disgusting. . Retrieved 2009-10-18.

[5] Sheila Roberts. "Exclusive : James Gunn Interview" (http://www.moviesonline.ca/movienews_8063.html). MoviesOnline. . Retrieved 2009-01-03.

[6] Brian Myers (2005-07-19). "Slither: Exclusive 1-on-1 Interview with James Gunn!" (http://www.bloody-disgusting.com/news/4340). Bloody-Disgusting. . Retrieved 2009-01-03.

[7] D_Davis (2006-04-05). "Genrebusters James Gunn - Interview 04/06" (http://www.genrebusters.com/film/interview_jamesgunn.htm). Genre Busters. . Retrieved 2009-01-03.

[8] Palopoli, Steve (April 5–11, 2006). "'Slither' Slugfest" (http://www.metroactive.com/bohemian/04.05.06/slither-0614.html). Metroactive. . Retrieved 2009-10-05.

[9] "'Slither' Oozes to HD DVD this October" (http://www.highdefdigest.com/news/show/Disc_Announcements/Universal/Slither_Oozes_to_HD_DVD_this_October/142). High-Def Digest. 2006-07-18. . Retrieved 2009-01-04.

[10] "JamesGunn.com" (http://www.jamesgunn.com). .

[11] Borys Kit (2006-04-05). "'Slither' leaves gloomy trail" (http://web.archive.org/web/20070418191254/http://www.hollywoodreporter.com/hr/search/article_display.jsp?vnu_content_id=1002277545). Hollywood Reporter. Archived from the original (http://www.hollywoodreporter.com/hr/search/article_display.jsp?vnu_content_id=1002277545) on 2007-04-18. . Retrieved 2007-09-21.

[12] "Slither (2006)" (http://www.boxofficemojo.com/movies/?id=slither.htm). Box Office Mojo. . Retrieved 2008-02-23.

[13] Conor Bresnan (2006-04-24). "Around the World Roundup: 'Ice Age' Spans Four Weeks, Tops $300M" (http://www.boxofficemojo.com/news/?id=2053&p=.htm). Box Office Mojo. . Retrieved 2007-09-21.

[14] "Slither (2006)" (http://www.boxofficemojo.com/movies/?page=main&id=slither.htm). Box Office Mojo. 2008-02-28. . Retrieved 2009-01-04.

[15] Brandon Gray (2006-04-03). "'Ice Age 2' Hot, 'Basic Instinct 2' Not" (http://www.boxofficemojo.com/news/?id=2041&p=.htm). Box Office Mojo. . Retrieved 2007-09-24.

[16] "US DVD Sales Chart for Week Ending Oct 29, 2006" (http://www.the-numbers.com/dvd/charts/weekly/2006/20061029.php). The Numbers. 2006-10-26. . Retrieved 2009-01-04.

[17] "USA DVD Rentals: 29 October 2006" (http://www.imdb.com/boxoffice/rentals?date=2006-12-24&region=us). IMDb. 2006-10-26. . Retrieved 2009-01-04.

[18] USA DVD Rentals: 24 December 2006 (http://www.imdb.com/boxoffice/rentals?date=2006-12-24&region=us)

[19] DVD sales as of 11/05/2006 (http://www.the-numbers.com/dvd/charts/weekly/2006/20061105.php)

[20] ROTTEN TOMATOES: 8th Annual Golden Tomato Awards (http://www.rottentomatoes.com/features/rtawards/movie_2006.php?r=21&mid=1159017&type=w)

[21] Slither - Movie Reviews, Trailers, Pictures - Rotten Tomatoes (http://www.rottentomatoes.com/m/slither/)

[22] The Must List: April 14, 2006 | Must List | News + Notes | Entertainment Weekly (http://www.ew.com/ew/article/commentary/0,6115,1181146_7||451056|0_0_,00.html)

[23] Chainsaw Awards - Nominees (http://horror.about.com/od/tvseriesminiseries/a/chain_award06.htm)

[24] "R.I.P. 2006 The Year in Review". RUE MORGUE. Jan/Feb 2007.

[25] Reviews from the Weekend of April 1–April 2, 2006 (http://tvplex.go.com/buenavista/ebertandroeper/060403.html). Ebert & Roeper, from movies.com.

[26] Travers, Peter (November 30, 2006). "Best 25 DVDs". ROLLING STONE.

External links

- Official website (http://www.slithermovie.net)
- *Slither* (http://www.allrovi.com/movies/movie/v1:319780) at AllRovi
- *Slither* (http://www.imdb.com/title/tt0439815/) at the Internet Movie Database

Trucker (film)

Trucker	
Directed by	James Mottern
Produced by	Scott Hanson Galt Niederhoffer Celine Rattray Daniela Taplin Lundberg Plum Pictures (company)
Written by	James Mottern
Starring	Michelle Monaghan Nathan Fillion Jimmy Bennett Benjamin Bratt Joey Lauren Adams
Distributed by	Monterey Media (U.S.)
Release date(s)	April 23, 2008 (Tribeca Film Festival)
Country	USA
Language	English

Trucker a 2008 dramatic independent film by Plum Pictures. It was written and directed by James Mottern, and produced by Scott Hanson, Galt Niederhoffer, Celine Rattray and Daniela Taplin Lundberg.

Plot

Diane Ford (Michelle Monaghan) is a long-haul truck driver. She spends her off time having one-night stands or out drinking with her married neighbor, Runner (Nathan Fillion). This life is upturned when her ex-husband Len (Benjamin Bratt) sends their 11-year-old son Peter (Jimmy Bennett) to stay with her while he recovers from cancer treatment.

Cast

- Michelle Monaghan as Diane Ford
- Nathan Fillion as Runner
- Benjamin Bratt as Leonard "Len" Bonner
- Joey Lauren Adams as Jenny Bell
- Jimmy Bennett as Peter Bonner
- Bryce Johnson as Rick
- Matthew Lawrence as Scott
- Brandon Hanson as Tom
- Maya McLaughlin as Molly
- Ricky Ellison as Robert
- Johnny Simmons as Teenager 1
- Stephen Sowan as Teenager 2
- Dennis Hayden as Trucker
- Mika Boorem as Young Woman

- Franklin Dennis Jones as Jonnie
- Amad Jackson as Doctor

Production

The film was shot on location in Hawthorne, CA, Bloomington, CA, and Mira Loma, CA.

Trucker has a reported budget of under 1.5 million dollars.[1]

Actress Michelle Monaghan learned to drive a truck in order to play her role; the movie was shot using authentic footage of her doing so.[2]

Reception

The film currently holds a 58% 'Rotten' rating on Rotten Tomatoes based on 36 reviews indicating mixed reviews.[3]

Roger Ebert chose it as one of his top ten independent films for 2009.[4]

Awards

List of awards for the film:[5]

- Michelle Monaghan – Excellence in Acting Award – Vail Film Festival
- Winner - Best Narrative Feature Film - Woods Hole Film Festival
- Official Selection Tribeca Film Festival
- Official Selection Austin Film Festival
- Official Selection Oxford Film Festival
- Official Selection Florida Film Festival
- Official Selection Vail Film Festival
- San Diego Film Critics: Best Actress (Michelle Monaghan)

References

[1] ComingSoon.net interview with [[Michelle Monaghan (http://www.comingsoon.net/news/tribecanews.php?id=44337)] April 22, 2008]
[2] James Mottern on Truckermovie.net (http://truckermovie.net/sf-forum/general-movie-discussion/questions-for-trucker-writer-james-mottern)
[3] "Trucker" (http://www.rottentomatoes.com/m/trucker/). Rotten Tomatoes. . Retrieved 2010-09-10.
[4] The best films of 2009 (http://blogs.suntimes.com/ebert/2009/12/the_best_films_of_2009.html)
[5] Official "Trucker" Theatrical Site (http://www.montereymedia.com/theatrical/films/trucker.html)

External links

- Trucker (http://www.montereymedia.com/theatrical/films/trucker.html)
- Official Fan Site (http://truckermovie.net/)
- *Trucker* (http://www.imdb.com/title/tt1087527/) at the Internet Movie Database

Waitress (film)

Waitress	
Theatrical release poster	
Directed by	Adrienne Shelly
Produced by	Todd King Jeff Rose Michael Roiff
Written by	Adrienne Shelly
Starring	Keri Russell Nathan Fillion Cheryl Hines Jeremy Sisto Andy Griffith Adrienne Shelly
Music by	Andrew Hollander
Editing by	Annette Davey
Distributed by	Fox Searchlight Pictures
Release date(s)	May 25, 2007
Running time	104 mins[1]
Country	United States
Language	English
Budget	$2,000,000
Box office	$22,179,430 (Worldwide)[1]

Waitress is a 2007 American comedy-drama film written and directed by Adrienne Shelly, who also appears in a supporting role. The film debuted at the 2007 Sundance Film Festival and went into limited theatrical release in the US on May 2, 2007.

Plot

Keri Russell plays Jenna, a waitress living in the American South, who is trapped in an unhappy marriage with the abusive Earl (Jeremy Sisto). She works in Joe's Pie Diner, where her job includes creating inventive pies with unusual titles inspired by her life, such as the "Bad Baby Pie" she invents after her unwanted pregnancy is confirmed. Jenna longs to run away from her dismal marriage, and is slowly accumulating money to do so. She pins her hopes for escape on a pie contest in a nearby town, which offers a $25,000 grand prize, but her husband won't let her go. Her only friends are coworkers Becky and Dawn (Cheryl Hines and Adrienne Shelly), and Joe (Andy Griffith), the curmudgeonly owner of the diner and several other local businesses, who encourages her to begin a new life elsewhere.

Jenna's life changes after she meets her new physician, Jim Pomatter (Nathan Fillion). He has moved to the small town to accommodate his wife, who is completing her residency at the local hospital, and is filling in for the woman who has been Jenna's doctor since childhood. The two are attracted to each other, and over the course of several pre-natal appointments the attraction grows. After Dr. Pomatter invites her into the office under a quickly exposed pretext, she impulsively initiates a passionate (and secret) affair.

Prompted by the gift of a baby journal, Jenna begins to keep a diary, ostensibly for her unborn child, with voiceovers giving the viewer access to her thoughts about that future child and her own plans. Between these entries, her relationship with Dr. Pomatter, and the thoughts she reveals as she describes the various pies she creates, the audience gets to know her evolving hopes and dreams, concerns and fears, and slowly growing attachment to the baby she at first didn't want.

After giving birth, Jenna bonds immediately with the baby girl she names Lulu. Earl, clearly disappointed it's a girl and witnessing that bonding, reminds Jenna of a promise he had forced her to make earlier not to love the baby more than she does him. That comment, the proverbial straw that broke the camel's back, wipes away any concerns she has about her lack of money and her fear of her husband. With determined frankness she tells him bluntly she hasn't loved him in years, will no longer put up with his possessiveness and abuse, and wants a divorce. Later, while Becky and Dawn are helping her prepare to leave the hospital and letting her know that Joe had lapsed and died, Jenna remembers an envelope Joe had brought to her before the birth, when she finds out he had been admitted as a patient in the same hospital. In the envelope she finds a handmade card with a sketch of her, a check for $270,450, and a message of friendship that urges her to start her life anew. While leaving the hospital, Dr. Pomatter wants to have a word with her in private regarding their affair and what is to happen now. She promptly breaks it off, handing him a chocolate Moon Pie and asks her friends to wheel her out. On the way out they ask her what that was all about, to which she coolly replies that she was having an affair with him and just ended it.

An epilogue depicts Jenna winning the pie contest, and becoming the new owner of the diner where she worked, now called Lulu's Pies, serving brightly colored pies to her customers and friends. The final shot shows her walking home hand-in-hand with the now toddler-aged Lulu (played by Shelly's actual daughter, Sophie).

Cast

- Keri Russell as Jenna Hunterson
- Nathan Fillion as Dr. Jim Pomatter
- Cheryl Hines as Becky
- Adrienne Shelly as Dawn
- Jeremy Sisto as Earl Hunterson
- Andy Griffith as Joe
- Eddie Jemison as Ogie
- Lew Temple as Cal
- Darby Stanchfield as Francine Pomatter

Reception

> Seeing *Waitress* at Sundance was a really emotional experience. The typical format for the festival is that the director is introduced to say a few words before the film begins. It was painful from the beginning to see that there was no director to introduce the film, since Adrienne had died. So the producer and Adrienne's husband Andy talked about how it had been Adrienne's dream to have a film at Sundance. It was very poignant.
>
> —Nancy Utley, COO at Fox Searchlight[2]

The film was accepted into the 2007 Sundance Film Festival, though its premiere there was bittersweet because writer/director Shelly (who also played Dawn in the film) was murdered less than three months before its debut[3] and just before she was about to learn the film had been accepted into the festival.[2] Its success there led Fox Searchlight Pictures to acquire the distribution rights for $4–5 million.[4] It opened the U.S. Comedy Arts Festival.[4]

The film received mostly positive reviews from critics, with an 89% "Fresh" rating among the 163 reviews tracked by Rotten Tomatoes,[5] and ending the year on that site's list of Top 100 films for 2007.[6] It got a 75 out of 100 at

Metacritic.[7] *Waitress* was called a "good-hearted, well-made comedy"[8] brimming with "quality star wattage".[9] The reviewer from *The A.V. Club* was less glowing, concluding:

> It would be tempting to compare the setting and ditzy sidekick/tough-talking blonde/soulful lead dynamic unfavorably to Martin Scorsese's *Alice Doesn't Live Here Anymore* if it aspired that high. With its snappy dialogue and broad characters, it's closer in spirit to that film's sitcom spin-off, *Alice*. Still, there's much to offset the shortcomings, particularly nice performances from Russell and Fillion and a rare, welcome role from Andy Griffith as the diner's gruff owner, even if he's largely there to set up a finale that cheats much of what's come before. It's an imperfect film, but it's the kind of imperfect film of which it would be nice to have seen Shelly make more.[10]

Mick LaSalle called it a "great American film" that transcends its "air of whimsicality and its emphasis on small-town characters and humble locations."[11]

References

[1] "Waitress (2007)" (http://www.boxofficemojo.com/movies/?id=waitress.htm). *Box Office Mojo*. Retrieved 2011-07-10.

[2] Wood, Gaby (2007-07-15). "The unbelievable truth" (http://www.guardian.co.uk/film/2007/jul/15/features.review1). *The Observer*. Retrieved 2011-07-10.

[3] Harvey, Dennis (2007-05-01). "Film Reviews - Waitress" (http://www.variety.com/review/VE1117932557.html). *Variety*. Retrieved 2011-07-10.

[4] Morfoot, Addie (2007-02-13). "Festival order for 'Waitress'" (http://www.variety.com/article/VR1117959391.html). *Variety*. Retrieved 2011-07-10.

[5] "Waitress" (http://www.rottentomatoes.com/m/waitress). *Rotten Tomatoes*. Flixter. Retrieved 2011-07-10.

[6] "Top Movies - 2007" (http://www.rottentomatoes.com/top/bestofrt_year.php?year=2007). *Rotten Tomatoes*. Flixter. Retrieved 2011-07-10.

[7] "Waitress Reviews, Ratings, Credits" (http://www.metacritic.com/movie/waitress). *Metacritic*. CBS. Retrieved 2011-07-10.

[8] Rocchi, James (2007-01-24). "Sundance Review: Waitress" (http://www.cinematical.com/2007/01/24/sundance-review-waitress). *Cinematical.com*. Retrieved 2011-07-10.

[9] (2007-01-23). "$UCCESS COMES TO ADRIENNE" (http://www.nypost.com/seven/01232007/news/columnists/uccess_comes_to_adrienne_columnists_lou_lumenick.htm). *NYPost.com*. Retrieved 2011-07-10.

[10] Phipps, Keith (2007-05-03). "Waitress | Film | Movie Review" (http://www.avclub.com/articles/waitress,3479). *The A.V. Club*. Retrieved 2011-07-10.

[11] LaSalle, Mick (2007-05-11). "Bittersweet film served up with heart and soul" (http://www.sfgate.com/cgi-bin/article.cgi?f=/c/a/2007/05/11/DDGF5POAC71.DTL). *San Francisco Chronicle*. Retrieved 2011-07-10.

External links

- Official website (http://www.foxsearchlight.com/waitress)
- *Waitress* (http://www.imdb.com/title/tt0473308/) at the Internet Movie Database
- *Waitress* (http://www.allrovi.com/movies/movie/v333784) at AllRovi
- Trailer (http://www.apple.com/trailers/fox_searchlight/waitress) at Apple.com

White Noise: The Light

White Noise: The Light	
Theatrical poster	
Directed by	Patrick Lussier
Produced by	Shawn Williamson
Written by	Matt Venne
Starring	Nathan Fillion Katee Sackhoff Craig Fairbrass Tegan Moss
Music by	Normand Corbeil
Cinematography	Brian Pearson
Editing by	Tom Elkins Patrick Lussier
Distributed by	Paramount Vantage
Release date(s)	January 5, 2007 (United Kingdom)
Running time	99 minutes
Country	Canada United States
Language	English
Budget	$10 million
Box office	$8.24 Million

White Noise: The Light, also marketed as ***White Noise 2***, is a 2007 horror thriller film, directed by Patrick Lussier and written by Matt Venne. The sequel stars Nathan Fillion and Katee Sackhoff in the lead roles. It is a stand-alone sequel to the 2005 film *White Noise*, directed by Geoffrey Sax. Lussier and Sax worked together on the 1996 television film *Doctor Who*.

Plot

After witnessing the murder of his wife and young son at the hands of Henry Caine (Craig Fairbrass) who then turned the gun on himself, Abe Dale (Nathan Fillion) is so distressed that he attempts to take his own life. A near-death experience follows that leaves Abe with the ability to identify those who are about to die. He acts on these premonitions to save three people from death, among them a nurse met during his recovery, Sherry Clarke (Katee Sackhoff).

Abe soon learns that Henry, before murdering Abe's wife and son, actually saved their lives. Abe concludes that Henry also had the ability to see death. Wanting to learn more about Henry, Abe visits his house only to learn that Henry survived his suicide. Investigating further, Abe discovers the phenomenon of "Tria Mera", The Third Day, when Christ was resurrected. Also on the third day the devil takes possession of the mortals who cheated death. Abe concludes that three days after he saved their lives, those he saved will be possessed and compelled to take the lives of others. Accepting this responsibility, Abe comes to terms with the horrible fact that he must consider killing to prevent further tragedy.

Cast

- Nathan Fillion as Abe Dale
- Katee Sackhoff as Sherry Clarke
- Craig Fairbrass as Henry Caine
- Adrian Holmes as Marty Bloom
- Kendall Cross as Rebecca Dale
- Teryl Rothery as Julia Caine
- William MacDonald as Dr. Karras
- Josh Ballard as Danny Dale
- David Milchard as Kurt
- Tegan Moss as Liz
- Chris Shields as Father Nathan
- David Orth as Dr. Serling

Production

Budgeted at approximately $10 million, the film is rated PG-13 for intense sequences of violence and terror, some disturbing images, thematic material and some language.

Release

The film was released to movie theaters internationally and was released direct-to-DVD in the United States on January 8, 2008.

Soundtrack

In the film, Abe witnesses a children's prayer concert that includes "The Spirit of Radio" by Rush, as arranged by Terry Frewer, a Vancouver-based composer, and performed by the Vancouver Bach Children's Chorus Soloists for this performance include Madeline Busby and Olivia Curth.

Box Office

White Noise: The Light grossed $8.24 million internationally as of January 27, 2008.

Reception

Unlike the original film, *White Noise*, the sequel received very positive reviews from most critics as well as the general public. As of November 2010, the review aggregate website Rotten Tomatoes reported that 86% of critics gave the film positive reviews with an average rating of 5.9 out of 10, based on seven reviews.[1]

References

[1] "White Noise 2: The Light (2008)" (http://www.rottentomatoes.com/m/white_noise_2/). Rotten Tomatoes. . Retrieved 2010-11-23.

External links

- *White Noise: The Light* (http://www.imdb.com/title/tt0496436/) at the Internet Movie Database
- *White Noise: The Light* (http://www.allrovi.com/movies/movie/v349932) at AllRovi

Super (2010 American film)

Super	
Theatrical release poster	
Directed by	James Gunn
Produced by	Ted Hope Miranda Bailey
Written by	James Gunn
Starring	Rainn Wilson Ellen Page Liv Tyler Kevin Bacon Nathan Fillion Michael Rooker
Music by	Tyler Bates
Cinematography	Steve Gainer
Editing by	Cara Silverman
Studio	This Is That Productions HanWay Films Ambush Entertainment
Distributed by	• IFC Films • (United States)[1] • StudioCanal • (International)
Release date(s)	September 12, 2010 (TIFF) April 1, 2011 (United States)
Country	United States
Language	English
Budget	$2.5 million[2]
Box office	$324,138[2]

Super is a 2010 American dark comedy written and directed by James Gunn, starring Rainn Wilson, Ellen Page, Liv Tyler, Kevin Bacon and Nathan Fillion. The film premiered at the 2010 Toronto International Film Festival and was released in theaters in the United States on April 1, 2011 and on Video on demand on April 13, 2011.[3] The film was released unrated[4] in U.S. theaters, and later received an R rating for its DVD/Blu-ray release.

Plot

The film opens with short-order cook Frank D'Arbo (Rainn Wilson) telling the audience of the only two good memories he's had in a life of disappointment: marrying his beautiful wife Sarah (Liv Tyler), and an incident in which he directed a police officer to catch a purse snatcher. Frank immortalizes these two events in a pair of crayon drawings he hangs on his wall for inspiration.

Later on, Sarah, a recovering addict, leaves Frank for Jacques (Kevin Bacon), a charismatic strip club owner who gets her hooked on drugs. Frank sinks into depression, where he has a vision in which he is touched by the hand of God and meets the Holy Avenger (Nathan Fillion), a superhero from a public-access television show on the All-Jesus Network who tells Frank that God has chosen him for a very special purpose. Frank believes that God has chosen him to become a superhero and goes to a local comic book shop for inspiration. His claim that he is designing a new superhero meets with enthusiastic appreciation from the foul-mouthed store clerk, Libby (Ellen Page). Frank creates a superhero costume and assumes the identity of "The Crimson Bolt". Armed primarily with a wrench, he begins to fight crime by delivering savage beatings to various rule breakers ranging from drug dealers and child molesters, to a man who cuts in line at the movies. The Crimson Bolt soon becomes a media sensation. Initially, the media views The Crimson Bolt as a violent psychopath, but he begins to gain public appreciation after the criminal backgrounds of many of his victims come to light. Frank later attempts to rescue Sarah, but Jacques's thugs recognize him under the costume and shoot Frank in the leg while he flees.

A wounded Frank goes to Libby for help, as his home is no longer safe with Jacques's thugs looking for him. Libby cajoles Frank into letting her become the Crimson Bolt's "kid sidekick", christening herself "Boltie" and designing a sexually suggestive costume. She proves to be even more unhinged than Frank, using her superhero guise to almost kill a man who may or may not have keyed her friend's car. Frank decides to let her go, but changes his mind when Libby rescues him from some of Jacques's thugs at a gas station. Libby soon becomes enamored with Frank, but her advances are turned down as Frank insists that he is still married. Deciding it is different when they are in their superhero identities, Libby rapes Frank while the two are in costume. Going in the bathroom to vomit, Frank encounters a vision of Sarah in the toilet and decides that now is the time to rescue her from Jacques.

Armed with guns, pipe bombs, and bulletproof vests, Frank and Libby sneak into Jacques's ranch killing the first few guards they encounter. Eventually, they are both shot; Frank is struck in the chest, his bulletproof vest sparing him, but Libby is struck in the head and dies instantly. Devastated by her death, Frank goes into a rage, killing all of Jacques's thugs. Inside, he has a final showdown with Jacques. Jacques shoots Frank and wounds him. Frank gains the upper hand, though, and stabs Jacques to death after a final monologue. Frank takes Sarah home, and she stays with him for a few months before leaving him again. This time, however, she manages to finally overcome her addiction and uses her experiences to help others with similar problems. She remarries and has children, but Frank is happy for her and decides that the reason why God chose him was so that he could rescue Sarah and help her get on with her life.

Frank, now with a pet bunny, looks on his wall of happy memories. Frank's entire wall is covered with pictures of his experiences from his time spent with Libby to pictures of Sarah's kids, who call him 'Uncle Frank'. Frank smiles with a tear running down his cheek.

Cast

- Rainn Wilson as Frank D'Arbo / The Crimson Bolt
- Ellen Page as Libby / Boltie
- Liv Tyler as Sarah Helgeland
- Kevin Bacon as Jacques
- Nathan Fillion as The Holy Avenger
- Michael Rooker as Abe
- Gregg Henry as Detective John Felkner
- Andre Royo as Hamilton
- Sean Gunn as Toby
- Stephen Blackehart as Quill
- Greg Ingram as Long-haired hood
- William Katt as Sgt. Fitzgibbon
- Linda Cardellini as Pet store employee
- Rob Zombie as God
- Don Mac as Mr. Range
- Steve Agee as Comic book store employee
- Mollie Milligan as Sarah's sister

Themes

Mike Stoklasa and Jay Bauman of *RedLetterMedia* analyzed various themes in their review show *Half in the Bag*.[5]

Personal journey

In stark contrast to most superhero films, Frank does not become a superhero because of a genuine interest in protecting the public, instead he uses the superhero motif to go on a journey of self-discovery. In a scene where someone cuts in line in front of him, Frank dons the superhero costume and severely hits the person for what are described as obviously "selfish" reasons.[5] Similarly, when James Gunn was asked about comparisons with *Kick-Ass*, he described *Super* as a movie "about a guy who's on his own sort of spiritual quest and he just happens to wear a superhero costume during it. But it's really about the guy and not the costume."[6]

Religion

In the film, Frank is often inspired by suggestions from the television show *The Holy Avenger* (similar to Bibleman) and by visions he sees relating to the Holy Avenger. Although the visions and thoughts are by Frank himself, he often attributes God, especially in one disturbing vision where the "Finger of God" touches his brain to inspire him to become a superhero.[5]

Glorification of violence

Stoklasa and Bauman also discussed how the film ironically mocks the glorification of violence.[5] In the film, there are many stylized acts of violence but it also has violence which is meant to make the audience "feel bad," for rooting for it.[5] Examples of this include when Libby beats an unarmed man for possibly vandalizing her friend's car. There is a scene where Frank splits a man's forehead with his wrench for cutting in line.

Production

Super was filmed between December 9, 2009 and January 24, 2010 in Shreveport, Louisiana with additional shooting at director James Gunn's home in Los Angeles, California (the comic book store shown in the film is a real store, ComicSmash, in Studio City, CA). Being a low-budget independent project, everyone involved in the film was paid scale (the minimum allowed by the Screen Actors Guild). Tyler Bates worked on the soundtrack.

Gunn has said in interviews that he had been working on the script for *Super* since 2002 but he had a hard time getting it made as producers felt that the content was too violent and esoteric. In addition, Gunn had a hard time deciding on the right actor to play Frank; John C. Reilly was Gunn's top choice, but he wasn't considered to be a big enough star for the film to get made.[7] After *Slither* was made, Gunn had effectively put the project on hold until his ex-wife Jenna Fischer encouraged him to go through with it and recommended Rainn Wilson, her co-star from *The Office*.[8] Wilson read the script while on set and decided he wanted to join the film, and in turn sent the script to Ellen Page, with whom he had worked in *Juno*, who immediately accepted the role of Libby.[9]

Super was Gunn's second film dealing with superheroes, the first being *The Specials* in 2000 that he wrote but did not direct. Gunn has said that examining superheroes from a different angle interests him, and that may do more films concerning the subject in the future.[10]

Reception

Critical response

Super received mixed reviews from critics. The review aggregator Rotten Tomatoes reported that 46% of critics made a positive review, classifying it as "rotten",[11] while Metacritic reported the film had an average score of 50 out of 100, indicating "mixed or average". Film4 wrote, "It's not that this type of movie shouldn't be made - this type of movie could be brilliant - but it plays like every first draft idea anyone had found its way to the screen because it made someone laugh over a few drinks...Some really interesting ideas and the odd flash of awesomeness, but overall a big old misfire with some ill-judged nastiness." [12] EW critic Owen Gleiberman wrote, "This trifle about a doofus who becomes a costumed superhero, even though he has no special powers, might have seemed funkier before Kick-Ass. Yet the movie is written and directed by James Gunn with a certain whimsical black-comic flair...It's really a one-joke movie, but the joke is a good one: Frank's *crusade* is just a geek's screw-loose revenge, which Wilson, digging into the character's misery, makes oddly sympathetic."[13] Conversely, Scott Weinberg of Cinematical wrote, "Chock full of insanely graphic violence, awash in thoroughly un-PC perspectives, and more than willing to keep on punching long after the audience is virtually incredulous, "Super" is fun and funny, dark and twisted, semi-schizophrenic and certifiably insane. What I liked most was its simple audacity. And Ellen Page." [14] Al Kratina reporting at the Fantasia Film Festival wrote, "There's a great movie somewhere inside James Gunn's dark comedy Super...Super is an undeniably entertaining film. But there's something off about it... *Super* is a funny film, a twisted story, and occasionally a very good movie, just rarely at the same time."[15]

Box office

Super made $46,549 on opening weekend with eleven theaters, averaging $4,232 per theater,[2] which was considered by analysts to be "a disappointing start" for the film.[16] Conversely, the film has fared better on VOD and has been anticipated to be the most successful film VOD for IFC so far.[17]

Awards

At the 2011 Fantasia Film Festival *Super* was tied with the documentary *Superheroes* for the AQCC Prize; "For two films that perfectly capture the Zeitgeist of our age and that present elaborate reflections on one of the biggest Americans trends, the AQCC Jury has awarded its best international film prize, in a tie, to the fiction film *Super* by

James Gunn and to the documentary *Superheroes* by Michael Burnett, two strong and complementary works."[18]

Controversy

Kick-Ass creator Mark Millar defended *Super* in light of accusations that it was copying his work with, "People have said to me, 'oh my God, he's ripping off *Kick-Ass*,' because it's coming out one year later, but James was doing this when I was doing *Kick-Ass* as well. Both projects were coming together at exactly the same time." Millar went on to screen *Super* at his *Kapow!* comic convention in London.[19] Gunn responded to the controversy with, "It sucks on the one hand and then on the other hand, who gives a shit? There are 4,000 bank heist movies. We can have five superheroes-without-powers movies", referring to *Defendor*, *Hero at Large* and *Special*, in addition to *Kick-Ass* and *Super*.[20]

References

[1] Kilday, Gregg (2010-09-12). "IFC Films nabs Rainn Wilson movie 'Super'" (http://www.hollywoodreporter.com/hr/content_display/news/e3iafc531ef3af052c7b017ee3a008f8d50). The Hollywood Reporter. . Retrieved 2010-09-13.

[2] *Super* (http://www.boxofficemojo.com/movies/?id=super2011.htm) at Box Office Mojo

[3] "The SUPER Release Date" (http://www.jamesgunn.com/2010/11/29/the-super-release-date-new-photos). 2010-11-29. . Retrieved 2011-01-01.

[4] Batts, Jim (2011-04-17). "James Gunn Brings SUPER to St. Louis" (http://wearemoviegeeks.com/2011/04/james-gunn-brings-super-to-st-louis/). . Retrieved 2011-09-25.

[5] Half in the Bag: Super and The Watchman Interview (http://redlettermedia.com/half-in-the-bag-super-and-the-watchman-interview/), RedLetterMedia

[6] " [SXSW Interview] James Gunn, Writer/Director of 'Super' (http://thefilmstage.com/2011/03/14/sxsw-interview-james-gunn-writerdirector-of-super/)", Jonathan Sullivan

[7] Moore, Brent (2011-03-24). "SXSW Interview: James Gunn, Director of Super" (http://www.geekscape.net/sxsw-interview-james-gunn-director-of-super.html). GeekScape.net. . Retrieved 2011-03-24.

[8] Douglas, Edward (2010-09-15). "TIFF Exclusive: Super Director James Gunn" (http://www.superherohype.com/features/articles/107172-tiff-exclusive-super-director-james-gunn). Superhero Hype. . Retrieved 2010-09-23.

[9] Riley, Janelle (2011-03-31). "'Super' Trouper" (http://www.backstage.com/bso/news-and-features-features/super-trouper-1005104312.story). Backstage. . Retrieved 2011-04-19.

[10] "SDCC 2011 EXCLUSIVE: James Gunn Talks Super on Blu-Ray" (http://www.movieweb.com/comic-con/2011/news/sdcc-2011-exclusive-james-gunn-talks-super-on-blu-ray). MovieWeb. 2011-06-26. . Retrieved 2011-06-30.

[11] "Rotten Tomatoes: Super" (http://www.rottentomatoes.com/m/super-2010/). Rotten Tomatoes.com. 2011-04-01. . Retrieved 2011-04-01.

[12] "Film4 Review" (http://www.film4.com/reviews/2010/super). .

[13] Gleiberman, Owen (2011-04-01). "Movie Review Super (2011)" (http://www.ew.com/ew/article/0,,20477552,00.html). EW.com. . Retrieved 2011-04-25.

[14] Weinberg, Scott (2010-09-12-10). "Review: James Gunn's 'Super' (TIFF 2010)" (http://blog.moviefone.com/2010/09/12/super-review-james-gunn/). Moviefone.com. . Retrieved 2011-04-02.

[15] Kratina, Al. "Fantasia 2011: Super | Montreal Gazette Blogs" (http://blogs.montrealgazette.com/2011/07/14/fantasia-2011-super/). Blogs.montrealgazette.com. . Retrieved 2011-08-25.

[16] Subers, Ray. "Arthouse Audit: 'Jane Eyre,' 'Win Win' Solid Again" (http://boxofficemojo.com/news/?id=3131&p=.htm). BoxOfficeMojo.com. . Retrieved April 25, 2011.

[17] Pond, Steve. "As VOD Explodes, a Flaw Exposed: You Can't Measure It" (http://www.thewrap.com/movies/column-post/and-top-vod-rental-who-knows-26214?page=0,2). The Wrap. . Retrieved April 28, 2011.

[18] Barton, Steve (August 7, 2011). "2011 Fantasia Film Festival Winners Announced" (http://www.dreadcentral.com/news/46264/2011-fantasia-film-festival-winners-announced). DreadCentral. . Retrieved August 10, 2011.

[19] Mortimer, Ben (2011-04-14). "Mark Millar on Upcoming Projects" (http://www.superherohype.com/features/articles/165435-exclusive-mark-millar-on-upcoming-projects). . Retrieved 2011-04-14.

[20] "Capone and SUPER writer-director James Gunn talk pipe-wrench justice and getting raped by a lady!!!" (http://www.aintitcool.com/node/49133). AintItCoolNews.com. 2011-04-04. . Retrieved 2011-04-29.

External links

- Official website (http://www.thecrimsonbolt.com/)
- *Super* (http://www.allrovi.com/movies/movie/v522035) at AllRovi
- *Super* (http://www.boxofficemojo.com/movies/?id=super2011.htm) at Box Office Mojo
- *Super* (http://www.ifcfilms.com/films/super) at IFC Films
- *Super* (http://www.imdb.com/title/tt1512235/) at the Internet Movie Database
- *Super* (http://www.rottentomatoes.com/m/super-2010/) at Rotten Tomatoes

Much Ado About Nothing (2012 film)

Much Ado About Nothing	
Directed by	Joss Whedon
Produced by	Joss Whedon
Based on	*Much Ado About Nothing* by William Shakespeare
Starring	<ul><li>Amy Acker</li><li>Alexis Denisof</li><li>Nathan Fillion</li><li>Clark Gregg</li><li>Reed Diamond</li><li>Fran Kranz</li><li>Sean Maher</li><li>Spencer Treat Clark</li><li>Riki Lindhome</li><li>Ashley Johnson</li></ul>
Cinematography	Jay Hunter
Studio	Bellwether Pictures
Country	United States
Language	English

Much Ado About Nothing is an independent film made by Joss Whedon and based on the Shakespeare play of the same name. The film is due to be released in 2012.[1]

Production

Much Ado About Nothing is the first feature from Bellwether, a micro-studio created by Whedon and his wife Kai Cole.[1][2] It was shot entirely on location at Whedon's house in Santa Monica in 12 days.[1] The film was shot in black and white by director of photography Jay Hunter, largely using hand-held cameras.[1][3] Whedon described the text as "a deconstruction of the idea of love, which is ironic, since the entire production is a love letter – to the text, to the cast, even to the house it's shot in." The film was produced by Whedon, line-produced by Nathan Kelly and M. Elizabeth Hughes, and co-produced by Kai Cole and Danny Kaminsky.[1]

Whedon asked the cast and crew to keep quiet about the project until principal photography was completed.[4] The first public hint of the film came on Twitter postings by actors Nathan Fillion and Sean Maher and costume designer Shawna Trpcic on October 23, 2011.[5]

Release

As of October 24, 2011, no distributor has been found for the film.[2] Whedon said that he hopes to take the film to film festivals "because it sounded like it would be festive".[2]

Cast

- Amy Acker as Beatrice
- Alexis Denisof as Benedick
- Nathan Fillion as Dogberry
- Clark Gregg as Leonato
- Reed Diamond as Don Pedro
- Fran Kranz as Claudio
- Jillian Morgese as Hero
- Sean Maher as Don John
- Spencer Treat Clark as Borachio
- Riki Lindhome as Conrade
- Ashley Johnson as Margaret
- Emma Bates as Ursula
- Tom Lenk as Verges
- Nick Kocher as First Watchman
- Brian McElhaney as Second Watchman
- Joshua Zar as Leonato's aide
- Paul M. Meston as Friar Francis
- Romy Rosemont as The Sexton

Clark Gregg, who was working with the director on *The Avengers* at the time, stepped in at very short notice to play the role of Leonato, which was originally intended for Anthony Head who was unavailable.[2]

References

[1] "Much Ado Press Release" (http://muchadothemovie.com/documents/MuchAdoPressRelease.pdf) (Press release). Bellweather Pictures. October 24, 2011. . Retrieved October 27, 2011.

[2] Vary, Adam B. (October 24, 2011). "Joss Whedon on his secret film of 'Much Ado About Nothing': 'This is the best vacation I've ever taken'" (http://insidemovies.ew.com/2011/10/24/joss-whedon-sean-maher-amy-acker-much-ado-exclusive/). *Entertainment Weekly*. . Retrieved October 27, 2011.

[3] "Director of Photography Jay Hunter Talks Much Ado About Joss" (http://www.whedonverse.net/features/interviews/much-ado-about-nothing-director-of-photography-jay-hunter/). *Whedonverse*. October 29, 2011. . Retrieved November 4, 2011.

[4] Nordyke, Kimberly (October 24, 2011). "Joss Whedon's Star Sean Maher Reveals 'Much Ado About Nothing' Secrets" (http://www.hollywoodreporter.com/news/joss-whedon-much-ado-about-nothing-sean-maher-nathan-fillion-252557). *The Hollywood Reporter*. . Retrieved October 27, 2011.

[5] Nordyke, Kimberly (October 23, 2011). "Joss Whedon Teases Mysterious New Project 'Much Ado About Nothing'" (http://www.hollywoodreporter.com/news/joss-whedon-nathan-fillion-much-ado-about-nothing-252323). *The Hollywood Reporter*. . Retrieved October 27, 2011.

External links

- Official Site (http://www.muchadothemovie.com/)
- *Much Ado About Nothing* (http://www.imdb.com/title/tt2094065/) at the Internet Movie Database

Two Guys and a Girl

Two Guys and a Girl	
Also known as	*Two Guys, a Girl and a Pizza Place (seasons 1 & 2)*
Genre	Sitcom
Created by	Danny Jacobson
Starring	- Ryan Reynolds - Richard Ruccolo - Traylor Howard - Nathan Fillion - Suzanne Cryer - Jillian Bach - Giuseppe Andrews
Composer(s)	- Freddy Curci - Tom Rizzo - Mark Vogel
Country of origin	United States
Language(s)	English
No. of seasons	4
No. of episodes	81 (List of episodes)
Production	
Executive producer(s)	- Mark Ganzel - Danny Jacobson - Kenny Schwartz - Marjorie Weitzman - Rick Wiener
Producer(s)	- Donald R. Beck - Vince Calandra - Jan Siegelman
Editor(s)	- Rick Blue - John Neal
Cinematography	Julius Metoyer
Running time	20–22 minutes
Production company(s)	- In Front Productions - Fox Television Studios
Broadcast	
Original channel	ABC
Original run	March 10, 1998 – May 16, 2001

Two Guys and a Girl (originally titled *Two Guys, a Girl and a Pizza Place*) is an American sitcom created by Kenny Schwartz and Danny Jacobson. It ran on ABC from March 10, 1998 to May 16, 2001. 81 episodes were transmitted over four seasons.

The series stars Ryan Reynolds, Traylor Howard and Richard Ruccolo as the primary characters. The second season saw the arrival of two recurring characters, Johnny Donnelly (Nathan Fillion) and Ashley Walker (Suzanne Cryer).

ABC bounced the sitcom from midweek to Friday night, leading to a steep drop in ratings. After the show moved back to Wednesday to try to revive the show's flagging support for a two-week trial, the plug was pulled, and the series was cancelled in May 2001. The series finale was titled "The Internet Show", an hour-long episode in which the fans of the show voted on the outcome online. In the end, they chose to have Ashley become pregnant with Pete's child, as opposed to either of the other two female characters, or nobody, becoming pregnant.

Overview

Based on the lives of Pete Dunville, Michael Bergen and Sharon Carter, the show was originally based on the life of its creator. The fictional "Beacon Street Pizza" is based on a real pizza restaurant named Theo's Pizza in Teele Square, Somerville, Massachusetts. It was where show creator Kenny Schwartz worked delivering pizzas while attending nearby Tufts University. The show was set in Boston and filmed at CBS Studio Center, in Studio City, Los Angeles, California.

The lives and loves of three close friends - Pete, a neurotic architecture student, Berg, the laid-back pre-med, and Sharon, a tough girl with a soft center. Pete and Berg are roommates and students at a local Boston university, while Sharon struggles with her work and relationships.

The series stars Ryan Reynolds as Michael Leslie "Berg" Bergen, and Richard Ruccolo as Peter "Pete" Dunville. The titular Two Guys were joined by Traylor Howard, who played Sharon Carter (later Carter-Donnelly). For the first two seasons, the series centered around the lives of Berg, an aimless graduate student, who was working at a Boston pizza parlor, Beacon Street Pizza, with Pete. They both attended graduate school together at Tufts University, unlike their college roommate, Sharon, who worked as the spokesperson (or apologist) for Immaculate Chemicals.

The format of the initial season varied considerably from that of subsequent seasons. The first season featured Jennifer Westfeldt, appearing as Melissa, Pete's girlfriend, and David Ogden Stiers as Mr. Bauer, a delusional old man who frequented the pizza place, pretending that experiences from films were his own. The second season abandoned these two characters, and focused more on the interplay between Pete and Berg, and their relationship with Sharon, who lived in the apartment above them. Berg eventually decided to attend medical school and become a doctor, while Pete dropped out of architecture classes to become a career counselor. The second season also introduced Johnny (Nathan Fillion), a jukebox repairman who started dating Sharon, and Ashley (Suzanne Cryer), a medical school classmate of Berg's who competed with him to be at the top of the class.

At the start of season three, the pizza place was abandoned entirely (hence the change in the show's title at this time), and Berg began his medical residency. Pete became a Vice President of a cosmetics company, and then a firefighter. Johnny and Sharon married and became the superintendents of the apartment building they lived in. Berg would go on to date Irene (Jillian Bach), the eccentric roommate across the hall, and Pete began dating a fellow firefighter named Marti (Tiffani Thiessen).

Cast and characters

Main cast

- Ryan Reynolds as Michael Eugene Leslie "Berg" Bergen (1998–2001) – the ditzy pretty boy who always managed to create chaos in the lives of his best friends, particularly Pete. While in college, he has difficulty settling on what he wants to do in life. Eventually he decides on becoming a doctor, where he meets Ashley, a worthy competitor at medical school. They begin a relationship, but he eventually breaks it off with her, due to her inability to reciprocate his feelings. Near the end of the show, he and Irene, Pete's former stalker, form a

relationship.
- Richard Ruccolo as Peter "Pete" Dunville (1998–2001) – often frantic and worried over what may occur with his professional and romantic life. Early in the show, he is conflicted with what he wants to do in life. He switches from his dreams of becoming an architect to becoming a fire fighter. He holds a very brief romance with Sharon. Later, near the end of the show he begins a lust-based relationship with Berg's ex-girlfriend, Ashley.
- Traylor Howard as Sharon Carter-Donnelly (1998–2001) – a complex woman who, strangely, manages to fit in with her best friends Pete and Berg. She is known for her confidence, yet inability to commit to relationships. Eventually, she manages to move past her fears and marries her boyfriend Johnny Donnelly.
- Nathan Fillion as Johnny Donnelly (1999–2001) – arrived in the second season as a jukebox repair man with eyes for Sharon. He and Sharon began dating with the occasional break-up due to Johnny's long-time friend Shaun, an attractive female who often got in the way of their relationship. The couple marry during the third season finale. Johnny's role as the super is embellished when he decides to become a fireman, against Sharon's wishes. Eventually, Sharon and Johnny decide that they are ready for children, as seen in the series finale.
- Suzanne Cryer as Ashley Walker (1999–2001) – did not arrive until the second season where she constantly rejected Berg, hoping to keep her long distance relationship with Justin (Jon Cryer) fresh. Ashley has hopes of becoming a doctor, which is where she and Berg meet. They become worthy competitors at the hospital and eventually start dating until Berg calls it off. At the end of the fourth season, she starts a sexual relationship with Pete and becomes pregnant in the series finale. This shocked viewers as they were unable to know what Ashley would do with the baby due to the show's cancellation.
- Jillian Bach as Irene (1999–2001) – arrives mid-season during season 2 where she is Pete's stalker. She continues stalking Pete until she forms a sexual relationship with Berg, while maintaining her love for Pete. Toward the end of season 3, she and Berg start dating but nevertheless break up due to Berg's other love interest, Katie Connor. Irene then forms a relationship with the mailman, causing Berg to become extremely jealous. The two get back together after an unexpected pregnancy scare.

Recurring cast

- Giuseppe Andrews as Germ (2000–2001) – the helper at Tufts Hospital who is recognized for his sluggish and premature attitude. He first appears in "Au Revoir Pizza Place", season 3 episode 2, but does not return until later on in the series where he becomes a close acquaintance of Pete, Berg, Sharon and Ashley.
- Julius Carry as Bill (1998) – the smart-mouth owner of Beacon Street Pizza. He only portrays his role during the first season.
- David Ogden Stiers as Mr. Bauer (1998) – hangs about the pizza place telling stories that are from movies which he claims to be his own experiences. The character of Mr. Bauer only occurred in the first season.
- Jennifer Westfeldt as Melissa (1998) – Pete's love interest during the first season. She arrives numerous times after "Two Guys, a Girl and an Apartment", where she and Pete break-up, which suggests that the episodes aired in the wrong order.
- Maury Ginsberg as Kamen (1998–1999) – is thwarted by Berg in "Two Guys, a Girl and Someone Better" where Berg ruins his life, more or less. He then continues to get Berg back on random occasions throughout season 2.
- Tiffani Thiessen as Marti (2000) – another love interest of Pete's who continually sasses him at the fire station. She and Pete start dating, to Irene's dislike. She broke up with Pete during the fourth season after having an affair with a baseball star.
- Dian Bachar as Roger (2001) – A mailman Irene dates after her breakup with Berg, Roger always wears shorts with his uniform. Like the *Cheers* character Cliff Clavin, Roger behaves as if his menial job requires a great amount of skill and effort. Despite his short stature, he behaves as if he were large and physically powerful, frequently challenging the much larger Berg to fights. In the finale, it is revealed this sense of self-confidence comes from his status as an army reservist who is trained to snap a mans neck with one hand.

Guest cast

- Carmen Electra as Isabella (1998) – the love interest of Pete and gets in the way of him and Berg. When Pete constantly feels he must dump on Melissa to go to 845 Arlington, Berg tries to stop him. ("Two Guys, a Girl and a Pizza Delivery")
- Jon Cryer as Justin (1999) – Ashley's long-distance boyfriend who moves to Boston to give the relationship a chance. Cryer only appeared in 1 episode. ("Two Guys, a Girl and Thanksgiving")
- Nomar Garciaparra as himself (2000) – he becomes a love interest of Ashley's until he falls for Pete's girlfriend Marti.
- Anthony Head as Dr. Staretski (1999) – he is a role model of Ashley's in the episode "Two Guys, a Girl and Mother's Day". Berg is surprised when he finds out that he paints nudes.
- Kathy Kinney as Mimi (1998) – Kinny played Mimi from *The Drew Carey Show* on the episode "Two Guys, a Girl and a Psycho Halloween". Her appearance is a short cameo role.
- Fred Willard as Frank Farber (1998) interviews Pete in "Two Guys, A Girl and a Vacation". He talks to Pete about woman he has conquered all around the world, until Berg uses a Scottish accent pretending to be his long lost love child to drive him away.
- Adam Carolla as himself (1998) – Carolla appeared as himself from the talkshow *Loveline*. Pete constantly asks him for advice on dating and career issues when Pete becomes a limo driver in "Two Guys, a Girl and a Limo".
- Conchata Ferrell as Shaun's mother (1999) – Ferrell plays Shaun's mother in the episode "Two Guys, a Girl and Valentine's Day". She shows excitement when meeting Berg after discovering that he is a doctor.
- blink-182 (1999) – The band appeared in the third season where they played at the pizza place naked. This showed reference to their latest single at the time, "What's My Age Again?". ("Au Revoir Pizza Place")
- Barenaked Ladies (1999) – The band made an appearance in "Two Guys, a Girl and Barenaked Ladies" where the group followed Pete around and sang about his current events."'
- Dan Finnerty & The Dan Band - made an appearance in "Bridesmaids Revisited" where Dan sang female songs throughout the episode as they followed Ashley.

Progression

Season 1

The series premiered on March 10, 1998 as *Two Guys, a Girl and a Pizza Place*. The episode entitled "The Pilot" was widely received by audiences around the U.S., having being watched by almost 18 million viewers. This allowed ABC to pick up the rest of the episodes to air mid-season.

The story of season 1 began around the premise of the pizza place. Characters such as Melissa (Jennifer Westfeldt) and Bill (Julius Carry) were credited as being the secondary cast members to Ryan Reynolds, Richard Ruccolo and Traylor Howard. Mr. Bauer, played by David Ogden Stiers, appeared around the pizza place, telling stories of his life events which have already occurred in movies. Pete would pay the rent every month and Berg (Reynolds) would test experimental drugs to help him. Pete, played by Richard Ruccolo would continue to structure his life around architecture and managing to graduate grad school, whilst Sharon (Howard), the friend upstairs, would continue to work for an evil corporation who exploit the Earth's natural resources, much to her dislike. This was the basic structure of the first season and the episodes were built around this. The episodes followed storylines such as: Pete preparing for a presentation which Berg ruins; Berg stealing the Celtic's '81 championship banner; Sharon joining the softball team and the story of how they all met. Although there is no real overall ongoing plot throughout season 1's structure is very disjointed if shown by the original production codes. This is demonstrated mainly by Pete's progress with Melissa: in episode 8 - *Party* Melissa and Pete are still together, having broken up in episode 5 - *Apartment*.

Season 2

Season 2 followed more of a structural basis for each episode. First, we see the arrival of two more primary characters, Ashley Walker (Suzanne Cryer) and Johnny Donnelly (Nathan Fillion). The involvement of these characters allowed the show to be more structural than the first season, as well as the dismissal of characters Bill, Mr. Bauer and Pete's long-time girlfriend Melissa.

The series started with Berg's realization that someone in his class, Walker, is cleverer than he is. This led to the anticipated romance between Berg and Ashley as they both headed down the path of becoming Physicians. Fillion's role as the jukebox repairman Johnny Donnelly lead to the relationship between him and character Sharon Carter (Howard). With more secondary characters (Irene, Kamen, Shaun) the show had the purpose to fill up a whole season of episodes, which it did. Other episodes of season 2 included: "Two Guys, a Girl and an Engagement", "Two Guys, a Girl and a Valentine's Day" and "Two Guys, a Girl and Ashley's Return" which all marked turning points in the story of the show. Johnny and Sharon broke up on Valentine's Day due to Sharon's jealousy of Shaun, Johnny's best friend. Berg and Ashley finally got together in "...And Ashley's Return" and Pete confesses his feelings towards Sharon and Johnny proposes in "...And an Engagement". The series ended with Sharon not giving Johnny an answer as well as her realizing that she may have feelings for Pete. This left the show at a cliffhanger after ABC had renewed the show for another season.

Season 3

The third season premiered in September, continuing the cliffhanger that occurred at the end of the second season. The pizza place had been completely abandoned so that the characters could pursue different dreams. Sharon answered Johnny's proposal with 'Yes, in theory', as she was still holding out on her feelings for Pete. Evidently, Pete flew to Paris after the night's events and returned completely over Sharon, with an ex-girlfriend. Berg and Ashley continued to build on their relationship and finally became doctors involved in Psych rotations. The series followed their relationship as being unsteady and completely built on hate of one another. This led to Berg breaking up with Ashley during the middle of the season.

Ashley continued to live with Pete and Berg during the third season before moving into her own apartment, originally Sharon and Johnny's who and moved to the basement to become the new supers. She started dating Boston Red Sox baseball star Nomar Garciaparra, who appeared as himself for a couple of episodes. Pete finds his true calling by becoming a firefighter. He enjoys the experiences of becoming an honorary firefighter until the feisty Marti, played by Tiffani Thiessen, comes along to thwart him at every turn. The two continue to take shots at each other until she starts dating Berg, to Pete's dislike. Pete and Berg get into a huge fight concerning Marti and consider not being roommates anymore.

When Pete gets his acceptance letter to Fireman Boot Camp, he goes to Marti in open arms and they become an item. Pete continues to hate Berg throughout the course of the final episodes of the season. Sharon and Johnny continue to bicker at one another until Johnny calls off the wedding. When they get back together, they decided that a quickie wedding is the best idea. Irene, Pete's alleged stalker, agrees to throw Sharon and Johnny a wedding on the roof of the building. This resulted in her inviting Robert Goulet, who appeared earlier on in season in the episode "Out With the Old". Goulet conducted the ceremony and evidently brought Pete and Berg back together as friends during the wedding.

At the end of the two part episode, Pete and Marti leave to go to Fireman Boot Camp, Sharon and Johnny go on their honeymoon and Ashley leaves to go sort out a joke that Pete told Nomar, causing him and Ashley to break up. Berg and Irene are left alone at the wedding as every one leaves and start to dance. The series ends with a cliffhanger again as the audience believes that something will happen between Berg and Irene. The series was renewed for another season due to the 10.2 million average viewers this season.

Season 4

ABC moved the sitcom from mid-week to Friday due to the shows popularity and possibility of removing the Friday night curse. However, the move proved ineffective and the show's average viewers dropped from 10.2 to 6.7 million.

Season 4 continued the story arc from where Season 3 left off. Johnny and Sharon are married, Pete and Marti are now firefighters and Berg and Irene...are sleeping together. After Berg gets over being on academic probation, he continues to be Irene's "sex buddy". The two start sleeping together secretly, hoping that Pete especially won't find out.

Johnny remains to be the superintendent until Sharon makes him an honorary fireman for the day on his birthday. Johnny decides that he wants to be a fireman to Sharon's dislike. Meanwhile, Berg and Irene become a couple and Pete and Marti break up. She leaves Pete for Ashley's ex, Nomar. Sharon feels unfulfilled after leaving her evil corporate job and decides that she wants to be a lawyer. This would have led to her being a lawyer in more depth rather than an assistant, but the plug was pulled mid-season.

When Berg tells Irene that he loves her and she has no reply, Berg goes out and meets someone else. Katie, the girl he meets, admits that she's been following him for 8 years. However, the two of them kiss and Berg tells Irene. Berg apologizes and Irene breaks up with him for the mailman Roger. In the final episode, Berg assumes that Irene may be pregnant and decides that he must win her back. The possibility of Irene, Sharon or Ashley being pregnant was tabulated online by the viewer's votes. The final episode saw Sharon and Johnny in a baby scare as well as Pete realizing that Ashley is pregnant with his baby. The series ended on a cliffhanger that would not be resolved, much to the viewer's dislike.

Series finale

The series finale was titled "The Internet Show", an episode in which the fans of the show voted on the outcome online. In the end, they chose to have Ashley become pregnant with Pete's child, as opposed to either of the other two female characters, or nobody, becoming pregnant.

The episode aired on May 16, 2001. It was written by Donald Beck and Vince Calandra and directed by Michael Lembeck. For the 2000-01 season finale, four different endings were filmed for viewers to vote online and decide which of the central female characters (Sharon, Ashley, or Irene) should become pregnant, while a fourth possible ending had no pregnancies at all. The plan was to have the pregnant one (which ultimately ended up being Ashley) give birth at the end of the proposed fifth season. However, a fifth season of the show never materialized; by the time the fourth season finale aired in May 2001, the show had just been cancelled because of low ratings. The episode was originally shown as a one hour episode split into two parts with "Should I Stay Or Should I Go?".[1]

Sharon thinks she may be pregnant and Ashley realizes she could be too. She goes into denial, despite showing the symptoms but agrees to take a pregnancy test with Sharon. When Berg finds out from a news report that a glow in the dark condom he used was defective he thinks Irene could be pregnant. Not wanting to worry her, he tries to get a urine sample from her without telling her. Pete is still annoyed at Ashley for giving up on their relationship to go to Stanford.

Ratings

The show had strong ratings success during its run, peaking in season 2 and averaging an 12.0 million viewers. Its key adult 18–49 audience was prevalently female (55%). It was ranked #1 in its time period with Total Viewers, outperforming *Beverly Hills, 90210*, *The Nanny* and *Dawson's Creek*. It was also #1 in its time period with key adults 18–49 and all male demos. Finally, it was the #3 sitcom on ABC with key Adults 18-34.[2]

Season	Timeslot (EDT)	Season Premiere	Season Finale	TV Season	Rank	Viewers (in millions)
1	Wednesday 8:30 P.M. (March 10, 1998 – July 22, 1998)	March 10, 1998	July 22, 1998	1997–1998	#36[3]	12.9[3]
2	Wednesday 8:30 P.M. (September 23, 1998 – May 26, 1999)	September 23, 1998	May 26, 1999	1998–1999	#44[4]	12.0[4]
3	Wednesday 8:30 P.M. (September 27, 1999 – April 26, 2000)	September 27, 1999	April 26, 2000	1999–2000	#57[5]	10.2[5]
4	Friday 8:00 P.M. (October 26, 2000 – May 16, 2001)	October 26, 2000	May 16, 2001	2000–2001	#104[6]	6.7[6]

Production notes

Theme song and opening sequences

The title sequence for the first two seasons consisted of a short collection of images of the three, and a few cartoon images of them drinking and eating pizza at the pizza place, which alternated with a logo saying *Two Guys, a Girl and a Pizza Place*. The title screen was accompanied by an instrumental cover of the song "Blister in the Sun" by the Violent Femmes.

Seasons 3 and 4 showed Pete, Berg and Sharon dancing around in front of a plain, white backdrop. They are seen wearing suits and dresses and dancing along to a more modern piece of music. The newly adapted logo (the show's name having changed) is seen overlaying the footage as the three dance and laugh in front of the backdrop.

The music for the series was composed by Freddy Curci, Tom Rizzo and Mark Vogel. The music for Seasons 1 and 2 were numerous variations of the title theme, a prime example of which is "Two Guys, a Girl and a Vacation" where the cast members do a short rendition of "Kokomo" by The Beach Boys. Steel drums and Caribbean instruments were used to variate the title theme within the scenes of the episode.

In Seasons 3 and 4, the music was more modern and used newer instruments, a change that coincided with the new title and title theme.

Crew

Directors	Writers
- Amanda Bearse	- Kevin Abbott
- Robby Benson	- Donald R. Beck
- Mark Cendrowski	- Paige Bernhardt
- Rich Correll	- Pat Bullard
- Dana DeVally Piazza	- Vince Calandra
- John Fortenberry	- Stevie Ray Fromstein
- Leonard R. Garner, Jr.	- Mark Ganzel
- Ellen Gittelsohn	- Danny Jacobson
- Gordon Hunt	- Liz Sagal
- Casey Johnson	- Kenny Schwartz
- Gil Junger	- Barry Wernick
- Kim Kozenfeld	- Rick Wiener
- Michael Lembeck	
- Gail Mancuso	
- Brian K. Roberts	
- Wil Shriner	
- Andrew Susskind	
- Rocco Urbisci	
- Ted Wass	
- Marjorie Weitzman	
- James Widdoes	
- David E. Windsor	

Episodes

Season	Episodes	Originally aired	
		Season premiere	**Season finale**
1	13	March 10, 1998	July 22, 1998
2	22	September 23, 1998	May 26, 1999
3	24	September 27, 1999	April 26, 2000
4	22	October 6, 2000	June 16, 2001

Reception

Two Guys, a Girl and a Pizza Place was very successful during its run on ABC. The first series premiere entitled "The Pilot" was watched by 17.94 million viewers, preceding the second highest rated episode of *The Drew Carey Show*.[7] The episode was given a 15.61 Nielsen rating and won its 18-49 adult demographic. This was ABC's biggest opening since *Spin City*.[7] The show continued to have success during the first few seasons but never reached the high rating of "The Pilot". On May 28, an episode known as "Two Guys, a Girl and How They Met" was given a 6.7 Nielsen rating,[8] a big drop from the series premiere. The estimated number of viewers was roughly 7.69 million.

The episode "Two Guys, a Girl and a Guy" was given a 9.4 Nielsen rating and was watched by roughly 8 million viewers. This never reached the standards of "The Pilot" but still had a very successful rating. Episodes from the series had substantially high and low Nielsen ratings.[8]

The Friday night curse

In the fall of 2000, ABC tried to reverse the curse of Friday nights by putting some of its top-rated shows into a programming block aimed at older viewers. Network execs took Wednesday night ratings winners *Two Guys, a Girl and a Pizza Place* (at this point retitled *Two Guys and a Girl*) and *The Norm Show* (starring *SNL* alum Norm Macdonald), and paired them with *Madigan Men* and *The Trouble with Normal*. All four shows would be gone before the end of the season. *Two Guys* held on the longest, even moving back to Wednesdays on television life support for a two-week trial to see if it could be revived. The season finale, "The Internet Show", was filmed with four different endings, with fans voting online to decide which female character would get pregnant. But the fifth season baby was never born. The show was canceled before the online vote was tabulated.[9]

Syndication

After being canceled by ABC, the series reaired in syndication on WE: Women's Entertainment in the United States. In 2010/2011, the showed aired on 5* in the UK. In 2011 it was aired on the ETC cable channel in the Philippines, and TVtropolis in Canada. It aired on Norwegian TV 2 as *Pizzagjengen*.

References

[1] "*Two Guys And A Girl The Series finale* The Internet Show" (http://www.tv.com/two-guys-and-a-girl/the-internet-show/episode/44688/trivia.html?tag=episode_header;trivia). TV.com. . Retrieved January 13, 2010.

[2] "*Two Guys, A Girl and a Pizza Place* Nielsen rating and demographic presentation" (http://google.com/search?q=cache:X8gGhrjBw5IJ:www.foxformats.com/scripted/two-guys-and-a-girl/Two-Guys-And-A-Girl-International-Format-Presentation.ppt+Two+Guys+a+girl+and+a+pizza+place+million+viewers&cd=62&hl=en&ct=clnk). . Retrieved December 24, 2009.

[3] "*Two Guys, A Girl and a Pizza Place* Nielsen rating 1997-1998" (http://fbibler.chez.com/tvstats/recent_data/1997-98.html). fbibler.chez.com. . Retrieved February 13, 2010.

[4] "*Two Guys, A Girl and a Pizza Place* Nielsen rating 1999-1999" (http://web.archive.org/web/20091029011819/http://geocities.com/Hollywood/4616/ew0604.html). geocities.com. Archived from the original (http://www.geocities.com/Hollywood/4616/ew0604.html) on 2009-10-29. . Retrieved February 13, 2010.

[5] "*Two Guys, A Girl and a Pizza Place* Nielsen rating 1999-2000" (http://www.variety.com/index.asp?layout=chart_pass&charttype=chart_topshows99&dept=TV). variety.com. . Retrieved February 13, 2010.

[6] "*Two Guys, A Girl and a Pizza Place* Nielsen rating 2000-2001" (http://fbibler.chez.com/tvstats/recent_data/2000-01.html). variety.com. . Retrieved February 13, 2010.

[7] "*Two Guys, A Girl and a Pizza Place* Nielsen rating March 10th" (http://www.mrpopculture.com/files/html/mar15-1998/). mrpopculture.com. . Retrieved December 23, 2009.

[8] "*Two Guys, A Girl and a Pizza Place* Nielsen rating May 28th" (http://www.sfgate.com/e/a/1998/05/28/STYLE8260.dtl). sfgate.com. . Retrieved December 23, 2009.

[9] "*Two Guys, A Girl and a Pizza Place* Friday Night Curse" (http://www.getback.com/gallery/the-friday-night-curse/3004897/7/). . Retrieved December 24, 2009.

External links

- *Two Guys and a Girl* (http://www.imdb.com/title/tt0137330/) at the Internet Movie Database
- *Two Guys and a Girl* (http://www.tv.com/show/221/summary.html) at TV.com
- *Two Guys and a Girl* (http://epguides.com/TwoGuysandaGirl) at epguides.com

Star Crossed (The Outer Limits)

"Star Crossed"	
The Outer Limits **episode**	
Episode no.	Season 5 Episode 21
Directed by	Helen Shaver
Written by	Chris Ruppenthal
Original air date	13 August 1999
Guest stars	
Angeline Ball, Nathan Fillion, Justin Louis, Robbi Chong, Natasha Vasiluk, Zoran Vukelic, Derek de Lint	

"**Star Crossed**" is an episode of *The Outer Limits* television show. It first aired on 13 August 1999, during the fifth season.

Introduction

> *In the year 2050 Earth was invaded by a humanoid race called The Hing. For six years a hard and reigning war was fought. At its conclusion, we were forced to agree that the Hing retain the control they had already won. It wasn't an easy truce, especially in a city called 'Archangel'.*

Opening narration

> *Some men lose themselves in war. Others, find themselves.*

Plot

It is 2056, six years after the Hing, a humanoid race, invaded Earth. While America fights on, Russia has reached an uneasy truce with the aliens, leaving some regions under their control and others declared neutral. In the neutral city of Archangel on the Barents Sea, cynical American expatriate Michael Ryan (Nathan Fillion) runs *Heaven*, a small coffee bar and music club, where shady Russians mingle with Hing soldiers and other dubious characters.

Everything is agreeably corrupt until Alexandra Nevsky (Natasha Vasiluk) informs Michael that Hing commander Sulat Ray (Derek de Lint) is on the lookout for two NATO soldiers who might be interested in buying a Hing scout vehicle that has gone missing. Those soldiers, Winston Meyerburg (Justin Louis) and Cass Trenton (Angeline Ball) have dodged Hing patrols and found their way to Michael's bar.

Cass, who was Michael's lover before the war — she only took up with Winston because she thought he was dead — suspects Michael can get them the scout vehicle. She appeals to his sense of patriotism, revealing that she is carrying a deadly parasite that she and Winston stole from the Hing and, if it can be replicated, might defeat the Hing.

But it becomes clear that it's going to take more than flag-waving and high ideals to get Michael to risk his neck in this situation.

Closing narration

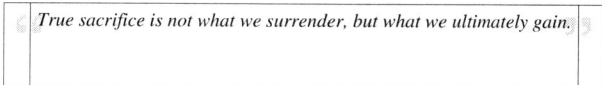
True sacrifice is not what we surrender, but what we ultimately gain.

Trivia

The story is a futuristic reinterpretation of "Casablanca" where a couple is carrying a parasite that might win the war for the humans. The couple flee to the city Archangel looking for a way to escape the Hing and gain the support of a former lover Michael who owns the cafe.

Cast

- Angeline Ball as Cass Trenton
- Nathan Fillion as Michael Ryan
- Justin Louis as Winston Meyerburg
- Robbi Chong as Teresita Arboleda
- Natasha Vasiluk as Alexandra Nevsky
- Zoran Vukelic as Hector
- Derek de Lint as Centurion
- Jim Shield as Duro
- Ian Marsh as Hing Centurion
- Ian Brown as Innocuous Man
- Stuart O'Connell as Hing Soldier
- Kevin Conway as The Control Voice

External links

- "Star Crossed" [1] at *The Outer Limits* official website [2]
- "Star Crossed" [3] at actor Derek de Lint's personal homepage [4]
- "Star Crossed" [5] at TV.com
- "Star Crossed" [6] at the Internet Movie Database

Season 5 of The Outer Limits (1995-2002)
Alien Radio • Donor • Small Friends • The Grell • The Other Side • Joyride • The Human Operators • Blank Slate • What Will The Neighbors Think • The Shroud • Ripper • Tribunal • Summit • Descent • The Haven • Deja Vu • The Inheritors • Essence of Life • Stranded • Fathers and Sons • Star Crossed • Better Luck Next Time
List of The Outer Limits episodes: Original Series (1963–1965) • The New Series (1995–2002)

References

[1] http://www.theouterlimits.com/episodes/season5/519.htm
[2] http://theouterlimits.com/noflash/index.html
[3] http://www.derekdelint.com/star_crossed.html
[4] http://www.derekdelint.com
[5] http://www.tv.com/episode/21528/summary.html
[6] http://www.imdb.com/title/tt0667953/

Firefly (TV series)

	Firefly
Genre	- Space Western - Drama
Created by	Joss Whedon
Starring	- Nathan Fillion - Gina Torres - Alan Tudyk - Morena Baccarin - Adam Baldwin - Jewel Staite - Sean Maher - Summer Glau - Ron Glass
Theme music composer	Joss Whedon
Opening theme	"The Ballad of Serenity" performed by Sonny Rhodes
Composer(s)	Greg Edmonson
Country of origin	United States
Language(s)	English
No. of seasons	1
No. of episodes	14 (List of episodes)
Production	
Executive producer(s)	- Joss Whedon - Tim Minear
Producer(s)	Ben Edlund
Editor(s)	Lisa Lassek
Cinematography	David Boyd
Camera setup	Single-camera
Running time	42 minutes
Broadcast	
Original channel	Fox
Picture format	- NTSC 480i - 16:9 HDTV 1080i - 16:9 Blu-ray Disc 1080p
Audio format	5.1 Surround Sound

Original run	September 20, 2002 – December 20, 2002
Chronology	
Followed by	*Those Left Behind* (comic) *Serenity* (film)

Firefly is an American space western television series created by writer and director Joss Whedon, under his Mutant Enemy Productions label. Whedon served as executive producer, along with Tim Minear.

The series is set in the year 2517, after the arrival of humans in a new star system, and follows the adventures of the renegade crew of *Serenity*, a "Firefly-class" spaceship. The ensemble cast portrays the nine characters who live on *Serenity*. Whedon pitched the show as "nine people looking into the blackness of space and seeing nine different things".[1] The show explores the lives of some people who fought on the losing side of a civil war and others who now make a living on the outskirts of society, as part of the pioneer culture that exists on the fringes of their star system. In addition, it is a future where the only two surviving superpowers, the United States and China, fused to form the central federal government, called the Alliance, resulting in the fusion of the two cultures. According to Whedon's vision, "nothing will change in the future: technology will advance, but we will still have the same political, moral, and ethical problems as today".[2]

Firefly premiered in the United States on the Fox network on September 20, 2002. Despite high expectations for the Joss Whedon-led project, by mid-December 2002, *Firefly* had averaged only 4.7 million viewers per episode and was 98th in Nielsen ratings.[3] It was canceled after eleven of the fourteen produced episodes were aired. Despite the series' relatively short life span, it received strong sales when it was released on DVD and has large fan support campaigns.[4] [5] It won an Emmy in 2003 for Outstanding Special Visual Effects for a Series. The post-airing success of the show led Whedon and Universal Pictures to produce a film based on the series, *Serenity*.[4] The *Firefly* franchise expanded from the series and film to other media including comics[6] and a role-playing game.[7]

Plot

Backstory

The series takes place in the year 2517, on a variety of planets and moons. The TV series does not reveal whether these celestial bodies are within one star system, only saying that *Serenity*'s mode of propulsion is a "gravity-drive". The film *Serenity* makes clear that all the planets and moons are in one large system, and production documents related to the film indicate that there is no faster-than-light travel in this universe. The characters occasionally refer to "Earth-that-was", and the film establishes that, long before the events in the series, a large population had emigrated from Earth to a new star system in generation ships:[8] "Earth-that-was could no longer sustain our numbers, we were so many". The emigrants established themselves in this new star system, with "dozens of planets and hundreds of moons". Many of these were terraformed, a process in which a planet or moon is altered to resemble Earth. The terraforming process was only the first step in making a planet habitable, however, and the outlying settlements often did not receive any further support in the construction of their civilizations. This resulted in many of the border planets and moons having forbidding, dry environments, well-suited to the Western genre.

Synopsis

The show takes its name from the "Firefly-class" spaceship, *Serenity*, that the central characters call home. It resembles a firefly in general arrangement, and the tail section, analogous to a bioluminescent insectoid abdomen, lights up during acceleration. The ship was named after the Battle of Serenity Valley, where Mal and Zoe were on the losing side. It is revealed in "Bushwhacked" that the Battle of Serenity Valley is widely considered the loss which sealed the fate of the Independents.

Throughout the series, the Alliance is shown to govern the star system through an organization of "core" planets, following its success in forcibly unifying all the colonies under a single government. DVD commentary suggests that the Alliance is composed of two primary "core" systems, one predominantly Western in culture, the other pan-Asian, justifying the series' mixed linguistic and visual themes. The central planets are firmly under Alliance control, but the outlying planets and moons resemble the 19th-century American West, with little governmental authority. Settlers and refugees on the outlying worlds ("out in the black" or "heading for the black") have relative freedom from the central government, but lack the amenities of the high-tech civilization that exists on the inner worlds. In addition, the outlying areas of space are inhabited by the Reavers, a cannibalistic group of nomadic humans that have become savage and animalistic.[9]

Into this mix are thrown the protagonists of the show. The captain of the crew of *Serenity* is Malcolm "Mal" Reynolds (Nathan Fillion) and the episode "Serenity" establishes that the captain and his first mate Zoe Washburne (Gina Torres) are veteran "Browncoats" of the Unification War, a failed attempt by the outlying worlds to resist the Alliance's assertion of control. A later episode, titled "Out of Gas", reveals that Mal bought the spaceship *Serenity* to continue living beyond Alliance control. Much of the crew's work consists of cargo runs or smuggling. One of the main story arcs is that of River Tam (Summer Glau) and her brother Simon (Sean Maher). River was a child prodigy, whose brain was subjected to experiments. As a result, she displays schizophrenia and often hears voices. It is later revealed that she is a "reader", one who possesses telepathic abilities. Simon gave up a highly successful career as a trauma surgeon to rescue her from the Alliance and as a result of this rescue they are both wanted fugitives. In the original pilot "Serenity", Simon joins the crew as a paying passenger with River smuggled on board as cargo. As Whedon states in an episodic DVD commentary, every show he does is about creating family.[10] By the last episode, "Objects in Space", the fractured character of River has finally become whole, partly because the others decided to accept her into their "family" on the ship.[10]

Signature show elements

The show blended elements from the space opera and Western genres, depicting humanity's future in a manner different from most contemporary science fiction programs in that there are no alien creatures or large space battles. *Firefly* takes place in a multi-cultural future, primarily a fusion of Occidental and Chinese cultures, where there is a significant division between the rich and poor. As a result of the Sino-American Alliance, Mandarin Chinese is a common second language; it is used in advertisements, and characters in the show frequently use Chinese words and curses. According to the DVD commentary on the episode "Serenity", this was explained as being the result of China and the United States being the two superpowers that expanded into space.[11]

The show also features slang not used in contemporary culture, such as adaptations of modern words, or new words altogether. For example, "shiny" is frequently used in a similar manner as the real world slang "cool". Written and spoken Chinese as well as Old West dialect are also employed. As one reviewer noted: "The dialogue tended to be a bizarre purée of wisecracks, old-timey Western-paperback patois, and snatches of Chinese".[4]

Tim Minear and Joss Whedon pointed out two scenes that, they believed, articulated the mood of the show exceptionally clearly.[10] One scene is in the original pilot "Serenity", when Mal is eating with chopsticks and a Western tin cup is by his plate; the other is in "The Train Job" pilot, when Mal is thrown out of a holographic bar window.[12] The DVD set's "making-of" documentary explains the series' distinctive frontispiece (wherein *Serenity* soars over a herd of unshod horses) as Whedon's attempt to capture "everything you need to understand about the series in five seconds".

One of the struggles that Whedon had with Fox was the tone of the show, especially with the main character Malcolm Reynolds. Fox pressured Whedon to make Mal more "jolly", as they feared he was too dark in the original pilot, epitomized by the moment he suggests he might 'space' Simon and River, throwing them out the airlock to die. In addition, Fox was not happy that the show involved the "nobodies" who "get squished by policy" instead of the actual policy makers.[10] [13]

Cast

Main characters

Firefly maintained an ensemble cast that portrayed the nine crew members of the ship, *Serenity*. These characters fight criminals and schemers, Alliance security forces, the utterly psychotic and brutal Reavers, and the mysterious men with "hands of blue"—who are apparently operatives of a secret agency which is part of the mega-corporation referred to in the DVD commentary only as The Blue Sun Corporation. The crew is driven by the need to secure enough income to keep their ship operational, set against their need to keep a low profile to avoid their adversaries. Their situation is greatly complicated by the divergent motivations of the individuals on board *Serenity*, but complex characterization was hampered by the show's brief run.

All nine of the main characters appeared in every episode, with the exception of "Ariel", from which Book is absent—it is explained that he was meditating at an abbey.

- Nathan Fillion as Malcolm "Mal" Reynolds—the owner of *Serenity* and former Independent sergeant in the pivotal Battle of Serenity Valley. Very little is known about the enigmatic Captain; the little he reveals about his past life betrays nothing of his character (a mystery of its own). Malcolm reveals that he grew up on a ranch, and was raised by his mother and the ranch hands. The only other scenes of his past life that are shown are about the Unification War, in which he and Zoe fought for the Independent Army, the "Browncoats", as a platoon sergeant in the 57th Overlanders. He is an efficient leader and is skilled with guns as well as in hand-to-hand combat. Mal's character is full of contradictions. He is constantly fighting his demons, and his true self remains something of a mystery.
- Gina Torres as Zoe Alleyne Washburne—second-in-command onboard *Serenity*, a loyal wartime friend of Captain Reynolds, and the wife of Wash. Described by her husband as a "warrior woman", she has great knowledge of combat. Her past is a mystery; the only thing known is that she was born and raised on a ship[14] and served under Mal during the war as a corporal.[15] She demonstrates an almost unconditional loyalty to Mal, the only exception noted being her marriage to Wash, which the captain claims was against his orders. Her surname during the Unification War was Alleyne.[16]
- Alan Tudyk as Hoban "Wash" Washburne—*Serenity*'s pilot and Zoe's husband. Wash expresses jealousy over his wife's "war buddy" relationship and unconditional support of their captain, most particularly in the episode "War Stories", in which he confronts Mal regarding their relationship. While more of Wash's past is disclosed than most other characters, his background is still sparse: he joined pilot training just to see the stars, which were invisible from the surface of his polluted homeworld, and he joined *Serenity* despite being highly sought after by other ships. He is very light-hearted and tends to make amusing comments, despite the severity of any situation.
- Morena Baccarin as Inara Serra—a Companion, which is the 26th century equivalent of a courtesan or oiran, who rents one of the Serenity's two small shuttles. Like her Renaissance counterparts, Inara enjoys high social standing. Her presence confers a degree of legitimacy and social acceptance the crew of *Serenity* would not have without her on board. She and Mal have a strained relationship, with unspoken romantic tension playing a significant part in several episodes, as well as in the movie. Inara arguably represents Mal's heart, and Mal is a noticeably darker character when Inara is absent (as during the first half of "Serenity").
- Adam Baldwin as Jayne Cobb—hired muscle. He and Mal met on opposite sides of a rivalry; Mal, while held at gunpoint, offered Jayne his own bunk and a higher cut than his current employer, so he turned coat and shot his then-partners. In the original Pilot "Serenity" he intimates to Mal that he didn't betray him because "The money wasn't good enough," however previously he'd pointedly asked the Alliance agent whether he'd be required to turn on the captain to help him, and in "Ariel" defends his actions alerting the authorities regarding Simon and River by claiming he'd not intended to betray Mal. He is someone who can be depended on in a fight.[17] He tends to act like a "lummox" who thinks he is the smartest person in space, but occasional hints of intelligence peek through this façade, giving the impression that he acts dumber than he is.[10] As Whedon states several times, Jayne is the man who will ask the questions that no one else wants to.[18] Even though he is a macho character, he has shown a

particularly intense fear of Reavers, more so than the rest of the crew. Despite his amoral mercenary persona, he sends a significant portion of his income to his mother.
- Jewel Staite as Kaywinnit Lee "Kaylee" Frye[19] [20] —the ship's mechanic. In the episode "Out of Gas", it is established that she has no formal training, but keeps *Serenity* running with an intuitive gift for the workings of mechanical equipment. Jewel Staite explains Kaylee's character as being wholesome, sweet, and "completely genuine in that sweetness", adding "She loves being on that ship. She loves all of those people. And she's the only one who loves all of them incredibly genuinely."[21] She has a crush on Dr. Simon Tam. Kaylee is the heart of the ship: according to creator Joss Whedon, if Kaylee believes something, it is true.[10]
- Sean Maher as Dr. Simon Tam—a medical researcher and trauma surgeon of the first caliber (top 3% in his class at a top core-planet institution), who is on the run after breaking his sister River out of a government research facility. In the episode "Safe", it is revealed that he and River had a privileged upbringing with access to the best education. It is also revealed that Simon sacrificed a highly-successful future in medicine, over his stern father's severe objections, when he rescued River. His bumbling attempts at a romantic relationship with Kaylee are a recurring subplot throughout the series, and at every turn he seems to find a way to unwittingly foil his own attempts at romance. His life is defined by caring for his sister.[10]
- Summer Glau as River Tam—smuggled onto the ship by her brother. River was a child prodigy of unparalleled genius, but she was experimented upon at the hands of Alliance doctors, leaving her delusional, erratic, and at times violent. Her personal journey of self-discovery is a running theme throughout the series and the movie. River is constantly at war with her own demons. She sees and hears things that others do not, and experiences waking dreams of her memories of the Alliance "academy" experiments. Opinions of her vary among the crew: some value her, Jayne fears her, and the rest just want her to stay out of trouble. She is also telepathic, or, as Captain Malcolm Reynolds puts it in the episode "Objects in Space", a "reader".
- Ron Glass as Derrial Book—a Shepherd (equivalent to a pastor). Although presented as a devout Christian man,[22] Book demonstrates a depth of knowledge about the activities of criminals (in "Our Mrs. Reynolds") and corrupt police (in "The Message"). He is also proficient in hand-to-hand combat and the use of firearms. When questioned on his non-Biblical intentions during the rescue in "War Stories", Book replies somewhat ironically that while the Bible is quite specific about killing, it's "somewhat fuzzier on the subject of kneecaps". In "Safe", he was shown to have sufficient status in the Alliance to receive medical treatment from the military with no questions asked. Book represents Mal's guide, conscience, and lost spirituality, while his hidden backstory was to have been gradually revealed, had the series continued.

Other roles

Five members of the *Firefly* cast appeared on Joss Whedon's other TV series as major villains. Fillion was cast as Caleb in the final season of *Buffy the Vampire Slayer* and later as Captain Hammer in the internet series *Dr. Horrible's Sing-Along Blog*, while Torres and Baldwin took on recurring roles on *Angel* in its fourth and fifth seasons respectively, as the characters of Jasmine and Marcus Hamilton. Tudyk portrayed the rogue character Alpha in Whedon's latest series, *Dollhouse*. Glau also portrayed an antagonist scientist who later helps the protagonists in the second season of *Dollhouse*, in the role of Bennett Halverson. She made her professional acting debut in the third-season *Angel* episode "Waiting in the Wings" before she was cast in *Firefly*.

Baccarin was originally intended to portray Eve in *Angel*'s final season, but in the end was unable to commit to the role due to other pursuits.[23] In addition, Staite appeared in several episodes of *Wonderfalls*, which was produced by Tim Minear. Fillion starred as Alex Tully in Tim Minear's short-lived series *Drive*. In a tribute to his character on *Firefly*, Fillion appears in a costume similar to Malcolm Reynolds in a Halloween episode of the television series *Castle*, a series in which he plays the lead role.[24]

Recurring characters

Despite the short run of the series, some recurring characters emerged from the inhabitants of the *Firefly* universe:

- Badger (Mark Sheppard) is an established smuggling middleman on the planet Persephone. He provided jobs for *Serenity* on at least two occasions. In the DVD commentary for the episode "Serenity", it was revealed that this part was originally written with the intention of Whedon himself playing the part. Badger appeared in the original pilot "Serenity" and in "Shindig", with a return in the comic book series *Serenity: Those Left Behind*.
- Adelei Niska (Michael Fairman) is a criminal kingpin who has a reputation for violent reprisals, including severe, prolonged torture, against those who fail him or even irritate him. He appeared in "The Train Job" and "War Stories".
- "Saffron" (Christina Hendricks) is a con artist whose real name is unknown. In the series she also used the aliases "Bridget" and "Yolanda", leading Mal to jokingly address her as "YoSaffBridge", a portmanteau of her three aliases, in the episode "Trash". She has a habit of marrying her marks during her scams. She first appeared in the episode "Our Mrs. Reynolds" as Mal's involuntarily acquired wife.
- "The Hands of Blue" (Jeff Ricketts and Dennis Cockrum): Two anonymous men wearing suits and blue gloves who pursue River, apparently to return her to the institute she escaped from, as shown in "The Train Job", "Ariel", and the *Serenity: Those Left Behind* comic. They kill anyone, including Alliance personnel, who had contact with her, using a mysterious hand-held device that causes brain hemorrhaging to anyone in its proximity, except them.

Production

Origin

Whedon developed the concept for the show after reading *The Killer Angels*, the Pulitzer Prize-winning novel by Michael Shaara chronicling the Battle of Gettysburg during the American Civil War. He wanted to follow people who had fought on the losing side of a war and their experiences afterwards as pioneers and immigrants on the outskirts of civilization, much like the post-American Civil War era of Reconstruction and the American Old West culture.[25] He intended the show to be "a *Stagecoach* kind of drama with a lot of people trying to figure out their lives in a bleak pioneer environment".[26] Whedon wanted to develop a show about the tactile nature of life, a show where existence was more physical and more difficult.[10] After reading *The Killer Angels*, Whedon read a book about Jewish partisan fighters in World War II that also influenced him.[25] Whedon wanted to create something for television that was more character-driven and gritty than most modern science fiction. Television science fiction, he felt, had become too pristine and rarefied.[27]

Whedon wanted to give the show a name that indicated movement and power, and felt that "Firefly" had both. This powerful word's relatively insignificant meaning, Whedon felt, added to its allure. He eventually wound up creating the ship in the image of a firefly.[10]

Format

During filming of the pilot episode, Whedon was still arguing with Fox that the show should be displayed in widescreen format. Consequently, he purposely filmed scenes with actors on the extreme edge of both sides so that they could only be shown in widescreen.[10] This led to a few scenes on the DVD (and later Blu-ray) where objects that should be visible (such as the ship's yoke) are not since they would not have been needed in a non-widescreen format. However, the pilot was rejected by the Fox executives, who felt that it lacked action and that the captain was too "dour".[12] They also disliked a scene in which the crew backed down to a crime boss, since the scene implied the crew was "being nothing".[10] Thus, Fox told Whedon on a Friday afternoon that he had to submit a new pilot script on Monday morning or the show would not be picked up.[12] Whedon and Tim Minear closeted themselves for the weekend to write what became the new pilot, "The Train Job".[12] At the direction of Fox, they added "larger than life" characters[12][13] such as the henchman "Crow", and the "hands of blue" men, who also introduced an

X-Files-type ending.[13]

For the new pilot, Fox made it clear that they would not air the episodes in the widescreen format. Whedon and company felt they had to "serve two masters" by filming widescreen for eventual DVD release, but keeping objects in frame so it could still work when aired in pan and scan full frame.[28] To obtain an immersive and immediate feel, the episodes were filmed in a documentary style with hand-held cameras, giving them the look of "found footage", with deliberately misframed or out-of-focus subjects.[10] [29] As Whedon related: "...don't be arch, don't be sweeping — be found, be rough and tumble and docu[mentary] and you-are-there".[30] Computer-generated scenes mimicked the motion of a hand-held camera. This style was not used, however, when shooting scenes that involved the central government, the Alliance. Tracking and steady cameras were used to show the sterility of this aspect of the *Firefly* universe.[10] Another style employed was lens flares harking back to 1970s television. This style was so desired that the director of photography, David Boyd, sent back the cutting-edge lenses which reduced lens flare in exchange for cheaper ones.[10]

Unlike most other science fiction shows, which add sound to space scenes for dramatic effect, *Firefly* portrays space as silent, because a vacuum cannot transmit sound.[31]

Set design

Production designer Carey Meyer built the ship *Serenity* in two parts (one for each level) as a complete set with ceilings and practical lighting installed as part of the set that the cameras could use along with moveable parts.[29] [32] The two-part set also allowed the second unit to shoot in one section while the actors and first unit worked undisturbed in the other. As Whedon recalled: "...you could pull it away or move something huge, so that you could get in and around everything. That meant the environment worked for us and there weren't a lot of adjustments that needed to be made."[32] There were other benefits to this set design. One was that it allowed the viewers to feel they were really in a ship.[29] For Whedon, the design of the ship was crucial in defining the known space for the viewer, and that there were not "fourteen hundred decks and a holodeck and an all-you-can-eat buffet in the back".[33] He wanted to convey that it was utilitarian and that it was "beat-up but lived-in and ultimately, it was home".[34] As Joss Whedon discusses in the DVD commentary, each room represented a feeling or character, usually conveyed by the paint color.[33] He explains that as you move from the back of the ship in the engine room, toward the front of the ship to the bridge, the colors and mood progress from extremely warm to cooler. Besides evoking a mood associated with the character who spends most time in each area, the color scheme also alludes to the heat generated in the tail of the ship. Whedon was also keen on utilizing vertical space; thus, having the crew's quarters accessible by ladder was important.[32] Another benefit of the set design was that it also allowed the actors to stay in the moment and interact, without having to stop after each shot and reset up for the next.[29] This helped contribute to the documentary style Whedon strove for.

The set had several influences, including the sliding doors and tiny cubicles reminiscent of Japanese hotels.[32] Artist Larry Dixon has noted that the cargo bay walls are "reminiscent of interlaced, overlapping Asian designs, cleverly reminding us of the American-Chinese Alliance setting while artistically forming a patterned plane for background scale reference".[35] Dixon has also remarked on how the set design contributed to the storytelling through the use of color, depth and composition, lighting, as well as its use of diagonals and patterned shadows.[35]

Their small budget was another reason to use the ship for much of the storytelling. When the characters did go off the ship, the worlds all had Earth atmosphere and coloring because they could not afford to design alien worlds. "I didn't want to go to Yucca Flats every other episode and transform it into Bizarro World by making the sky orange", recalled Whedon.[30] As Meyer recalled: "I think in the end the feel was that we wound up using a lot of places or exteriors that just felt too Western and we didn't necessarily want to go that way; but at some point, it just became the lesser of two evils—what could we actually create in three days?"[32]

Music

Firefly	
Soundtrack album by Greg Edmonson, Joss Whedon	
Released	November 8, 2005
Genre	Classical, Country
Length	60:15
Label	Varèse Sarabande

Professional ratings	
Review scores	
Source	Rating
Allmusic	★★★★☆/★★★★★ [36]
SoundtrackNet	★★★★☆ [37] [38]

Greg Edmonson composed the musical score for the series. He stated that he wrote for the emotion of the moment. However, one reviewer averred that he also wrote for the characters, stating: "... Edmonson has developed a specialized collection of musical symbolism for the series ..."[39] To help illustrate the collection, the reviewer gave key "signatures" various names, noting that "Serenity" recalls the theme of the show and is used when they return to the ship, or when they were meeting clandestinely; it was "the sound of their home". The slide guitar and fiddle used in this piece are portable instruments which fit the lifestyle of the crew: "... the music they make calls up tunes played out in the open, by people who were hundreds of miles away yesterday. 'Serenity' conjures the nomadic lifestyle the crew leads and underlines the western aspect of the show."[39] Another emotional signature was "Sad Violin". It was used at the end of the Battle of Serenity Valley, but also helped set up the joke for when Mal tells Simon that Kaylee is dead in the episode "Serenity". The most memorable use of "Sad Violin", however, is at the end of "The Message", when the crew mourned the death of Tracey. This was also the last scene of the last episode the actors shot, and so this was seen by them, and Edmonson, as *Firefly*'s farewell. To denote impending danger, "Peril" was used, which is "a low pulse, like a heartbeat, with deep chimes and low strings".[39] The reviewer also noted character signatures. The criminal Niska has his own signature: Eastern European or Middle Eastern melodies over a low drone. Simon and River's signature was a piano played sparsely with a violin in the background. This is in contrast to the portable instruments of "Serenity": the piano is an instrument that cannot be easily moved and evokes the image of "the distant house and family they both long for". The various signatures were mostly established in the first pilot, "Serenity", and helped enhance the narrative.

> In every episode, the musical score intensified my experience of this intelligent, remarkable show. Using and combining all these signatures, Greg Edmonson brought out aspects of *Firefly*'s story and characters that were never explicitly revealed in the other elements of the series.[39]

The musical score expressed the cultural fusion depicted in the show. Cowboy guitar blended with Asian influence produced the atmospheric background for the series. As one reviewer stated:

> Old music from the future—the music of roaring campfires and racous [*sic*] cowboys mixed with the warm, pensive sounds of Asian culture and, occasionally, a cold imperial trumpet, heralding the ominous structural presence of a domineering government. Completely thrilling.
> — Steve Townsley[40]

The show's theme song, "The Ballad of Serenity", was written by Joss Whedon and performed by Sonny Rhodes. Whedon wrote the song before the series was greenlit and a preliminary recording performed by Whedon can be found on the DVD release. The soundtrack to the series was released on CD on November 8, 2005 by Varèse Sarabande, although a 40 minute soundtrack was released by Fox Music in September 2005 as a digital EP.[41] "The Ballad of Serenity" was used by NASA as the wake-up song for astronaut Robert L. Behnken and the other crewmembers of STS-130 on February 12, 2010.[42]

Track listing[43] (tracks 1–17 appear in both the digital and CD releases)		
No.	Title	Length
1.	"Firefly - Main Title"	0:52
2.	"Big Bar Fight" (from "The Train Job")	1:56
3.	"Heart of Gold Montage" (from "Heart of Gold")	2:10
4.	"Whitefall/Book" (from "Serenity", "The Message")	2:20
5.	"Early Takes Serenity" (from "Objects in Space")	2:36
6.	"The Funeral" (from "The Message")	2:36
7.	"River's Perception/Saffron" (from "Objects in Space", "Our Mrs. Reynolds")	2:14
8.	"Mal Fights Niska/Back Home" (from "War Stories", "Shindig")	1:54
9.	"River Tricks Early" (from "Objects in Space")	3:30
10.	"River Understands Simon" (from "Safe")	2:04
11.	"Leaving/Caper/Spaceball" (from "Trash", "Objects in Space", "Bushwhacked")	2:39
12.	"River's Afraid/Niska/Torture" (from "Ariel", "The Train Job", "War Stories")	3:21
13.	"In My Bunk/Jayne's Statue/Boom" (from "War Stories", "Jaynestown", "Bushwhacked")	2:28
14.	"Inara's Suite" (from "The Train Job", "Serenity", "War Stories")	3:29
15.	"Out of Gas/Empty Derelict" (from "Out of Gas", "Bushwhacked")	1:50
16.	"Book's Hair/Ready for Battle" (from "Jaynestown", "Heart of Gold")	1:59
17.	"Tears/River's Eyes" (from "Serenity", "Objects in Space")	1:59
18.	"Cows/New Dress/My Crew" (from "Safe", "Shindig", "Safe")	2:11
19.	"Boarding the Serenity/Derelict" (from "War Stories", "Bushwhacked")	2:02
20.	"Burgess Kills/Captain & Ship" (from "Heart of Gold", "Out of Gas")	3:26
21.	"Saved/Isn't Home?/Reavers" (from "Out of Gas", "Train Job", "Serenity")	2:55
22.	"Reavers Chase Serenity" (from "Serenity")	3:22
23.	"River's Dance" (from "Safe")	1:50
24.	"Inside the Tam House" (from "Safe")	2:22
25.	"Dying Ship/Naked Mal" (from "Out of Gas", "Trash")	2:10

Casting

In casting his nine-member crew, Whedon looked first at the actors and considered their chemistry with others. Cast member Sean Maher recalls, "So then he just sort of put us all together, and I think it was very quick, like right out of the gate, we all instantly bonded".[44] All nine cast members were chosen before filming began. However, while filming the original pilot "Serenity", Whedon decided that Rebecca Gayheart was unsuitable for the role of Inara Serra, and shot her scenes in singles so that it would be easier to replace her.[10] Morena Baccarin auditioned for the role and two days later was on the set in her first television show. "Joss brought me down from the testing room like a proud dad, holding my hand and introducing me,"[45] Baccarin recalled.

(*From left to right, top to bottom*) Adam Baldwin, Ron Glass, Summer Glau, Alan Tudyk, Sean Maher, Jewel Staite, Morena Baccarin, and Nathan Fillion: eight of the nine main actors in 2005 (not pictured: Gina Torres)

Whedon approached Nathan Fillion to play the lead role of Malcolm Reynolds; after explaining the premise and showing Fillion the treatment for the pilot, Fillion was eager for the role.[46] Fillion was called back several times to read for the part before he was cast. He noted that "it was really thrilling. It was my first lead and I was pretty nervous, but I really wanted that part and I wanted to tell those stories."[47] Fillion later said he was "heartbroken" when he learned the series had been cancelled.

Alan Tudyk auditioned through a casting office and several months later was called in for a test audition, where he met with Whedon. He was then told to come back in to test with the possible Zoes (Wash's wife) and that it was down to him and one other candidate. The Zoes did not work out (Gina Torres eventually received the role) and Tudyk was sent home, but received a call informing him he had the part anyway.[48] His audition tape is included in the special features of the series' DVD release.

Gina Torres, a veteran of several science fiction/fantasy works (*Cleopatra 2525*, *The Matrix Reloaded*, *Alias*, *Hercules: The Legendary Journeys*), was at first uninterested in doing another science fiction show, but "was won over by the quality of the source material".[49] As she recalled, "you had these challenged characters inhabiting a challenging world and that makes for great storytelling. And no aliens!"[49]

For Adam Baldwin, who grew up watching westerns, the role of Jayne Cobb was particularly resonant.[50]

Canadian actress Jewel Staite videotaped her audition from Vancouver and was asked to come to Los Angeles to meet Whedon, at which point she was cast for the role of Kaylee Frye, the ship's engineer.[51]

Sean Maher recalls reading for the part and liking the character of Simon Tam, but that it was Whedon's personality and vision that "sealed the deal" for him.[44] For the role of Simon's sister, River Tam, Whedon called in Summer Glau for an audition and test the same day. Glau had first worked for Whedon in the *Angel* episode "Waiting in the Wings". Two weeks later, Whedon called her to tell her she had the part.[52]

Veteran television actor Ron Glass has said that until *Firefly*, he had not experienced or sought a science-fiction or western role but he fell in love with the pilot script and the character of Shepherd Book.[53]

Production staff

Tim Minear was selected by Whedon to be the show runner, who serves as the head writer and production leader. According to Whedon "[Minear] understood the show as well as any human being, and just brought so much to it that I think of it as though he were always a part of it".[54] Many of the other production staff were selected from people Whedon had worked with in the past, with the exception of the director of photography David Boyd, who was the "big find" and who was "full of joy and energy".[55]

The writers were selected after interviews and script samplings. Among the writers were José Molina, Ben Edlund, Cheryl Cain, Brett Matthews, Drew Z. Greenberg and Jane Espenson.[55] Espenson wrote an essay on the writing process with Mutant Enemy.[56] A meeting is held and an idea is floated, generally by Whedon, and the writers brainstorm to develop the central theme of the episode and the character development. Next, the writers (except the one working on the previous week's episode) meet in the anteroom to Whedon's office to begin 'breaking' the story into acts and scenes. For the team, one of the key components to devising acts is deciding where to break for commercial and ensuring the viewer returns. "Finding these moments in the story help give it shape: think of them as tentpoles that support the structure". For instance, in "Shindig", the break for commercial occurs when Malcolm Reynolds is gravely injured and losing the duel. "It does not end when Mal turns the fight around, when he stands victorious over his opponent. They're both big moments, but one of them leaves you curious and the other doesn't."

Next, the writers develop the scenes onto a marker-filled whiteboard, featuring "a brief ordered description of each scene". A writer is selected to create an outline of the episode's concept—occasionally with some dialogue and jokes—in one day. The outline is given to showrunner Tim Minear, who revises it within a day. The writer uses the revised outline to write the first draft of the script while the other writers work on developing the next. This first draft is usually submitted for revision within three to fourteen days; afterward, a second and sometimes third draft is written. After all revisions are made, the final draft would be produced as the 'shooting draft'.

Costume

Jill Ohanneson, *Firefly*'s original costume designer, brought on Shawna Trpcic as her assistant for the pilot. When the show was picked up, Ohanneson was involved in another job and declined *Firefly*, suggesting Trpcic for the job.

The costumes were chiefly influenced by World War II, the American Civil War, the American Old West, and 1861 samurai Japan. Trpcic used deep reds and oranges for the main cast, to express a feeling of "home", and contrasted that with grays and cool blues for the Alliance.[57] Since the characters were often getting shot, Trpcic would make up to six versions of the same costume for multiple takes.[58]

- For River, mostly jewel tones were used to set her apart from the rest of the *Serenity* crew. River had boots to contrast with the soft fabrics of her clothes, "because that's who she is—she's this soft, beautiful, sensitive girl, but with this hardcore inner character," recalled Trpcic.[59]
- The designers also wanted to contrast Simon, River's brother, with the rest of the crew. Whereas they were dressed in cotton, Simon wore wool, stiff fabrics, satins and silk. He was the "dandy", but as the show progressed, he loosened up slightly.[60]
- For Kaylee, Trpcic studied up on Japanese and Chinese youth, as originally the character was Asian. Other inspirations for Kaylee's costumes were Rosie the Riveter and Chinese Communist posters.[61]
- Inara's costumes reflect her high status, and are very feminine and attractive.
- Trpcic designed and created the clothes for the minor character of Badger with Joss Whedon in mind, since he intended to play that part. When Mark Sheppard played the role instead, he was able to fit into the clothes made for Whedon.[62]
- For the Alliance, besides the grays and cool blues, Trpcic had in mind Nazi Germany, but mixed it with different wars, as the first sketches were "too Nazi".[63] The uniforms of the Alliance soldiers are surplus armor from the 1997 film *Starship Troopers*.[64]

Reception

Critical review

Many reviews focused on the show's fusion of Wild West and outer space motifs. *TV Guide*'s Matt Roush, for instance, called the show "oddball" and "offbeat", and noted how literally the series took the metaphor of space operas as Westerns. Roush opined that the shift from space travel to horseback was "jarring", but that once he got used to this, he found the characters cleverly conceived, and the writing a crisp balance of action, tension and humor.[65] Several reviewers, however, criticized the show's setting; Tim Goodman of the *San Francisco Chronicle* felt that the melding of the western and science fiction genres was a "forced hodgepodge of two alarmingly opposite genres just for the sake of being different" and called the series a "vast disappointment",[66] and Carina Chocano of Salon.com said that while the 'space as Wild West' metaphor is fairly redundant, neither genre connected to the present.[67] Emily Nussbaum of the *New York Times*, reviewing the DVD set, noted that the program featured "an oddball genre mix that might have doomed it from the beginning: it was a character-rich sci-fi western comedy-drama with existential underpinnings, a hard sell during a season dominated by *Joe Millionaire*".[68]

The *Boston Globe* described *Firefly* as a "wonderful, imaginative mess brimming with possibility". The review further notes the difference between the new series and other programs to be that those shows "burst onto the scene with slick pilots and quickly deteriorate into mediocrity..."Firefly" is on the opposite creative journey."[67] Jason Snell called the show one of the best on television, and one "with the most potential for future brilliance".[69]

Reviewers also compared *Firefly* to Whedon's other series, *Buffy the Vampire Slayer*. Chocano noted that the series lacks the psychological tension of *Buffy*, and suggests that this might be attributable to the episodes being aired out of order.[67] MSN, on the other hand, pointed out that after viewing the DVD boxed set it was easy to see why the program had attracted many die-hard fans. "All of Whedon's fingerprints are there: the witty dialogue, the quirky premises and dark exploration of human fallacy that made *Buffy* brilliant found their way to this space drama".[70]

Fandom

Firefly generated a loyal base of fans during its three-month original broadcast run on Fox in late 2002. These original fans, self-styled Browncoats, first organized to try to save the series from being canceled by Fox. Their efforts included raising money for an ad in *Variety* magazine and a postcard writing campaign to UPN. While unsuccessful in finding a network that would continue the show, their support led to a release of the series on DVD in December 2003.[5] A subsequent fan campaign then raised over $14,000 in donations to have a purchased *Firefly* DVD set placed aboard 250 U.S. Navy ships by April 2004 for recreational viewing by their crews.[71]

These and other continuing fan activities eventually persuaded Universal Studios to produce a feature film, *Serenity*.[4] (The title of *Serenity* was chosen, according to Whedon, because Fox still owned the rights to the name 'Firefly'). Numerous early screenings were held for existing fans in an attempt to create a buzz and increase ticket sales when it was released widely on September 30, 2005.[4] The film was not as commercially successful as fans had hoped, opening at number two and making only $40 million worldwide during its initial theatrical release.

On June 23, 2006, fans organized the first worldwide charity screenings of *Serenity* in 47 cities, dubbed as Can't Stop the Serenity or CSTS, an homage to the movie's tagline, "Can't stop the signal".[72] The event raised over $65,000[73] for Whedon's favorite charity, Equality Now. In 2007, $106,000 was raised;[74] in 2008, $107,219; and in 2009, $137,331.[75]

Another campaign on June 23, 2006 referred to the date as *Serenity* Day,[76] on which fans bought—and got others to buy—copies of the *Serenity* and *Firefly* DVDs in hopes of convincing Universal that creating a sequel was a good business decision. On this day, *Serenity* and *Firefly* were ranked second and third, respectively, on the DVD Best Sellers list. The dates for both campaigns were chosen because it is series creator Joss Whedon's birthday.

In July 2006, a fan-made documentary was released, titled *Done the Impossible*, and is commercially available. The documentary relates the story of the fans and how the show has affected them, and features interviews with Whedon and various cast members. Part of the DVD proceeds are donated to Equality Now.

NASA Browncoat astronaut Steven Swanson took the *Firefly* and *Serenity* DVDs with him on Space Shuttle Atlantis' STS-117 mission in June 2007.[77] [78] [79] The DVDs were added to the media collection on the International Space Station as entertainment for the station's crews.[80] [81]

A fan-made, not-for-profit, unofficial sequel to *Serenity*, titled *Browncoats: Redemption*, premiered at Dragon*Con 2010 on September 4, 2010. According to the film's website, Whedon gave "his blessing" to the project. The film was sold on DVD and Blu-ray at the film's website, with all proceeds being distributed among five charities.[82] The film was also screened at various science-fiction conventions across the United States, with admission receipts similarly being donated. All sales ended on September 1, 2011, one year after its premiere, with total revenues exceeding $115,000.[83] Community discussion continues regarding screenings in conjunction with the *Can't Stop the Serenity* project.

Cult status

In 2005, *New Scientist* magazine's website held an internet poll to find "The World's Best Space Sci-Fi Ever". *Firefly* came in first place, with its cinematic follow-up *Serenity* in second.[84] On May 9, 2006, the *Firefly* episodes were added to the iTunes Music Store for download as part of Fox Television Classics along with *Buffy the Vampire Slayer* and *Lost in Space*. Hulu.com lists five consecutive episodes, with a newer one added and the oldest removed once a week.[85] In April 2010, Netflix added the entire series to their streaming on demand service.[86]

Brad Wright, co-creator of *Stargate SG-1* has said that the 200th episode of SG-1, is "A little kiss to *Serenity* and *Firefly*, which was possibly one of the best canceled series in history". In the episode, "Martin Lloyd has come to the S.G.C. [Stargate Command] because even though "Wormhole X-Treme!" was canceled after three episodes, it did so well on DVD they're making a feature [film]".[87] The follow-up film, *Serenity*, was voted the best science fiction movie of all time in an *SFX* magazine poll of 3,000 fans.[88] *Firefly* was later ranked #25 on *TV Guide's* Top Cult Shows Ever.[89] The name for the Google beta app Google Wave was inspired by this TV series.[90] [91]

On the CBS sitcom, *The Big Bang Theory*, Sheldon Cooper is a fan of *Firefly*. When he and Leonard Hofstadter are discussing their roommate agreement, they instill a passage in which they dedicate Friday nights to watching *Firefly*, as Sheldon believes it will last for years, but since it was canceled, he brands Rupert Murdoch, the owner of Fox, a traitor.[92]

On the NBC comedy *Community*, the characters Troy and Abed are fans of the show. They have an agreement that if one of them dies, the other will stage it to look like a suicide caused by the cancellation of *Firefly*, in the hopes that it will bring the show back.[93]

In the 2003 *Battlestar Galactica* miniseries/pilot, a ship resembling *Serenity* appears in the background of the scene where Laura Roslin (Mary McDonnell) is diagnosed with breast cancer.[94] *Serenity* is one of several spaceships inserted as cameos into digital effects scenes by Zoic Studios, the company responsible for digital effects in both *Firefly* and *Battlestar Galactica*.[94]

In an interview on February 17, 2011, with *Entertainment Weekly*, Nathan Fillion joked that: "If I got $300 million from the California Lottery, the first thing I would do is buy the rights to *Firefly*, make it on my own, and distribute it on the Internet".[95] This quickly gave rise to a fanbased initiative to raising the funds to purchase the rights.[96] On March 7, 2011, the organizers announced the closure of the project due to lack of endorsement from the creators, with $1 million pledged at the time it was shut down.[97] Those fans are now working on creating their own fan-funded science fiction production company.[98]

Awards

Firefly won the following awards:

- Emmy Award: *Outstanding Special Visual Effects for a Series*, 2003
- Visual Effects Society: *Best visual effects in a television series*, 2003 (episode "Serenity")
- Saturn Award: *Cinescape Genre Face of the Future Award, Male*, 2003 (Nathan Fillion)
- Saturn Award: *Saturn Award for Best DVD Release (television)*, 2004
- SyFy Genre Awards: *Best Series/Television*, 2006[99]
- SyFy Genre Awards: *Best Actor/Television* Nathan Fillion, 2006
- SyFy Genre Awards: *Best Supporting Actor/Television* Adam Baldwin, 2006
- SyFy Genre Awards: *Best Special Guest/Television* Christina Hendricks for "Trash", 2006
- SyFy Genre Awards: *Best Episode/Television* "Trash", 2006

The series was also nominated for the following awards:

- Visual Effects Society: *Best compositing in a televised program, music video, or commercial*, 2003
- Motion Picture Sound Editors, USA, "Golden Reel Award": *Best sound editing in television long form: sound effects/foley*, 2003
- Hugo Award: *Best Dramatic Presentation, Short Form*, 2003 (episode "Serenity")
- Hugo Award: *Best Dramatic Presentation, Short Form*, 2004 (episodes "Heart of Gold" and "The Message", which at that time had not been shown on television in the USA)
- Golden Satellite Award: *Best DVD Extras*, 2004

Ratings

At the time the series was cancelled by Fox, it averaged 4.48 million viewers and ranked 125th.[3]

Broadcast history

Firefly consists of one two-hour pilot and thirteen one-hour episodes. The series originally aired in the United States on Fox in September 2002. The episodes were aired out of the intended order. Although Whedon had designed the show to run for seven years,[100] and the show had a loyal following during its original broadcast,[101] low ratings resulted in cancellation by Fox in December 2002 after only 11 of the 14 completed episodes had aired in the United States and Canada.[102] Prior to cancellation, some fans, worried about low ratings, formed the *Firefly* Immediate Assistance campaign whose goal was to support the production of the show by sending in postcards to Fox. After it was canceled, the campaign worked on getting another network such as UPN to pick up the series. The campaign was unsuccessful in securing the show's continuation.[103]

The *Onion A.V. Club* cited several actions by the Fox network that contributed to the show's failure, most notably airing the episodes out of sequence, making the plot more difficult to follow.[104] For instance, the double episode "Serenity" was intended as the premiere, and therefore contained most of the character introductions and back-story. However, Fox decided that "Serenity" was unsuitable to open the series, and "The Train Job" was specifically created to act as a new pilot.[12] In addition, *Firefly* was promoted as an action-comedy rather than the more serious character study it was intended to be, and the showbiz trade paper *Variety* noted Fox's decision to occasionally preempt the show for sporting events.[102]

A box set containing the fourteen completed episodes (including those which had not yet aired in the United States) was released on region 1 DVD on December 9, 2003, region 2 on April 19, 2004, and region 4 on August 2, 2004. The box features the episodes in the original order in which the show's producers had intended them to be broadcast, as well as seven episode commentaries, outtakes and other features. The DVDs feature the episodes as they were shot in 16:9 widescreen, with anamorphic transfers and Dolby Surround audio. By September 2005, its DVD release had sold approximately 500,000[105] copies and was one of the top movers at Amazon.com for months. At

Amazon.com the DVDs had average daily rankings of between 1st and 75th in 2003, 22nd and 397th in 2004, 2nd and 232nd in 2005, and 2nd and 31st in 2006 as of June 27, 2006.[106]

Fox remastered the complete series in 1080i high-definition for broadcast on Universal HD, which began in April 2008.[107] The series was re-released on Blu-ray Disc on November 11, 2008, comprising three discs; exclusive extras to the Blu-ray release include extra audio commentary from Joss Whedon, Nathan Fillion, Alan Tudyk and Ron Glass for the episode "Our Mrs. Reynolds", as well as an additional featurette, *"Firefly" Reunion: Lunch with Joss, Nathan, Alan and Ron*.[108]

On March 12, 2009, the series was the winner of the first annual Hulu awards in the category "Shows We'd Bring Back".[109]

The Science Channel began airing the series on March 6, 2011.[110] All episodes aired in the intended order, including episodes "Trash", "The Message" and "Heart of Gold", which were not aired in the original Fox series run. Along with each episode, Dr. Michio Kaku will give commentary about the real-life science behind the science fiction of the show.[95]

Episode #	Title	Original air date	Broadcast #	Production #
1	"Serenity"	December 20, 2002[111]	11	1AGE79
2	"The Train Job"	September 20, 2002[111]	1	1AGE01
3	"Bushwhacked"	September 27, 2002[111]	2	1AGE02
4	"Shindig"	November 1, 2002[112]	6	1AGE03
5	"Safe"	November 8, 2002[112]	7	1AGE04
6	"Our Mrs. Reynolds"	October 4, 2002[112]	3	1AGE05
7	"Jaynestown"	October 18, 2002[112]	4	1AGE06
8	"Out of Gas"	October 25, 2002[113]	5	1AGE07
9	"Ariel"	November 15, 2002[113]	8	1AGE08
10	"War Stories"	December 6, 2002[113]	9	1AGE09
11	"Trash"	June 28, 2003	12	1AGE12
12	"The Message"	July 15, 2003	13	1AGE13
13	"Heart of Gold"	August 19, 2003	14	1AGE10
14	"Objects in Space"	December 13, 2002[114]	10	1AGE11

Home video releases

Firefly: The Complete Series	
Set details: <ul><li>14 episodes</li><li>4 disc set (3 disc Blu-ray)</li></ul> **Features:** <ul><li>Anamorphic widescreen (1.78:1 aspect ratio)</li><li>Dolby Digital 5.1 (DVD)</li><li>DTS-HD Master Audio 5.1 (Blu-ray)</li><li>Subtitles vary depending on region</li></ul>	**Bonus features:** <ul><li>Audio commentary on "Serenity" by writer/director Joss Whedon and actor Nathan Fillion</li><li>Audio commentary on "The Train Job" by co-writer/director Joss Whedon and co-writer Tim Minear</li><li>Audio commentary on "Shindig" by writer Jane Espenson, actor Morena Baccarin and costume designer Shawna Trpcic</li><li>Audio commentary on "Our Mrs. Reynolds" by writer Joss Whedon and actors Nathan Fillion, Alan Tudyk and Ron Glass (Blu-ray exclusive)</li><li>Audio commentary on "Out of Gas" by writer Tim Minear and director David Solomon</li><li>Audio commentary on "War Stories" by actors Nathan Fillion and Alan Tudyk</li><li>Audio commentary on "The Message" by actors Alan Tudyk and Jewel Staite</li><li>Audio commentary on "Objects in Space" by writer/director Joss Whedon</li><li>Four deleted scenes</li><li>"Here's How it Was: The Making of *Firefly*" featurette</li><li>"Serenity: The Tenth Character" featurette</li><li>Joss' Tour of the Set</li><li>*Firefly* Reunion: Lunch with Joss, Nathan, Alan and Ron (Blu-ray exclusive)</li><li>Alan Tudyk's audition</li><li>Gag Reel</li><li>Joss Sings the *Firefly* theme</li><li>Easter Egg: Adam Baldwin sings "Hero of Canton"</li></ul>

Release dates:	Region 1	Region 2	Region 4	
	December 9, 2003 November 11, 2008 (Blu-ray)	April 19, 2004 September 19, 2011 (Blu-ray)[115]	August 2, 2004 December 3, 2008 (Blu-ray)	

Media franchise

The popularity of the short-lived series served as the launching point for media franchise within the *Firefly* universe, including a feature film *Serenity* which addresses many plot points left unresolved by the cancellation of the series.

Additionally there were three comic-book mini-series, *Serenity: Those Left Behind* (104 pages, 2006), *Serenity: Better Days* (80 pages, 2008) and *Serenity: The Shepherd's Tale* (56 pages, 2010) in which Whedon explored plot strands he had intended to explore further in the series. The comics are set, in plot terms, between the end of the TV series and the opening of the feature film. The mini-series were later published in collected form as hardback and softcover graphic novels.

References

[1] Brioux, Bill. "Firefly series ready for liftoff" (http://jam.canoe.ca/Television/TV_Shows/F/Firefly/2002/07/22/734323.html). jam.canoe.ca. . Retrieved 2006-12-10.

[2] Whedon, *Serenity: Relighting the Firefly*, DVD extra

[3] "Fox Squashes "Firefly"" (http://www.eonline.com/uberblog/b44314_fox_squashes_firefly.html). E! Online. 2002-12-13. . Retrieved 2009-12-30.

[4] Russell, M.E. (June 24, 2006). "The Browncoats Rise Again" (http://www.weeklystandard.com/Content/Public/Articles/000/000/005/757fhfxg.asp). The Daily Standard. . Retrieved 2006-07-16.

[5] Chonin, Neva (2005-06-08). "When Fox canceled 'Firefly,' it ignited an Internet fan base whose burning desire for more led to 'Serenity'" (http://www.sfgate.com/cgi-bin/article.cgi?f=/c/a/2005/06/08/DDGQJD4D2O1.DTL&hw=firefly&sn=001&sc=1000). San Francisco Chronicle. . Retrieved 2006-11-09.

[6] "Serenity" (http://www.darkhorse.com/Search/serenity). Dark Horse Comics. . Retrieved June 29, 2011.

[7] "Review of Serenity Role Playing Game" (http://www.rpg.net/reviews/archive/11/11650.phtml). RPGnet. . Retrieved June 29, 2011.

[8] Serenity Blu-ray databanks

[9] The film adaptation explains how the Reavers came to exist in the Firefly universe.

[10] Whedon, *Firefly: the complete series: "Serenity" commentary*
[11] This Sino-American heritage is illustrated by labels on crates in the episode "The Train Job", consisting of a Chinese flag superimposed over a United States flag.
[12] Whedon, *Firefly: the complete series: "Train Job" commentary*, track 1
[13] Whedon, *Firefly: the complete series: "Train Job" commentary*, track 7
[14] Shooting script for "Heart of Gold", in *Firefly: The Official Companion, Volume 2*, p 169.
[15] "Gina Torres as Zoe Washburne - The Women of Joss Whedon" (http://www.ugo.com/tv/joss-whedon-spotlight-zoe-washburn). UGO.com. . Retrieved 2009-02-01.
[16] Whedon, *Serenity: The Official Visual Companion*
[17] Whedon, *Firefly: the complete series: "Train Job" commentary*, track 10
[18] Whedon, *Serenity: Director's Commentary*, track 7 "Mr. Universe"
[19] Staite, Jewel (2004). "Kaylee speaks: Jewel Staite on Firefly". In Jane Espenson, Glenn Yeffeth. *Finding Serenity, anti-heroes, lost shepherds and space hookers in Joss Whedon's Firefly*. Dallas: BenBella books. p. 227. ISBN 1-932100-43-1. PN1992.77.F54F56 2005. "Aside from playing Kaywinnit Lee "Kaylee" Frye in Firefly and Serenity"
[20] "Shindig" (http://titanbooks.com/firefly-the-official-companion-volume-one-3081/). *Firefly: the official companion, volume one* (Paperback ed.). London: Titan books. July 2006. p. 112. ISBN 978-1-84576-314-5. . "Miss Kaywinnit Lee Frye and escort [...] Mal and Kaylee make their way into the party."
[21] Lee, Michael J. (2005-09-15). "Interview with Jewel Staite" (http://www.radiofree.com/profiles/jewel_staite/interview02.shtml). Radio Free Entertainment. . Retrieved 2007-07-13.
[22] *Firefly: the official companion, volume one*, p. 166
[23] IF Magazine interview with Morena Baccarin (http://www.whedon.info/Morena-Baccarin-Heartland-Tv,22816.html)
[24] "The return of Firefly's Mal Reynolds" (http://www.tvsquad.com/2009/10/27/the-return-of-fireflys-mal-reynolds/). *TV Squad*. October 27, 2009. . Retrieved December 9, 2010.
[25] Whedon, *Serenity: The Official Visual Companion*, p. 8
[26] Whedon, *Firefly Companion, Vol 1*, 6
[27] Whedon, "Interview with Joss Whedon", *Done the Impossible*
[28] Whedon, *Firefly: the complete series: "Train Job" commentary*, track 6
[29] Whedon, *Firefly: the complete series: "Train Job" commentary*, track 3
[30] Whedon, *Firefly Companion, Vol 1*, 12
[31] McDuffee, Keith (September 8, 2006). "Firefly: Objects in Space (series finale)" (http://www.tvsquad.com/2006/09/08/firefly-objects-in-space-series-finale/). TVSquad. . Retrieved 2007-12-11.
[32] Whedon, *Firefly Companion, Vol 1*, 11
[33] Whedon, *Firefly Companion, Vol 1*, 10
[34] Whedon, *Firefly Companion, Vol 1*, 10–11
[35] Dixon, "The Reward, the Details, the Devils, the Due", *Finding Serenity*, 8
[36] Monger, James Christopher. "Firefly [Original Television Soundtrack (http://www.allmusic.com/album/w132571) - Greg Edmonson"]. *AllMusic*. Rovi Corporation. .
[37] Jarry, Jonathan (2005-11-16). "Firefly Soundtrack" (http://www.soundtrack.net/albums/database/?id=3922). *SoundtrackNet*. SoundtrackNet, LLC. .
[38] Jarry, Jonathan (2005-10-1). "Firefly Soundtrack" (http://www.soundtrack.net/albums/database/?id=3862). *SoundtrackNet*. SoundtrackNet, LLC. .
[39] Goltz, "Listening to *Firefly*", *Finding Serenity*, 209–215
[40] Steve, Townsley. "Music in the 'Verse: Firefly and Serenity" (http://www.tracksounds.com/reviews/firefly_serenity.htm). tracksounds.com. . Retrieved 2006-07-01.
[41] Jarry, Jonathan (2005-10-01). "SoundtrackNet: Firefly Soundtrack" (http://www.soundtrack.net/albums/database/?id=3862). SoundtrackNet. . Retrieved 2008-02-22.
[42] "Twitter / NASA: Shuttle crew awoke @4:14pET to theme song from "Firefly"." (http://twitter.com/NASA/status/9026148546). *Twitter*. NASA. 2010-02-12. . Retrieved 22 March 2011.
[43] Henry, Susan. "Track and Cue List for Published Version of Firefly Soundtrack" (http://www.itasca.net/~sgh/fireflystk.html). . Retrieved 2008-03-02.
[44] Whedon, *Firefly Companion, Vol 1*, 132
[45] Whedon, *Firefly Companion, Vol 1*, 68
[46] "Interview with Nathan Fillion - Dreamwatch Magazine 107" (http://www.whedon.info/article.php3?id_article=1531&img=). whedon.info. 2003-09-09. . Retrieved 2006-07-11.
[47] Whedon, *Firefly Companion, Vol 1*, 26
[48] Whedon, *Firefly Companion, Vol 1*, 60
[49] Whedon, *Firefly Companion, Vol 1*, 40
[50] Whedon, *Firefly Companion, Vol 1*, 94
[51] Whedon, *Firefly Companion, Vol 1*, 114

[52] Whedon, *Firefly Companion, Vol 1*, 142
[53] Whedon, *Firefly Companion, Vol 1*, 166
[54] Whedon, *Firefly Companion, Vol 1*, 6, 8
[55] Whedon, *Firefly Companion, Vol 1*, 8
[56] Espenson, Jane. "The Writing Process" (http://www.fireflyfans.net/firefly/espenson.htm). Fox Broadcasting Company. . Retrieved 2006-11-05.
[57] Whedon, *Firefly Companion*, Vol. 1, 150.
[58] Whedon, *Firefly Companion*, Vol. 1, 154.
[59] Whedon, *Firefly Companion*, Vol. 1, 128.
[60] Whedon, *Firefly Companion*, Vol. 1, 127.
[61] Whedon, *Firefly Companion*, Vol. 1, 24.
[62] Whedon, *Firefly Companion*, Vol. 1, 120.
[63] Whedon, *Firefly Companion*, Vol. 1, 66.
[64] Whedon: "... That would be because we rented the suits from the *Starship Troopers* people ... again, no money". DVD commentary for "The Train Job", 17:30 minutes.
[65] Matt Roush. "Out (Or Up) Yonder" *TV Guide*; November 9, 2002
[66] Goodman, Tim (September 20, 2002). "Sci-fi 'Firefly' is a bonanza of miscues from 'Buffy' creator" (http://www.sfgate.com/cgi-bin/article.cgi?f=/c/a/2002/09/20/DD141692.DTL&hw=firefly&sn=003&sc=537). The San Francisco Chronicle. . Retrieved 2006-11-09.
[67] Chocano, Carina (October 3, 2002). "Giddyup, spaceman" (http://www.salon.com/entertainment/tv/diary/2002/10/03/firefly/). Salon.com. . Retrieved 2006-07-15.
[68] Nussbaum, Emily (December 21, 2003). "A DVD Face-Off Between the Official and the Homemade" (http://www.nytimes.com/2003/12/21/arts/television/21NUSS.html?ei=5007&en=c508df9532d71a84&ex=1387342800&adxnnl=1&partner=USERLAND&adxnnlx=1152994428-SRzXGWQ2CEWBejqgzRixZQ). New York Times. . Retrieved 2006-07-15.
[69] Snell, Jason (December 12, 2002). "*Firefly* vs. the Firing Squad" (http://web.archive.org/web/20060814235449/http://www.teevee.org/archive/2002/12/13/index.html). teevee. Archived from the original (http://www.teevee.org/archive/2002/12/13/index.html) on 2006-08-14. . Retrieved 2006-07-15.
[70] "Canceled TV Shows" (http://tv.msn.com/tv/article.aspx?news=150653&mpc=2). MSN.com. . Retrieved 2006-07-15.
[71] "Sci-Fi Series "Firefly" Available through Navy's Afloat Library Program" (http://www.navy.mil/search/display.asp?story_id=12580). . Retrieved 2009-09-30.
[72] "Can't Stop the Serenity" (http://www.cantstoptheserenity.com/). Cantstoptheserenity.com. . Retrieved 2009-02-01.
[73] "Can'tStopTheSerenity.com | The Global Event" (http://www.cantstoptheserenity.com/2006/). Cantstoptheserenity.com. . Retrieved 2009-02-01.
[74] "The Global Charity Event" (http://www.cantstoptheserenity.com/2007/). Cantstoptheserenity.com. . Retrieved 2009-02-01.
[75] "Past Events" (http://www.cantstoptheserenity.com/events/). . Retrieved 2010-06-10.
[76] ""Serenity" Day" (http://www.fireflyfans.net/mthread.asp?b=2&t=21111&newsid=0). Fireflyfans.net. . Retrieved 2009-12-30.
[77] "Meet Your Browncoat Astronaut" (http://www.breakingatmo.com/status/2007/06/meet-your-browncoat-astronaut). Breaking Atmo. June 8, 2007. . Retrieved March 22, 2011.
[78] Welker, DeAnn (June 27, 2007). ""Firefly" and "Serenity" arrive at the space station" (http://blog.oregonlive.com/peteramescarlin/2007/06/firefly_and_serenity_arrive_at.html). *The Oregonian*. OregonLive.com. . Retrieved March 22, 2011.
[79] Taylor, Dawn. "Quick Reviews: Serenity: Collector's Edition" (http://www.dvdjournal.com/quickreviews/s/serenity.q.shtml). The DVD Journal. . Retrieved March 22, 2011.
[80] "Firefly and Serenity DVDs to the International Space Station aboard the shuttle Atlantis" (http://www.whedon.info/Firefly-and-Serenity-DVDs-to-the.html). Whedon.info. June 27, 2007. . Retrieved February 21, 2011.
[81] Johns, Anna (June 28, 2007). "Firefly & Serenity in space" (http://www.aoltv.com/2007/06/28/firefly-and-serenity-in-space/). AOL TV. . Retrieved September 9, 2011.
[82] "Browncoats: Redemption; Charities" (http://browncoatsmovie.com/?page_id=74). . Retrieved 2010-01-01.
[83] "Browncoats: Redemption" (http://browncoatsmovie.com/). . Retrieved 2011-09-13.
[84] "The World's Best Space Sci-Fi Ever: Your verdict" (http://www.newscientist.com/article/dn8211). NewScientistSpace.com. October 26, 2005. . Retrieved 2006-08-06.
[85] "Firefly - Full Episodes and Clips streaming online" (http://www.hulu.com/firefly). *Hulu*. . Retrieved February 22, 2011.
[86] "This Week on Netflix Instant: Fargo, It Might Get Loud & More" (http://www.firstshowing.net/2010/this-week-on-netflix-instant-fargo-it-might-get-loud-more/). Firstshowing. April 20, 2010. . Retrieved 2010-09-23.
[87] "Wright on Target" (http://www.gateworld.net/interviews/wright_on_target.shtml). GateWorld.net. July 14, 2006. . Retrieved 2006-07-17.
[88] "Serenity named top sci-fi movie" (http://news.bbc.co.uk/2/hi/entertainment/6517155.stm). BBC Online. 2007-04-02. . Retrieved 2007-03-02.
[89] "TV Guide Names the Top Cult Shows Ever" (http://www.tvguide.com/news/top-cult-shows-40239.aspx). *TVGuide*. . Retrieved 2007-06-29.

[90] Cochrane, Nate (May 29, 2009). "Opinion: Google's wave drowns the bling in Microsoft's Bing" (http://www.itnews.com.au/News/146353,opinion-googles-wave-drowns-the-bling-in-microsofts-bing.aspx). iT News Australia. . Retrieved June 3, 2009.

[91] "Google's new "Wave"; was the name actually inspired by Firefly?" (http://whedonesque.com/comments/20516). Whedonesque. May 29, 2009. . Retrieved 2009-09-29.

[92] Townsend, Allie (May 18, 2010). "CBS' Big Bang Theory Sets Record High Syndication Price, Makes A Great Firefly Reference" (http://techland.time.com/2010/05/18/the-big-bang-theorys-hilarious-firefly-quip-and-record-syndication-deal/). *TIME*. Techland. . Retrieved July 15, 2011.

[93] Sepinwall, Alan (February 17, 2011). "Review: 'Community' - 'Intermediate Documentary Filmmaking': Pierce the puppet-master" (http://www.hitfix.com/blogs/whats-alan-watching/posts/community-intermediate-documentary-filmmaking-pierce-the-puppet-master). HitFix. . Retrieved July 15, 2011.

[94] David Bassom (2007), *Battlestar Galactica: the official companion*, p. 148

[95] Hibberd, James (February 17, 2011). "'Firefly' returning to cable; Fillion says he'd play Mal again -- EXCLUSIVE" (http://insidetv.ew.com/2011/02/17/firefly-returns/). *Entertainment Weekly*. . Retrieved February 20, 2011.

[96] Kuhn, Thor (March 29, 2011). "History of Help Nathan Buy Firefly" (http://unstoppablesignals.com/hnbf/). *Unstoppable Signals*. . Retrieved March 29, 2011.

[97] "According to Joss's..." (http://www.facebook.com/HelpNathanBuyFF/posts/185893901452455). Facebook. March 7, 2011. . Retrieved June 29, 2011.

[98] "The State of Affairs" (http://unstoppablesignals.com/2011/04/where-we-are/). Unstoppable Signals. April 7, 2011. . Retrieved June 29, 2011.

[99] "SyfyPortal Awards" (http://web.archive.org/web/20061126081755/http://www.syfyportal.com/news.php?id=2895). Archived from the original (http://syfyportal.com/news.php?id=2895) on 2006-11-26. . Retrieved 2006-10-08.

[100] "Serenity Set Visit: IGN visits the set of the Firefly movie" (http://movies.ign.com/articles/564/564677p1.html). IGN. 2004-11-08. . Retrieved 2007-08-02.

[101] "Push Record" (http://www.tvguide.com/news/PUSH-RECORD-49078.aspx). TV Guide. October 7, 2002. . Retrieved 2006-11-09.

[102] Snyder, Gabriel (March 21, 2004). "'Firefly' feature alights" (http://www.variety.com/article/VR1117901954?refCatId=13). Variety. . Retrieved 2006-06-24.

[103] "The Fan Campaign: A Timeline of Fan Efforts to Keep Firefly on the Air" (http://www.browncoats.com/index.php?ContentID=42e95a1f27c00). Browncoats.com. . Retrieved 2006-07-01.

[104] "Firefly: The Complete Series - Review" (http://www.avclub.com/articles/firefly-the-complete-series,11623/). The A. V. Club. January 12, 2004. . Retrieved 2007-02-05.

[105] Breznican, Anthony (September 21, 2005). "'Firefly' alights on big screen as 'Serenity'" (http://www.usatoday.com/life/movies/news/2005-09-21-serenity_x.htm). USA Today, . Retrieved 2006-06-04.

[106] "Real time Firefly DVD pricing and ranking from Amazon.com" (http://fireflyfans.net/amazon.asp). FireflyFans.net. June 27, 2006. . Retrieved 2006-06-27.

[107] "'Firefly' Gets Hi-Def Makeover" (http://www.tvweek.com/?pageId=212). TelevisionWeek. 2006-08-03. . Retrieved 2006-08-04.

[108] "Fox Announces Firefly Blu-ray, Specs" (http://www.highdefdigest.com/news/show/Fox/TV_on_High-Def/Disc_Announcements/Fox_Announces_Firefly_Blu-ray,_Specs/2010). High-Def Digest. 2008-08-19. . Retrieved 2008-08-19.

[109] "Firefly wins 1st annual Hulu award for "Shows we'd bring back"" (http://whedonesque.com/comments/19461). Whedonesque. . Retrieved 2010-09-23.

[110] "Firefly premieres Sunday, Mar 6" (http://press.discovery.com/us/sci/programs/firefly/). Science Channel. . Retrieved 2011-02-14.

[111] *Firefly: the complete series*, disk one backcover

[112] *Firefly: the complete series*, disk two backcover

[113] *Firefly: the complete series*, disk three backcover

[114] *Firefly: the complete series*, disk four backcover

[115] "Firefly - The Complete Series" (http://www.amazon.co.uk/dp/B003EI0TF6/). Amazon.co.uk. . Retrieved July 27, 2011.

Further reading

- *Firefly: the official companion, volume one*. Abbie Bernstein, Bryan Cairns, Karl Derrick, Tara Di Lullo. London, UK: Titan Books. July 2006. ISBN 139781845763145.
- *Firefly: the official companion, volume two*. Abbie Bernstein, Bryan Cairns, Karl Derrick, Tara Di Lullo. London, UK: Titan Books. April 2007. ISBN 139781845763725.
- Jane Espenson, ed., with Glen Yeffeth, ed (2004). *Finding Serenity: Anti-heroes, Lost Shepherds and Space Hookers in Joss Whedon's "Firefly"*. Dallas, Texas: Benbella Books. ISBN 1-932100-43-1.
- Joss Whedon (2005). *Serenity: the official visual companion*. UK: Titan Books. ISBN 1-84576-082-4.
- *Firefly — The Complete Series* (DVD). 20th Century Fox. December 9, 2003. ISBN 6308024716.
- *Done the Impossible: The Fans' Tale of Firefly & Serenity* (http://www.donetheimpossible.com) (DVD). 2006.

External links

- *Firefly* (http://www.imdb.com/title/tt0303461/) at the Internet Movie Database
- *Firefly* (http://www.tv.com/show/7097/summary.html) at TV.com
- *Firefly* (http://www.dmoz.org/Arts/Television/Programs/Science_Fiction_and_Fantasy/F/Firefly/) at the Open Directory Project
- *Firefly-Serenity* Chinese Pinyinary (http://fireflychinese.kevinsullivansite.net/)—English translations of the Chinese words and phrases used in *Firefly* and *Serenity*

Buffy the Vampire Slayer (TV series)

Buffy the Vampire Slayer	
Genre	Supernatural drama Comedy-drama Action Horror
Created by	Joss Whedon
Starring	Sarah Michelle Gellar Nicholas Brendon Alyson Hannigan Anthony Stewart Head Charisma Carpenter David Boreanaz Seth Green James Marsters Marc Blucas Emma Caulfield Michelle Trachtenberg Amber Benson
Theme music composer	Nerf Herder
Composer(s)	Christophe Beck Thomas Wanker Robert Duncan Sean Murray
Country of origin	United States
Language(s)	English
No. of seasons	7
No. of episodes	144 (List of episodes)
Production	
Executive producer(s)	Joss Whedon David Greenwalt Marti Noxon
Running time	43 minutes
Broadcast	
Original channel	The WB (1997–2001) UPN (2001–2003)
Picture format	NTSC 480i 4:3 PAL 576i 16:9 (Seasons 4–7)
Original run	March 10, 1997 – May 20, 2003
Chronology	
Preceded by	*Buffy the Vampire Slayer* (1992 film)
Followed by	*Buffy the Vampire Slayer Season Eight* (comic book)
Related shows	*Angel*

Buffy the Vampire Slayer is an American television series that aired from March 10, 1997, until May 20, 2003. The series was created in 1997 by writer-director Joss Whedon under his production tag, Mutant Enemy Productions with later co-executive producers being Jane Espenson, David Fury, David Greenwalt, Doug Petrie, Marti Noxon, and David Solomon. The series narrative follows Buffy Summers (played by Sarah Michelle Gellar), the latest in a line of young women known as "Vampire Slayers" or simply "Slayers". In the story, Slayers are "called" (chosen by fate) to battle against vampires, demons, and other forces of darkness. Like previous Slayers, Buffy is aided by a Watcher, who guides, teaches, and trains her. Unlike her predecessors, Buffy surrounds herself with a circle of loyal friends who become known as the "Scooby Gang".

The series received critical and popular acclaim and usually reached between four and six million viewers on original airings.[1] Although such ratings are lower than successful shows on the "big four" networks (ABC, CBS, NBC, and Fox),[2] they were a success for the relatively new and smaller WB Television Network.[3] Reviews for the show were positive; it has been included in many "best of" lists, including being ranked #41 on the list of TV Guide's 50 Greatest TV Shows of All Time, #2 on *Empire*'s 50 Greatest TV Shows of All Time, voted #3 in 2004 and 2007 on *TV Guide*'s Top Cult Shows Ever[4][5] and listed in *Time* magazine's "100 Best TV Shows of All-*TIME*."[6] It was nominated for Emmy and Golden Globe awards, winning a total of 3 Emmys. However, snubs in lead Emmy categories resulted in outrage among TV critics and the decision by the academy to hold a tribute event in honor of the series after it had gone off the air in 2003.[7]

The WB network ceased operation on September 17, 2006, after airing a homage to its "most memorable series", including the premiere episodes of *Buffy* and its spin-off *Angel*.[8] *Buffy*'s success has led to hundreds of tie-in products, including novels, comics, and video games. The series has received attention in fandom (including fan films), parody, and academia, and has influenced the direction of other television series.[9]

Production

Origins

Writer Joss Whedon says that "Rhonda the Immortal Waitress" was really the first incarnation of the *Buffy* concept, "just the idea of some woman who seems to be completely insignificant who turns out to be extraordinary".[10] This early, unproduced idea evolved into *Buffy*, which Whedon developed to invert the Hollywood formula of "the little blonde girl who goes into a dark alley and gets killed in every horror movie".[11] Whedon wanted "to subvert that idea and create someone who was a hero".[11] He explained, "The very first mission statement of the show was the joy of female power: having it, using it, sharing it".[12]

The idea was first visited through Whedon's script for the 1992 movie *Buffy the Vampire Slayer*, which featured Kristy Swanson in the title role. The director, Fran Rubel Kuzui, saw it as a "pop culture comedy about what people think about vampires".[13] Whedon disagreed: "I had written this scary film about an empowered woman, and they turned it into a broad comedy. It was crushing."[14] The script was praised within the industry,[15] but the movie was not.[16]

Buffy creator Joss Whedon also served as executive producer, head writer, and director on the series.

Several years later, Gail Berman, a Fox executive, approached Whedon to develop his *Buffy* concept into a television series.[17] Whedon explained that "They said, 'Do you want to do a show?' And I thought, 'High school as a horror movie'. And so the metaphor became the central concept behind *Buffy*, and that's how I sold it."[18] The supernatural elements in the series stood as metaphors for personal anxieties associated with adolescence and young adulthood.[19] Whedon went on to write and partly fund a 25-minute non-broadcast pilot[20] that was shown to networks and eventually sold to the WB Network. The latter promoted the premiere with a series of *History of the Slayer* clips,[21] and the first episode aired on March 10, 1997.

Executive producers

Joss Whedon was credited as executive producer throughout the run of the series, and for the first five seasons (1997–2001) he was also the show runner, a role that involves serving as head writer and being responsible for every aspect of production. Marti Noxon took on the role for seasons six and seven (2001–2003), but Whedon continued to be involved with writing and directing *Buffy* alongside projects such as *Angel*, *Fray*, and *Firefly*. Fran Rubel Kuzui and her husband, Kaz Kuzui, were credited as executive producers[22] but were not involved in the show. Their credit, rights, and royalties over the franchise relate to their funding, producing, and directing of the original movie version of *Buffy*.[23]

Writing

Script-writing was done by Mutant Enemy, a production company created by Whedon in 1997. The writers with the most writing credits[24] include: Joss Whedon, Steven S. DeKnight, Jane Espenson, David Fury, Drew Goddard, Drew Greenberg, David Greenwalt, Rebecca Rand Kirshner, Marti Noxon and Doug Petrie. Other authors with writing credits include: Dean Batali, Carl Ellsworth, Tracey Forbes, Ashley Gable, Howard Gordon, Diego Gutierrez, Elin Hampton, Rob Des Hotel, Matt Kiene, Ty King, Thomas A. Swyden, Joe Reinkemeyer, Dana Reston and Dan Vebber.[25]

Jane Espenson has explained how scripts came together.[26] First, the writers talked about the emotional issues facing Buffy Summers and how she would confront them through her battle against evil supernatural forces. Then the episode's story was "broken" into acts and scenes. Act breaks were designed as key moments to intrigue viewers so that they would stay with the episode following the commercial break. The writers collectively filled in scenes surrounding these act breaks for a more fleshed-out story. A whiteboard marked their progress by mapping brief descriptions of each scene. Once "breaking" was done, the credited author wrote an outline for the episode, which was checked by Whedon or Noxon. The writer then wrote a full script, which went through a series of drafts, and finally a quick rewrite from the show runner. The final article was used as the shooting script.

Casting

Actresses who auditioned for Buffy Summers and got other roles include Julie Benz (Darla), Elizabeth Anne Allen (Amy Madison), Julia Lee (Chanterelle/Lily Houston/Anne Steele), Charisma Carpenter (Cordelia Chase), and Mercedes McNab (Harmony Kendall). Bianca Lawson, who played vampire slayer Kendra Young in season 2 of the show, originally auditioned for the role of Cordelia Chase before Charisma Carpenter was cast in the role.

The title role went to Sarah Michelle Gellar, who had appeared as Sydney Rutledge on *Swans Crossing* and Kendall Hart on *All My Children*. At age 18 in 1995, Gellar had already won a Daytime Emmy Award for Outstanding Younger Leading Actress in a Drama Series.[27] In 1996, she was initially cast as Cordelia Chase during a week of auditioning. She decided to keep trying for the role of Buffy, and after several more auditions, she landed the lead.[28]

Nathan Fillion auditioned for the role of Angel back in early 1996. David Boreanaz had already been cast at the time of the unaired *Buffy* pilot, but did not appear.

Anthony Stewart Head had already led a prolific acting and singing career,[29] but remained best known in the United States for a series of twelve coffee commercials with Sharon Maughan for Nescafé.[30] He accepted the role of Rupert Giles. Unlike other *Buffy* regulars, Nicholas Brendon had little acting experience, instead working various jobs — including production assistant, plumber's assistant, veterinary janitor, food delivery, script delivery, day care counselor, and waiter — before breaking into acting and overcoming his stutter.[31] [32] He landed his Xander Harris role following only four days of auditioning.[33] Ryan Reynolds and Danny Strong (Jonathan Levinson) also auditioned for the part.

Alyson Hannigan was the last of the original six to be cast. Following her role in *My Stepmother Is an Alien*,[34] she appeared in commercials and supporting roles on television shows throughout the early 1990s.[34] In 1996, the role of Willow Rosenberg was initially played by Riff Regan for the unaired *Buffy* pilot, but Hannigan auditioned when the role was being recast for the series proper. Hannigan described her approach to the character through Willow's reaction to a particular moment: Willow sadly tells Buffy that her Barbie doll was taken from her as a child. Buffy asks her if she ever got it back. Willow's line was to reply "most of it". Hannigan decided on an upbeat and happy delivery of the line "most of it", as opposed to a sad, depressed delivery. Hannigan figured Willow would be happy and proud that she got "most of it" back. That indicated how she was going to play the rest of the scene, and the role, for that matter, and defined the character.[35] Her approach subsequently got her the role.

Broadcast history and syndication

Buffy the Vampire Slayer first aired on March 10, 1997, (as a mid season replacement for the show *Savannah*) on the WB network, and played a key role in the growth of the Warner Bros. television network in its early years.[36] After five seasons, it transferred to the United Paramount Network (UPN) for its final two seasons. In 2001, the show went into syndication in the United States on local stations and on cable channel FX; the local airings ended in 2005, and the FX airings lasted until 2008. Beginning in January 2010, it began to air in syndication in the United States on Logo.[37] Reruns also briefly aired on MTV. In March 2010, it began to air in Canada on MuchMusic and MuchMore.[38] On November 7, 2010, it began airing on Chiller with a 24-hour marathon; the series airs weekdays. Chiller has also aired a 14-hour Thanksgiving Day marathon on November 25, 2010.[39] In 2011, it began airing on Oxygen and TeenNick.

While the seventh season was still being broadcast, Sarah Michelle Gellar told *Entertainment Weekly* she was not going to sign on for an eighth year; "When we started to have such a strong year this year, I thought: 'This is how I want to go out, on top, at our best".[40] Whedon and UPN gave some considerations to production of a spin-off series that would not require Gellar, including a rumored Faith series, but nothing came of those plans.[41] The *Buffy* canon is continuing outside the television medium in the Dark Horse Comics series, *Buffy* Season Eight. This has been produced since March 2007 by Whedon, who also wrote the first story arc, "The Long Way Home".[42]

As of July 15, 2008, *Buffy the Vampire Slayer* episodes are available to download for PlayStation 3 and PlayStation Portable video game consoles via the PlayStation Network.[43]

In the United Kingdom, the entire series aired on Sky1 and BBC2. After protests from fans about early episodes being edited for their pre-watershed time-slot, from the second run (mid-second season onwards), the BBC gave the show two time slots: the early-evening slot (typically Thursday at 6:45 pm) for a family-friendly version with violence, objectionable language and other stronger material cut out, and a late-night uncut version (initially late-night Sundays, but for most of the run, late-night Fridays; exact times varied).[44] Sky1 aired the show typically at 8:00 pm on Thursdays. From the fourth season onwards, the BBC aired the show in anamorphic 16:9 widescreen format. Whedon later said that *Buffy* was never intended to be viewed this way.[45] Despite his claims, Sky1 and FX UK now air repeat showings in the widescreen format.

Opening sequence

The *Buffy* opening sequence provides credits early in each show. The music was performed by the rock band Nerf Herder. The melody is similar to that of an Austrian pop song from the 1980s called "Codo" by DÖF, but Nerf Herder have said that they had "never heard of DÖF" and the similarity was coincidental.[46] In the DVD commentary for the first *Buffy* episode, Whedon said his decision to go with Nerf Herder's theme was influenced by cast member Alyson Hannigan, who had made him listen to the band's music.[47] Janet Halfyard, in her essay "Music, Gender, and Identity in *Buffy the Vampire Slayer* and *Angel*", describes the opening:

> It begins with the sound of an organ, accompanied by a wolf's howl, with a visual image of a flickering night sky overlaid with unintelligible archaic script: the associations with both the silent era and films such as Nosferatu and with the conventions of the Hammer House of Horror and horror in general are unmistakable.[48]

But the theme changes: "The opening sequence removes itself from the sphere of 1960s and '70s horror by replaying the same motif, the organ now supplanted by an aggressively strummed electric guitar, relocating itself in modern youth culture".[48] This music is heard over images of a young cast involved in the action and turbulence of adolescence. The sequence provides a post-modern twist on the horror genre.[48]

The brief clips of characters and events which compose the opening sequence are updated from season to season. The only shots that persist across all seven seasons are those of a book titled *Vampyr* and of the cross given to Buffy by Angel in the first episode. Each sequence ends with a lingering shot of Buffy, which changes between seasons. In seasons six and seven, the final shots of Gellar are respectively as Buffybot in "The Gift" (season five finale) and the First Evil posing as Buffy in "Lessons" (season seven premiere). The only exception was in the season four episode "Superstar", which featured a long shot of Jonathan Levinson.

Four episodes feature an opening sequence that is unique to that specific episode. The fourth season episode "Superstar" is the same as the season four credits except numerous clips of Jonathan are added in. The fifth season premiere "Buffy vs. Dracula" has the regular season five credits with the omission of the Michelle Trachtenberg (Dawn) scenes from the title sequence. She is instead credited as a guest star. The season six episode "Once More, with Feeling" has a different opening theme song and credits. The season six episode "Seeing Red" added Amber Benson (Tara) into the regular season six opening credits for her final episode.

Music

Buffy features a mix of original, indie, rock and pop music. The composers spent around seven days scoring between fourteen to thirty minutes of music for each episode.[49] Christophe Beck revealed that the *Buffy* composers used computers and synthesizers and were limited to recording one or two "real" samples. Despite this, their goal was to produce "dramatic" orchestration that would stand up to film scores.[49]

Alongside the score, most episodes featured indie rock music, usually at the characters' venue of choice, The Bronze. *Buffy* music supervisor John King explained that "we like to use unsigned bands" that "you would believe would play in this place".[49] For example, the fictional group Dingoes Ate My Baby were portrayed on screen by front group Four Star Mary.[50] Pop songs by famous artists were rarely featured prominently, but several episodes spotlighted the sounds of more famous artists such as Sarah McLachlan,[51] [52] The Brian Jonestown Massacre, Blink-182,[53] Third Eye Blind,[54] Aimee Mann[55] (who also had a line of dialogue), The Dandy Warhols,[56] Cibo Matto,[57] Coldplay, Lisa Loeb, and Michelle Branch.[58] The popularity of music used in *Buffy* has led to the release of four soundtrack albums: *Buffy the Vampire Slayer: The Album*,[59] *Radio Sunnydale*,[60] the *"Once More, with Feeling" Soundtrack*,[61] [62] [63] and *Buffy the Vampire Slayer: The Score*.

Setting and storylines

Setting and filming locations

Main articles: Sunnydale, Hellmouth and Filming locations

Most of *Buffy* was shot on location in Los Angeles, California. The main exterior set of the town of Sunnydale, including the infamous "sun sign", was located in Santa Monica, California in a lot on Olympic Boulevard.[64] The show is set in the fictional California town of Sunnydale, whose suburban Sunnydale High School sits on top of a "Hellmouth", a gateway to demon realms. The Hellmouth, located beneath the school library, is a source of mystical energies as well as a nexus for a wide variety of evil creatures and supernatural phenomena. In addition to being an open-ended plot device, Joss Whedon has cited the Hellmouth and "High school as Hell" as one of the primary metaphors in creating the series.[65]

The high school used in the first three seasons is actually Torrance High School, in Torrance, California. This school was used until the residents of Torrance complained about loud sounds at night.[66] The school exterior has been used in other television shows and movies, most notably *Beverly Hills, 90210*, *Bring It On*, *She's All That* and the spoof *Not Another Teen Movie*.[66] In addition to the high school and its library, scenes take place in the town's cemeteries, a local nightclub (The Bronze), and Buffy's home (located in Torrance), where many of the characters live at various points in the series.

Some of the exterior shots of the college Buffy attends, UC Sunnydale, were filmed at UCLA. Several episodes include shots from the Oviatt Library at CSUN.[67][68]

Format

Buffy is told in a serialized format, with each episode involving a self-contained story while contributing to a larger storyline,[19] which is broken down into season-long narratives marked by the rise and defeat of a powerful antagonist, commonly referred to as the "Big Bad". While the show is mainly a drama with frequent comic relief, most episodes blend different genres, including horror, martial arts, romance, melodrama, farce, science fiction, comedy, and even, in one episode, musical comedy.

The series' narrative revolves around Buffy and her friends, collectively dubbed the "Scooby Gang", who struggle to balance the fight against supernatural evils with their complex social lives.[19] The show mixes complex, season-long storylines with a villain-of-the-week format; a typical episode contains one or more villains, or supernatural phenomena, that are thwarted or defeated by the end of the episode. Though elements and relationships are explored and ongoing subplots are included, the show focuses primarily on Buffy and her role as an archetypal heroine.

In the first few seasons, the most prominent monsters in the *Buffy* bestiary are vampires, which are based on traditional myths, lore, and literary conventions. As the series continues, Buffy and her companions fight an increasing variety of demons, as well as ghosts, werewolves, zombies, and unscrupulous humans. They frequently save the world from annihilation by a combination of physical combat, magic, and detective-style investigation, and are guided by an extensive collection of ancient and mystical reference books. Hand-to-hand combat is chiefly undertaken by Buffy and Angel, later by Spike, and to a far lesser degree by Giles and Xander. Willow eventually becomes an adept witch, while Giles contributes his extensive knowledge of demonology and supernatural lore.

Inspirations and metaphors

During the first year of the series, Whedon described the show as "*My So-Called Life* meets *The X-Files*".[69] *My So-Called Life* gave a sympathetic portrayal of teen anxieties; in contrast, *The X-Files* delivered a supernatural "monster of the week" storyline. Alongside these series, Whedon has cited cult film *Night of the Comet* as a "big influence",[70] and credited the *X-Men* character Kitty Pryde as a significant influence on the character of Buffy.[71] The authors of the unofficial guidebook *Dusted* point out that the series was often a pastiche, borrowing elements from previous horror novels, movies, and short stories and from such common literary stock as folklore and mythology.[72] Nevitt and Smith describe *Buffy*'s use of pastiche as "post modern Gothic".[73] For example, the Adam character parallels the *Frankenstein* monster, the episode "Bad Eggs" parallels *Invasion of the Body Snatchers*, and so on.

Buffy episodes often include a deeper meaning or metaphor as well. Whedon explained, "We think very carefully about what we're trying to say emotionally, politically, and even philosophically while we're writing it... it really is, apart from being a pop-culture phenomenon, something that is deeply layered textually episode by episode".[74] Academics Wilcox and Lavery provide examples of how a few episodes deal with real life issues turned into supernatural metaphors:

> In the world of *Buffy* the problems that teenagers face become literal monsters. A mother can take over her daughter's life ("Witch"); a strict stepfather-to-be really is a heartless machine ("Ted"); a young lesbian fears that her nature is demonic ("Goodbye Iowa" and "Family"); a girl who has sex with even the nicest-seeming guy may discover that he afterwards becomes a monster ("Innocence").[19]

The love affair between the vampire Angel and Buffy was fraught with metaphors. For example, their night of passion cost the vampire his soul. Sarah Michelle Gellar said: "That's the ultimate metaphor. You sleep with a guy and he turns bad on you."[75]

Buffy struggles throughout the series with her calling as Slayer and the loss of freedom this entails, frequently sacrificing teenage experiences for her Slayer duties. Her difficulties and eventual empowering realizations are reflections of several dichotomies faced by modern women and echo feminist issues within society.[76]

In the episode "Becoming (Part 2)", when Joyce learns that Buffy is the Slayer, her reaction has strong echoes of a parent discovering their child is gay, including denial, suggesting that she try "not being a Slayer", and ultimately kicking Buffy out of the house.[77]

Plot summary

Season one exemplifies the "high school as hell" concept. Buffy Summers has just moved to Sunnydale after burning down her old school's gym and hopes to escape her Slayer duties. Her plans are complicated by Rupert Giles, her new Watcher, who reminds her of the inescapable presence of evil. Sunnydale High is built atop a Hellmouth, a portal to demon dimensions that attracts supernatural phenomena to the area. Buffy meets two schoolmates, Xander Harris and Willow Rosenberg, who help her fight evil through the series, but they must first prevent The Master, an ancient and especially threatening vampire, from opening the Hellmouth and taking over Sunnydale.

The emotional stakes are raised in season two. New vampires Spike and Drusilla (weakened from a mob in Prague, which presumably caused her debilitating injury), come to town along with the new slayer, Kendra Young, who was activated as a result of Buffy's brief death in the season one finale. Xander becomes involved with Cordelia, while Willow becomes involved with witchcraft and Daniel "Oz" Osbourne, who becomes a werewolf after being bitten by his young cousin Jordy who happens to be a werewolf. Buffy and the vampire Angel develop a relationship over the course of the season, but after they sleep together, Angel's soul, given to him by a curse, is lost and he once more becomes Angelus, a sadistic killer. He torments much of the "Scooby Gang" throughout the rest of the season and murders multiple innocents and Giles' new girlfriend Jenny Calendar, a gypsy who had been sent to make sure that the curse that gave Angel his soul was never broken. Buffy is forced to kill him (right after Willow restores his soul) and leaves Sunnydale, emotionally shattered.

After attempting to start a new life in Los Angeles, Buffy returns to town in season three. Angel is resurrected, but after he and Buffy realize that a relationship between them can never happen, he leaves Sunnydale at the end of the season. A new watcher named Wesley is put in Giles's place when he is fired from the Watcher's Council because he had developed a "father's love" for Buffy, and towards the end of the season Buffy announces that she will also no longer be working for the council. Early in the season she is confronted with an unstable Slayer, Faith, who was called up after Kendra's death near the end of season two, as well as affable Sunnydale Mayor Richard Wilkins, who has plans to "ascend" (become a giant snake demon) on Sunnydale High's Graduation Day. Although she works with Buffy at first, after accidentally killing a human, Faith becomes irrational and sides with Mayor Wilkins, eventually landing in a coma after a fight with Buffy. At the end of the season, Buffy and the entire graduation class defeat Mayor Wilkins by blowing up Sunnydale High, killing him in the process.

Season four sees Buffy and Willow enroll at UC Sunnydale while Xander joins the workforce and begins dating Anya, a former vengeance demon. Spike returns as a series regular and is abducted by The Initiative, a top-secret military installation based beneath the UC Sunnydale campus. They implant a microchip in his head which prevents him from harming humans. He reluctantly helps the Scooby Gang throughout the season and eventually begins to fight on their side after learning that he can harm other demons. Oz leaves town after realizing that he is too dangerous as a werewolf, and Willow falls in love with Tara Maclay, another witch. Buffy begins dating Riley Finn, a grad student whom she later realizes is a member of The Initiative. Although appearing to be a well-meaning anti-demon operation, The Initiative's sinister plans are revealed when Adam, a demon/human/computer hybrid secret project, escapes and begins to wreak havoc on the town.

During season five, a younger sister to Buffy, Dawn, suddenly appears in Buffy's life, and although she is new to the series, to the characters it is as if she has always been there. Buffy is confronted with Glory, an exiled hell-God that is searching for a "Key" that will allow her to return to her Hell dimension and in the process would blur the lines between dimensions and unleash Hell on Earth. It is later discovered that the Key's protectors had turned the Key into human form as Buffy's sister Dawn, concurrently implanting everybody with lifelong memories of her. The Watcher's Council aids in Buffy's research of Glory, and she and Giles are both reinstated by the Council. Riley leaves early in the season after deducing that Buffy does not love him and joins a military demon-hunting operation, while Spike, still implanted with the Initiative chip, realizes he is in love with Buffy and continually helps the Scoobies in their fight. Buffy's mother, Joyce, dies of a brain aneurysm, while at the end of the season, Xander proposes to Anya. Glory later discovers that Dawn is the key and kidnaps her. Buffy sacrifices her own life to save Dawn's and prevent the portal to the Hell dimensions from opening.

At the beginning of season six, Buffy's friends resurrect her through a powerful spell, believing that they have rescued her from Hell. Buffy reveals she was in Heaven during her death and she falls into a deep depression for most of the season. Giles returns to England after deciding that Buffy has become too reliant on him, while Buffy takes up a fast-food job for money and develops a secret, mutually abusive relationship with Spike. Dawn suffers from kleptomania and feelings of alienation, Xander leaves Anya at the altar, after which Anya once again becomes a vengeance demon, and Willow becomes addicted to magic, causing Tara to temporarily leave her. They also begin to deal with The Trio, a group of nerds led by Warren Mears who use their technological proficiency to attempt to kill Buffy and take over Sunnydale. Warren is shown to be the only competent villain of the group and, after Buffy thwarts his plans multiple times and the Trio breaks apart, he comes unhinged and attacks Buffy with a gun, killing Tara in the process. This causes Willow to descend into darkness and unleash all of her dark magical powers, killing Warren. Giles returns to face her in battle and infuses her with light magic, tapping into her remaining humanity. This causes Willow to attempt to destroy the world to end everyone's suffering, although it eventually allows Xander to reach through her pain and end her rampage. At the end of the season, after attacking Buffy, Spike leaves Sunnydale and travels to see a demon and asks him to "return him to what he used to be" so that he can "give Buffy what she deserves". After passing a series of tests, the demon restores his soul.

During season seven, it is revealed that Buffy's resurrection caused an instability which allows the First Evil to begin tipping the balance between good and evil. It begins hunting down and killing the inactive Potential Slayers, and raises an army of ancient, powerful Turok-Han vampires. After the Watchers' Council is destroyed, a number of the Potential Slayers (some brought by Giles) take refuge in Buffy's house. Faith returns to help fight the First Evil, and the new Sunnydale High School's principal, Robin Wood, also joins the cause. The Turok-Han vampires and a sinister preacher known as Caleb begin causing havoc for the Scoobies. As the Hellmouth becomes more active, nearly all humans and demons flee Sunnydale. In the series finale, the Scoobies descend into the Hellmouth while

Willow casts a spell that activates all of the Potential Slayers, granting them Slayer powers. Angel comes to Sunnydale with an amulet, which Buffy gives to Spike. Anya, now human again, dies in the fight, as do some of the new Slayers. Spike's amulet channels the power of the sun and kills all of the vampires in the Hellmouth, incinerating Spike in the process. This causes the Hellmouth to collapse, and the entirety of Sunnydale collapses into the resulting crater, while the survivors of the battle escape in a school bus.

Characters

Main characters

Buffy Summers (played by Sarah Michelle Gellar) is "the Slayer", one in a long line of young women chosen by fate to battle evil forces. This mystic calling endows her with dramatically increased physical strength, as well as endurance, agility, accelerated healing, intuition, and a limited degree of clairvoyance, usually in the form of prophetic dreams.

Buffy receives guidance from her Watcher, Rupert Giles (Anthony Stewart Head). Giles, rarely referred to by his first name, is a member of the Watchers' Council, whose job is to train and assist the Slayers. Giles researches the supernatural creatures that Buffy must face, offering insights into their origins and advice on how to kill them.

Buffy is also helped by friends she meets at Sunnydale High: Willow Rosenberg (Alyson Hannigan) and Xander Harris (Nicholas Brendon). Willow is originally a bookish wallflower; she provides a contrast to Buffy's outgoing personality, but shares the social isolation Buffy suffers after becoming a Slayer. As the series progresses, Willow becomes a more assertive character, a powerful witch, and comes out as a lesbian. In contrast, Xander, with no supernatural skills, provides comic relief and a grounded perspective. It is Xander who often provides the heart to the series, and in season six, becomes the hero in place of Buffy who defeats the "Big Bad". Buffy and Willow are the only characters who appear in all 144 episodes; Xander is missing in only one.

Supporting characters

> *Main articles: List of Buffy characters, Buffy minor characters, List of Buffy villains, and Scooby Gang (Buffy the Vampire Slayer).*

The cast of characters grew over the course of the series. Buffy first arrives in Sunnydale with her mother, Joyce Summers (portrayed by Kristine Sutherland), who functions as an anchor of normality in the Summers' lives even after she learns of Buffy's role in the supernatural world ("Becoming, Part Two"). Buffy's teenage sister Dawn Summers (Michelle Trachtenberg) does not appear until season five.

A vampire with a soul, Angel (portrayed by David Boreanaz), is Buffy's love interest throughout the first three seasons. He leaves Buffy to make amends for his sins and search for redemption in his own spin-off, *Angel*.

James Leary, Adam Busch, Iyari Limon, Danny Strong and Tom Lenk on a panel at the 2004 Moonlight Rising fan convention

At Sunnydale High, Buffy meets several other students willing to join her fight for good (alongside her friends Willow and Xander), an informal group eventually tagged the "Scooby Gang" or "Scoobies". Cordelia Chase (Charisma Carpenter), the archetypal shallow cheerleader, reluctantly becomes involved, and Daniel "Oz" Osbourne (Seth Green), a fellow student, rock guitarist and werewolf, joins the group through his relationship with Willow. Anya (Emma Caulfield), a former vengeance demon (Anyanka) who specialized in avenging scorned women, becomes Xander's lover after losing her powers, and joins the group in season four.

In Buffy's senior year at high school, she meets Faith (Eliza Dushku), the second current-Slayer who was brought forth when Slayer Kendra Young (Bianca Lawson) was killed by vampire Drusilla (Juliet Landau), in season two. Although she initially fights on the side of good with Buffy and the rest of the group, she comes to stand against them and sides with Mayor Richard Wilkins (Harry Groener) after accidentally killing a human in season three. She reappears briefly in the fourth season, looking for vengeance, and moves to *Angel* where she voluntarily goes to jail for her murders. Faith reappears in season seven of *Buffy*, having helped Angel and crew, and fights with Buffy against The First Evil.

Buffy gathers other allies: Spike (James Marsters), a vampire, is an old companion of Angelus and one of Buffy's major enemies in early seasons, although they later become allies and lovers. At the end of season six, Spike regains his soul. Spike is known for his Billy Idol-style peroxide blond hair and his black leather coat, stolen from a previous Slayer, Nikki Wood; her son, Robin Wood (D. B. Woodside), joined the group in the final season. Tara Maclay (Amber Benson) is a fellow member of Willow's Wicca group during season four, and their friendship eventually turns into a romantic relationship. Buffy became involved personally and professionally with Riley Finn (Marc Blucas), a military operative in "the Initiative", which hunts demons using science and technology. The final season sees geeky wannabe-villain Andrew Wells (Tom Lenk) come to side with the Scoobies, who regard him more as a nuisance than an ally.

Buffy featured dozens of recurring characters, both major and minor. For example the "Big Bad" (villain) characters were featured for at least one season (e.g. Glorificus was a character that appeared in 13 episodes, spanning much of season five). Similarly, characters who allied themselves to the group and characters which attended the same institutions were sometimes featured in multiple episodes.

Spin-offs

Buffy has inspired a range of official and unofficial works, including television shows, books, comics and games. This expansion of the series encouraged use of the term "Buffyverse" to describe the fictional universe in which *Buffy* and related stories take place.[78]

The franchise has inspired *Buffy* action figures and merchandise such as official *Buffy/Angel* magazines and *Buffy* companion books. Eden Studios has published a *Buffy* role-playing game, while Score Entertainment has released a *Buffy* Collectible Card Game.

Possible film or series continuation

Joss Whedon was interested in a film continuation in 1998,[79] but such a film has yet to materialize.

Angel

The spin-off *Angel* was introduced in October 1999, at the start of *Buffy* season four. The series was created by *Buffy*'s creator Joss Whedon in collaboration with David Greenwalt. Like *Buffy*, it was produced by the production company Mutant Enemy. At times, it performed better in the Nielsen ratings than its parent series did.[1]

The series was given a darker tone focusing on the ongoing trials of Angel in Los Angeles. His character is tormented by guilt following the return of his soul, punishment for more than a century of murder and torture. During the first four seasons of the show, he works as a private detective in a fictionalized version of Los Angeles, California, where he and his associates work to "help the helpless" and to restore the faith and "save the souls" of those who have lost their way. Typically, this mission involves doing battle with evil demons or demonically allied humans (primarily the law firm Wolfram & Hart), while Angel must also contend with his own violent nature. In season five, the Senior Partners of Wolfram and Hart take a bold gamble in their campaign to corrupt Angel, giving him control of their Los Angeles office. Angel accepts the deal as an opportunity to fight evil from the inside.

In addition to Boreanaz, *Angel* inherited *Buffy* regular Charisma Carpenter (Cordelia Chase). When Glenn Quinn (Doyle) left the series during its first season, Alexis Denisof (Wesley Wyndam-Pryce), who had been a recurring character in the last nine episodes of season three of *Buffy*, took his place. Carpenter and Denisof were followed later by Mercedes McNab (Harmony Kendall) and James Marsters (Spike). Several actors and actresses who played *Buffy* characters made guest appearances on *Angel*, including Seth Green (Daniel "Oz" Osbourne), Sarah Michelle Gellar (Buffy Summers), Eliza Dushku (Faith), Tom Lenk (Andrew Wells), Alyson Hannigan (Willow Rosenberg), Julie Benz (Darla), and Juliet Landau (Drusilla). Angel also continued to appear occasionally on *Buffy*.

Expanded universe

Outside of the TV series, the Buffyverse has been officially expanded and elaborated on by authors and artists in the so-called "Buffyverse Expanded Universe". The creators of these works may or may not keep to established continuity. Similarly, writers for the TV series were under no obligation to use information which had been established by the Expanded Universe, and sometimes contradicted such continuity.

Dark Horse has published the *Buffy* comics since 1998.[80] In 2003, Whedon wrote an eight-issue miniseries for Dark Horse Comics titled *Fray*, about a Slayer in the future. Following the publication of *Tales of the Vampires* in 2004, *Dark Horse Comics* halted publication on Buffyverse-related comics and graphic novels. The company is currently producing Whedon's *Buffy the Vampire Slayer Season Eight* with forty issues beginning in March 2007, to pick up where the television show left off – taking the place of an eighth canonical season.[42] The first story arc is also written by Whedon, and is called "The Long Way Home" which has been widely well-received, with circulation rivalling industry leaders DC and Marvel's top-selling titles.[81] Also after "The Long Way Home" came other story arcs like Faith's return in "No Future for You" and a *Fray* cross-over in "Time of Your Life".

Pocket Books hold the license to produce *Buffy* novels, of which they have published more than sixty since 1998. These sometimes flesh out background information on characters; for example, *Go Ask Malice* details the events that lead up to Faith arriving in Sunnydale. The most recent novels include *Carnival of Souls*, *Blackout*, *Portal Through Time*, *Bad Bargain*, and *The Deathless*.

Five official *Buffy* video games have been released on portable and home consoles.[82] Most notably, *Buffy the Vampire Slayer* for Xbox in 2002 and *Chaos Bleeds* for GameCube, Xbox and PlayStation 2 in 2003.[83]

Undeveloped spinoffs

The popularity of *Buffy* and *Angel* has led to attempts to develop more on-screen ventures in the fictional 'Buffyverse'. These projects remain undeveloped and may never be greenlit. In 2002, two potential spinoffs were in discussion: *Buffy the Animated Series* and *Ripper*. *Buffy the Animated Series* was a proposed animated TV show based on *Buffy*; Whedon and Jeph Loeb were to be executive producers for the show, and most of the cast from *Buffy* were to return to voice their characters. 20th Century Fox showed an interest in developing and selling the show to another network. A three-minute pilot was completed in 2004, but was never picked up. Whedon revealed to *The Hollywood Reporter*: "We just could not find a home for it. We had six or seven hilarious scripts from our own staff – and nobody wanted it."[84] Neither the pilot nor the scripts have been seen outside of the entertainment industry, though writer Jane Espenson has teasingly revealed small extracts from some of her scripts for the show.[85]

Ripper was originally a proposed television show based upon the character of Rupert Giles portrayed by Anthony Stewart Head. More recent information has suggested that if *Ripper* were ever made, it would be a TV movie or a DVD movie.[86] There was little heard about the series until 2007 when Joss Whedon confirmed that talks were almost completed for a 90 minute *Ripper* special on the BBC[87] with both Head and the BBC completely on board.

In 2003, a year after the first public discussions on *Buffy the Animated Series* and *Ripper*, *Buffy* was nearing its end. Espenson has said that during this time spinoffs were discussed, "I think Marti talked with Joss about *Slayer School* and Tim Minear talked with him about Faith on a motorcycle. I assume there was some back-and-forth pitching."[88] Espenson has revealed that *Slayer School* might have used new slayers and potentially included Willow Rosenberg, but Whedon did not think that such a spinoff felt right.[89]

Dushku declined the pitch for a Buffyverse TV series based on Faith and instead agreed to a deal to produce *Tru Calling*. Dushku explained to IGN: "It would have been a really hard thing to do, and not that I would not have been up for a challenge, but with it coming on immediately following *Buffy*, I think that those would have been really big boots to fill".[90] Tim Minear explained some of the ideas behind the aborted series: "The show was basically going to be Faith meets *Kung Fu*. It would have been Faith, probably on a motorcycle, crossing the earth, trying to find her place in the world."[91]

Finally, during the summer of 2004 after the end of *Angel*, a movie about Spike was proposed.[92] The movie would have been directed by Tim Minear and starred Marsters and Amy Acker and featured Alyson Hannigan.[93] Outside the 2006 Saturn Awards, Whedon announced that he had pitched the concept to various bodies but had yet to receive any feedback.[94]

In September 2008, *Sci-Fi Wire* ran an interview with Sarah Michelle Gellar in which she said she would not rule out returning to her most iconic role: "Never say never," she said. "One of the reasons the original *Buffy* movie did not really work on the big screen—and people blamed Kristy, but that's not what it was—the story was better told over a long arc," Gellar said. "And I worry about Buffy as a 'beginning, middle and end' so quickly. ... You show me a script; you show me that it works, and you show me that [the] audience can accept that, [and] I'd probably be there. Those are what my hesitations are."[95]

Cultural impact

Buffy has had a cultural impact on a number of media. It has impacted television studies and inspired fan-made films, it has been parodied and referenced, and has influenced other television series.

Academia

Buffy is notable for attracting the interest of scholars of popular culture as a subset of popular culture studies. Some academic settings include the show as a topic of literary study and analysis.[96] [97] National Public Radio describes *Buffy* as having a "special following among academics, some of whom have staked a claim in what they call 'Buffy Studies.'"[98] Though not widely recognized as a distinct discipline, the term "Buffy studies" is commonly used amongst the peer-reviewed academic *Buffy*-related writings.[99] The response to this attention has had its critics. For example, Jes Battis, who authored *Blood Relations in Buffy and Angel*, admits that study of the Buffyverse "invokes an uneasy combination of enthusiasm and ire", and meets "a certain amount of disdain from within the halls of the academy".[100] Nonetheless *Buffy* eventually led to the publication of around twenty books and hundreds of articles examining the themes of the show from a wide range of disciplinary perspectives including sociology, Speech Communication, psychology, philosophy, and women's studies.[101] The Whedon Studies Association produces the online academic journal *Slayage* and sponsors a biennial academic conference on the works of Joss Whedon.

Anthony Stewart Head and Nicholas Brendon at the Oakland Super SlayerCon fan convention

Fandom and fan films

The popularity of *Buffy* has led to websites, online discussion forums, works of *Buffy* fan fiction and several unofficial fan-made productions.

Buffy in popular culture

The series, which employed pop culture references as a frequent humorous device, has itself become a frequent pop culture reference in video games, comics and television shows, and has been frequently parodied and spoofed. Sarah Michelle Gellar has participated in several parody sketches, including a *Saturday Night Live* sketch in which the Slayer is relocated to the *Seinfeld* universe,[102] and adding her voice to an episode of *Robot Chicken* that parodied a would-be eighth season of *Buffy*.[103]

"Buffy" is the code-name used for the mobile phone created by the social networking website Facebook.[104]

U.S. ratings

	Season	Timeslot (ET)	U.S. ratings	Network	Rank	Network rank
1	1997	Monday 9:00 pm	3.7 million	The WB	#144	#6
2	1997–1998	Monday 9:00 pm (September 15, 1997 – January 19, 1998) Tuesday 8:00 pm (January 20 – May 19, 1998)	5.2 million		#133	#3
3	1998–1999	Tuesday 8:00 pm	5.3 million[105]		#133	#2 (tied)
4	1999–2000		4.7 million[106]		#122	#2 (tied)
5	2000–2001		4.4 million[107]		#120	#3
6	2001–2002		4.6 million[108]	UPN	#124	#3
7	2002–2003		3.6 million[109]		#140	#4

Buffy helped put The WB on the ratings map, but by the time the series landed at UPN in 2001, viewing figures had fallen. *Buffy the Vampire Slayer* had a series high during the third season with 5.3 million viewers, this probably due to the fact that both Gellar and Hannigan had hit movies out during the season (*Cruel Intentions* and *American Pie* respectively), and a series low with 3.6 million during the seventh season. The show's series finale "Chosen" pulled in a season high of 4.9 million viewers on the UPN network.

Buffy did not compete with shows on the big four networks (CBS, ABC, NBC, and Fox), but The WB was impressed with the young audience that the show was bringing in. Because of this, The WB ordered a full season of 22 episodes for the series' second season. After the episode "Surprise", which was watched by 8.2 million people, *Buffy* was moved from Monday at 9 pm to launch The WB's new night of programming on Tuesday. Due to its large success in that time slot, it remained on Tuesdays at 8 pm for the remainder of its original run. With its new timeslot on The WB, the show quickly climbed to the top of The WB ratings and became one of their highest-rated shows for the remainder of its time on the network. The show always placed in the top 3, usually only coming in behind *7th Heaven*. Between seasons three and five, *Buffy* flip-flopped with *Dawson's Creek* and *Charmed* as the network's second highest-rated show.

In the 2001–2002 season, the show had moved to UPN after a negotiation dispute with The WB. While it was still one of their highest rated shows on their network, The WB felt that the show had already peaked and was not worth giving a salary increase to the cast and crew. UPN on the other hand, had strong faith in the series and quickly grabbed it along with *Roswell*. UPN dedicated a two-hour premiere to the series to help re-launch it.

Impact on television

Commentators of the entertainment industry including *Allmovie*, *The Hollywood Reporter* and *The Washington Post* have cited *Buffy* as "influential".[110] Autumn 2003 saw several new shows going into production in the U.S. that featured strong females who are forced to come to terms with supernatural power or destiny while trying to maintain a normal life.[111] These post-*Buffy* shows include *Dead Like Me* and *Joan of Arcadia*. Bryan Fuller, the creator of *Dead Like Me*, said that "*Buffy* showed that young women could be in situations that were both fantastic and relatable, and instead of shunting women off to the side, it puts them at the center".[111] In the United Kingdom, *Buffy* became a blueprint for the revived *Doctor Who* series (2005–present),[112] and executive producer Russell T Davies has said:

> *Buffy the Vampire Slayer* showed the whole world, and an entire sprawling industry, that writing monsters and demons and end-of-the world is not hack-work, it can challenge the best. Joss Whedon raised the bar for every writer—not just genre/niche writers, but every single one of us.[113]

As well as influencing *Doctor Who*, *Buffy* influenced its spinoff series *Torchwood*.[114]

Several *Buffy* alumni have gone on to write for or create other shows. Such endeavors include *Tru Calling* (Douglas Petrie, Jane Espenson and lead actress Eliza Dushku), *Wonderfalls* (Tim Minear), *Point Pleasant* (Marti Noxon), *Jake 2.0* (David Greenwalt), *The Inside* (Tim Minear), *Smallville* (Steven S. DeKnight), and *Lost* (Drew Goddard and David Fury).

Meanwhile, the Parents Television Council complained of efforts to "deluge their young viewing audiences with adult themes".[115] The U.S. Federal Communications Commission (FCC), however, rejected the Council's indecency complaint concerning the violent sex scene between Buffy and Spike in "Smashed"[116] The BBC, however, chose to censor some of the more controversial sexual content when it was shown on the pre-watershed 6:45 pm slot.[117]

Series information

The first season was introduced as a mid-season replacement for the short-lived night-time soap opera *Savannah*, and therefore was made up of only 12 episodes. Each subsequent season was built up of 22 episodes. Discounting the unaired *Buffy* pilot, the seven seasons make up a total of 144 *Buffy* episodes aired between 1997 and 2003.

Awards and nominations

Buffy has gathered a number of awards and nominations which include an Emmy Award nomination for the 1999 episode "Hush", which featured an extended sequence with no character dialogue.[118] The 2001 episode "The Body" revolved around the death of Buffy's mother. It was filmed with no musical score, only diegetic music; it was nominated for a Nebula Award in 2002.[118] The fall 2001 musical episode "Once More, with Feeling" received plaudits, but was omitted from Emmy nomination ballots by "accident". It has since been featured on *Channel 4's* "100 Greatest Musicals".[119] In 2001, Sarah Michelle Gellar received a Golden Globe-nomination for Best Actress in a TV Series-Drama. Recently, the series was both nominated and won in the Drama Category for Television's Most Memorable Moment at the 60th Primetime Emmy Awards for "The Gift" beating *The X Files*, *Grey's Anatomy*, *Brian's Song* and *Dallas* although the sequence for this award was not aired.

DVD releases

DVD	Release date		
	United States/Canada[120]	United Kingdom	Australia
The Complete First Season	January 15, 2002	November 27, 2000	November 20, 2000
The Complete Second Season	June 11, 2002	May 21, 2001	June 15, 2001
The Complete Third Season	January 7, 2003	October 29, 2001	November 22, 2001
The Complete Fourth Season	June 10, 2003	May 13, 2002	May 20, 2002
The Complete Fifth Season	December 9, 2003	October 28, 2002	November 29, 2002
The Complete Sixth Season	May 25, 2004	May 12, 2003[121]	April 20, 2003
The Complete Seventh Season	November 16, 2004	April 5, 2004[122]	May 15, 2004
The Chosen Collection (Seasons 1–7)	November 15, 2005[123]	–	—
The Complete DVD Collection (Seasons 1–7)	–	October 30, 2005	November 23, 2005

References

[1] Wahoske, Matthew J.. "Nielsen Ratings For Buffy The Vampire Slayer, Angel, And Firefly" (http://web.archive.org/web/20080216043137/http://home.insightbb.com/~wahoskem/buffy.html). *Insightbb.com*. Archived from the original (http://home.insightbb.com/~wahoskem/buffy.html) on February 16, 2008. .

[2] " The Dual Network Rule. (http://www.fcc.gov/Bureaus/Mass_Media/Orders/2001/fcc01133.txt)", *Federal Communications Commission* (May 15, 2001): "the four major broadcast networks are unique among the media in their ability to reach a wide audience"

[3] Kaiser Family Foundation", Generation M: Media in the Lives of 8–18 Year Olds (http://www.kff.org/entmedia/upload/Speaker-Biographies-Generation-M-Media-in-the-Lives-of-8-18-Year-olds.pdf#search=" Dawson's Creek, Buffy is often associated with the early success of the Warner Brothers Network.")", *Kff.org* (March 9, 2005). The article says that "Mr. Levin was a key player in establishing The WB's distinct brand and youth appeal through programming such as *Dawson's Creek, Buffy the Vampire Slayer, 7th Heaven, Charmed, Felicity, Smallville, Gilmore Girls, Everwood* and *One Tree Hill*."

[4] "TV Guide's 25 Top Cult Shows" (http://forums.tannerworld.com/showthread.php?t=4001). TannerWorld Junction. May 26, 2004. . Retrieved July 11, 2011.

[5] "TV Guide Names the Top Cult Shows Ever" (http://www.tvguide.com/news/top-cult-shows-40239.aspx). *TV Guide*. June 29, 2007. . Retrieved July 11, 2011.

[6] Poniewozik, James (September 6, 2007). "The 100 Best TV Shows of All-*TIME*" (http://www.time.com/time/specials/2007/article/0,28804,1651341_1659188_1652063,00.html). *Time* (Time.com). . Retrieved March 4, 2010.

[7] O'Neil, Tom (July 9, 2010). "'True Blood' breaks the Emmy vampire curse" (http://goldderby.latimes.com/awards_goldderby/2010/07/true-blood-anna-paquin-vampires-emmy-nominations-news.html). *Los Angeles Times* (latimes.com). . Retrieved July 8, 2010.

[8] Schneider, Michael & Adalian, Josef, " WB revisits glory days (http://www.variety.com/article/VR1117946199?cs=1&s=h&p=0)", *Variety.com* (June 30, 2006).

[9] For example: Dillard, Brian J., " Buffy the Vampire Slayer [TV Series] (http://www.allmovie.com/cg/avg.dll?p=avg&sql=A174873)", *Allmovie* (2003 or after): "wildly influential cult hit". Harrington, Richard, " Joss Whedon's New Frontier (http://www.washingtonpost.com/wp-dyn/content/article/2005/09/29/AR2005092900594.html)", *The Washington Post* (September 30, 2005): "One of the best, most influential, genre-defining television series in decades".

[10] "Buffy: Television with Bite" *Buffy sixth season DVD set*, Disc six (2003), two minutes, fifteen seconds onwards.

[11] Billson, Anne, *Buffy the Vampire Slayer (BFI TV Classics S.)*. British Film Institute (December 5, 2005), pp24–25.

[12] Gottlieb, Allie, " Buffy's Angels (http://www.metroactive.com/papers/metro/09.26.02/buffy1-0239.html)", *Metroactive.com* (September 26, 2002).

[13] Havens, Candace, *Joss Whedon: The Genius Behind Buffy* Benbella Books (May 1, 2003), p51. Fran Kuzui also discussed *Buffy* in Golden, Christopher, & Holder, Nancy, *Watcher's Guide Vol. 1*. Simon & Schuster (October 1, 1998), pp247–248.

[14] Havens, Candace, *Joss Whedon: The Genius Behind Buffy* Benbella Books (May 1, 2003), p23.

[15] Brundage, James, "Buffy the Vampire Slayer" film review (http://www.filmcritic.com/reviews/1992/buffy-the-vampire-slayer/?OpenDocument). *Filmcritic.com* (1999). An example of the praise given to the script and dialogue behind the *Buffy* movie.

[16] "*Buffy the Vampire Slayer* at *Rottentomatoes.com*" (http://www.rottentomatoes.com/m/buffy_the_vampire_slayer/). .

[17] Golden, Christopher, and Holder, Nancy, *Watcher's Guide Vol. 1*. Simon & Schuster (October 1, 1998), pp249–250

[18] 'Said, SF', " Interview with Joss Whedon by SF Said (http://www.shebytches.com/SFSaidgb.html)", *Shebytches.com* (2005).
[19] Wilcox, Rhonda V.; David Lavery (April 2002). "Introduction" (http://books.google.com/?id=amKx_wH-PDYC&pg=PR17&dq=buffy+forces+introduction). *Fighting the Forces: What's at Stake in Buffy the Vampire Slayer*. Rowman & Littlefield. xix. ISBN 9780742516816. .
[20] Topping, Keith "Slayer". Virgin Publishing, (December 1, 2004), p7
[21] " Buffy, The Vampire Slayer, Forgotten Premiere Trailer (http://www.tvobscurities.com/articles/forgotten_buffy.php)" *Tvobscurities.com* (July 16, 2003).
[22] Various authors, " Fran Kuzui (http://www.imdb.com/name/nm0476900/)" and " Kaz Kuzui (http://www.imdb.com/name/nm0476901/)", *Internet Movie Database* (updated 2006).
[23] Golden, Christopher, and Holder, Nancy, *Watcher's Guide Vol. 1*. Simon & Schuster (October 1, 1998), "Gail Berman and Fran Kuzui came to Whedon to ask if he wanted to do the TV series" (p241). Also see *Watcher's Guide Vol. 1*, pp246–249.
[24] BBC " Buffy Episode Guide (http://www.bbc.co.uk/cult/buffy/indetail/)", *BBC* .
[25] TV.com " List of Buffy Writers (http://www.tv.com/buffy-the-vampire-slayer/show/10/cast.html?flag=3&tag=subtabs;writers_directors)", *TV.com* .
[26] Espenson, Jane, " The Writing Process (http://www.fireflyfans.net/firefly/espenson.htm)", *Fireflyfans.net* (2003).
[27] Various authors, " Awards for Sarah Michelle Gellar (http://www.imdb.com/name/nm0001264/awards)" *Internet Movie Database* (updated 2006).
[28] Havens, Candace, *Joss Whedon: The Genius Behind Buffy* Benbella Books (May 1, 2003), p35–36.
[29] Various authors, " Anthony Head (http://www.imdb.com/name/nm0372117/)" *Internet Movie Database* (updated 2006).
[30] Golden, Christopher, & Holder, Nancy *Watcher's Guide Vol. 1*. Simon & Schuster (October 1, 1998), "His long-lasting fame as the romantic and intriguing coffee guy is gradually being replaced by his new image as librarian in *Buffy*, p210 (October 1, 1998).
[31] Anonymous, " NickBrendon.com; biography (http://nickbrendon.com/biography/)" *Nickbrendon.com* (updated 2006).
[32] Kappes, Serena, " Xander Slays His Demon (http://nickbrendon.com/2001/05/01/xander-slays-his-demon/)", *Nickbrendon.com*, originally from *People.com*, (May 2001).
[33] Golden, Christopher, and Holder, Nancy, *Watcher's Guide Vol. 1*. Simon & Schuster (October 1, 1998), Brendon said "Four days. That's fast.", p199.
[34] Various authors, " Alyson Hannigan (http://www.imdb.com/name/nm0004989/)" *Internet Movie Database* (updated 2006).
[35] Golden, Christopher, and Holder, Nancy, *Watcher's Guide Vol. 1*. Simon & Schuster (October 1, 1998), p202.
[36] See: Kaiser Family Foundation " Generation M: Media in the Lives of 8–18 Year Olds (http://www.kff.org/entmedia/upload/Speaker-Biographies-Generation-M-Media-in-the-Lives-of-8-18-Year-olds.pdf)", *Kff.org* (March 9, 2005), Schneider, Michael & Adalian, Josef, " WB revisits glory days (http://www.variety.com/article/VR1117946199?cs=1&s=h&p=0)", *Variety.com* (June 30, 2006).
[37] "Buffy wants her MTV, and Logo too" (http://www.afterellen.com/blog/dorothysnarker/buffy-wants-her-mtv-and-logo-too) AfterEllen.com. December 14, 2009. . Retrieved March 6, 2010.
[38] "Buffy the Vampire Slayer at MuchMusic.com" (http://www.muchmusic.com/tv/buffy/). MuchMusic.com. . Retrieved March 13, 2010.
[39] ""Buffy" Tv Series to air on Chiller Network from November 2010" (http://www.whedon.info/Buffy-Tv-Series-to-air-on-Chiller.html). *Variety*. October 20, 2010. . Retrieved October 21, 2010.
[40] " Stake Out (http://www.ew.com/ew/article/0,,426799~10~0~gellarexplainswhybuffy,00.html)", *Entertainment Weekly* (February 26, 2003).
[41] Haberman, Lia, " A Buffy-less "Buffy"? Have Faith (http://www.eonline.com/uberblog/b44610_A_Buffy-less_quotBuffyquot_Have_Faith.html)", *E! Online* (February 11, 2003).
[42] Brown, Scott (July 18, 2006). "First Look: The new 'Buffy' comic" (http://popwatch.ew.com/2006/07/18/the_new_buffy_c/). *Entertainment Weekly*. . Retrieved January 10, 2009.
[43] " (http://store.playstation.com/video/index.vm#category/PN.PC.US-PN.PC.VIDEO.US-ACTION_BUFFY/PN.PC.US-PN.PC.VIDEO.US-TV_GENRE_ACTION)" *PlayStation Store* (July 15, 2008)
[44] Burr, Vivien, " Buffy vs the BBC: Moral Questions and How to Avoid Them (http://slayageonline.com/essays/slayage8/Burr.htm)" *Slayageonline.com* (March 2003), p1.
[45] " Angel Creator Joss Whedon Sees Evolution of TV Shows on DVD (http://web.archive.org/web/20070927190217/http://www.videostoremag.com/news/html/breaking_article.cfm?sec_id=2&article_ID=5243)" *Video Store Mag* (August 28, 2003).
[46] " Before Nerf Herder, the original Buffy theme: "Codo" by 1980s Austrian band, DÖF. (http://whedonesque.com/comments/11527)" *Whedonesque.com* (October 2006).
[47] *Buffy the Vampire Slayer* first season DVD set. *20th century Fox* (region 2, 2000), disc one.
[48] Halfyard, Janet K. " Love, Death, Curses and Reverses (in F minor): Music, Gender, and Identity in Buffy the Vampire Slayer and Angel (http://slayageonline.com/essays/slayage4/halfyard.htm)", *Slayageonline.com* (http://slayageonline.com/) (December 2001).
[49] "Buffy: Inside the Music" from "Buffy the Vampire Slayer Complete Fourth Season DVD set *20th century Fox* (May 13, 2002), disc three.
[50] "Four Star Mary Bios" (http://www.fourstarmary.com/bioscontent.html). Four Star Mary. . Retrieved July 22, 2008.
[51] "BBC Cult Buffy Trivia – 'Becoming, Part Two'" (http://www.bbc.co.uk/cult/buffy/indetail/becomingtwo/trivia.shtml). BBC. . Retrieved July 22, 2008.
[52] "BBC Cult Buffy Trivia – 'Grave'" (http://www.bbc.co.uk/cult/buffy/indetail/grave/trivia.shtml). BBC. . Retrieved July 22, 2008.

[53] "BBC Cult Buffy Trivia – 'Something Blue'" (http://www.bbc.co.uk/cult/buffy/indetail/somethingblue/trivia.shtml). BBC Cult Buffy Trivia. . Retrieved July 22, 2008.
[54] "'Faith, Hope, and Trick' at BuffyGuide" (http://www.buffyguide.com/episodes/faithhope.shtml). BuffyGuide. . Retrieved July 22, 2008.
[55] "BBC Cult Buffy Trivia – 'Sleeper'" (http://www.bbc.co.uk/cult/buffy/indetail/sleeper/trivia.shtml). BBC. . Retrieved July 22, 2008.
[56] "BBC Cult Buffy Trivia – 'Triangle'" (http://www.bbc.co.uk/cult/buffy/indetail/triangle/trivia.shtml). BBC. . Retrieved July 22, 2008.
[57] "Cibo Matto Press Release" (http://www.wbr.com/laramie/laramie_press.html). Cibo Matto Official Website. . Retrieved July 22, 2008.
[58] "BBC Cult Buffy Trivia – 'Tabula Rasa'" (http://www.bbc.co.uk/cult/buffy/indetail/tabularasa/trivia.shtml). BBC. . Retrieved July 22, 2008.
[59] "'Buffy the Vampire Slayer: The Album' at Amazon" (http://www.amazon.com/dp/B00001R3O2). Amazon. . Retrieved July 22, 2008.
[60] "'Radio Sunnydale' Album at Amazon" (http://www.amazon.com/dp/B0000E6EFX). Amazon. . Retrieved July 22, 2008.
[61] "'Once More With Feeling!' Album at Amazon" (http://www.amazon.com/dp/B00006J3WH). Amazon. . Retrieved July 22, 2008.
[62] "List of Buffy Albums at Buffy World" (http://www.buffyworld.com/buffy/music.php). BuffyWorld. . Retrieved July 22, 2008.
[63] "Buffy Albums List at BuffyGuide" (http://www.buffyguide.com/merchandise/soundtrack.shtml). BuffyGuide. . Retrieved July 22, 2008.
[64] Various authors, " Sets and Locations (http://www.imdb.com/title/tt0118276/locations)", *The Ultimate Buffy and Angel Trivia Guide* (updated 2007).
[65] Yovanovich, Linda, "Young Blood", *Smgfan.com*, originally from *OnSat* (July 14, 1997), Whedon said: "[High school as hell] was always the basis of the show. When they said, 'Do you want to turn it into a show?' The character was not enough alone to sustain it. But you know when I thought of the idea of the horror movies as a metaphor for high school, [I said] okay this is something that will work week to week."
[66] " Buffy the Vampire Slayer film locations (http://www.movie-locations.com/movies/b/buffy.html)", *Movie-locations.com*
[67] Various authors, "California State University, Northridge#Film and television shoots", "California State University, Northridge: Film & Television Shoots."
[68] CSUN Oviatt Library Website, " (http://library.csun.edu/About/InMedia)", "Oviatt Library In The Media"
[69] " Joss Whedon: Executive Producer of Angel (http://www.cityofangel.com/council/joss.html)", *Cityofangel.com* (2006). Also see Flowers, Phoebe, " Sixth season was last great one for Buffy – Dvd Review (http://www.tvshows.nu/article.php3?id_article=4984)", *Tvshows.nu* (June 16, 2004). Executive Producer Marti Noxon stated: "I'm basically trying to write *My So-Called Life* with vampires".
[70] P., Ken, " An Interview with Joss Whedon (http://uk.tv.ign.com/articles/425/425492p6.html)", *Ign.com* (June 23, 2003), web-page 6.
[71] Whedon, Joss " Kitty Pryde influenced Buffy (http://whedonesque.com/comments/3095)" *Whedonesque.com* (February 27, 2004).
[72] Miles, Lawrence, *Dusted*, Mad Norwegian Press (November 2003).
[73] Nevitt, Lucy, & Smith, Andy William, " Family Blood is always the Sweetest: The Gothic Transgressions of Angel/Angelusby (http://blogs.arts.unimelb.edu.au/refractory/2003/03/18/family-blood-is-always-the-sweetest-the-gothic-transgressions-of-angelangelus-lucy-nevitt-andy-william-smith/)", *Refractory: a Journal of Entertainment Media* Vol. II (March 2003): Nevitt and Smith bring attention to *Buffy*'s use of pastiche: "Multiple pastiche without enabling commentary is doubtless self-canceling, yet, at the same time, each element of pastiche calls into temporary being what and why it imitates."
[74] Shuttleworth, Ian, " Bite me, professor (http://web.archive.org/web/20040202205347/http://news.ft.com/servlet/ContentServer?pagename=FT.com/StoryFT/FullStory&c=StoryFT&cid=1059479741556)" *Financial Times*, citing interview from *The New York Times* (September 11, 2003)
[75] " Bye-Bye Buffy (http://www.cbsnews.com/stories/2003/05/20/entertainment/main554813.shtml)", *CBSnews.com* (May 20, 2003).
[76] Kaveny, C. (2003, November 7). What Women Want: 'Buffy,' the Pope, and the New Feminists. Commonweal, 18-24.
[77] Stafford, Nikki (December 1, 2007). *Bite Me!: The Unofficial Guide to Buffy the Vampire Slayer: The Chosen Edition*. ECW Press. p. 182. ISBN 1550228072.
[78] Walton, Andy, " Slang-age in the Buffyverse (http://www.cnn.com/2003/SHOWBIZ/TV/05/19/buffy.sidebar/)", *CNN* (February 18, 2004).
[79] Jenny Hontz, Chris Petrikin (June 5, 1998). "Whedon, Fox vamping" (http://www.variety.com/article/VR1117471584). *Variety*. . Retrieved November 25, 2008.
[80] " Buffy the Vampire Slayer#1 (http://www.darkhorse.com/Comics/98-372-a/Buffy-the-Vampire-Slayer-1-photo-cover)" *Dark Horse Comics* ("Buffy the Vampire Slayer #1" released September 23, 1998).
[81] "DC Comics Month-to-month Sales: April 2007 (Other Publishers: Dark Horse)" (http://www.comicsbeat.com/2007/06/05/dc-comics-month-to-month-sales-april-2007/). *The Beat*. . Retrieved June 4, 2007.
[82] "Gamespot List of Buffy Games" (http://uk.gamespot.com/search.html?type=11&stype=all&tag=search;button&om_act=convert&om_clk=search&qs=Buffy+the+Vampire+Slayer&x=10&y=12). Gamespot. . Retrieved July 22, 2008.
[83] "BBC – Buffy: Chaos Bleeds" (http://www.bbc.co.uk/cult/buffy/buffystuff/videogame/chaosbleeds.shtml). BBC. . Retrieved July 22, 2008.
[84] Hockensmith, Steve, " Dialogue with 'Buffy' creator Joss Whedon (http://www.hollywoodreporter.com/h/search/index_form.jsp)", *Hollywoodreporter.com*, requires subscription, (May 16, 2003)
[85] Espenson, Jane, " Reading what's been written to sound written as it's spoken (http://www.janeespenson.com/archives/00000095.php)", *Janeespenson.com* (May 9, 2006) & " Sorry, JVC, but it's simply true (http://www.janeespenson.com/archives/00000097.php)", *Janeespenson.com* (May 11, 2006).
[86] *UK Buffy the Vampire Slayer and Angel Magazine*. Titan Magazines, Issue 80, (December 2005), p19.

[87] "Comic-Con: Joss Whedon panel report" (http://www.tvsquad.com/2007/07/28/comic-con-joss-whedon-panel-report/). Tvsquad.com. . Retrieved June 16, 2010.

[88] " Dear Jane (http://www.bbc.co.uk/cult/news/buffy/2003/07/03/5522.shtml)", *BBC.co.uk* (July 3, 2003).

[89] 'Hercules', " Way Interesting Buffy Bits (Courtesy Jane E & Others) (http://www.aintitcool.com/display.cgi?id=14787)", *Aintitcool.com* (March 21, 2003). Also see " Spin-offs stop spinning (http://www.bbc.co.uk/cult/news/buffy/2003/03/24/3421.shtml)", *BBC.co.uk* (March 24, 2003).

[90] Kuhn, Sarah, " An Interview with Eliza Dushku (http://uk.tv.ign.com/articles/421/421047p2.html)", *Ign.com* (May 28, 2003), web-page 2.

[91] *Femme Fatales*, (May–June 2003). Details archived online: Matt (transcriber), " Eliza Talks Faith Spinoff (http://spoiledrotten.tvheaven.com/buffy.html)", *Spoiledrotten.tvheaven.com* (April 11, 2003). Also see " Kung Fu Faith (http://www.bbc.co.uk/cult/news/buffy/2003/04/14/3812.shtml)", *BBC.co.uk* (April 14, 2003) and *Whedonesque.com* (http://whedonesque.com/comments/1131).

[92] Spike TV movie on the cards? (http://whedonesque.com/comments/3877), *Whedonesque.com* (May 9, 2004). Marsters is indirectly quoted about the possibility of a Spike movie in May 2004.

[93] Saney, Daniel, " Whedon eyes Willow for Spike movie (http://www.digitalspy.co.uk/tv/news/a24796/whedon-eyes-willow-for-spike-movie.html)", *Digitalspy.co.uk* (September 28, 2005). Originally reported by *Tvguide.com*.

[94] " Video interview with Joss from the Saturn Awards (http://whedonesque.com/comments/10310)", *Whedonesque.com* (February 15, 2006). Originally reported by *Iesb.net*.

[95] "Sarah Michelle Gellar - New "Buffy" Movie - A Film Wouldn't Work" (http://www.whedon.info/Sarah-Michelle-Gellar-New-Buffy.html). Sci-Fi Wire. January 22, 2008. . Retrieved September 10, 2010.

[96] Scholars lecture on 'Buffy the Vampire Slayer' (http://www.ctv.ca/CTVNews/Entertainment/20040529/scholars_buffy_040529/), *Ctv.ca* (May 29, 2004).

[97] " Study Buffy at university (http://www.metro.co.uk/weird/13473-study-buffy-at-university)", *Metro.co.uk* (May 16, 2006) MA course at Brunel University, West London.

[98] Ulaby, Neda (http://www.npr.org/templates/story/story.php?storyId=3850482), ' – 'Buffy Studies' (http://www.npr.org/templates/story/story.php?storyId=1262180)", *National Public Radio* (May 13, 2003)

[99] Lavery, David, & Wilcox, Rhonda V., *Slayageonline.com* (http://slayageonline.com/) (2001–). The term is in use from the subtitle of *Slayage: The Online International Journal of Buffy Studies*, and thus has become used in essays by those who contribute to scholarship relating to *Buffy*.

[100] Battis, Jes, *Blood Relations*, McFarland & Company (June 2005), page 9.

[101] See: Hornick, Alysa, " *Whedonology* an Academic Buffy Studies and Whedonesque Bibliography (http://www.alysa316.com/Whedonology/)", *Alysa316.com* (updated 2006). See Buffy studies published books.

[102] SNL (aired Jan. 17, 1998) see 'doggans' (transcriber) SNL Transcripts: "Buffy the Vampire Slayer" (http://snltranscripts.jt.org/97/97kbuffy.phtml), *Snltranscripts.jt.org* (1997).

[103] "Buffy Season 8" from *Robot Chicken* Season 1, episode 4 (aired March 13, 2005). See: *IMDb* entry (http://www.imdb.com/title/tt0687782/), *Whedonesque.com* (http://whedonesque.com/comments/6038).

[104] "The Facebook Phone: It's Finally Real and Its Name Is Buffy" (http://allthingsd.com/20111121/the-facebook-phone-its-finally-real-and-its-name-is-buffy/). AllThingsD. November 21, 2011. . Retrieved November 22, 2011.

[105] Final ratings for the 1998–1999 TV season (http://web.archive.org/web/20091029011819/http://geocities.com/Hollywood/4616/ew0604.html)

[106] "– US-Jahrescharts 1999/2000" (http://www.quotenmeter.de/cms/?p1=n&p2=9946&p3=). Quotenmeter.de. May 30, 2002. . Retrieved March 20, 2011.

[107] "TV Ratings 2000–2001" (http://fbibler.chez.com/tvstats/recent_data/2000-01.html). .

[108] "How did your favorite show rate?" (http://www.usatoday.com/life/television/2002/2002-05-28-year-end-chart.htm). *USA Today*. May 28, 2002. . Retrieved April 27, 2010.

[109] "– 2002–2003 TV Ratings" (http://groups.google.com/group/rec.arts.tv/browse_thread/thread/ee82c0640bcaeb06/82c78e0fe7710443?lnk=st&q="practice"++2002-03+"primetime"+friends+survivor&rnum=1&hl=en#82c78e0fe7710443). Groups.google.com. . Retrieved March 20, 2011.

[110] For example: Dillard, Brian J., " Buffy the Vampire Slayer [TV Series] (http://www.allmovie.com/work/174873)", *Allmovie* (2003 or after): "wildly influential cult hit". Harrington, Richard, " Joss Whedon's New Frontier (http://www.washingtonpost.com/wp-dyn/content/article/2005/09/29/AR2005092900594.html)", *The Washington Post* (September 30, 2005): "One of the best, most influential, genre-defining television series in decades". Kit, Borys, " Whedon lassos 'Wonder' helm for Warners (http://today.msnbc.msn.com/id/7224008/ns/today-entertainment/)", *The Hollywood Reporter*, requires subscription (March 17, 2005): "the influential WB Network/UPN drama series"

[111] Salem, Rob, " The season to talk to dead people (http://www.whedon.info/article.php3?id_article=1319&img=)", *Thestar.com*, transcribed to *Whedon.info* (August 25, 2003)

[112] B, KJ, " Doctor Who Report: New Theme Music?; Buffy a Template for New Doctor Who? (http://uk.tv.ign.com/articles/595/595354p1.html)", *Ign.com* (March 11, 2005): "Producer Steve Moffat admits that the blueprint for the new series was *Buffy the Vampire Slayer*"

[113] Moore, Candace, " John Barrowman Plays Bisexual Time Traveler on New Dr. Who (http://www.afterelton.com/TV/2005/5/drwho.html)", *Afterelton.com* (May 19, 2005).

[114] Stokes, Richard; Hugo, Simon (March 2008). "Like a Kid in a Candy Store". *Torchwood Magazine* (Titan Magazines) (2): 64–65. ISSN 17560950.

[115] " The 2001–2002 Top 10 Best and Worst Shows on Network TV (http://www.parentstv.org/PTC/publications/reports/top10bestandworst/2002/main.asp)" & " TV Bloodbath: Violence on Prime Time Broadcast TV (http://www.parentstv.org/PTC/publications/reports/stateindustryviolence/main.asp)" *Parentstv.org* (2002 & 2003 respectively).

[116] FCC, In the Matter of Complaints Against Various Broadcast Licensees Regarding Their Airing of the UPN Network Program "Buffy the Vampire Slayer" on November 20, 2001 (http://www.fcc.gov/eb/Orders/2004/FCC-04-196A1.html).

[117] Burr, Vivien. "Buffy vs. the BBC: Moral Questions and How to Avoid Them" (http://slayageonline.com/essays/slayage8/Burr.htm).

[118] Various authors, "Awards for *Buffy the Vampire Slayer* (http://www.imdb.com/title/tt0118276/awards)", *Internet Movie Database* (updated 2005)

[119] " 100 Greatest Musicals: The Results (http://www.channel4.com/film/newsfeatures/microsites/M/musicals/results_15to11.html)", *Channel4.com* (Autumn 2003)

[120] "North American Buffy DVD Release Dates" (http://www.tvshowsondvd.com/shows/Buffy-Vampire-Slayer/1147). TVShowsOnDVD. . Retrieved July 22, 2008.

[121] "United Kingdom Buffy Season 6 Release Date" (http://www.bbc.co.uk/cult/news/buffy/2003/03/17/3261.shtml). BBC. . Retrieved July 22, 2008.

[122] "United Kingdom Buffy Season 7 Release Date" (http://homecinema.thedigitalfix.co.uk/content.php?contentid=10746). DVDTimes. . Retrieved July 22, 2008.

[123] "The Chosen Collection Review" (http://uk.dvd.ign.com/articles/673/673077p1.html). IGN. . Retrieved July 22, 2008.

Further reading

- James B. South and William Irwin: "Buffy the Vampire Slayer and Philosophy: Fear and Trembling in Sunnydale". Open Court Books, Chicago 2003, ISBN 0-8126-9531-3
- Gregory Stevenson: *Televised Morality. The Case of Buffy the Vampire Slayer*. Hamilton Books, Dallas 2003, ISBN 0-7618-2833-8
- Rhonda Wilcox and David Lavery (Hrsg.): *Fighting the Forces. What's at Stake in Buffy the Vampire Slayer*. Rowman and Littlefield Publ., Lanham 2002, ISBN 0-7425-1681-4
- Lorna Jowett: *Sex and the Slayer. A Gender Studies Primer for the Buffy Fan*. Wesleyan University Press, Middletown 2005, ISBN 0-8195-6758-2
- Michael Adams: *Slayer Slang: A Buffy the Vampire Slayer Lexicon*, Oxford University Press, 2003, ISBN 0-19-516033-9

External links

- *Buffy the Vampire Slayer* (http://www.allrovi.com/movies/movie/v174873) at AllRovi
- *Buffy the Vampire Slayer* (http://www.imdb.com/title/tt0118276/) at the Internet Movie Database
- *Buffy the Vampire Slayer* (http://www.tv.com/show/10/summary.html) at TV.com
- *Buffy the Vampire Slayer* (http://www.thewb.com/shows/buffy-the-vampire-slayer) at The WB
- Buffyverse Wiki (http://buffy.wikia.com/wiki/Buffyverse_Wiki)

Miss Match

Miss Match	
Genre	Dramedy
Created by	Darren Star and Jeff Rake
Starring	Alicia Silverstone Ryan O'Neal James Roday Lake Bell David Conrad Nathan Fillion
Opening theme	"Love Is Gonna Get You" by Macy Gray
Country of origin	United States
Language(s)	English
No. of episodes	18 (7 unaired)
Production	
Running time	43 minutes
Broadcast	
Original channel	NBC
Original run	September 26 – December 15, 2003

Miss Match is a 2003 American television series created by Jeff Rake and Darren Star and produced by Twentieth Century Fox, Darren Star Productions and Imagine Entertainment. It aired in the U.S. on NBC, Australia on Network Seven, Arena and FOX8, and in the UK on Living, Channel 4 and is currently on E4. The series filmed at least 18 episodes but only 8 aired in the US. The entire series aired in both the UK & Canada.

Starring Alicia Silverstone and Ryan O'Neal, the show garnered poor ratings, which could have been due to its inability to compete in the Friday 8pm ET timeslot (aka "Friday night death slot"). It was based on the real-life story of Samantha Daniels.

Premise

A Los Angeles matrimonial attorney (Alicia Silverstone) doubles as a high-end matchmaker, Kate Fox, even though her own love life is far from perfect.

Characters

Kate Fox (Alicia Silverstone) - Kate Fox is a divorce lawyer by day who ends up becoming a match maker. Her own romantic life is complicated to say the least. Throughout the series she is involved with Michael and later his best friend, Adam. Kate often finds herself getting involved in the relationships she sets up for people. Various characters mention to her that she addicted to love and lives through the lives of others.

Jerry Fox (Ryan O'Neal) - Kate's father who owned the law firm she works for. He was not a perfect father to Kate but they bonded over law. He is shown to still have feelings for Kate's mother but is not hung up on her. Later in the series he is linked with Serena.

Nick Paine (James Roday)- Kate's co-worker who is a womanizer. He and Kate tolerate each other, at best. He later dates Victoria.

Claire (Jodi Long) - Fox & Associates secretary.

Victoria (Lake Bell) - Kate's best friend who is a bartender. She often overlooks the dates Kate sets people up with. She tends to only have flings with men, like the one she starts with Nick. The only man we see her like as more than a hookup is Adam.

Michael Mendelson (David Conrad) - Kate's on and off again boyfriend after she sets him up on several dates. His ex girlfriend is Lauren who left him for his best friend Adam.

Adam Logan (Nathan Fillion) - Adam comes to town after Lauren hires Kate as her divorce lawyer. He and Michael end up repairing their friendship but he soon becomes involved with Kate and Victoria.

Lauren Logan (Dina Meyer) - Michael's ex girlfriend and Adam's ex-wife. After finding out that Michael & Kate are involved she makes Kate break it off. After finding out Adam & Kate are involved she sues Kate's law firm for malpractice.

Serena Lockner (Charisma Carpenter) - Serena is an old classmates of Kate who comes back into her life. Kate helps her adopt a baby and give it back to the mother when she realizes she made a mistake. She later returns and starts a romance with Kate's father.

NBC had a cross promotion where Galen Gering & McKenzie Westmore, who starred on NBC's soap opera Passions, appeared in an episode of the series.

Nielsen ratings

- Episode 1: Pilot (9/26/03) - Viewers: 7.7 million
- Episode 2: Who's Your Daddy? (10/03/03) - Viewers: 5.9 million
- Episode 3: Something Nervy (10/10/03) - Viewers: 6.0 million
- Episode 4: Kate In Ex-Tasy (10/17/03) - Viewers: 6.5 million
- Episode 5: I Got You, Babe (10/24/03) - Viewers: 6.7 million
- Episode 6: Addicted To Love (11/07/03) - Viewers: 5.9 million
- Episode 7: Jive Turkey (11/14/03) - Viewers: 5.7 million
- Episode 8: The Love Bandit (11/21/03) - Viewers: 5.7 million
- Episode 9: Bad Judgement (12/05/03) - Viewers: 6.8 million
- Episode 10: Santa, Baby (12/12/03) - Viewers: 5.9 million
- Episode 11: Who's Sari Now? (12/19/03) - Viewers: 6.1 million

International broadcasts

- Austria – ORF1
- Australia – FOX8, Arena
- Belgium – VTM, Kanaal 2
- Brazil – FOX
- Brunei - Star World
- Croatia - HRT
- Estonia - TV3
- Finland - MTV3
- Germany – Super RTL
- Greece - ANT1
- Hong Kong - Star World, TVB Pearl
- India – Star World
- Italy - Canale 5
- Malaysia - Star World

- Mexico - Fox Latin America
- Netherlands - Veronica
- New Zealand - TV2
- Norway – ZTV, TV3
- Pakistan – Star World
- Philippines – Studio 23
- Portugal – Fox Life
- Romania – B1 TV
- Serbia – RTS
- Slovenia – Kanal A
- South Africa - SABC 3
- Spain – Antena neox
- Sweden - TV4
- Switzerland - TSR 1, TSI 1
- Thailand – True Series
- Turkey - CNBC-e
- UK – Living, Channel 4 and E4

External links
- *Miss Match* [1] at the Internet Movie Database
- *Miss Match* [2] at TV.com
- *Miss Match* [3] at epguides.com

References
[1] http://www.imdb.com/title/tt0362867/
[2] http://www.tv.com/show/17081/summary.html
[3] http://epguides.com/MissMatch

I Do (Lost)

"I Do"	
Lost episode	
Kate and Sawyer kiss in their cage.	
Episode no.	Season 3 Episode 6
Directed by	Tucker Gates
Written by	Damon Lindelof & Carlton Cuse
Production code	306
Original air date	November 8, 2006
Guest stars	
Nathan Fillion as Kevin Callis Michael Bowen as Danny Pickett M. C. Gainey as Tom Friendly Tania Raymonde as Alex Fredric Lane as Marshal Edward Mars Ariston Green as Jason Eden-Lee Murray as Suzanne Callis Mark Dillen Stitham as Minister Michael Vendrell as Guy Teddy Wells as Ivan	

"**I Do**" is the sixth episode of the third season of *Lost*, and the 55th episode overall. It aired on November 8, 2006 on ABC. The episode was written by Damon Lindelof and Carlton Cuse and directed by Tucker Gates. The character of Kate Austen (Evangeline Lilly) is featured in the episode's flashbacks, where her brief marriage to a police officer, Kevin Callis (Nathan Fillion), is shown. In the present events, Jack Shephard (Matthew Fox) considers whether or not to perform surgery on Ben Linus (Michael Emerson), and is motivated by Kate's claims that if he does not comply, Sawyer (Josh Holloway) will be killed.

This was the last episode to air before a 13-week hiatus, so it was written so that it would fit as a "mini-series finale", and also had a major theme in the contrast between Kate's relationships with Kevin and Sawyer. "I Do" gained mostly positive reviews, with much praise to the cliffhanger ending, and had 17.15 million American viewers upon release.

Plot

Flashbacks

While on the run from the law, Kate goes to Miami, where under the name "Monica" she meets and gets engaged to a police officer, Kevin Callis (Nathan Fillion). Before their wedding, Kevin's mother, Suzanne, gives Kate a gold locket that had been passed down on the female side of the family at weddings. A while after the ceremony, Kate calls U.S. Marshal Edward Mars (Fredric Lane). She does not want to run any more and pleads for him to stop chasing her. Mars guesses that Kate has got involved with a man, and tells her that if Kate can really stay put, settle down, he will stop chasing her, but that they both know it is unlikely that Kate will ever stop running. Later, Kate shows signs of relief after getting a negative pregnancy test, and decides to reveal the truth about her life to her husband. She drugs Kevin, places her mother-in-law's locket in his hands and leaves.

On the Island

On the main island, John Locke (Terry O'Quinn) tells Nikki Fernandez (Kiele Sanchez), Paulo (Rodrigo Santoro), Sayid Jarrah (Naveen Andrews) and Desmond Hume (Henry Ian Cusick) that Mr. Eko (Adewale Akinnuoye-Agbaje) was killed by an animal, and decides to bury Eko where he died as he thinks the other castaways have seen have "too many funerals" recently. As Locke goes to the beach to get shovels, Sayid follows him and asks what really killed Eko. Locke says that the survivors call it "The Monster", and further speculates that The Monster may be what brought them there and that Eko died for a reason, he just does not know what it is yet. After the burial, Locke sees a message on Eko's stick: "Lift up your eyes and look north, John 3:05".

On Hydra island, Jack Shephard (Matthew Fox) checks Ben Linus's (Michael Emerson) x-rays and medical file, and tells Ben that the tumor in his spine will become inoperable in a week. Jack however adds he is not going to operate on Ben because he does not trust the Others' promise of freeing him, Kate and Sawyer (Josh Holloway).

After the quarry where Kate and Sawyer are working suffers an invasion by Alex (Tania Raymonde), who demands to know where her boyfriend Karl (Blake Bashoff) is, Juliet Burke (Elizabeth Mitchell) brings Kate to talk to Jack, telling her that it is the only way to prevent Danny Pickett (Michael Bowen) from killing Sawyer. When Jack and Kate see each other, Kate asks him to operate on Ben to prevent Sawyer from getting killed, but Jack gets angry and refuses.

After returning to her cage, Kate and Sawyer have an argument, and she climbs out of her cage and breaks open Sawyer's, saying if he does not want Jack to save his life, then he is going to save his own. Sawyer then tells her that they cannot run because of being on another island, something he did not tell her "because I wanted you to believe that we had a damn chance." Kate and Sawyer then have sex, unknowingly in full view of the cameras. At the Hydra station, Jack finds his door unlocked and unguarded, and outside reaches a surveillance room, where he sees Kate and Sawyer cuddling together on a monitor. Ben appears behind him, and after a brief exchange Jack decides to do the surgery, but wants Ben to keep his promise to let Jack off the island.

As Juliet anesthetizes Ben and Jack begins the operation, Pickett goes with another man to Sawyer's cage. Kate and Sawyer attempt to fight, but Pickett's companion overpowers Kate and holds her at gunpoint, leading Sawyer to surrender. Meanwhile, Jack sabotages the operation by cutting Ben's kidney sack, and demands for Tom (M.C. Gainey) to speak with Kate. Before Pickett can shoot Sawyer, Tom calls over the walkie-talkie. As Pickett gives the walkie to Kate, Jack tells her she has an hour head start, and directs her to call him on the radio when she is safe.

Production

"It's actually more difficult for her to stay in that house and cook breakfast and be a little housewife, than it is for her to break rocks and work in a quarry and sleep in a cage."

—Evangeline Lilly[1]

Show runners Damon Lindelof and Carlton Cuse wrote "I Do" as a "mini-season finale", as it was the last episode before mid-season hiatus, and would end in a cliffhanger. It also served as a climax and beginning of a closure of Jack, Kate and Sawyer's captivity on Hydra Island,[1] with the writers saying that afterwards there would be a return to the beach and the six-episode block would be "more palatable" and make more sense, comparing them to the first seven episodes of season 2 where the tail section survivors are introduced.[2] Executive producer Bryan Burk also said the pre-hiatus episodes were "our season 2.5. Like, this is kind of like wrapping up a lot of where we were last year", considering season three would really begin in the seventh episode.[3]

Nathan Fillion played Kevin Callis.

A main theme of the episode is Kate's inability to commit to other people, always running from difficult emotional situations, and having barriers between her and her interests – physical, as in Sawyer's cage or Jack's aquarium, or metaphorical, as in her inability to settle down as Kevin's wife. Kate's marriage, which was first alluded in the season one episode "Outlaws", is meant to be a contrast with her relationship with Sawyer in the realtime events – Kate and Kevin is a heartfelt and passionate relationship where Kate tries to get involved but her lifestyle ends up on making the marriage fail, whereas with Sawyer both are afraid of intimacy and connection yet still end up together.[1]

Nathan Fillion was cast as Kevin because the producers thought he fit as "someone to believe that Kate had actually married and settled down with" for being "really good and kinda fun and intelligent", and also because Cuse and Lindelof were fans of Fillion's work on *Firefly*.[2] Fillion said that he was a *Lost* fan and described his experience working at the show as "a dream".[4]

Reception

17.15 million American viewers watched this episode live, standing as the ninth most-seen program of the week.[5] It also had 1.1 million viewers in the United Kingdom.[6]

Chris Carabott of IGN gave a 9.3 out of 10 to "I Do", describing it as "delivering some key moments in the series' history and leaving viewers with a spectacular cliffhanger ending."[7] Carabott complimented Locke's scenes as "short but nonetheless powerful" and praised Matthew Fox's acting, saying he "steals the show with one of his best performances to date".[7] Writing for *Entertainment Weekly*, Christine Fenno considered that the flashbacks "weren't as exciting as the action on the island, but they were full of fun details" and liked Jack's scenes at the operating room.[8] Jonathan Toomey of AOL's TV Squad called "I Do" "an episode worthy of being called a mid-season finale", thinking that the romantic scenes between Kate and Sawyer worked for "the tension that existed".[9] BuddyTV's Oscar Dahl considered "I Do" as "a worthy end to Lost's truncated Fall season", having a good reaction to the cliffhanger and saying the episode "set up incredible possibilities for the rest of the season".[10] Not all reviews were positive, with *Slant Magazine*'s critic Andrew Dignan feeling it was "lacking both the immediacy and urgency that keeps viewers clamoring for months on end", and being critical of the writing, particularly on most of the essential plot elements occurring in the final minutes.[11]

"I Do" was selected as one of the "25 Sexiest TV Shows on DVD" by *Entertainment Weekly*.[12] IGN ranked the episode 28th out of the 115 Lost episodes, describing it as a "turning point episode of the third season."[13] On the other hand, a similar list by *Los Angeles Times* ranked "I Do" as the 91st, saying it "mostly botched" the plot point of Kate's wedding despite Nathan Fillion's presence, and feeling it was an episode that "probably shouldn't have had to have as much pressure on it as it did (acting as a mini-cliffhanger in early Season 3)".[14] Evangeline Lilly submitted this episode for consideration on her behalf in the category of "Outstanding Lead Actress in a Drama Series" at the 2007 Emmy Awards.[15]

References

[1] Carlton Cuse, Evangeline Lilly, Josh Holloway (2007). *Audio commentary for "I Do"* (DVD). *Lost: The Complete Third Season* Disk 2: Buena Vista Home Entertainment.

[2] Lindelof, Damon; Carlton Cuse (2006-12-06). "Official *Lost* Audio Podcast" (http://ll.media.abc.com/podcast/audio/itunes/Lostpodcast_3X1_abc.mp3). American Broadcasting Company. . Retrieved 2008-03-24.

[3] dos Santos, Kristin (2006-11-09). "Lost Redux: Swim for it!" (http://www.eonline.com/print/index.jsp?uuid=893efed6-f85b-48ef-a894-a8e4901cea56&contentType=watchWithKristin). E! Online. . Retrieved 2011-07-12.

[4] "MeeVee Exclusive! Interview with Drive Star Nathan Fillion" (http://replay.web.archive.org/20081101161022/http://blog.meevee.com/my_weblog/2007/04/canadianborn_ac.html). MeeVee. 2007-04-13. Archived from the original (http://blog.meevee.com/my_weblog/2007/04/canadianborn_ac.html) on 2008-11-01. . Retrieved 2011-04-16.

[5] "Weekly Program Rankings" (http://abcmedianet.com/web/dnr/dispDNR.aspx?id=111406_09). ABC Medianet. November 14, 2006. . Retrieved 2008-07-23.

[6] Holmwood, Leigh (2006-12-18). "Hogfather scores for Sky One" (http://www.guardian.co.uk/media/2006/dec/18/overnights). *The Guardian*. . Retrieved 2011-07-16.

[7] Carabott, Chris (2006-11-09). "Lost: "I Do" review" (http://tv.ign.com/articles/744/744980p1.html). IGN. . Retrieved 2011-07-16.

[8] Fenno, Christine (2007-06-07). "*Lost*: Caged Heat" (http://www.ew.com/ew/article/0,,1557074,00.html). *Entertainment Weekly*. . Retrieved 2011-07-16.

[9] Toomey, Jonathan (2006-11-08). "Lost: I Do" (http://www.aoltv.com/2006/11/08/lost-i-do). TV Squad. . Retrieved 2011-07-16.

[10] Dahl, Oscar (2006-11-09). "Lost: "I Do"" (http://www.buddytv.com/articles/lost/lost-i-do-sixpack.aspx). BuddyTV. . Retrieved 2011-07-16.

[11] Dignan, Andrew (2006-11-06). "Lost Thursdays: Season Three, Ep. 6: "I Do"" (http://www.slantmagazine.com/house/2006/11/lost-thursdays-season-three-ep-6-i-do/). *Slant Magazine*. . Retrieved 2011-07-16.

[12] "25 Sexiest TV Shows on DVD" (http://www.ew.com/ew/article/0,,20240932_18,00.html). *Entertainment Weekly*. Time, Inc. 2008-11-11. . Retrieved 2008-11-19.

[13] "Ranking Lost" (http://tv.ign.com/articles/109/1094268p8.html). IGN. 2010-06-02. . Retrieved 2010-12-13.

[14] VanDerWerff, Todd (2010-05-23). "'Lost' 10s: Every episode of 'Lost,' ever (well, except the finale), ranked for your enjoyment" (http://latimesblogs.latimes.com/showtracker/2010/05/lost-10s-every-episode-of-lost-ever-well-except-the-finale-ranked-for-your-enjoyment.html). *Los Angeles Times*. . Retrieved 2010-07-27.

[15] "2007 Emmys CONFIRMED Episode Submissions" (http://goldderbyforums.latimes.com/eve/forums/a/tpc/f/1106078764/m/53610293). The Envelope Forum, *Los Angeles Times*. . Retrieved 2007-06-18.

External links

- *I Do* (http://www.imdb.com/title/tt0883770/) at the Internet Movie Database

Drive (TV series)

Drive	
Genre	Drama Action
Created by	Tim Minear Ben Queen
Starring	Nathan Fillion Kristin Lehman Mircea Monroe Riley Smith Kevin Alejandro J. D. Pardo Dylan Baker Emma Stone Rochelle Aytes Taryn Manning Melanie Lynskey
Opening theme	"Can't Stop the World" by Gavin Rossdale
Composer(s)	Keith Power
Country of origin	United States
Language(s)	English
No. of seasons	1
No. of episodes	6 (List of episodes)
Production	
Executive producer(s)	Tim Minear Ben Queen Greg Yaitanes
Running time	42 minutes
Broadcast	
Original channel	Fox
Picture format	480i (SDTV) 720p (HDTV)
Original run	April 13, 2007 – April 23, 2007

Drive is a short-lived American action drama television series created by Tim Minear and Ben Queen, produced by Minear, Queen, and Greg Yaitanes, and starring Nathan Fillion, four episodes of which aired on the Fox network in April 2007. Two unaired episodes were later released directly to digital distribution.

The series is set across the backdrop of an illegal automobile road race with the central focus being on the unwitting competitors and, as the plot develops, the unseen puppet masters who sponsor the race. Minear has described the show's thematic tone by saying "a secret, illegal, underground road race can be anything from *Cannonball Run* to *The Game* to *North by Northwest* to *Magnolia*-on-wheels. Ours is all those things."[1]

Firefly and *Serenity* star Nathan Fillion, a longtime friend of series creator Tim Minear, plays the lead role of Alex Tully. Ivan Sergei played Tully in the unaired pilot.[2]

The show premiered on April 13, 2007 on CTV in Canada.[3] It debuted in the United States on April 15, 2007 on Fox, and moved into its regular time slot on Mondays the next day; in that slot it faced stiff competition from NBC's *Deal or No Deal* and ABC's *Dancing with the Stars*. On April 25, Fox canceled *Drive* only after four episodes had aired.[4] As of 2010 the series has not been released to international markets (with the exception of Canada) or on DVD.

Cast and characters

Actor	Role	Vehicle	Notes
Nathan Fillion	Alex Tully	1972 Ford F-100 (tan) 1972[5] Dodge Challenger (black)	Protagonist
Kristin Lehman	Corinna Wiles		Partners with Alex Tully
Kevin Alejandro	Winston Salazar	1964 Chevrolet Impala lowrider (gold)	
J.D. Pardo	Sean Salazar		Winston Salazar's partner and half-brother
Dylan Baker	John Trimble	1999 Ford Taurus (silver-blue)	
Emma Stone	Violet Trimble		John Trimble's partner and daughter
Michael Hyatt	Susan Chamblee	Land Rover LR3 (light blue) Ford Focus (red)	
Rochelle Aytes	Leigh Barnthouse	Pontiac Solstice (black)	Originally partners with Susan Chamblee and Ivy Chitty
Melanie Lynskey	Wendy Patrakas	Dodge Grand Caravan SXT (silver)	
Taryn Manning	Ivy Chitty		Originally partners with Susan Chamblee and Leigh Barnthouse, then partners with Wendy Patrakas, then steals the Trimbles' Ford Taurus
Riley Smith	Rob Laird	1979 Pontiac Trans Am (white)	
Mircea Monroe	Ellie Laird		Rob Laird's partner and wife
Wayne Grace	Jimmy Cousins	Harley Davidson touring motorcycle (black)	
K Callan	Ceal Cousins		Jimmy Cousins's partner and wife
Brian Bloom	Allan James	2007 Dodge Charger (black) 2002 Chevrolet Impala (red)	Not a race participant
Richard Brooks	Detective Ehrle		Not a race participant
Charles Martin Smith	Mr. Bright		One of the race organizers; not a race participant
Katie Finneran	Becca Freeman		Alex Tully's sister; not a race participant
Amy Acker	Kathryn Tully		Alex Tully's wife; not a race participant

Route

The following are the checkpoints passed, clues and/or instructions before arrival, and the specifics regarding them.

Checkpoint	Clue/Instructions	Specifics
Key West, Florida	Text message: "Mainland Go" (announced the start of the race, not a destination)	The starting line of the race.
Jupiter, Florida	Text message: "Fly to Jupiter and find the red eye."	The Jupiter Inlet lighthouse.
Cape Canaveral, Florida	Text message: "Kennedy killed in '73." The message is accompanied by a countdown clock.	In 1973, Cape Kennedy was renamed to Cape Canaveral, thus "killing" the name "Kennedy." Drivers met at the Kennedy Space Center, where the countdown corresponded with a space shuttle launch.
Rome, Georgia	Each driver was given a red ticket stub with instructions to go to Rome, "After sunset, before dark." NOTE: in the ticket was written "ADMIT".	After Sunset drive-in movie theater.
Appomattox Court House, Virginia	Text message: "Surrender, America"	Appomattox Court House was where Confederate general Robert E. Lee surrendered to Union general Ulysses S. Grant, thus ending the Civil War.
Cleveland, Ohio	Most of the racers received two hot candies, while Alex, Corinna, Sean and Winston, who had taken advantage of their head start, received a note reading "Great Balls of Fire: The Rock 'n' Roll Hall of Fame - Cleveland"	The Rock 'n' Roll Hall of Fame.
Unknown	Alex Tully received the address to the next checkpoint on a slip of paper after arriving at The Rock 'n' Roll Hall of Fame.	The slip of paper is passed hand-to-hand, and the checkpoint is never revealed in the six produced episodes.

Episodes

A total of six episodes of *Drive* were produced, four of them were aired prior to its cancellation. The series premiered on April 13, 2007 in Canada and on April 15, 2007 in the United States.

#	Title	Directed by	Written by	Original air date	Production code[6]	U.S. viewers (millions)
0	Unaired Pilot	Greg Yaitanes	Tim Minear & Ben Queen	Unaired		
1	**"The Starting Line"**	Greg Yaitanes	Tim Minear & Ben Queen	April 13, 2007 (CTV)	1AMP01	6.04[7]
	An illegal cross country race is being run. Contestants in the race are not all there by their own choice – Alex Tully is searching for his missing wife; a mother is somehow involved for her baby's safety--others may simply be after the 32 million dollar prize.					
2	**"Partners"**	Greg Yaitanes	Tim Minear & Tom Szentgyorgyi	April 13, 2007 (CTV)	1AMP02	6.04[7]
	The race continues in Jupiter, Florida, where Tully, Wiles, and the other racers prepare for the next clue. Wendy Patrakas prepares to kill Ivy Chitty to stay in the race. Corinna's interest in the race is revealed.					
3	**"Let the Games Begin"**	Marita Grabiak	Eoghan Mahony & Ben Queen	April 16, 2007 (Fox)[8]	1AMP03	5.66[9]
	The race continues on the next stage. Alex meets an old acquaintance after getting in trouble with the police while Wendy gets a new co-driver.					
4	**"No Turning Back"**	Elodie Keene	Lauren Schmidt & Craig Silverstein	April 23, 2007 (Fox)[10]	1AMP04	4.60[11]
	Alex and Corinna are offered a chance to move ahead of the other racers; Corinna is unsure of how safe the move would be. Susan and Leigh wish to stay in the race even after their betrayal by another. Wendy fears for her baby's safety. Susan and Leigh are eliminated from the race.					

5	"The Extra Mile"	Paul Edwards	Salvatore J. Stabile & Juan Carlos Coto	July 15, 2007 (Online)	1AMP05	N/A
Alex, Corinna and the Salazar brothers are faced with the ramifications of their jump-start; Leigh gets a new partner; and Ivy puts Sam in danger.							
6	"Rear View"	Michael Katleman	Kristen Reidel & Scott M. Gimple	July 15, 2007 (Online)	1AMP06	N/A
Alex risks everything to find Kathryn; Violet picks up a hitchhiking Ivy; Wendy hurries to save Sam from her husband; and the military finally catches up with Rob.							

Production notes

Fox greenlit series production on *Drive* in October 2006. In addition to the series pilot, another twelve episodes were ordered as a midseason replacement for spring 2007.[12]

Filming locations

Drive was shot in the Los Angeles area, using road footage and green-screen technology. According to Tim Minear, "because of technology, we can actually create a cross-country road race and shoot it all in Santa Clarita."[13] This led to geographic inconsistencies in the series, including mountains and desert settings visible during highway scenes set near Gainesville, Florida, when there are no actual mountain ranges or deserts in that area.

Highway scenes were shot on Interstate 210 in Rialto, California on the finished but unopened portion between Alder Ave. and Linden Ave. The exit for Alder Ave can be seen as the exit in most of the freeway scenes. In the first episode, the Alder Ave. sign for the exit is clearly legible. Scenes at the "Kennedy Space Center" were filmed at the Ambassador Auditorium in Pasadena, California.

Music

- Gavin Rossdale - "Can't Stop the World"
- The Doors - "Roadhouse Blues (Crystal Method Remix)"
- Bloc Party - "Kreuzberg"
- Nine Pound Hammer - "Radar Love"
- X - "The Hungry Wolf"
- Lunatic Calm - "Leave You Far Behind"
- Ghost in the Machine - "King of My World"
- Yonderboi - "Soulbitch"
- The Rhones - "Quitter"

Cancellation

The two-hour premiere of *Drive* in the United States, broadcast on April 15, 2007 at 8:00 pm, was watched by six million viewers.[14] The program did not deliver the ratings Fox desired, and on April 25, 2007, the network announced that it had cancelled *Drive*.[4] The final two remaining unaired episodes of *Drive* were made available for online streaming on Fox on Demand beginning Sunday, July 15, 2007, in addition to the previously aired episodes. All six episodes of the show have been made available for purchase and download from the iTunes Store[15] and Amazon Video on Demand exclusively for United States residents.[16]

Fox initially announced that the final two episodes would air on July 4, 2007. The network rescheduled them for July 13 and later pulled them entirely.[17] The two remaining episodes were posted online on July 15, 2007. Executive producers Tim Minear and Craig Silverstein subsequently gave an interview that described what might have happened if the series had continued.[18]

Awards

Drive, while short-lived, is the first series to be nominated for an Emmy Award under the organization's new "broadband" eligibility guidelines. The show's title sequence had originally been submitted for consideration in the category of "best outstanding visual effects in a drama series". However, Emmy regulations require a series to air at least six episodes in order to be eligible, whereas *Drive* had only aired four episodes prior to its cancellation. After the sequence was posted for streaming on the Internet, it became eligible under the new "special visual effects" category.[19]

In popular culture

- In the September 2007 issue of Marvel Comics' *Friendly Neighborhood Spider-Man*, Peter Parker comments that "ever since Fox cancelled *Drive*, it's been one piece of bad luck after another."[20]

References

[1] "The Tim Minear Interview" (http://www.whedon.info/Tim-Minear-Drive-Tv-Series-Pilot.html). *The Drive News Blog*. 2006-07-01. .

[2] Andreeva, Nellie (December 15, 2006). "'Drive' time for Fillion at Fox" (http://web.archive.org/web/20070104045228/http://www.hollywoodreporter.com/hr/content_display/television/news/e3i0123c6f82e9d75a960daf0920816a410). *The Hollywood Reporter*. Archived from the original (http://www.hollywoodreporter.com/hr/content_display/television/news/e3i0123c6f82e9d75a960daf0920816a410) on January 4, 2007. .

[3] "CTV adds 'Drive' to schedule, premieres April 13" (http://www.ctv.ca/CTVNews/Entertainment/20070409/drive_show_070409/). CTV.ca. . Retrieved 2011-02-21.

[4] Schneider, Michael (2007-04-25). "'Drive' runs out of gas" (http://www.variety.com/article/VR1117963779?refCatId=14). Variety. . Retrieved 2007-04-26.

[5] While referred to in the show as a 1972 model, the vehicle's distinctive front and rear mark it as a 1970 model, markedly different from the 1972–1974 models.

[6] "DRIVE" (http://www.foxinflight.com/tv/44/). FoxInFlight.com. 20th Century Fox. . Retrieved October 16, 2010.

[7] "WEEKLY PROGRAM RANKINGS FROM 04/09/07 THROUGH 04/15/07" (http://abcmedianet.com/web/dnr/dispDNR.aspx?id=041707_06) (Press release). ABC Medianet. April 17, 2007. . Retrieved October 16, 2010.

[8] "(DRV-103) "Let the Games Begin"" (http://www.thefutoncritic.com/listings.aspx?id=20070220fox01). The Futon Critic. . Retrieved June 23, 2007.

[9] "WEEKLY PROGRAM RANKINGS FROM 04/16/07 THROUGH 04/22/07" (http://abcmedianet.com/web/dnr/dispDNR.aspx?id=042407_06) (Press release). ABC Medianet. April 24, 2007. . Retrieved October 16, 2010.

[10] "(DRV-104) "No Turning Back"" (http://www.thefutoncritic.com/listings.aspx?id=20070410fox01). The Futon Critic. . Retrieved June 23, 2007.

[11] "WEEKLY PROGRAM RANKINGS FROM 04/23/07 THROUGH 04/29/07" (http://abcmedianet.com/web/dnr/dispDNR.aspx?id=050107_08) (Press release). ABC Medianet. May 1, 2007. . Retrieved October 16, 2010.

[12] Adalian, Josef (2006-10-30). "Fox springs into 'Drive'" (http://www.variety.com/article/VR1117952974?refCatId=1300). Variety. .

[13] Miller, Gerri. "Inside "Drive"" (http://electronics.howstuffworks.com/drive.htm). *HowStuffWorks*. . Retrieved 2011-02-21.

[14] Bauder, David (2007-04-17). "Ratings: NBC Sinks; Fox's 'Drive' Stalls" (http://web.archive.org/web/20071015230645/http://forbes.com/feeds/ap/2007/04/17/ap3622233.html). *Forbes*. Archived from the original (http://www.forbes.com/feeds/ap/2007/04/17/ap3622233.html) on October 15, 2007. . Retrieved April 18, 2007.

[15] "Drive, Season 1" (http://phobos.apple.com/WebObjects/MZStore.woa/wa/viewTVSeason?id=251903353&s=143441). . Retrieved August 17, 2007.

[16] "Drive: Unbox Video" (http://www.amazon.com/dp/B000PH2DUI/). . Retrieved August 17, 2007.

[17] "*Drive:* Fox Hijacks Last Two Episodes" (http://tvseriesfinale.com/tv-show/drive-fox-hijacks-last-two-episodes/). *TVSeriesFinale.com*. 2007-07-06. .

[18] "*Drive:* What Would've Happened on the Cancelled Series" (http://tvseriesfinale.com/tv-show/drive-what-wouldve-happened-on-the-cancelled-series/). *TVSeriesFinale.com*. 2007-07-11. .

[19] Michael Schneider (2007-07-20). "'Drive' makes primetime Emmy history: Fox show the first broadband nominee" (http://www.variety.com/article/VR1117968898?refCatId=14). Variety. . Retrieved 2008-03-03.

[20] David, Peter (w). *Friendly Neighborhood Spider-Man* v2, 22 (September 2007), Marvel Comics

External links

- *Drive* (http://www.imdb.com/title/tt0770521/) at the Internet Movie Database
- *Drive* (http://www.tv.com/show/58334/summary.html) at TV.com

Robot Chicken

Robot Chicken	
Title Card	
Genre	Black comedy
Format	Stop motion animation Sketch comedy
Created by	Seth Green Matthew Senreich
Voices of	(Complete list)
Opening theme	"Robot Chicken" by Les Claypool
Composer(s)	Michael Suby
Country of origin	United States
No. of seasons	5
No. of episodes	100 (and 4 specials) (List of episodes)
Production	
Executive producer(s)	Seth Green Matthew Senreich Alex Bulkley Corey Campodonico
Running time	11-12 minutes
Production company(s)	ShadowMachine Films Stoop!d Monkey Sony Pictures Digital Williams Street
Broadcast	
Original channel	Adult Swim
Picture format	4:3 SDTV (2005-2009) 16:9 HDTV (2010-present)
Original run	February 20, 2005 – present
Chronology	
Related shows	*Titan Maximum*
External links	
Website [1]	

Robot Chicken is an American stop motion animated television series created and executive produced by Seth Green and Matthew Senreich along with co-head writers Douglas Goldstein and Tom Root. Green provides many voices for the show. Senreich, Goldstein, and Root were former writers for the popular action figure hobbyist magazine *ToyFare*. The show's reception is good, with some calling it a cult classic. It has won an Annie Award and been nominated for an Emmy award.

Series genre and creation

Robot Chicken is a sketch comedy that parodies a number of pop culture conventions using stop motion animation of toys, action figures, and claymation (usually for special effects) and various other objects, such as tongue depressors, The Game of Life pegs and popsicle sticks during a joke about loss of budget. The show's name was inspired by a dish on the menu at a West Hollywood Chinese restaurant, Kung Pao Bistro, where Green and Senreich had dined, although the series originally was intended to be titled "*Junk in the Trunk*".[2]

The show premiered on Sunday, February 20, 2005. It is produced by Stoop!d Monkey, ShadowMachine Films, Williams Street, and Sony Pictures Digital, and currently airs in the US as a part of Cartoon Network's Adult Swim block, in the United Kingdom and Ireland as part of FX's Adult Swim block, in Canada on Teletoon's TELETOON at Night block, in Australia on The Comedy Channel's Adult Swim block, in Russia on 2x2's Adult Swim block, in Germany on TNT Serie's Adult Swim block and in Latin America on the I.Sat Adult Swim block (after being cancelled from Latin Cartoon Network's Adult Swim block in 2008 for unknown reasons).

The series was renewed for a 20-episode third season, which ran from August 12, 2007 to September 28, 2008. After an eight month hiatus, during the third season, the show returned on August 31, 2008 to air the remaining five episodes. The series was renewed for a fourth season which premiered on December 7, 2008 and ended September 20, 2009. In early 2010, the show was renewed for a 5th and 6th season (40 more episodes total).[3] Season 5 premiered on December 12, 2010. The second group of episodes began broadcasting on October 23, 2011.

In 2007 *Robot Chicken* was the highest rated original show on Adult Swim and the second highest on the network, after *Family Guy*.[4]

Overview

The show focuses on mocking pop culture, referencing toys, films, television, and popular fads, as well as more obscure references like anime cartoons and older television programs. One particular motif often involves the idea of fantastical characters being placed in a more realistic world or situation (such as Stretch Armstrong requiring a corn syrup transplant after losing his abilities because of aging, Optimus Prime performing a prostate cancer PSA, and Godzilla having problems in the bedroom). The program even had a 30 minute episode dedicated to *Star Wars* which premiered June 17, 2007 in the US featuring the voices of Star Wars notables George Lucas, Mark Hamill (from a previous episode), Billy Dee Williams, and Ahmed Best. (The Star Wars episode was nominated for a 2008 Emmy Award: Outstanding Animated Program (for Programming Less Than One Hour)). Another recurring segment is "Hilarious Bloopers", a parody of the Bob Saget era of *America's Funniest Home Videos* featuring the host constantly moving around in various exaggerated, disjointed motions. Unlike that show, this skit ends with the host using various household methods of suicide. Another recurring character is the "nerd"; (Whose name was mentioned as Gary in an early episode) a dorky middle school kid with broken glasses and a plaid shirt who talks with a lisp, spitting when he says the letter S. Every season finale to date has ended with Mike Lazzo, the head of Adult Swim, saying that "Robot Chicken is canceled", although thus far it has still returned for an additional season following each joke proclamation.

Opening sequence

A mute Mad Scientist finds a road-killed chicken, which he takes back to his laboratory to re-fashion into a cyborg. Midway through the opening sequence, the titular chicken turns its laser eye towards the camera, and the title appears amidst the 'laser effects' as Les Claypool of Primus can be heard screaming "It's alive!" in typical *Frankenstein* fashion. Claypool also composed and performed the show's theme song. The Mad Scientist then straps the re-animated Robot Chicken into a chair, uses calipers to hold its eyes open, and forces it to watch a bank of television monitors (an allusion to *A Clockwork Orange*); this scene segues into the body of the show. (In the episode "1987", Michael Ian Black claims that this sequence tells the viewer that they *are* the Robot Chicken, being forced to watch the skits); as a result, the show does not actually focus on the robot chicken. The first episode of the fifth season debuted a new opening, a parody of the film Saving Private Ryan, but returned to normal in following episodes.

Voice cast

Main cast

Besides Seth Green voicing himself and many of the characters for the show, major recurring actors/writers are:

- Candace Bailey
- Donald Faison
- Jordan Ladd
- Amy Smart
- Abraham Benrubi
- Tamara Garfield
- Seth MacFarlane
- Kevin Shinick
- Alex Borstein
- Sarah Michelle Gellar
- Breckin Meyer
- Adam Talbott
- Leah Cevoli
- Ginnifer Goodwin
- Dan Milano
- Zeb Wells
- Rachael Leigh Cook
- Clare Grant
- Chad Morgan
- Victor Yerrid
- Hugh Davidson
- Jamie Kaler
- Tom Root
- Eden Espinosa
- Mila Kunis
- Matthew Senreich

Celebrity guest stars

Among those celebrities that contributed to this show are:

- Scott Adsit
- Sean Astin
- Sebastian Bach
- Kevin Bacon
- Robin Bain
- Diora Baird
- Sasha Barrese
- Lance Bass
- Kristen Bell
- Ahmed Best
- Michael Ian Black
- Wayne Brady
- Amy Brenneman
- Eugene Byrd
- Dean Cain
- Bruce Campbell
- Linda Cardellini
- Robert Carradine
- Emma Caulfield
- Kyle Chandler
- Kristin Chenoweth
- Phyllis Diller
- Snoop Dogg
- Dr. Drew
- Clark Duke
- Zac Efron
- Chris Evans
- Joey Fatone
- David Faustino
- Jon Favreau
- Corey Feldman
- Miguel Ferrer
- Nathan Fillion
- Carrie Fisher
- Dan Fogler
- Megan Fox
- Alfonso Freeman
- Nick Frost
- Soleil Moon Frye
- Peter Gallagher
- Barry Gibb
- Donald Glover
- Ethan Hawke
- Jon Heder
- Hugh Hefner
- Mike Henry
- Hulk Hogan
- Michael Hogan
- Kelly Hu
- Vanessa Hudgens
- Gregory Itzin
- Scarlett Johansson
- Rashida Jones
- Monica Keena
- Jimmy Kimmel
- Don Knotts
- Ashton Kutcher
- Phil LaMarr
- Mike Lazzo
- Stan Lee
- Matthew Lillard
- Christopher Lloyd
- Mario Lopez
- Sir Mix-a-Lot
- Katy Mixon
- Ronald D. Moore
- Pat Morita
- Olivia Munn
- Conan O'Brien
- Pat O'Brien
- Raymond Ochoa
- Sandra Oh
- Masi Oka
- Master P
- Adrianne Palicki
- Hayden Panettiere
- Chris Parnell
- Simon Pegg
- Ron Perlman
- Katelin Peterson
- Roddy Piper
- Scott Porter
- Freddie Prinze, Jr.
- Zachary Quinto
- J.K. Simmons
- Nick Simmons
- Christian Slater
- Jean Smart
- Robert Smigel
- Kurtwood Smith
- Hal Sparks
- Emma Stone
- Patrick Stump
- Cree Summer
- Marc Summers
- T-Pain
- Tila Tequila
- Charlize Theron
- Lea Thompson
- Rory Thost
- Stuart Townsend
- Michelle Trachtenberg
- Triple H
- Alan Tudyk
- Robin Tunney

- Emmanuelle Chriqui
- Michael Chiklis
- Erika Christensen
- Diablo Cody
- Gary Coleman
- Kevin Connolly
- Josh Cooke
- Abbie Cornish
- Dave Coulier
- Chace Crawford
- Macaulay Culkin
- Robert Culp
- Alan Cumming
- Jean-Claude Van Damme
- Anthony Daniels
- Rosario Dawson
- Dom DeLuise
- Dustin Diamond
- Zachary Gordon
- Mark-Paul Gosselaar
- Topher Grace
- Spencer Grammer
- Brian Austin Green
- Cee-Lo Green
- Melanie Griffith
- Josh Groban
- Greg Grunberg
- Corey Haim
- Mark Hamill
- Alyson Hannigan
- Colin Hanks
- Neil Patrick Harris
- Melissa Joan Hart
- Dennis Haskins
- David Hasselhoff
- George Lucas
- Ludacris
- Holly Madison
- Jena Malone
- Lee Majors
- Bridget Marquardt
- James Marsden
- Danny Masterson
- Ming-Na
- William Mapother
- Malcolm McDowell
- John C. McGinley
- Julian McMahon
- Rove McManus
- Shane McRae
- Jim Meskimen
- Josh Radnor
- Efren Ramirez
- Marion Ramsey
- Jeremy Renner
- Burt Reynolds
- Alfonso Ribeiro
- Andy Richter
- Paul Rudd
- Debra Jo Rupp
- Katee Sackhoff
- Meredith Salenger
- Rick Schroder
- Ryan Seacrest
- Dave Sheridan
- Dax Shepard
- Sarah Silverman
- Gene Simmons
- Skeet Ulrich
- Wilmer Valderrama
- James Van Der Beek
- Milo Ventimiglia
- Lark Voorhies
- Patrick Warburton
- Erik Weiner
- Joss Whedon
- Mae Whitman
- Kendra Wilkinson
- Billy Dee Williams
- Harland Williams
- Michael Winslow
- Elijah Wood
- Matthew Wood
- "Weird Al" Yankovic
- Tay Zonday

Other voice actors

Besides the celebrities above, many famous voice actors work on this series including:

- Michael Benyaer
- Bob Bergen
- Julianne Buescher
- Keith Crofford
- Jim Cummings
- Jeannie Elias
- Mike Fasolo
- Bill Farmer
- Rachael MacFarlane
- Keith Ferguson
- Quinton Flynn
- Danny Goldman
- Tom Kane
- George Lowe
- Roger L. Jackson
- Drew Massey
- Patrick Pinney
- Bill Ratner
- Adam Reed
- Susan Silo
- Danny Smith
- Dana Snyder
- Stephen Stanton
- Fred Tatasciore
- Frank Welker

DVD releases

DVD Name	Release Date			Ep #	Discs
	Region 1	Region 2	Region 4		
Season One	March 28, 2006	September 29, 2008	April 4, 2007	1–20	3
This two disc boxset includes all 20 episodes from Season 1 in production order. While it contains many sketches that were edited from the TV airings, several of the original Sony Screenblast webtoons, and the words "Jesus" and "Christ" as an oath unbleeped (though "fuck" and "shit" are still censored out), the episodes are not all uncut. One particular segment that featured the Teen Titans meeting Beavis and Butt-head was omitted from the DVD because of legal problems. The Voltron/"You Got Served" sketch shown on the DVD has a replacement song because of legal issues over the song that was used on the TV version. At a performance of *Family Guy Live* in Chicago, during the Q&A session that ends each performance, Seth Green was asked how they came up with the name *Robot Chicken*. He explained that the title of each episode was a name Adult Swim rejected for the name of the show. A Region 2 version of the set was released in the UK on September 29, 2008.[5]					
Season Two: Uncensored	September 4, 2007	September 28, 2009	November 11, 2007	21–40	3

This two disc boxset includes all 20 episodes from Season 2 in production order and uncensored, with the words "fuck" and "shit" uncensored (except for one instance in the episode "Easter Basket" in the Lego sketch). It is currently available for download on iTunes (though the episode "Veggies for Sloth" is absent because of copyright issues involving the "Archie's Final Destination" segment.)[6] Seth Green stated at Comic-Con 2006 that the second DVD set will contain the "Beavis and Butt-head meet the Teen Titans" sketch, which had been removed from the first DVD set because of copyright issues. However, the sketch is absent from the DVD (Although it is available on iTunes). Bonus features include the Christmas Special. A secret Nerf gun fight can be found on the disc 1 extras menu, and pushing "up" over the extras and set-up items on the menu reveals more special features.					
Season Three: Uncensored	October 7, 2008	January 25, 2010	December 3, 2008	41–60	3
This two disc boxset includes all 20 episodes from Season 3 in production order. This DVD is Uncensored except for the "Cat in the Hat" sketch from episode 7 on Disc 1. It also intentionally censored in episode 5 in the "Law and Order" KFC sketch. This DVD has special features such as deleted scenes and animatics. It also includes commentary for all of the episodes and has "Chicken Nuggets" commentary for episodes 1 and 3-5. The bonus features also include a gag reel and audio takes.					
Star Wars Special	July 22, 2008	TBA	August 6, 2008	1	1
This single DVD features the Star Wars special in its TV-edited version (i.e. with bleeps in place of profane words) and several extras about the crew and their work on the special, including a photo gallery, alternate audio, and an easter egg demonstrating the crew's difficulty in composing a proper musical score for the sketch "Empire on Ice". Also features various audio commentaries, featuring members of the cast and crew.					
Star Wars Episode II	July 21, 2009	TBA	August 5, 2009	1	1
This single DVD features the main Star Wars special extras, including normal Robot Chicken episodes and common DVD extras; The Making Of, deleted scenes etc.					
Season Four: Uncensored	December 15, 2009	August 30, 2010	December 2, 2009	61–80	3
This two disc boxset includes all 20 episodes from Season 4 in production order. The special features include Chicken Nuggets, San Diego Comic-Con '08 Panel, Day in the life, New York Comic-Con '09 Panel, Video Blogs, Australia Visit, Alternate Audio, Deleted Scenes and Deleted Animations. Plus Commentary on all 20 episodes.					
Season Five: Uncensored	October 25, 2011		November 30, 2011	81-100	3
This two disc boxset includes all 20 episodes from Season 5, in production order. Nine of the episodes were previously unaired before DVD release. The set includes commentary on all episodes, Chicken Nuggets on a few episodes, a featurette on Episode 100. Deleted Scenes and Deleted Animations are also included. In Deleted Scenes are the sketches Beavis and Butthead Meet the Teen Titans (deleted from Season One due to copyright issues) and the Riverdale: Final Destination Sketch (deleted from Season 2 sets).					

Revolver Entertainment have released the first four seasons and all three Star Wars specials in the United Kingdom.[7] A box set including the first 3 seasons has also been released.[8]

Madman Entertainment have released up to date all Robot Chicken releases in Australia and New Zealand.

References

[1] http://www.adultswim.com/shows/robot-chicken/index.html
[2] "G4 - The Screen Savers - Robot Chicken, Constantine, Dark Tip" (http://www.g4tv.com/screensavers/episodes/3902/Robot_Chicken_Constantine_Dark_Tip.html). G4tv.com. 2005-02-16. . Retrieved 2010-07-13.
[3] "Robot Chicken Gets Unprecedented Two-Season, 40 Episode Pick-Up - TV Ratings, Nielsen Ratings, Television Show Ratings" (http://tvbythenumbers.com/2010/01/21/robot-chicken-gets-unprecedented-two-season-40-episode-pick-up/39625). TVbytheNumbers.com. 2010-01-21. . Retrieved 2010-04-27.
[4] "Toon Zone - Your Source for Toon News!" (http://www.toonzone.net/news/articles/20353/adult-swim-ends-2007-with-its-highest-ratings-ever-for-young-adults). News.toonzone.net. 2007-12-13. . Retrieved 2010-07-13.
[5] "Robot Chicken - Season 1 Box Set (Region 2) (Pal): DVD" (http://www.amazon.co.uk/dp/B001D12ZKI). Amazon.co.uk. . Retrieved 2010-07-13.
[6] "Robot Chicken - Season 2 Review" (http://www.tvshowsondvd.com/reviews/Robot-Chicken-Season-2/6795). TVShowsOnDVD.com. 2007-08-31. . Retrieved 2010-07-13.
[7] "sitcomsondvd.co.uk" (http://sitcomsondvd.co.uk/dvds/dvd/511/Robot-Chicken-Season-1). sitcomsondvd.co.uk. . Retrieved 2010-04-27.
[8] "sitcomsondvd.co.uk" (http://sitcomsondvd.co.uk/dvds/dvd/513/Robot-Chicken-Seasons-1-3). sitcomsondvd.co.uk. . Retrieved 2010-04-27.

External links

- *Robot Chicken* (http://www.adultswim.com/shows/robot-chicken/index.html) at Adultswim.com
- *Robot Chicken* (http://www.imdb.com/title/tt0437745/) at the Internet Movie Database
- *Robot Chicken* (http://www.tv.com/show/33630/summary.html) at TV.com
- *Robot Chicken* (http://www.adultswim.co.uk/shows/robot-chicken) at Adultswim.com (UK)
- *Robot Chicken* – Star Wars Review (http://www.variety.com/review/VE1117933920.html?categoryid=32&cs=1) at Variety.com

|group1 = Animated TV series |list1 = *Family Guy* (1999–2002, 2005–present) • *American Dad!* (2005–present) • *The Cleveland Show* (2009–present) • *The Flintstones* (2013–)

|group2 = Live-action TV series |list2 = *The Winner* (2007) |group3 = Animated web series |list3 = *Seth MacFarlane's Cavalcade of Cartoon Comedy* (2008–2009)

|group5 = Voices |list5 =Peter Griffin • Brian Griffin • Stewie Griffin • Glenn Quagmire • Stan Smith • Roger • Tim the Bear

|group6 = Films |list6 = *Ted* (2012)

|group7 = Studio albums |list7 = *Music Is Better Than Words* (2011)

|group8 = See also |list8 =Fuzzy Door Productions • *The Life of Larry and Larry & Steve* • *Zoomates* • Rachael MacFarlane • *Robot Chicken* • *Night of the Hurricane*

}}

List of *Desperate Housewives* characters

Following is a comprehensive list of every supporting fictional character in the ABC television series *Desperate Housewives*.

Acquaintances of Edie Britt

The following characters are all family members and acquaintances of **Edie Britt**, one of the protagonists of the series.

Dave Williams

Dave Williams, previously **David Dash** (Neal McDonough) is a twice-widowed, mysterious man introduced in the fifth season premiere as Edie's motivational speaker husband and the focus of the season's mystery. Dave convinced Edie to return to Wisteria Lane and persuade her tenant to move out. During their welcoming party, Edie learns the women forgive her for what happened instead of asking for her forgiveness. Annoyed by this, she asks Dave why he would force her to return to Wisteria Lane. Dave tells her that they can be happy here.

Dave learns that Edie was insulted by Karen McCluskey, and is getting tired of the hostility towards her. Dave asks Mrs. McCluskey to apologize, but when she refused, her cat Toby mysteriously disappeared. She asks Dave to help her find him, and Dave tells her he might help if she apologizes to Edie. Karen promises reluctantly, and after she does, she notices that Toby is back at her house. Assuming that Dave was responsible, Karen tried doing some research on Dave, resulting in him making everyone think that Karen is going senile. Karen is temporarily sent to the hospital. On her release, she continues her research with her sister and they call Dr. Heller, Dave's psychiatrist. Meanwhile, Dave forms a garage rock band with Tom, Orson, Carlos and Mike, who he helped move to the Lane in order to be closer to him. Dave arranges for the band to play at the "Battle of the Bands" competition at "The White Horse Club". Dr. Heller arrives in Fairview and learns that Mike, the man Dave is after, is in Dave's band. Dave strangles Dr. Heller in the club's storage room and sets the body ablaze, which later expands fire to the whole club. He later tells the police that Porter Scavo might have set the club on fire.

Dave constantly sees hallucinated visions of his wife and daughter, the people Mike and Susan accidentally killed in their car crash a few years back. Dave tells his dead family he will be with them soon. Edie catches Dave talking to himself in the middle of the night, and as she tries to understand what is going on, he attacks her. Edie kicks him out of the house. While leaving, Dave flashes back to when he learned he lost his family and how his anger got him admitted to a mental facility. He also remembers that when he got out, he met Edie and, after learning she used to live on the same street as Mike, married her. Mike sees Dave with his luggage and invites Dave to stay with him until things get better. Later, Edie realizes she does not want to be alone, and takes Dave back. Lee learns from Bob that Dave told the cops Porter set the fire to the club and tells Tom. Tom confronts Dave, and Dave explains that he had to tell the detectives what he thought he saw. Their friendship ends there.

Dave then plans a camping trip with Mike and Katherine, trying to trick Edie not to go and not to tell Katherine that she is not going. Edie and Dave are at a liquor store when a priest, recognizing Dave, comes up to them. Dave distracts Edie and tells the priest he does not want to recall his past. Edie finds this strange, and begins looking up Dave's past. In the camping trip which Dave arranged to exact his revenge on Mike by killing Katherine, his plan is botched when Edie texts him just as he was about to shoot Katherine, causing him to lose his aim. Edie had discovered his secret and demanded to confront him. Dave goes home and finds Edie, who reveals that she was now aware of his intentions. As she dials Mike's number to warn him, Dave grabs her by the throat. He almost strangles her, but releases her at the last moment. Tearful and disoriented, Edie rushes out and drives away in the car, but avoids running over Orson and collides with an electric post and receives a fatal shock, killing her in a matter of minutes. Dave later realizes that instead of Katherine it is M.J. he should have been trying to kill all this time in order to hurt Susan who was actually driving the car that killed his wife and daughter. When Jackson, Susan's boyfriend, returns, Dave fears he knows information from the incident in the club that he will tell the police. When he overhears a conversation that reveals Jackson is in the country illegally, he tips off immigration and gets Jackson arrested.

Dave makes one last attempt to take revenge on Susan by taking her and M.J. on a trip for fishing, while Mike discovers that Dave is really David Dash and his wife and daughter were killed in the car crash that broke up their marriage. Mike calls and warns Susan that Dave is a killer, and Susan and M.J. try to escape, but when Susan sprains her ankle, Dave catches her, and when M.J. is hiding, Dave bribes him. Back in the car, when Mike calls Susan back, Dave answers and reveals his intentions and is about to kill M.J. when Mike tells Dave to let Susan and M.J. go and to take him instead. Dave revises his plan and plans on making Susan watch as Mike hits the car with himself and M.J. in it, on the road of the accident because he thought it would be "poetic" to the protests of Susan, who asks Dave what his daughter would think of him killing an innocent child. His daughter reappears in the form of an hallucination and, as a result, Dave lets M.J. go. Mike crashes into Dave's car with only Dave in it, but both survive. Dave imagines what would have happened if his wife and daughter stayed home. After this confrontation, it is revealed that Dave was sent to a mental hospital in Boston, having clearly lost his mind.

Umberto Roswell

Umberto Roswell (Matt Cedeno) - Umberto is seen for the first time in the series' 100th episode, "The Best Thing That Ever Could Have Happened" during Edie's flashback remembering Eli Scruggs. Edie recalls one time that when she was having marital problems with her second ex-husband, Umberto. Feeling insecure about her appearance Eli reassures Edie and makes her feel better. Umberto reveals he is gay and leaves Edie. Eli, working in the bathroom, overhears the conversation and consoles Edie. A drunk Edie decides to cheer herself up by having sex with Eli. This episode marks the only appearance by Umberto in the series.

Charles McLain

Charles McLain (Greg Evigan) is Edie's first husband, and Travers's dad. He's a doctor, who's been working with Doctors Without Borders. He and Edie got divorced when Travers was two years old, and the parents decided to let Travers grow up with his dad, giving Charles full custody.

Travers McLain

Travers McLain (Jake Cherry, season 3; Stephen Lunsford, season 5) is Edie's son with her first husband Charles McLain. He lives with his father full time and was first mentioned in the pilot episode of the series, when he was said to be staying at Martha Huber's while Edie was "entertaining" a man. However he was never seen nor mentioned again until the sixteenth episode of the third season. His father Charles McLain left him with Edie whilst he went on a Doctors without Borders trip in Africa. Edie tried to leave Travers with Carlos while she went to a party, but as Carlos had a date, he declined. Seeing Travers playing by himself in the street, Carlos brings him to his home and later criticizes an intoxicated Edie for not supervising her son. She in turn reveals that she didn't take custody of him because she didn't feel she was capable of it and was being a realistic mother.

Later on Edie uses him as a way to get closer to Carlos and he is on to it the whole time but seems to take part in the plan willingly. Later in the episode, Edie and Carlos are in bed together. Edie's ex-husband, Charles, comes to pick up Travers. Edie tries to get shared custody of Travers when she suspects Carlos might be losing interest in their relationship. Charles learns about this and he and Edie get into an argument. Edie threatens to hire a lawyer so she can get full custody of Travers. Carlos learns of Edie's plan and tells her that she should think of what is best for Travers which is for him to stay with Charles and not have to go back and forth. He comforts her, saying that he will be there for her and Edie decides to call off her lawyer.

When Edie leaves Wisteria Lane for what she thinks is for good, she tells Travers she would have to spend Mother's Day with him. In fact, she would have to spend a lot more time with him from now on. Travers is next seen in season 5 when the Housewives visit him at Beecher's Academy (about 4 hours outside of Fairview) to inform him of his mother's death and to give him her ashes. While he is sad about his mother's death, he harbors anger toward her for her abandonment of the family. He eventually forgives her after a conversation with Karen McCluskey, and asks the Housewives to dispose of Edie's ashes as they see fit.

Ilene Britt

Ilene Britt (K Callan) is Edie's dead mother who appears in one of her dreams in the season three finale. She blames Edie for tricking Carlos into a relationship, and warns her that she will die alone, just like her mother. Edie would later die in a car accident moments after leaving her husband, but dies with all of the residents of Wisteria Lane around her.

Austin McCann

Austin McCann (Josh Henderson) is a troubled 17-year-old kid who was having problems with his mother's new boyfriend. When Edie, Austin's aunt, catches him trying to break into her house, she lets him stay with her for some time instead of going to Mexico like he was planning to, since he fought his mother's boyfriend, but she chose her boyfriend instead of Austin.

He is instantly attracted to Julie Mayer, and whilst she is also attracted to him, she doesn't immediately let him know. They spend some time playing cat and mouse but begin a relationship after both being held hostage by Carolyn Bigsby, much to Susan's displeasure, as she considers him a trouble-maker, and fears he will break her daughter's heart. In episode 3.11, "No Fits, No Fights, No Feuds", Julie gives up her virginity to Austin. Shortly afterwards, it was revealed that Austin had been sleeping with Danielle Van De Kamp, who is also a friend of Julie's. Austin plans to break it off with her to keep Julie from finding out, but it ends with Danielle threatening to reveal their relationship to Julie if Austin quits having sex with her.

In episode 3.12, "Not While I'm Around", Edie and Susan caught Austin and Danielle having sex. At the end of the episode, Susan tells Julie about Austin and Danielle, and Julie is seen crying on her mother's shoulder. It's suspected that Julie's relationship with Austin is over, as well as Julie and Danielle's friendship. As of the episode "I Remember That", it is established that Julie dumped Austin, as said by Edie to Tom Scavo when Edie broached him about hiring Austin for a job. This was later confirmed by Austin himself who proceeded to get high on the job, telling Lynette his reason was that "Julie dumped me and I'm very.... very upset." Lynette fired Austin for smoking marijuana on the job, but Tom hired him back because "teenage girls think he's hot...he'll bring in all the high school girls and half the men's chorus."

Later on he discovers that he got Danielle pregnant just when he managed to mend his relationship with Julie. Orson Hodge told Austin he would need to leave town. Although Austin refused, Andrew pointed out that sooner or later he would just hurt Julie again. Austin agreed to leave; said goodbye to Julie and told her she was the only person who ever gave him a second chance, and then rode away on his motorcycle for parts unknown.

Lila and Paige Dash

Lila and Paige Dash (**Marie Caldare** and **Madeleine Michelle Dunn**) were respectively Dave Williams's first wife and their daughter. Both of them died in car accident, involving Susan and Mike. Paige was born approximately the same time as Susan's boy M.J. Delfino in the same hospital.

Dr. Samuel Heller

Dr. Samuel Heller (Stephen Spinella) was a psychiatrist, who worked with the criminally insane. David Dash was one of his patients. When Dr. Heller discovers that Dave has changed his name to Dave Williams, and returned to Fairview to live, he becomes very concerned about what might happen. He comes to Fairview looking for Dave, and confronts him in a nightclub. Dave strangles him to death, and sets the club on fire. It would be several months before the body is identified, prompting Karen McCluskey and her sister Roberta to put all the pieces together of Dave's revenge plan against Mike and Susan.

Acquaintances of Betty Applewhite

The following characters are all family members and acquaintances of **Betty Applewhite**, one of the protagonists of the series.

Virgil Applewhite

Virgil Applewhite is Betty's deceased husband and the father of their children Caleb and Matthew. He does not appear in the series.

Caleb and Matthew Applewhite

Caleb (Page Kennedy and NaShawn Kearse) and **Matthew Applewhite** (Mehcad Brooks and in Flashbacks Hendrix Henrie-Erhahon) are Betty Applewhite's sons. Before the Applewhites moved to Fairview, Matthew was dating a young woman named Melanie Foster. He tried to break up with her, but she wouldn't let go. Matthew asked Melanie to meet at the Lumberjack warehouse garden, but Caleb turns up first and when he tells Melanie he loves her, she laughs in his face. Caleb then tries to kiss her, but she slaps him and hits him with a pole. Caleb gets scared and hits her with it over the head. Melanie falls and, thinking that he killed her, Caleb flees. Matthew returned later and told Melanie, who was still alive, that Caleb didn't mean to do what he did but she tells him unless they get back together, she's going to the police, Matthew begged Melanie not to say anything, but she walks away. He hits her with the pole three times, which kills the young woman, and he places his jacket on her.

Matthew and Betty locked Caleb in the basement as punishment for Melanie's death, but Betty did not know that Matthew was the real killer. Matthew starts dating Danielle Van de Kamp, and her mother, Bree, is not happy with this. Matthew and Danielle create a plan to get Caleb out of the way. Matthew tells Caleb that Danielle likes him and she wants to kiss him. Caleb goes to the Van De Kamp house and into Danielle's room but Danielle freaks and screams for Bree. Bree enters with her gun and frightens Caleb away. After this Betty decides to kill Caleb peacefully with some pills disguised in ice cream but Caleb tells Betty that Matthew said he should go to Danielle's room. She does not kill Caleb and instead locks Matthew in the basement. Danielle finds Matthew and when Betty brings Matthew some food Danielle attacks her and Matthew and Danielle run away. Betty learns that Matthew killed Melanie and tells Bree. Bree rushes home to find Danielle and Matthew there with money they stole from Bree's safe and she won't let Matthew and Danielle out of the house. Matthew brings out a gun and tells Bree to move or he'll shoot her and she challenges him to in order to prove to her watching daughter that Matthew is a murderer. However before he can pull the trigger, Matthew is shot in the heart by a police sniper and dies. Caleb and Betty leave Wisteria Lane after Matthew's death.

Melanie Foster

Melanie Foster was a high school aged girl from Chicago who was involved with Matthew Applewhite. (Portrayed by Joy Bisco) She is seen in flashbacks in the season 2 episode "Remember, Part 1". When Matthew tried to end their relationship, Melanie reacted angrily and asked him to meet her at a lumberyard. When Caleb shows up first and tries to kiss Melanie, she reacts violently and pushes him away. But he persists and eventually hits her with the back of an axe and knocks her unconscious. Minutes later, Matthew arrives to find a groggy Melanie, but when she persistently bashes Caleb, Matthew beats her to death and covers her with his sweater. Because Caleb arrived home first with blood on his hands, Betty is convinced it is he that murdered Melanie. Melanie's family hired Curtis Monroe (played by Michael Ironside) to look for Caleb; however, he accidentally shot himself to death while falling on the stairs in the Applewhite basement.

Acquaintances of Katherine Mayfair

The following characters are all family members and acquaintances of **Katherine Mayfair**, one of the protagonists of the series.

Adam Mayfair

Adam Mayfair (Nathan Fillion) is Katherine's ex-husband and a doctor. Adam moves in Wisteria Lane with Katherine and Dylan Mayfair. He and Katherine go into an attic room in their house and Adam asks her "Is this the room?" Katherine tells him that it is, and that Dylan wants to move into it but she will not allow it. When he questions whether they made a mistake moving to Wisteria Lane, she tells him that they did not have a choice.[1] It is often implied he has a history as a ladies' man[2] and it is revealed that he left Chicago because of a patient who sued him for sexual assault after he left her, although he let Katherine believe she was just an erotomaniac.[3] When she finds out, she asks him to leave and he does. While packing his stuff, he finds Lilian's note and discovers Katherine's mystery, making him decide to actually walk out on her.[4] In episode 4.11, Dylan wants to talk to Adam because she is willing to know the truth about her father. Adam meets Katherine before talking to Dylan and they decide that he should learn what Dylan knows and what she doesn't and Adam would make up something. After this, Katherine tells him that she wants to patch things up with him but Adam guarantees that he will give her one last alibi, but then he is done with her.

In the season four finale, Adam and Katherine seemed to have re-kindled their marriage. They even go to Dylan's cello recital together, as a family. Since Adam had never seen a photo or ever met Wayne, he didn't know he was also at the recital. Wayne asked Adam during the intermission to help with some car trouble he was having. Wayne knocks Adam unconscious with a tire iron, takes him to an abandoned shack and beats him so badly that he thinks

Adam has died. After Wayne leaves to deal with Katherine, Adam who had only feigned being dead, steals a car and heads to Wisteria Lane to save Katherine from Wayne. He shows up just as Wayne is about to shoot Katherine. The two men engage in an off-screen scuffle and Adam was successful in wrestling the gun away from Wayne. Bree then takes Adam to get cleaned up and he isn't seen after that, during which time Katherine is holding Wayne at gun point. He taunts her that even if gets jail time, he will come after her. Bree and Adam hear a gunshot, and walk in to find Katherine over Wayne's body. In the 5-year leap, it is assumed that Katherine and Adam are divorced because there is no sign of Adam.

Dylan Mayfair

Dylan Mayfair (Lyndsy Fonseca) is Katherine's daughter, adopted from an orphanage in Romania, and the adoptive maternal step-sister of the original Dylan, who was killed by a bookshelf. Dylan has no memory of "her" past life. So Dylan, her mother Katherine and her stepfather Adam move into Wisteria Lane and it is revealed that Katherine and Dylan lived there twelve years ago. Dylan finds a note that Katherine threw into the fireplace, which implies that Katherine killed Dylan's real father. Throughout Season 4, she unearths more surprising news about her past. She and Julie participate in the Founder's Day Ball.

One day, Dylan is driving, and a police officer pulls her over for speeding. Later, she finds out he is her father, Wayne, who she always thought had died. Wayne asks Dylan not to tell Katherine that they have met. Dylan meets Wayne a few times for dinner, telling Katherine that she's out on a date. Katherine follows Dylan one evening and discovers the truth. In fact, that night Dylan and Wayne resolve to tell Katherine that they have been meeting. When she hears the news, Katherine pretends she is no longer afraid of Wayne - but keeps a gun hidden under the counter. Wayne later discovers that Dylan is not his biological daughter. He realizes this after watching home videos of Dylan when she was young. Most striking is the fact that while his daughter had a scar from a bike accident that needed 11 stitches but Dylan's skin is unmarked. Katherine has no choice but to tell Dylan the truth about all the secrets she has kept her and she ran off when her dad came back with a gun.

Katherine says that Wayne abused her. She reported him to the police twice but because Wayne was a police officer, they "lost the paperwork" the first time. The second time, a policewoman advises Katherine to leave town so she packs her things and leaves with her daughter. Eventually, Wayne finds them but Katherine has gone out for the evening. When she returns, Mary Alice (who was babysitting) tells her that Wayne came by and gave Dylan a doll, which the little girl would not let go of. Katherine takes the doll and puts it on top of a bookcase. Wayne visits again and they have a fight, only ending when Katherine hits him with a candlestick so he leaves. Lillian offers Katherine a drink and she later falls asleep on the couch, waking up only when she hears a scream. She rushes upstairs and finds Dylan under the bookcase where Katherine had hidden the doll. Lillian says "I came to see if she needed a blanket and found her - she is ice cold." The original Dylan is now dead. Katherine feels like she cannot go to the police because she believes Wayne will find a way to pin Dylan's death on her. She buries her daughter in the woods. She flies to a Romanian orphanage and adopts a girl who bears a striking resemblance to Dylan. The girl's biological mother had died in childbirth and her father had been murdered.

After the five year jump in the Season 4 finale, Dylan leaves a message for Katherine saying she has just returned from Paris, where her fiance proposed under the Eiffel Tower. In the fifth season Katherine reveals that Dylan has married and the she and her husband, Bradley, have had a baby. Katherine briefly thinks of leaving Wisteria Lane because Dylan informs her that her husband travels frequently and that she could use help with the baby. It is learned that Dylan and her family live in Baltimore. Katherine eventually turns down the offer due to her budding romance with Mike Delfino.

She makes her return to Wisteria Lane when her mother intentionally stabs herself. Katherine claims that Mike was the one who stabbed her to get back at him for telling her he never loved her. When Susan tries to reason with Katherine she realizes that she needs serious mental help and upon learning that only a family member can commit someone to a mental institution, she calls Dylan, pretending to be a doctor, and tells her she should come to

Fairview. Dylan returns and when Susan tries to talk to her Dylan is increasingly hostile and mean towards Susan. However, this is due to the fact that Dylan was under the assumption that Mike was married to her mother and that Susan was the one who stabbed her mother. After Susan shows Dylan her wedding album, Dylan realizes that her mother has been lying to her and living in delusion. When she visits her at the hospital she catches her in her lies and tells her that she has spoken to Mike and tells her that she knows Mike and Susan are married. Upon learning this Katherine goes into a full blown meltdown and both Susan and Dylan watch as she is restrained. Katherine then looks at her daughter and repeats the phrase, "I asked you not to come" as she breaks down in tears. There is no mention of her husband or baby.

Wayne Davis

Wayne Davis (Gary Cole) was a police officer, Katherine's first husband, and the father of the "real" Dylan. It is shown in flashbacks that he beat his wife and also had a drinking problem, causing Katherine to leave him. He spent twelve years trying to track Katherine and his daughter down and discovered Katherine is back on Wisteria Lane. He wanted a relationship with his daughter, or who he thought to be his daughter, until Katherine informed him that Dylan is not his child. Upon hearing this, he had a blood test done at the hospital under the guise of it being a homicide. The test results come back concluding that he is not Dylan's father. He tries everything in his power to find out what actually happened to his daughter, even threatening to kill Katherine so she would tell him. He then held Katherine hostage along with her best friend, Bree Hodge, until Katherine finally told him the truth about what happened to his daughter. It turns out that she was accidentally killed by a fallen bookshelf after Katherine placed the doll that he had bought her on the top shelf. Katherine and her aunt buried her in her backyard so Wayne would not convince the police that she had killed her in order to keep her from him and have them both arrested for murder. After this, she went to a Romanian orphanage and found a girl who looked a lot like her recently deceased daughter. Katherine then adopted the young girl and changed her name to Dylan Mayfair, to cover up the real death of her daughter, Dylan Davis. When he found this out from Katherine, he was going to kill her, until Adam, came to her rescue. After a fight between the two ensues, Wayne winds up shooting himself in the abdomen. Then as Bree goes to clean Adam up, Katherine is left holding a gun to Wayne, who lays conscious on the floor. As he lays there he tells her that he'll do some time in jail but his buddies will help him get out and that he'll come after her again. After realizing the truth in his statements, Katherine shoots him in the chest, killing him instantly.

Lillian Simms

Lillian Simms (Ellen Geer) was Katherine's aunt – the elderly woman who owned the house on 4356 Wisteria Lane. After getting too ill to live there on her own she moved to a nursing home, but kept leasing the house in order to pay for her living arrangements. For the first three seasons of the show, Mike rented the house. When Mike moved out, Mrs. Simms was convinced by Edie not to let Carlos rent her house. When Katherine moved in in the season four premiere, Katherine claimed that she is back on Wisteria Lane in order to care for her aunt. In the episode "If There's Anything I Can't Stand", Lillian Simms comes to live in her home again to be cared for in her last days alive. Lillian arrived on a Saturday and the day she arrived she told Katherine that she had been feeling guilty and thought that Katherine and she should tell Dylan about what had happened twelve years earlier. Days later Lillian pretended to take a sleeping pill before Katherine left and then when she had thought that Katherine was gone she used the bell she was given to call Dylan to her room. When Dylan came into her room she tried to tell Dylan what happened and why Dylan did not remember living on Wisteria Lane twelve years ago. But Katherine arrived and sent Dylan away and then took the bell with her. Later that evening while Dylan was practicing her cello, Lillian wrote a note, folded it and died while dropping the note on the floor. Lillian was taken away in an ambulance and her note went unnoticed as Katherine closed her aunt's door.

Sylvia Greene

Sylvia Greene (Melora Walters) was a woman from Adam's past; when she shows up, Adam angrily tells her she already ruined his life once. It is later revealed that she was Adam's mistress in Chicago, and she was threatening Adam because he ended the affair, which led to an accusation of sexual assault. In the tornado episode, Bree invites her into her house and Sylvia locks herself in the bathroom where Bree, Orson and Benjamin are supposed to take shelter. They find a closet to stay in, where it is revealed that Adam did indeed sleep with Sylvia Greene. During the worst part of the tornado, Sylvia comes out of the room and begs Adam to come with her and love her. When Adam does nothing, she threatens to tell exactly what happened in Chicago. She was yelling "I'm leaving!!" at an attempt to get Adam to come out when the door swings open and the tornado sweeps her up. She is later found dead in a tree by Kayla Scavo, and is identified by Adam and Katherine.

Robin Gallagher

Robin Gallagher (Julie Benz) was a stripper at *Double D's*, a strip club left to Susan Mayer when her ex-husband, Karl Mayer, was killed in the plane crash. When Susan sells her half of the business she convinces Robin to leave stripping when she learns that she wants to be a teacher and has higher hopes and dreams. Susan manages to get Robin a job at her school but she is fired after it is revealed she used to be a stripper. Susan and Mike then invite Robin to stay with them. Robin accepts the offer but the other women of Wisteria Lane are less than pleased to have their husbands, boyfriends and sons leering at Robin. This causes them all to judge her prematurely, but they all later come around and see that Robin is genuinely a nice person and much more than a reformed stripper. Robin decides to become roommates with Katherine Mayfair, and the two become fast friends. After a night out together, Robin admits to being a lesbian and kisses Katherine. This confuses Katherine, but she ends up sleeping with her. Robin becomes frustrated as Katherine is unwilling to define their relationship, or show affection in front of the neighbors. Katherine admits that she cares too much about what other people think. Robin is afraid that Katherine is kicking her out, but instead Katherine suggests they go away together, so she can figure things out. Robin says "I've always wanted to go to Paris". They pack and leave that evening.

Acquaintances of Angie Bolen

The following characters are all family members and acquaintances of **Angie Bolen**, one of the protagonists of the series.

Nick Bolen

Nick Bolen (formerly Dominic) (Jeffrey Nordling) is the manipulative husband of new housewife Angie Bolen. He shares a past with one of the ladies of Wisteria Lane. It is revealed the woman he was involved with was Susan Delfino's daughter, Julie Mayer. When she dropped out of medical school and began waitress she was seeing a married man with the initial "D". Nick is revealed to be this man when he secretly visits her at the hospital. He then reveals that his real name is Dominic. It was revealed he is not Italian like his wife when she told Katherine Mayfair. Nick goes over to Susan's house because he is trying to get Julie back. Lynette came over to give Susan something and she overhears the altercation between Julie and Nick. After Nick leaves, Julie admits that Nick was the married man with whom she had the affair. Lynette goes over to tell Nick to stay away from Julie, but Nick threatens Lynette. It was revealed that his wife, Angie knew about his affair with Julie and punches him in the face, telling him that they're even now. At a coffee shop, he's friendly with a waitress before using a disposable cell phone to tell an agent that he "wants to come in" and wants to be sure "she" gets a free pass.

Danny Bolen

Danny Bolen (formerly Tyler) (Beau Mirchoff) is the tightly wound son of Angie and Nick Bolen. He is known to have dated Rosie and Tine. He appears to be somewhat disturbed. He comments that he did not want to move to Fairview, to which his mother replied "Oh, honey. Whose fault was that?" He has feelings for Julie Mayer, but is prone to random fits of anger around her. He was also seen saying to his father after Nick was chatting up some younger ladies "I know", which might mean he either knows that his father was dating Julie or that he strangled Julie and blamed Danny. Danny seems to share more of a connection with Angie than with Nick. When he asked Julie did she think the man she dated strangled her, she said no. Danny appeared doubtful over that and later gave her a gun. He then warned his dad if he ever saw Nick with Julie again, he would tell his mother about the affair. After Julie tells Danny she will never be with him, he attempts to commit suicide, but fails. Later at the hospital, he is being looked after by Nurse Mona Clark, who lives on Wisteria Lane. When Mona calls him by name, a dazed Danny says that his name is Tyler. He starts dating Ana, which concerns Angie, as she is afraid that Ana is going to break his heart someday. He goes to New York City to talk Ana about her supposed modelling job and reconects with his grandmother. It also reavealed that Patrick Logan is his biological father, but he does not know this and thinks of Nick as his real dad. However it is implied that Danny's inherited his father (Patrick's) violent and aggressive tendencies which Angie and Nick are trying to stamp out. In episode 6x13 Ana reveals to Angie that Danny has a passion for poetry and writing which came as a surprise to Angie. When he meets Patrick in 6x19 he reveals to Danny that he is writing a novel to which Danny thinks is "cool" and the two strike an instant bond over the subject. It is clear that Danny's inherited Patrick's love for writing. However Patrick is writing a novel about how he and Angie first met and their story but Danny thinks it is all fiction. Patrick asks Danny's advice as to how the story of their family should end to which Danny replies that the guy should kill the girl. Patrick smiles almost proudly and says that killing her was his first instinct too, which shows how alike they are in many ways. The next day Patrick visits Danny again who memorizes his drink and asks if he was sticking around to which Patrick replied that he's not going anywhere until he's finished his "book." Danny takes an interest to the plot and they talk about how it could end. Patrick basically tells Danny that it would be too easy to kill the girl (Angie) as he wants to get revenge on her for taking his kid. He reveals to Danny that he's going to take something from her to which Danny guesses "the kid" and seems excited by the idea, thinking it's all fiction and not knowing that it's him. In episode 6x21 Danny unknowingly reveals to Patrick that Nick will be out running later that night which makes it easier for Patrick to kill him, which he attempts to in a direct hit and run but Nick survives and ends up in hospital. He suspects instantly that Patrick Logan is in town and warns Angie that it's not safe and she should get Danny out of town. She gives Danny money to tide him over and tells him about Patrick Logan and the eco-terrorist group he started, but missing out the important fact of their relationship. Danny leaves against his will but Patrick breaks into his house when he's gone. He receives a text from Patrick pretending to be Angie and tells him to hurry home. He does so, much to the shock of his mother, late at night and she tells him to get out of the house, until Patrick turns on the light and says "what's the rush?" then points a gun straight at Danny. The three of them held in the same room together forces Angie to build Patrick his bomb. Meanwhile Patrick tells Danny the truth about his paternity and ties him up, calmly apologizes for doing so and reveals that he wants to have a traditional father, son relationship with him. Danny finds the whole thing half-funny, half-infuriating as he replies "are you serious?" Patrick and him both laugh before Patrick admits to how ridiculous he sounded and mentions that he'll untie him and they can get to know each other once he's finished doing something important. Danny furiously says "if you ever untie me I'll kill you!" to which Patrick dismisses as him being angry. He then tells him that he'll realize who he's really mad at. "The guy who spent 20 years looking for you, or the people who spent 20 years lying to you?" to which Danny realizes is true. His whole life is a lie. The end of episode 6x22 shows Patrick either untying or tying Danny, never taking his eyes off him while Danny tries not to cry. Danny is saved at the last minute by Gabrielle Solis while Angie kills Patrick with the bomb which was in the detonator. Later, while Angie and Nick relocate to Atlanta, Danny is seen relocating to New York to be with his grandmother and Ana Solis. During a tearful goodbye at the bus station Nick tells Danny he turned out a better man than he ever could have imagined. Danny responds by saying. "If I am, it's because you were my father." This signals he never wanted anything to do with Patrick and still thinks of Nick as his father.

Rose De Luca

Rose De Luca is Angie's mother who resides in New York. She has a strained relationship with her daughter, due to her being on the run.

Emily Portsmith

Emily Portsmith (Julie McNiven) was a waitress seen working at The Coffee Cup, a café in Fairview. She becomes acquainted with Nick Bolen, a regular customer. Emily is seen wiping bread crumbs from his shirt and is supposedly flirting with him several times. One night, after Nick leaves the coffee shop, Emily is left to close up the joint and when she prepares to go she is stopped by someone she knows, and who ends up strangling her, just like Julie was strangled. Emily is left for dead in the floor of the café. In the episode "Would I Think of Suicide?" Emily is found dead prompting people to take self-defense classes as the strangler might be out there.

Patrick Logan

Patrick Logan (John Barrowman) is the man Angie Bolen has been on the run from for nearly 20 years. It is revealed in "Chromolume No. 7", that he is Danny's real father. In "My Two Young Men", he killed Iris Beckley (Ellen Crawford), Rose's neighbor in order to cover up his tracks when she asked him about his intentions to find Angie. Patrick also told her calmly but firmly that Angie had taken something from him and he wants it back. It is implied that this something is Danny. He then stages a fake break in before apparently strangling Iris Beckley. The end of the episode shows Patrick watching Danny leave the house from his car and then we see him looking at the house, a mixture of anger, sadness and hate in his expression. Nick reveals in this episode that he, Rose, Patrick and Angie are the only ones who knew about Danny's true paternity. In "We All Deserve to Die", he meets his son Danny for the first time and asks him for inspiration for writing his novel and the two strike up an instant bond. It is clear that they both share a love for writing. He tells Danny the story of how he and his mother met and how she broke his heart, kidnapped his baby and ran off with another man to which Danny replies "damn, she sounds like a bitch!" Patrick then asks Danny for advice on how the "story" regarding their family should end. Danny ponders for a moment before replying that the guy should kill the girl to which Patrick wickedly replies "funny, that was my first instinct too," meaning that he wanted to see how his son's opinion should affect his actions on Angie. He then waits outside Angie's house late at night but doesn't do anything. The next day Patrick visits Danny again who memorizes his drink and asks if he was sticking around to which Patrick replied that he's not going anywhere until he's finished his "book." Danny takes an interest to the plot and they talk about how it could end. Patrick basically tells Danny that it would be too easy to kill the girl (Angie) as he wants to get revenge on her for taking his kid. He reveals to Danny that he's going to take something from her to which Danny guesses "the kid" and seems excited by the idea, thinking it's all fiction and not knowing that it's him. He runs over Nick Bolen to get Angie. He gets her to make another bomb by threatening to take Danny's life and when he handcuffs Angie to her bed. He takes her cellphone pretending to be her telling Danny to come back home. It dawns on Danny that he is Patrick's kid when Patrick holds a gun to and later ties him up saying when its over. Patrick wants him and Danny to have a traditional father and son relationship. Danny replies "Are you serious?", showing he wants nothing to do with him. But Patrick asks him to think about if he wants to live with someone who spent 20 years searching for him, or someone who spent 20 years lying to him. Patrick Logan is finally killed in "I Guess This is Goodbye" when Angie plants the bomb inside the detonator and Patrick activates the bomb without knowing he is going to commit suicide.

Acquaintances of Renee Perry

The following characters are all family members and acquaintances of **Renee Perry**, one of the protagonists of the series.

Doug Perry

Doug Perry (Reggie Austin) is the husband of Renee Perry. He is a Major League Baseball player from New York. Renee and Doug are currently divorced. One year later he got married with his mistress, Tina.

Ben Faulkner

Ben Faulkner (Charles Mesure). An Australian businessman new to the lane, he immediately becomes a target for Renee's affections. After a bit of resistance, he sees a part of Renee rarely seen by most and becomes quite fond of her. Meanwhile, he hires Mike Delfino for one of his construction projects, knowing of his criminal past. Later some of his workers discover Alejandro's body. When Bree tries to get him to re-bury the body he tells her he is going to turn the body over to the police, but later after witnessing Chuck Vance harass Bree, Ben comes to her rescue and scares Chuck away he then hires Mike to re-bury Alejandro's body.

Acquaintances of Karen McCluskey

The following characters are all family members and acquaintances of **Karen McCluskey**, one of the protagonists of the series.

Roberta Simmons

Roberta Simonds[5] (Lily Tomlin) is Karen McCluskey's older sister. She first appears in Season 5 when Karen is hospitalized due to Dave's plot to make her look crazy. Karen asks for Roberta's help in digging into Dave's past. Thanks to her job on a telephone company, Roberta found out that Dave was being contacted several times every month by Dr. Samuel Heller, a criminal psychiatrist. The two sisters travel back east to visit Heller, but they do not find him because at the time he had already been murdered by Dave. Roberta tells Karen she is tired of all the snooping around so she leaves her sister alone in her investigation. However, when Heller's receptionist learns he is dead, she calls Roberta to warn her about this, and the two sisters team up yet again, and break into Dave's house to get some evidence of what he's up to. Detectives Lyons and Collins find them in Dave's house (and it is implied at this time that Roberta does drugs), and bring them in for questioning, where everyone finally discovers that Dave must be after Susan and Mike for killing his previous family in an accident.

Roy Bender

Roy Bender (Orson Bean) is a retired steak salesman, who begins dating Karen at the start of the sixth season. Together they discover Julie Mayer after she is strangled. He and Karen later confess that they are in love with each other. Lynette later hires Roy as a handyman, at Karen's request. It is where Roy is revealed to be a little old fashioned when it comes to women and doesn't like that Lynette bosses Tom around and goes behind her back to get his approval on things. He and the Scavos later come to an understanding. He is present with Karen when the plane crashes on Wisteria Lane, both he and Karen manage to get out of harms way in time. He is also hired by Bree to watch Orson when she fears he will commit suicide. However instead of watching Orson, Roy leaves him in the laundry room, puts a broom through Orson's wheelchair spokes and goes to sleep. It is revealed in the seventh season (By Mary Alice's opening narration) that he and Karen have married.

Acquaintances of Mary Alice Young

The following characters are all family members and acquaintances of **Mary Alice Young**, the narrator of the series.

Zach Young

Zachary "Zach" Young, formerly **Dana Taylor** (Cody Kasch) is the "adopted" son of Paul and Mary Alice. Zach's birth parents are Deirdre Taylor and Mike Delfino and his paternal half-brother is M.J. Delfino. However, Zach's true identity is revealed in "One Wonderful Day", the final episode of the first season.

Zach went missing, after holding Susan hostage, until she saw him in a park. She bought him lunch and told him that she wanted to help until he said he hoped he and Julie would reconcile. Susan, visibly shaken by this, suggested he go to Utah and find Paul and gave him money to get there. Months later, after Felicia Tilman framed Paul Young for her murder, Paul begged Zach to ask his grandfather, Noah Taylor, for money to pay a lawyer, claiming it was for a car. Noah refused, telling Zach that he would not inherit his fortune because of Zach's supposed lack of bravery. Wanting to prove him wrong, Zach turned off Noah's respirator and found that he had inherited a vast fortune and no longer wanted anything to do with Paul Young. Zach moved to his grandfather's mansion.

Zach reappeared in "Not While I'm Around", as Gabrielle's secret admirer. Zach was semi-stalking Gabrielle Solis, sending her flowers, a dress and an expensive bracelet, revealing himself when she met him at a restaurant. Zach unsuccessfully tried to impress Gabrielle with luxurious gifts and his wealth, including a chateau in Switzerland. When Zach discovered Gabrielle was dating one of his employees, he made sure that he dumped Gabrielle, claiming she was too old. She was upset and got drunk. When she woke the next morning and found herself in bed with Zach. He claimed that they had sex and she couldn't remember. Zach used this to assume an escalation of their relationship. Gabrielle asked Carlos to scare Zach off but Carlos told her that Zach had such a large penis that she could not possibly forget sleeping with him. Gabrielle lectured Zach about how not to behave towards his friends and told him to leave her alone after he proposes to her at the Pizzeria. She told him that she didn't want a relationship with him so he left, after telling Gabrielle that when she's middle aged and alone, she will only have herself to blame.

In Season Seven, Zach made his first appearance since Season Three, in "Where Do I Belong", appearing as a delivery guy, delivering flowers to Bree. Later in the episode, a gun matching the one used to shoot Paul Young popped up on Bree's couch. As Paul hunts for Zach, he discovers that his son was overwhelmed by his wealth, losing himself to drugs and gambling and lost his fortune. He goes to Mike, asking for help finding Zach, revealing that he knows Zach shot him. It turns out Mike has been keeping tabs on Zach but the boy refuses to answer his phone. Mike confronts him at a motel and Zach admits shooting Paul. Mike is jarred at how Zach is strung out on drugs and goes to Paul, saying that whatever the man plans to do, it can't be worse than what Zach is doing to himself. The two men are seen at Zach's doorstep, ready to confront him.

Martha Huber

Martha Huber (Christine Estabrook) lived at 4350 Wisteria Lane. She first appeared in the pilot episode as a nosey neighbour who discovered Mary Alice Young's suicide. After hearing a loud sound from her kitchen, she went to the Young house on the pretence of returning a blender, and found Mary Alice dead.

When Edie's house burns down, Martha discovers a measuring cup that Edie said wasn't her in the ruins, making Martha curious. When she finds a new measuring cup in Susan's groceries, she realises that Susan burned Edie's house down. Martha, currently suffering financial difficulties, consequently blackmails Susan. Susan and her daughter, Julie, break into Martha's home to retrieve the cup and destroy it.

It is revealed that while on a visit to her sister, Martha discovered that Mary Alice's real name is Angela Forrest and that she stole a baby in Utah, moving to Wisteria Lane to escape her past. Martha decides to solve her financial difficulties by blackmailing Mary Alice by letter but Mary Alice commits suicide after receiving it. Mary Alice's friends find the note when packing up her belongings and give it to Paul. He hires a private eye/hit man to discover who was responsible and kill them. Paul discovers Edie has the same stationery but Edie stole it while living with Martha. Paul confronts Martha and she explains that she was desperate for money and Mary Alice killed herself because of "what she did to that poor baby", Zach Young, whose true identity is Dana Taylor. In a rage, Paul kills Martha by bludgeoning her with the blender and strangling her. He then buries her next to a forest hiking trail.

Martha Huber has made few appearances since season one. In season five, she appears gossiping to the residents of Wisteria Lane about finding Mary Alice Young's body. Martha was seen again in the season seven premiere episode "Remember Paul?" via flashbacks.[6]

It should be noted that twelve years after her murder, Paul finally confesses to the crime and is arrested. Her sister, Felicia, is presumably killed after driving into a semi-truck.

Felicia Tilman

Felicia Tilman (Harriet Sansom Harris) first arrives on Wisteria Lane in the eleventh episode of the first season to aid with the search for her sister Martha Huber, who has gone missing. However, as Felicia informs Edie Britt upon her arrival, she knows that her sister is dead and has come to Wisteria Lane to discover who is behind her sister's murder.

After finding and reading Martha's journals, Felicia discovered that Martha was blackmailing Paul and Mary Alice Young because they had bought a baby named Dana from drug addict Deirdre Taylor and then moved to Fairview and changed the baby's name to Zach Young. Incidentally, Martha found this out from Felicia, who had worked in the same rehab center as Mary Alice did back in Utah. Felicia then realized that it was Paul who had murdered her sister as he had obviously found out that Martha was blackmailing Mary Alice and wanted to avenge his wife's suicide. After revealing that she knows everything, Felicia tells Paul to leave town for good or she will expose Zach's true identity and the fact that he murdered Martha. Paul agrees to go but Felicia then informs him that Zach shall be staying with her from now on. Felicia then informs Zach that his father is not planning on coming back and that he shall be living with her. This then results in Zach attacking Felicia with a hockey stick which causes Felicia to fall down a flight of stairs, causing severe injury to her neck.

In season two, Felicia has been discharged from the hospital, but is still badly bruised and wearing a neck brace. Mike goes to visit Felicia to see if she knows where Zach is, as he has recently disappeared after failing to murder Mike. Felicia informs Mike that she does not know where Zach is and that she herself is going back to Utah for a few months to recuperate. Felicia then returns to Wisteria Lane a biological grandfather). Both Felicia and Mike comfort Zach after hearing the news that Paul has been killed, as Noah instructed Paul to be arrested and then killed in the back of an armored truck. However, Paul is revealed to be alive.

This results in Felicia planning her final act of revenge against Paul. After sneaking into his home through the backdoor, Felicia steals the spare key to Paul's house. Upon discovering her in his kitchen, Paul instructs Zach to throw out the food as Felicia may have tried to poison them both. Felicia then calls the police from her home and reports that Paul has been threatening her. Whilst phoning the police, she is in the process of pumping large quantities of her own blood from her body. The police inform Felicia that no action can be taken against Paul by just making threats, to which she replies that she will just have to deal with the problem herself. That following evening, Paul walks into his kitchen only to slip and discover blood on the floor and on the kitchen walls. The police quickly come upon the scene and place Paul in handcuffs when they discover two of Felicia's fingers in the trunk of his car. While Paul is escorted to prison, Felicia escapes to the mountains and retreats to a log cabin where she (with her hand heavily bandaged and missing two fingers) checks in under the alias of her dead sister "Mrs.Huber". A flashback in the seventh season reveals that Karen McClusky knew all along Felicia had faked her death and kept it quiet.

Felicia Tilman returns in the seventh season premiere episode "Remember Paul?" It emerges that Felicia has been pulled over for speeding and was arrested for having no identification, prompting Paul to be freed. Felicia is sent to prison for eighteen months, where she is visited by Paul Young, who gloats that she is now in prison and he is now free. When Felicia accuses him of murdering her sister, he hangs up the phone, and through the plexiglass, admits that he did, much to her surprise.. Back in prison, Felicia sticks up a newspaper cutting of Paul in her prison cell. Her roommate claims that he looks like a killer and says it is a shame he was released. "It's all for the best," Felicia replies. "Paul can receive the punishment he's entitled to. Just between us, Paul will be dead within six months." When her roommate asks how that's possible, she replies: "Paul Young doesn't have friends on that street. I do."

In "A Humiliating Business", it is revealed that Paul's new wife Beth Young is actually Felicia's daughter, when Beth visits her in prison. Felicia appears again in the following episode "Sorry Grateful", In which she is disgusted to learn that Beth slept with Paul Young, in order to gain his trust. However, she instructs Beth to use it to her advantage, in order to gain proof that Paul did, in fact, murder her sister, Martha Huber. When Beth visits her again she tells her that she hasn't gained any evidence of Paul's misdeeds, but rather doubts her mother's mental stability, Felicia flys into an uncontrollable rage after learning that Beth is beginning to develop feelings for Paul, when she refuses to leave his house. Through Mary Alice's voice-over, we also learn that Felicia will not hesitate to punish both Beth and Paul, if Beth is 'stupid enough' to fall in love with him. It is also revealed in "Sorry Grateful" that Felicia's husband left her and Beth, when Beth was at an early age. Since then, contrary to tradition on Thanksgiving, Felicia and Beth never shared a meal with anyone, let alone each other. The reason being that Felicia felt there was nothing to be thankful for, and refused to allow a male classmate of Beth's into the house. In Assassins, Beth questions Felicia to know if she had anything to do with Paul being shot. Felicia denies but secretly calls Mike, assuming he accepted an offer she made to take care of Paul. Meeting her at the prison, Mike tells Felicia he had nothing to do with it, making her wonder who could have been the shooter. When Paul confronts Beth and kicks her out of the house, revealing he did murder Martha, Beth goes to Felicia to talk about it. However, Felicia dismisses Beth as being a fool for not getting the confession on tape, dismisses her as useless and tells the guards to remove her daughter from the visitor list.

When Beth shoots herself, Felicia has Paul visit her in prison, grief-stricken that the war between them has claimed her daughter's life. She says it's time for Paul to let Beth go and for both of them to put the fight behind them. At the end of the episode, Felicia is told that because of her personal tragedy, the parole board has granted her a release. Felicia smiles secretly, hinting that she plans to use her freedom to get at Paul. It turns out that Paul had put Katherine Mayfair's old house in Beth's name when he purchased it, and thus Felicia inherits it upon her release. She talks Paul into taking her out to a lake to scatter Beth's ashes. Paul brings a gun for protection but Felicia manages to get it away from him and holds it on him, saying she could shoot him and plead self-defense. Instead, she throws the gun in the lake and tells Paul it's time to let the hate go. They scatter the ashes and then leave. However, at her new home, it's revealed Felicia kept the real ashes and tells Beth's real ashes that she'll take revenge on Paul in a much more satisfying way than just shooting him. She tells Karen McCluskey that Paul knew who Beth was all along and seduced her to get at Felicia, driving her to suicide. Convinced, Karen tells Felicia she'll help her keep an eye on Paul.

When Felicia begins to poison Paul's food (by sabotaging meals that Susan has been cooking for him), Paul suspects that Susan is trying to kill him and has her arrested, but when the police suspect that Felicia was the culprit afterall, they contact her to come to the police station for questioning. This causes Felicia to flee from Wisteria Lane. After Paul is convinced of Susan's innocence, he decides to move out of the lane and give Susan her house back. However, as he is about to leave, he is knocked unconscious by Felicia. When Paul awakens that night, Felicia has bound him to a chair and hooked him to an antifreeze drip which slowly weakens and poisons him; although Felicia has an extra syringe filled with potassium chloride that she will plunge into Paul's chest if he tries to yell for help, which will kill him instantly. However, Susan comes by the house and discovers Paul being tortured. She calls the police and distracts Felicia by using a toy police car and activating its siren, tricking Felicia into thinking that the police were coming for her. As Felicia briefly flees, Susan helps cut away some of Paul's bindings, but when Felicia realises that she's been tricked, she returns and attacks Susan, attempting to kill her with the potassium chloride syringe. Paul, finally breaking free, quickly pushes Felicia of Susan and into the wall, where he begins to strangle her; a scene eerily similar to Martha's death. However, Susan manages to convince Paul that he's not a killer and Paul finally lets

Felicia go. Felicia then escapes the house with her daughter's ashes avoiding capture from the police.

While driving down the highway the next morning, Beth's ashes spill and cause Felicia to lose control of her car. She is last seen about to crash head-on with a semi-truck, and is presumed to have died in the collision.

Beth Young

Beth Young (née **Tilman**; Emily Bergl) was Paul Young's second wife introduced in "You Must Meet My Wife". Beth met Paul while writing to him in prison where he was serving time for the apparent murder of Felicia Tilman. She arrives on Wisteria Lane distressed and lost, looking for Paul. Paul tells her that the letters she wrote to him kept him going and since he was not allowed conjugal visits, this is like their wedding night. However Beth did not want to rush into sex. Paul doesn't listen and later that night he brings her a gift that is wrapped away in a shopping bag. Beth is shocked that it is lingerie and she says to him that she thought they were going to take it slowly. Paul gets her to read a letter she wrote to him, but Beth gets wound-up and said it was just fantasy. She then blurts out 'I thought you would stay in prison. Paul is instantly made upset by this remark. Paul kisses her on the head and tells her that he will not be patient forever.

In "Truly Content" Susan, Lynette and Bree show up at Beth and Paul Young's house. They invite Beth to their weekly poker game. Paul asks her what Susan, Lynette and Bree wanted. Beth replies saying that they invited her to play cards with them, and that they were just being friendly, Paul says to Beth to never confuse being nosey to being friendly, saying that they were digging for dirt. Beth asks Paul if he does not want her to go, to which he replies that she will go and hopefully later they will start to become friends. He adds that it will be useful in time.

During a poker game, Beth talks to the other five housewives about her life when she was younger. Beth says that when she was eight her father left her mother, and that they were pretty much alone, saying that most of her friends were either stuffed or plastic. Then Beth talk about her mothers boyfriends, but says that as soon as she learned their names that her mother would kick them out, and that there would be a new toothbrush in the bathroom. When everyone looks at her strangely and puzzled Beth asks to let her know if she is sharing too much, which causes Susan to say no, but whisper to Lynette, who is sitting next to her saying that Beth is cracking like an egg. Beth later says that she saw Paul's picture at trial, and that there was just something about his eyes that she really liked and spoke to her. Susan asks if the headline "Arrested For Murder" did not speak to Beth, which she admits gave her a pause but that then Beth and Paul started corresponding while he was in jail behind bars, and that she discovered what a wonderful man Paul really is, which gives everyone the shivers. Beth tells Renee that you cannot help who you fall in love with, and jokes that Paul is a real lady killer. They all stare at her as if she is crazy. Beth says that in her heart she always knew that Paul was innocent, and that she was correct for thinking that.

Beth asks Karen McCluskey why she does not like her husband, Paul. Mrs. McCluskey says that people think he is a murderer. Beth says that he was exonerated and that Felicia Tillman framed him, and Karen McCluskey reveals that everyone's blaming Paul for the murder of Felicia's sister, Martha Huber.

Beth tells Paul she had a lovely time at the poker game. He asks what the neighborhood is saying about him. Beth says, that a bunch of people think that he killed Martha Huber. Paul tells her that she should know that he is not a murderer. Beth tells him that she knows, but that she fell in love with him before she knew that, and that even if he was that she is always going to be on his side, she also tells him that no matter if he is innocent or not, she would still love him, and that he should remember that. When Beth refuses to sleep with Paul, she eventually reveals she is a virgin and her continuing refusal makes her demand she leave him. When Susan discovers Paul got her fired from her job as a teacher, she attacks him in his home and Beth pulls a gun on her to make her leave. Realizing how his wife aided him, Paul kisses her and they end up in bed.

Beth is worried about Paul's plans for Wisteria Lane. When his former cellmate moves into the neighborhood, Beth threatens to tell people he attacked her unless he tells her Paul's plans. She meets Paul at home in sexy underwear, revealing what she knows but she supports him, saying she knows all about revenge. It is soon revealed that Beth is actually Felicia Tilman's daughter, aiding her mother in revenge on Paul. After she and Paul sleep together, Beth questions her mother's sanity and if she knew for certain Paul killed her sister, the two women have a fight, Beth leaves. When Paul is shot later in the season, Beth returns to jail, convinced her mother had something to do with it but Felicia is honestly surprised to hear it happened. Unknown to Beth, the detectives investigating the shooting told Paul how she was Felicia's daughter, making him realize how she has been using him all along. While Paul develops hatred for Beth, Beth falls in love with Paul, and has turned against Felicia to support Paul. After a confrontation with Zach, Paul realizes that "no one can ever love him" and decides to kick Beth out of the house. Beth confesses her love to Paul but he remembers what Zach told him, and doesn't listen to her, he closes the door on her face, leaving her with nowhere to go. Beth tries to get back with Paul, telling him how she believed her mother's claims of Paul killing her aunt but now that she knows him, doesn't believe it. She's thus shocked when Paul confesses to having killed Martha after all. Beth goes to see Felicia in prison where her mother berates her for being so stupid as to not get the confession on tape and that Beth is useless to her, telling the guards to remove her daughter from the visitor list. Bree comes to Beth's motel to reveal they're both a match to be a kidney donor for Susan but Bree wants to do it in order to feel needed. With nothing else left in her life, Beth goes to the hospital and makes sure the nurse in the waiting room files the paperwork ensuring her kidney will go to Susan. Beth then pulls a gun out of her purse and shoots herself in the head, leaving her brain dead.

Told of Beth's shooting, Susan and the other women are thrown as Beth is on life support, declared brain dead. Paul is shown to be affected by all this, telling Susan that he will not let Beth go and won't allow her to take his wife's kidney. Felicia meets Paul in prison, saying that their battle cost them Beth's life and she truly loved Paul. In the end, Paul decides to let Susan have the kidney and mourns his wife. Felicia Tilman, Beth's mother, is released from prison at the end of the episode, and decides to get revenge on Paul for murdering Martha, and for the death of her daughter.

Jerry Shaw

Jerry Shaw (Richard Roundtree) is private investigator and hitman of Fairview. Mr. Shaw first appears in "Who's That Woman?" where Paul hires him to find out who sent Mary Alice the blackmail note. He appears again in the episode "Anything You Can Do" after Paul finds out that Edie used the same type of stationery that the blackmail note was written on. Jerry Shaw tracks down Edie at the same Saddle Ranch Bar Deirdre was last seen before she proceeded to the Young residence only to find a watery grave. Edie traveled there with Susan who both teamed up to spy on Kendra and Mike. He confronts Edie, masquerading as a partner in real estate and makes a smooth deal with her. In the next episode, "Guilty", Mr. Shaw confronts Edie at an abandoned site in the middle of a rural highway. He finds out that the paper came from Martha Huber just before he was about to shoot her. Shaw then proceeds to tell Paul that Mrs. Huber was the writer of the note. Paul decides to take it upon himself to kill Mary Alice's blackmailer. Jerry Shaw disappears until the twentieth episode, when Susan hires Mr. Shaw himself, of all PIs, to investigate the Young Family after Zach set fire to her kitchen. His last appearance being in the episode "Sunday in the Park with George", where he delivers falsified information regarding the Young family. Susan finally asks him to run a complete background check on Mike Delfino. Susan finds out that Mike had killed a cop, and sees Noah and Kendra in a photo, recognizing Kendra instantly setting her straight to getting back with Mike.

Other characters

Ida Greenberg

Ida Greenberg (Pat Crawford Brown) was a neighbor on Wisteria Lane, who was close friends with Karen McCluskey. She first appeared in the episode, "Come In, Stranger", as a neighbor at the watch-meeting complaining that somebody was watching her whenever she took a shower. In season two, we discover that Ida has a drinking problem. But that ends because, when she asks for God to end her alcoholism, her bottle is shot due to an event taking place at Mike's house, and she quits. In the same episode, it is also revealed that Ida attends a Methodist church. When Mike awakes from his coma, Ida's nephew, Dr. Lee Craig, tells her about this, and she starts spreading the news around Wisteria Lane. Also, when she planned to go on a trip somewhere, in episode 3.06, Susan steals her cab. In season four, Ida has gotten back to drinking.[7] When a neighborhood meeting is done for elections of the street president, Ida objects against the gay neighbors, not because of their fountain, but because they're gay.[8] During the tornado warning, she takes cover in Mrs. McCluskey's basement with the Scavos, and the house is destroyed due to the tornado.[7] It is soon confirmed she has died, sacrificing herself to save Lynette's children and husband. After her death, we learn that Ida was a professional baseball player during World War II. Her ashes are scattered by Lynette and Mrs. McCluskey at a baseball field where she had her glory days.[9]

Alberta Fromme

Alberta Fromme (Betty Murphy) lives on a street neighboring Wisteria Lane. It hasn't been determined on which address. Mrs. Fromme is a single woman. It is unknown whether she has been divorced or widowed. Alberta owns a cat, Mr. Whiskers who always needs to be watched when she goes out of town. Therefore she must rely on her neighbor friends to take responsibility. When Susan watches Mr. Whiskers, Alberta's house is broken into by Mike; however, the cat was unharmed. Alberta continues to be a recurring character who is mostly seen during neighborhood gatherings and when one of the housewives needs something or vice versa. Alberta hasn't been seen since season three, indicating that over the years she has moved or died.

Edwin Mullins

Edwin Mullins (Cheyenne Wilbur) and his wife lived at 4351 Wisteria Lane. Mr Mullins was a taxidermist, and kept a lot of stuffed animals in his home, as revealed by Susan, who also states that he often invites people in, and then introduces them to all his "pets". They also had a problem with teenagers spreading toilet paper across their yard, and kept a spare key to Mrs. McCluskey's house. They also trusted Bree by giving her a key to their home. They left Wisteria Lane because of all the action happening there: murder, suicide, blackmail, violence, and arson. It was never determined where they went. Mr. Mullins's brother was Susan's divorce attorney.

Art Shepherd

Arthur "Art" Shepherd (Matt Roth) and his ill sister Rebecca lived at 4352 Wisteria Lane. He moved to Wisteria Lane in season three, and was introduced in the episode "Bang", where he saves Lynette from being killed by Carolyn Bigsby during the supermarket hostage situation. By doing so he became a hero of Parker's. However, while bringing over a cake to Art, Lynette found his basement full of toys, and filled from floor to ceiling with polaroids of half-naked boys. When confronted, he claims they are photos of past students, as he is a swim coach. Convinced that Art was a pedophile, she asked Karen McCluskey for advice and soon there were massive demonstrations outside the Shepherd's house. After Rebecca died, Lynette came to rethink what she had seen, and begged for Art's forgiveness. He responded by saying that he never acted on his feelings because of his sister, but now he was free of those restrictions. He then ominously stated that he's going to be moving to a new neighborhood.

Rebecca Shepherd

Rebecca Shepherd (Jennifer Dundas) was Art's wheelchair bound sister whom Art cared for at their home. When the accusations towards Art grew stronger, Rebecca came to her brother's defense, claiming that his love for boys was completely pure, only being that of a swimming coach's pride of his students. While the protests were going on, Rebecca died of cardiac arrest.

Eli Scruggs

Eli Scruggs (Beau Bridges) was the neighborhood handyman who had been described as quiet, helpful, and tidy. He is the central focus in the series' 100th episode, "The Best Thing That Ever Could Have Happened", which is also his only appearance in the series. Eli first appeared on Wisteria Lane while looking for work. Out of sympathy, Mary Alice asks him to fix her broken vase and then suggests him to other neighbors on the lane. About two years later, Mary Alice gives Eli the vase he fixed and asks him to leave. Shortly after, she kills herself. Eli also witnesses Rex Van de Kamp telling Bree that she could not possibly live out her dream by writing her own cookbook. When Bree throws a collection of recipes and ideas for her book in the garbage, Eli retrieves them without her knowledge. Following Rex's death, he gives them back and tells her he enjoyed some of her recipes. This is presumably what leads Bree to published her own cookbook in between seasons four and five. When Gabrielle moves onto Wisteria Lane, Eli overhears her complaining about how bored she is and offers to get her into the neighborhood poker game with Susan, Lynette, Bree, and Mary Alice. Gabrielle agrees, but she comes off as a "rude, obnoxious bitch" during the game and the women do not invite her to any further games. With Eli's advice, Gabrielle shows up unannounced at one of the games and explains that her behavior stems from her loneliness and that she misses her life in the city. Seeing the raw, sincere emotion, the women invite Gabrielle to the poker game. Eli also had a sexual encounter with Edie while she was drunk and divorcing her gay second husband. Eli also saves an infant Penny Scavo when Lynette accidentally leaves her in the car. This allows Lynette to reevaluate the balance between her work life and home life. When Susan is divorcing Karl, she asks Eli to change her locks. She asks him to do the same following her divorce from Mike.

After over a decade of working on Wisteria Lane, Eli decides to retire. His last job is repairing Susan's roof. However, during the job, he suffers a heart attack and dies. His body is discovered by Juanita Solis. All the ladies, Gabrielle, Edie, Bree, Lynette and Susan, all reflect on how Eli had helped them get where they are today. Eli is buried on a Saturday. Bree fixes a flower which had come loose on his coffin, she says she wanted to fix something for Eli for a change. A voiceover of Mary Alice then reveals that in a place reserved for only the very best of people, Eli smiled and said "Thank you".

Eddie Orlofsky

Eddie Orlofsky (Josh Zuckerman) is a friend of Danny's, one of the few that remained friends with him even when Danny was being accused of assaulting Julie. Eddie was first seen when he came over to the Bolen house to ask his buddy Danny to help fix his car. Eddie is shown working at The Coffee Cup, a local café where Emily Portsmith, a waitress, becomes the second known victim of the Fairview strangler. Eddie mentions that he was glad he was late to work, because he doesn't think he could have handled discovering Emily's body. Eddie invites Julie and Danny to watch him do stand up comedy at a local club. Julie doesn't want to go but Ana wants to date Danny and convinces Julie to take her to Eddie's act so she can get closer to Danny. Eddie picks up Irina after she is dumped by Preston Scavo on their wedding night. After hitting on her she tells him she is way out of his league and says that she did not come all the way to America to hook up with a greasy haired boy. Angry and obviously hurt by the comments, he pulls the car to the side of the road. He is then seen lunging for her throat. He is then seen digging a hole in the woods next to Irina's dead body. In the April 2010 episode, "Epiphany", Eddie's past relationship to the women on Wisteria Lane is explained and why he strangles and kills women. He was always rejected by the women he was attracted to, and developed strong hatred towards the women who rejected him. Since he was a child, Eddie has had a friendly relationship with the women on Wisteria Lane. For example: Susan paid for him to attend an artist's seminar to encourage his artistic ability; Gaby let him unpack boxes in her house when she first moved in; Bree gave him some love advice, unaware his affections would be towards her daughter Danielle; Lynette tried to include him in the Scavo family's game night to help him fit in. Eddie had such a desperately lonely childhood because his mother Barbara (played by Diane Farr) was abandoned by his father when he was four years old, claiming he never wanted children. Barbara becomes an alcoholic and also claims that she never loved or wanted him. When she discovers that he had strangled a teenager, she tries to call the police. In a rage, Eddie strangles Barbara to death, and minutes later, Lynette invites him to move in to her house, which he tearfully accepts. Lynette realizes he's the Fairview strangler when she sees a remorse face and can't look her in the eyes when she tells him about the police finding his mother in the woods. He locks Lynette in his childhood home. In the season finale, Eddie holds the fate of Lynette and her unborn child in his hands. In the end he has Lynette call police and he turns himself in, thanks in part to Lynette stepping in and saying she believes in him.

Mona Clarke

Mona Clarke (**Maria Cominis**) was a wife and mother that lived on Wisteria Lane. She was a registered nurse who worked at Fairview Hospital. Mona had a reputation for having a big mouth. On different occasions she has been shown to annoy Lynette, Gabrielle, and Edie. Susan and Mike did not invite her to their wedding, unlike most the other residents of Wisteria Lane.

While caring for Danny Bolen after his attempted suicide, he awakes, and Mona calls him Danny, to which he replies that his real name is actually Tyler. Mona figures out what she believes happened to the Bolens, and tells them she understands their situation and won't tell anyone about it, offering to be a confidante to Danny should he need to talk about it. However, her attitude changes once Danny tells her the actual story, and Mona blackmails the Bolens, asking for $67,000 so she can start a new life at a new job. Shortly after a heated confrontation with Angie at a Christmas block party, Mona is struck by the wing of a crashing airplane. In the following episode it is revealed that Mona has fallen into a coma and Angie and Nick are hoping she dies. Finally Mona succumbs to her injuries and dies.

Detective Lyons

Detective Lyons (**Billy Mayo**) is a detective for the Fairview Police Department. He is involved in many of Fairview's crimes and mysteries, and is often seen on Wisteria Lane. He investigated the disappearance of Victor Lang as well as the suspected arson of Warren Shilling's nightclub.

Mitzi Kinsky

Mitzi Kinsky (**Mindy Sterling**) is a resident on Wisteria Lane living at 4347, the house formerly owned by Ida Greenberg. She has a reputation in the neighborhood of being a bitter, cynical and shrewd widow. She is first seen in "The Glamorous Life", where she is seen having two disputes with Angie Bolen. She is later seen in the season six finale "I Guess This is Goodbye", this time arguing with both Susan and Karen. She reappeared in season seven's "Pleasant Little Kingdom" where Paul Young considers buying her house. Mitzi considers selling but decides she will not screw over her friends. She stays on Wisteria Lane. Weeks later, Bree asks if Mitzi would be a possible kidney donor for Susan, but Mitzi slams the door in her face. Later on, Mitzi finally gives in and gets herself tested; however she is not a match for Susan.

Animals

Bongo

Bongo is a dog who once belonged to Mike Delfino. He first appeared in the pilot. When Susan Mayer is competing for Mike's affections against Edie Britt in season one, she uses Bongo to impress him. However, Bongo eats one of Susan's earrings and has to go to the vet. Mike explains that Bongo is very important to him because he belonged to his late wife. In the second season premiere, Bongo attacks Susan while she is holding a gun to Zach Young because he thinks she is putting Mike in danger. Bongo is last seen in "The Sun Won't Set", when he takes down Caleb Applewhite during a neighborhood search for the man who attacked Gabrielle Solis. No explanation for Bongo's absence has been given in the series. However, Marc Cherry has explained that he was either given away or died after Mike fell into a coma, noting that Bongo was cut from the series because of story complications and budget reductions.[10]

Rafael

Rafael is the dog of Bob and Lee. In one episode, Susan locked him in her garage in attempt to befriend Lee. However, the dog ran out revealing her secret, leaving yellow footprints behind.

Toby

Toby the cat was the previous pet and companion of Ida Greenberg until her death in Something's Coming. After this he is taken into the care of Karen McCluskey. He is still currently in her care after five and a half years. In season five, Toby was kidnapped by Dave Williams after Karen refused to apologize to Edie Britt. Once she did, however, he returned to her care and stayed there for the rest of the season and has not been seen since.

Roxy

Roxy was the previous guide dog (Golden Retriever) to Carlos Solis when he was blind. She joined the family near the end of season four and had a rivalry with Gabrielle Solis which caused her to kidnap her and send her back to the school, however Roxy just followed the car back and remained in the house. In the season 4 finale, Roxy attacks Ellie while she and Gaby struggle over the duffle bag of money, prompting Ellie to flee the house and run to the Mayfair's, inadvertently walking in on Wayne holding Katherine hostage. Carlos regained his sight in season five and Roxy has not made any appearances since then.

Mr. Whiskers

Mr. Whiskers was the cat owned by Alberta Fromme. She was once taken care of by Susan Mayer.

The Scavo Dog

The unnamed dog was bought by Lynette Scavo as a distraction after her son, Parker Scavo started to have an interest in sex. The dog hasn't been seen since season three, but has been talked about up until late season 4.

References

[1] Desperate Housewives Episode 4x01: Now You Know
[2] Desperate Housewives Episode 4x03: The Game
[3] Desperate Housewives Episode 4x09: Something is Coming
[4] Desperate Housewives Episode 4x10: Welcome to Kanagawa
[5] Desperate Housewives Season 5 episode 23, *Everybody Says Don't*
[6] http://www.abcmedianet.com/web/dnr/dispDNR.aspx?id=090310_10
[7] Desperate Housewives Episode 4.09 Something's Coming
[8] Desperate Housewives Episode 4.05 Art Isn't Easy

[9] Desperate Housewives Episode 4.10 Welcome to Kanagawa
[10] 'Desperate Housewives': 'The truth about my gals in the suburbs' (http://weblogs.variety.com/season_pass/2008/09/desperate-hou-1. html) *Variety*. Retrieved on 2009-07-28.

Dr. Horrible's Sing-Along Blog

Dr. Horrible's Sing-Along Blog	
Promotional image	
Genre	Musical Tragicomedy Neo-Noir
Creator	Joss Whedon Jed Whedon Zack Whedon Maurissa Tancharoen
Directed by	Joss Whedon
Produced by	David M. Burns Michael Boretz
Written by	Joss Whedon Jed Whedon Zack Whedon Maurissa Tancharoen
Starring	Neil Patrick Harris Felicia Day Nathan Fillion Simon Helberg
Music by	Joss Whedon Jed Whedon
Editing by	Lisa Lassek
Country	United States
Language	English
Original run	July 15, 2008 – July 20, 2008
Running time	42 minutes
No. of episodes	3

Dr. Horrible's Sing-Along Blog is a 2008 musical tragicomedy miniseries in three acts, produced exclusively for Internet distribution. Filmed and set in Los Angeles, the show tells the story of Dr. Horrible (played by Neil Patrick Harris), an aspiring supervillain; Captain Hammer (Nathan Fillion), his nemesis; and Penny (Felicia Day), their shared love interest.

The movie was written by writer/director Joss Whedon, his brothers Zack Whedon (a television writer) and Jed Whedon (a composer), and Jed's wife, actress Maurissa Tancharoen. The team wrote the musical during the 2007–2008 Writers Guild of America strike. The idea was to create something small and inexpensive, yet professionally done, in a way that would circumvent the issues that were being protested during the strike.[1][2] On October 31, 2008, *Time* magazine named it #15 in *Time*'s Top 50 Inventions of 2008.[3][4] It also won the People's Choice Award for "Favorite Online Sensation", and the 2009 Hugo Award for Best Dramatic Presentation, Short

Form.[5] In the inaugural 2009 Streamy Awards for web television, *Dr. Horrible* won seven awards: Audience Choice Award for Best Web Series, Best Directing for a Comedy Web Series, Best Writing for a Comedy Web Series, Best Male Actor in a Comedy Web Series (Harris), Best Editing, Best Cinematography, and Best Original Music.[6] It also won a 2009 Creative Arts Emmy Award for Outstanding Special Class – Short-format Live-Action Entertainment Programs.[7] [8]

Plot

Dr. Horrible's Sing-Along Blog consists of three acts of approximately 14 minutes each. They were first released online in July 2008 as individual episodes, with two-day intervals between each release.

Act I

Dr. Horrible is filming an entry for his video blog, giving updates on his schemes and responding to various emails from his viewers. Asked about the "her" that he often mentions, he launches into a song about Penny, the girl he likes from the laundromat ("My Freeze Ray").

The song is cut short by his "evil moisture buddy" Moist, who brings up a letter from Bad Horse, the leader of the Evil League of Evil. The letter informs Dr. Horrible that his application for entry into the League will be evaluated, and that they will be watching for his next heinous crime ("Bad Horse Chorus").

The following day, Horrible prepares to steal a case of wonderflonium for his time-stopping Freeze Ray by commandeering the courier van using a remote control device. Penny happens to be on the same street ("Caring Hands"), and appears asking him to sign a petition to turn a condemned city building into a homeless shelter. However, the remote requires his attention, and he appears uninterested in her and her cause. As Penny leaves, Horrible is conflicted, but opts to steal the wonderflonium, telling himself that 'A man's gotta do what a man's gotta do' ("A Man's Gotta Do").

When Horrible remotely drives the van away, Captain Hammer appears and takes over Horrible's song, smashing the remote control receiver and inadvertently causing the van to veer towards Penny. Hammer pushes her out of the way (into a pile of garbage) just as Horrible regains control of the van and stops it, making it appear that Captain Hammer stopped the van with his bare hands. The two confront each other, with Hammer slamming Horrible's head on the van's hood, but Penny emerges to thank Hammer, making him forget about beating up Dr. Horrible. As Hammer and Penny serenade each other, Horrible makes off with the wonderflonium.

Act II

Dr. Horrible stalks Penny and Captain Hammer on their dates; Horrible sings of the misery of the human condition, and Penny sings of hope and the possibility of redemption ("My Eyes"). Penny and Horrible, known to her as Billy, begin to talk openly as friends.

On his blog, Horrible reveals that his Freeze Ray has been completed, and that he plans to use it the next day. The following post reveals that he has failed, as Hammer and the LAPD watch his blog, and they were ready for him. He then receives a phone call from Bad Horse and is reprimanded, saying that the only way to be inducted now is to commit an assassination ("Bad Horse Chorus (Reprise)"). Horrible is conflicted and can't decide on a victim, or even if he wants to commit a murder at all, even though the League will deny his application or even kill him, if he doesn't.

Billy chats with Penny over frozen yogurt, at the laundromat, about his problems ("Penny's Song"). As they grow closer, Penny mentions that Captain Hammer is planning to drop by. Billy panics and tries to leave, only to run into Hammer as he walks in. They feign ignorance on recognizing each other, but when Penny leaves them alone, Hammer taunts Horrible about his crush on Penny, happy to be taking the thing that Dr. Horrible wants most. It becomes obvious that Hammer doesn't really care about Penny but just wants to sleep with her to spite Horrible.

Horrible decides to kill Hammer as his heinous crime for admission to Bad Horse's Evil League of Evil ("Brand New Day").

Act III

The city is abuzz with Captain Hammer's crusade to help the homeless and he is considered the city's new hero; Penny ponders her relationship with Captain Hammer, waiting at the laundromat to share frozen yogurt with an absent Billy; and Dr. Horrible goes into seclusion while obsessively constructing a Death Ray to kill Captain Hammer once and for all ("So They Say").

At the opening for the new homeless shelter, where a statue of Captain Hammer will be unveiled, Captain Hammer begins a speech of encouragement to the homeless, but it degenerates into selfish, condescending praise of his own excellence and relationship with Penny ("Everyone's a Hero"). Penny, embarrassed and disillusioned, quietly tries to leave as the crowd joins in singing Hammer's song, but they are interrupted by the appearance of Dr. Horrible, who uses the Freeze Ray on Captain Hammer, cutting his song short. Dr. Horrible taunts the shocked crowd and declares that they cannot recognize that Hammer's disguise is "slipping", and he reveals a second, more lethal laser gun: his completed Death Ray ("Slipping").

At last, Horrible aims the lethal weapon at the frozen form of Captain Hammer, but hesitates. At that moment the Freeze Ray unexpectedly fails, and a suddenly revived Hammer punches Horrible across the room. The Death Ray falls from his hands, damaging it. Hammer then picks up the Death Ray, turns it on Horrible, and triumphantly completes the final note of his prior song. However, ignoring Dr. Horrible's warnings, Hammer pulls the trigger and the damaged Death Ray misfires. The weapon explodes in Hammer's hands, injuring him and causing him to feel pain, apparently for the first time in his life. He flees, a wailing wreck, asking for "someone maternal." Dr. Horrible realizes suddenly that he has succeeded in vanquishing his nemesis, but still having not committed the murder required by the League. Unfortunately, he discovers Penny slumped against a wall, gored by shrapnel from the exploding gun. Tragically, she dies in Horrible's arms, deliriously reassuring him that Captain Hammer will save them.

Dr. Horrible declares Pyrrhic victory, with "the world [he] wanted, at [his] feet," seeing that her death is ironically the murder he required. In the aftermath, Horrible gains infamy and is free to commit additional crimes unfettered by Captain Hammer. Horrible becomes a member of the League, striding into a party in celebration of his induction, attended by Moist and the villains Pink Pummeller and Purple Pimp. Captain Hammer is seen on a psychiatric couch sobbing to his therapist. Dr. Horrible, donning a new outfit – red coat, black gloves and his goggles covering his eyes – takes his seat at the League, composed of Tie-Die, Snake Bite, Professor Normal, Dead Bowie, Fake Thomas Jefferson, Fury Leika, and Bad Horse (an actual horse). He addresses the camera, saying, "now the nightmare's real," and in working "to make the whole world kneel," that "[He] won't feel...". He completes the line "...a thing," in a final blog post as a numb-looking Billy, out of costume and looking lost in the midst of his lab. ("Everything You Ever")

Soundtrack

The musical contains 14 songs, including credits and reprises, but at the time of broadcast the song titles were not identified. The soundtrack was released through the iTunes Store on September 1, 2008[9] and was released on CD in the US on December 15, 2008.

Dr. Horrible's Sing-Along Blog Soundtrack made the top 40 Album list on release, despite being a digital exclusive only available on iTunes.[10]

Musical numbers

Act I

- "Dr. Horrible Theme" – Instrumental
- "My Freeze Ray" – Dr. Horrible
- "Bad Horse Chorus" – Bad Horse Chorus
- "Caring Hands" – Penny
- "A Man's Gotta Do" – Dr. Horrible, Penny & Captain Hammer

Act II

- "Dr. Horrible Theme" – Instrumental
- "My Eyes" – Dr. Horrible & Penny
- "Bad Horse Chorus (Reprise)" – Bad Horse Chorus
- "Penny's Song" – Penny
- "Brand New Day" – Dr. Horrible

Act III

- "Dr. Horrible Theme" – Instrumental
- "So They Say" – Movers, Captain Hammer Groupies, Penny, Captain Hammer, News Anchors & Dr. Horrible
- "Everyone's a Hero" – Captain Hammer & Groupies
- "Slipping" – Dr. Horrible
- "Everything You Ever/Finale" – Dr. Horrible & Groupies
- "End Credits" – Instrumental

Cast

- Neil Patrick Harris as Billy/Dr. Horrible: An aspiring supervillain of the mad scientist variety with the catchphrase, "I've got a Ph.D in Horribleness." He desires to become a member of Bad Horse's Evil League of Evil and use his inventions to take over the world and enact social change for the betterment of humanity. His socio-political beliefs include the paradoxical idea of autocratic anarchy: "The world is a mess, and I just... need to rule it." As Billy, he struggles to make a romantic connection with Penny.

From left to right: Maurissa Tancharoen, Joss Whedon, Nathan Fillion, Jed Whedon, Felicia Day, Neil Patrick Harris

- Felicia Day as Penny: Dr. Horrible's love interest. She is idealistic and generous and volunteers at a homeless shelter.
- Nathan Fillion as Captain Hammer: Dr. Horrible's archenemy. Hammer is self-centered and possesses super-human strength and near-invulnerability. He enjoys harassing Dr. Horrible even when the situation does not warrant it.
- Simon Helberg as Moist: Dr. Horrible's friend and sidekick, who has the underwhelming ability to dampen things. Dr. Horrible calls him "my evil moisture buddy."

Several colleagues of Joss Whedon have cameo roles in the series. Marti Noxon, an executive producer on *Buffy the Vampire Slayer*, portrays a newsreader alongside *Buffy* and *Angel* writer David Fury. *Buffy* and *Angel* writers Doug

Petrie and Drew Goddard cameo as supervillains Professor Normal and Fake Thomas Jefferson, respectively. Jed, Joss, and Zack Whedon all provide the singing voices of Bad Horse Chorus. Zack also plays the man who rolls the gurney with Penny on it out of frame, and Jed Whedon also appears as the supervillain Dead Bowie, while Maurissa Tancharoen plays a superhero/supervillain groupie as well as the background voice on "Everything You Ever."

Production

Joss Whedon funded the project himself (at just over $200,000[11]) and enjoyed the independence of acting as his own studio. "Freedom is glorious," he comments. "And the fact is, I've had very good relationships with studios, and I've worked with a lot of smart executives. But there is a difference when you can just go ahead and do something." As a web show, there were fewer constraints imposed on the project, and Whedon had the "freedom to just let the dictates of the story say how long it's gonna be. We didn't have to cram everything in—there is a lot in there—but we put in the amount of story that we wanted to and let the time work around that. We aimed for thirty minutes, we came out at forty two, and that's not a problem."[12] Some of the music was influenced by Stephen Sondheim.[13]

The production of the DVD included a contest, announced at Comic-Con, in which fans submitted a three-minute video explaining why they should be inducted into the Evil League of Evil. Ten winning submissions have been added to the DVD release.

Recording locations

Dr. Horrible was recorded at a number of Los Angeles area locations:

- Songs were recorded in a small studio set up in Joss Whedon's loft.[14]
- The Coin Wash laundromat is located at 1372 Sunset Boulevard, near Echo Park.
- There are a number of photos posted in numerous places on the Web of the cast and crew taken at DC Stages [15], 1360 East 6th Street (at Mateo Street), Los Angeles.
- The outdoor scenes featuring the Captain Hammer "groupies" were recorded on East 6th Street near the northeast corner of South Central Avenue, within walking distance of DC Stages.
- The lake with the paddleboat is Echo Park Lake.
- Dr. Horrible's home, used for blogging scenes as well as the final party scene, is the house featured in the "Mad Scientist House" episode of *Monster House*.

Distribution

Whedon has said that the plan was to find a venue for the series that would enable it to earn its money back and pay the crew. This plan was to release the show onto the Internet, with an iTunes[16] release to follow. If successful enough, an official DVD would be greenlit, which Whedon planned to have some "amazing extras".[17]

The musical's fansite launched in March 2008 (despite the official site containing nothing more than a poster at the time) and was the first place to publicly release the teaser trailer three months later on June 25, 2008.[18]

Online

The episodes first aired at the Official *Dr. Horrible* website, hosted on Hulu, accessible internationally (unusual for the US-based service whose videos are typically not accessible to Internet users who reside outside the US) and free to watch (ad-supported). Act I premiered on Tuesday, July 15, 2008 – Act II followed two days later on July 17, and Act III surfaced on July 19. The episodes were taken offline on July 20 as planned, but became available again on July 28. The show was later (date unknown) restricted to the United States only.[19]

On October 10, 2009, all three acts were made available via iTunes for the UK and Australia. The film is also available from Amazon Video on Demand. On November 29, 2009 all three acts, both separate and together, were taken off Hulu. On February 22, 2010, the full feature became available to stream on Netflix, with all three episodes appearing sequentially.

DVD and Blu-ray

On November 28, 2008, the Official *Dr. Horrible* website announced that pre-orders were being taken for the DVD. The following day Tubefilter reported that pre-orders of the *Dr. Horrible* DVD were "booming".[20]

The DVD was released exclusively at Amazon.com on December 19, 2008 in the United States and on January 13, 2009 in Canada at Amazon.ca.

The DVD is region free. During pre-ordering the Amazon page stated the discs would be manufactured on demand using recordable media. Although some customers report receiving DVD-R discs (identified by a purple data-side), most are receiving pressed discs.[21]

On June 2, 2009, a new release of *Dr. Horrible's Sing-Along Blog* was produced by New Video Group, which included the same materials as the Amazon DVD but was distributed through regular retail outlets.[22] A Blu-ray version was released on May 25, 2010 from New Video Group.[23]

Special features on the DVD and Blu-ray include *Commentary! The Musical*; commentary by the cast and creators; behind-the-scenes featurettes on the making of the movie and the music; the top 10 Evil League of Evil application videos from fans; and four easter eggs.

Commentary! The Musical

The DVD and Blu-ray versions of *Dr. Horrible* include as an extra *Commentary! The Musical*, a commentary track comprising entirely new songs performed by the cast and crew, thus creating a whole other musical on its own. The actors and writers sing various songs both as solos and with the entire company, playing versions of themselves. *Commentary!* is partly self-referential, and one of the co-creators, Jed Whedon, self-referentially comments that one song "wasn't even about the movie, it was about itself", which he claims is "like breaking the ninth wall".[24] As of January 5, 2010, *Commentary! The Musical* has been for sale on the iTunes Music Store.

Musical numbers

- "Commentary!" — Company
- "Strike" — Company
- "Ten-Dollar Solo" — Stacy Shirk (as Groupie #2), Neil Patrick Harris
- "Better (Than Neil)" — Nathan Fillion
- "It's All About the Art" — Felicia Day
- "Zack's Flavor" — Zack Whedon, female backups, Joss Whedon
- "Nobody Wants To Be Moist" — Simon Helberg (as Moist)
- "Ninja Ropes" — Jed Whedon, Neil Patrick Harris, Nathan Fillion
- "All About Me" — Extras
- "Nobody's Asian in the Movies" — Maurissa Tancharoen
- "Heart (Broken)" — Joss Whedon, backups (Jed Whedon, Zack Whedon, Maurissa Tancharoen)
- "Neil's Turn" — Neil Patrick Harris
- "Commentary! (Reprise)" — Company
- "Steve's Song" — Steve Berg

Profits

All proceeds from iTunes and DVD sales will go toward paying the cast and crew of *Dr. Horrible*, who were not compensated at the time.[25]

On November 29, 2008, Joss Whedon blogged about *Dr. Horrible's Sing-Along Blog* and stated that, "We've been able to pay our crew and all our bills".[26]

Comic books

Tie-in comic books for *Dr. Horrible's Sing-Along Blog* have been released by Dark Horse Comics. The first three were through its online comics anthology *Dark Horse Presents*, the fourth was a special release as part of the "One Shot Wonders" series. All were written by Zack Whedon.

- "Captain Hammer: Be Like Me!" was released in issue #12 and featured art by Eric Canete.[27]
- "Moist: Humidity Rising" was released in issue #17 with art by Farel Dalrymple.[28]
- "Penny: Keep Your Head Up" appears in issue #23 with art by Jim Rugg.[29]
- "Dr. Horrible" was released a special one-shot comic, detailing Dr. Horrible's origin story, with art by Joëlle Jones.[30]

All four stories were collected in *Dr. Horrible, and Other Horrible Stories* by Dark Horse Comics, in September 2010 (ISBN 978-1-59582-577-3). The collection also features an additional story about the Evil League of Evil.

Book

On March 29, 2011, *Dr. Horrible's Sing-Along Blog Book* (ISBN 978-1-84856-862-4) was published by Titan Books. The book contains essays by Whedon, Fillion, Harris, Day, and Helberg; the complete shooting script; the script for *Commentary: The Musical*; and piano/vocal sheet music for *Dr. Horrible's Sing-Along Blog*.[31]

Events

On August 29, 2008, the first authorized sing-along version of *Dr. Horrible's Sing-Along Blog* was hosted at Dragon*Con in Atlanta, Georgia, with showings reaching standing-room-only capacity. Felicia Day showed up to one of the showings.[32]

Stage productions of the show have become very popular at colleges and high schools.[33] [34] [35] [36]

In November 2010, Cult Classic Theatre in Glasgow, Scotland, performed the first official UK production of Dr. Horrible's Sing-Along Blog.[37]

In January 2011, Balagan Theatre performed *Dr. Horrible's Sing-Along Blog* at the ACT Theatre's Allen Theatre in Seattle. The production was reviewed by *Broadway World*.[38] A televised performance of a concert version of "Freeze Ray" can also be viewed.[39]

In Ireland, an official production of the musical was performed in Trinity College Dublin by the college's drama society; The DU Players. The show took place from October 25–29, 2010.[40]

Awards and nominations

Awards

2009 Streamy Awards[41]

- Audience Choice Award for Best Web Series
- Best Male Actor in a Comedy Web Series – Neil Patrick Harris
- Best Directing for a Comedy Web Series
- Best Writing for a Comedy Web Series

2009 Hugo Awards

- Best Dramatic Presentation, Short Form

2009 People's Choice Awards

- Best Internet Phenomenon Award

2009 Primetime Creative Arts Emmy Awards

- Outstanding Special Class – Short-format Live-Action Entertainment Programs[42][43]

During the broadcast of the 2009 Primetime Emmy Awards ceremony, which was hosted by Harris, a speech by representatives of Ernst & Young was "interrupted" by a sketch featuring Harris as Dr. Horrible and Nathan Fillion as Captain Hammer, with cameos by Felicia Day and Simon Helberg.[44]

Nominations

2008 Constellation Awards

- Best Science Fiction Film, TV Movie, or Mini-Series of 2008
- Best Male Performance in a 2008 Science Fiction Film, TV Movie, or Mini-Series (Neil Patrick Harris as Dr. Horrible)[45]

Sequel

Joss Whedon has announced that a sequel is in the works which may take the form of another web series or even a feature film.[46] Nathan Fillion has also said that he knows the title of the sequel, but is unwilling to reveal it at this time.[47]

On April 3, 2010, Zack and Jed Whedon announced to representatives of fan site Whedonopolis that they were starting work on the script that afternoon, although verifying this claim could be difficult.[48]

In a *New York Times* interview in April 2011, Whedon said, "We've got several songs near completion and we've got a very specific structure," and that the stars of *Dr. Horrible* have sung the songs at casual gatherings.[49]

Neil Patrick Harris says that a possible date for *Dr. Horrible 2's* principal photography is during the 2011 *How I Met Your Mother* hiatus.[50]

References

[1] Whedon, Joss (June 28, 2008). "Comment on "Doctor Horrible website is live"" (http://whedonesque.com/comments/16734#236716). *Whedonesque.com*. . Retrieved June 28, 2008.

[2] Roush, Matt (June 30, 2008). "Exclusive: First Look at Joss Whedon's "Dr. Horrible"" (http://web.archive.org/web/20080822100528/http://community.tvguide.com/blog-entry/TVGuide-Editors-Blog/Roush-Dispatch/Joss-Whedon-Dr/800042425). *Roush Dispatch*. TV Guide. Archived from the original (http://community.tvguide.com/blog-entry/TVGuide-Editors-Blog/Roush-Dispatch/Joss-Whedon-Dr/800042425) on August 22, 2008. . Retrieved June 30, 2008.

[3] "TIME's Best Inventions of 2008" (http://www.time.com/time/specials/packages/article/0,28804,1852747_1854195_1854133,00.html). Time. October 29, 2008. . Retrieved December 7, 2008.

[4] "TIME's Top 10 TV Series of 2008" (http://www.time.com/time/specials/packages/article/0,28804,1855948_1863395_1863399,00.html). TIME. November 3, 2008. . Retrieved February 17, 2009.

[5] "The Hugo Awards : 2009 Hugo Award Nominations" (http://www.thehugoawards.org/2009/03/2009-hugo-award-nominations/). . Retrieved March 20, 2009.

[6] "The Streamy Awards: 2009 Winners" (http://www.streamys.org/winners/). . Retrieved April 9, 2009.

[7] "Nominations: Official 2009 Primetime Emmy Award Nominees" (http://www.emmys.com/nominations?tid=73). Academy of Television Arts & Sciences. . Retrieved June 26, 2010.

[8] "2009 Emmy Nominations: Outstanding Special Class – Short-format Live-Action Entertainment Programs" (http://www.emmys.com/nominations/2009?tid=73). Academy of Television Arts & Sciences. . Retrieved October 14, 2010.

[9] "Lyrics and liner notes coming soon on our site. For now, let your ears enjoy the soundtrack on iTunes." (http://twitter.com/drhorrible/statuses/906450423). Dr. Horrible Twitter. . Retrieved September 2, 2008.

[10] "Dr. Horrible Soundtrack makes Top 40!" (http://doctorhorrible.net/dr-horribles-sing-along-blog-soundtrack-makes-billboards-top-40-album-list/313/). DoctorHorrible.net. September 12, 2008. . Retrieved June 26, 2010.

[11] "Meet Joss Whedon the Web Slayer." (http://www.wga.org/writtenby/writtenbysub.aspx?id=3438). Written By Magazine. . Retrieved January 6, 2009.

[12] Baldwin, Drew (July 14, 2008). "Joss Whedon Interview: The Web Has Been Wonderful For "Horrible"" (http://news.tubefilter.tv/2008/07/14/joss-whedon-interview-the-web-has-been-wonderful-for-horrible-2/). Tubefilter. . Retrieved July 14, 2008.

[13] Nussbaum, Emily (July 21, 2008). "Joss Whedon on 'Dr. Horrible,' Stephen Sondheim, and Bad Horse" (http://nymag.com/daily/entertainment/2008/07/joss_whedon_on_dr_horrible_ste.html). NY Magazine. . Retrieved July 23, 2008.

[14] "Dr. Horrible's Sing-Along Blog (Soundtrack from the Motion Picture)" (http://www.drhorrible.com/linernotes.html). DrHorrible.com. . Retrieved June 26, 2010.

[15] http://www.destages.com/

[16] Spelling, Ian (May 19, 2008). "Whedon's Dr. Horrible Almost Done" (http://web.archive.org/web/20080727093131/http://www.scifi.com/scifiwire/index.php?category=4&id=54390). *SCI FI Wire*. SCI FI. Archived from the original (http://www.scifi.com/scifiwire/index.php?category=4&id=54390) on July 27, 2008. . Retrieved June 27, 2008.

[17] Spelling, Ian (June 2, 2008). "Joss Whedon offers a sneak peak [*sic*] at his brand-new Dollhouse" (http://web.archive.org/web/20080727131242/http://www.scifi.com/sfw/interviews/sfw18953.html). *SCI FI Wire*. SCI FI. Archived from the original (http://www.scifi.com/sfw/interviews/sfw18953.html) on July 27, 2008. . Retrieved June 27, 2008.

[18] Gelman, Vlada (June 25, 2008). "Whedon's 'Horrible' Trailer" (http://www.tvweek.com/blogs/blink/2008/06/whedons_horrible_trailer.php). *Television Week: Blink*. Crain Communications Inc.. . Retrieved July 18, 2008.

[19] Sharma, Arjun (July 29, 2008). "'Dr. Horrible' Free Again on Hulu, Shortly After Fourth Part Confirmed" (http://news.tubefilter.tv/2008/07/29/dr-horrible-free-again-on-hulu-shortly-after-fourth-part-confirmed-2/). Tubefilter. . Retrieved July 29, 2008.

[20] Hustvedt, Marc (November 29, 2008). "'Dr. Horrible' DVD Ships December 19th, Pre-Orders Booming" (http://news.tubefilter.tv/2008/11/29/dr-horrible-dvd-ships-december-19th-pre-orders-booming/). Tubefilter. . Retrieved June 26, 2010.

[21] "Dr. Horrible's Sing-Along Blog (Amazon.com Exclusive)" (http://www.amazon.com/dp/B001M5UDGS/). Amazon.com. . Retrieved December 20, 2008.

[22] "Dr. Horrible's Sing-Along Blog" (http://www.newvideo.com/new-video-nyc/dr-horribles-sing-along-blog/). New Video Group. . Retrieved June 2, 2009.

[23] "Dr. Horrible's Sing-Along Blog [Blu-ray]:" (http://www.amazon.com/dp/B0025KW29U/). Amazon.com. . Retrieved June 26, 2010.

[24] Davis, Erick (July 1, 2008). "Joss Whedon To Record First Ever Musical DVD Commentary" (http://blog.moviefone.com/2008/07/01/joss-whedon-to-record-first-ever-musical-dvd-commentary/). *Cinematical*. Weblogs Inc.. . Retrieved July 1, 2008.

[25] "It's Dr. Horrible ... It's (Dr.) Gone!" (http://www.inews880.com/Channels/Reg/iReports/Story.aspx?ID=1017368). iNews 880 AM. July 20, 2008. . Retrieved November 13, 2008.

[26] Whedon, Joss (November 29, 2008). "Comment on "Dr. Horrible DVD available for pre-order on Amazon"" (http://whedonesque.com/comments/18243#270186). *Whedonesque.com*. . Retrieved June 26, 2010.

[27] "Captain Hammer: Be Like Me! (Nemesis of Doctor Horrible)" (http://www.myspace.com/darkhorsepresents?issuenum=12&storynum=2). Dark Horse Comics. . Retrieved August 6, 2008.

[28] "Moist: Humidity Rising" (http://www.myspace.com/darkhorsepresents?issuenum=17&storynum=1). Dark Horse Comics. . Retrieved December 3, 2008.
[29] "Penny: Keep Your Head Up" (http://myspace.com/darkhorsepresents?issuenum=23&storynum=1). Dark Horse Comics. . Retrieved June 7, 2009.
[30] Rogers, Vaneta (October 23, 2009). "Zack Whedon's DR. HORRIBLE: DHC's Latest One-Shot Wonder" (http://www.newsarama.com/comics/091023-dr-horrible.html). Newsarama. . Retrieved June 26, 2010.
[31] Whedon, Joss; Maurissa Tancharoen, Jed Whedon, and Zack Whedon (March 2011). *Dr. Horrible's Sing-Along Blog Book*. London: Titan Books. pp. 160. ISBN 978-1-84856-862-4.
[32] Jackson, Josh (August 31, 2008). "Dr. Horrible & The Buffy Horror Picture Show" (http://www.pastemagazine.com/high_gravity/2008/08/dr-horrible-the-buffy-horror-picture-show.html). Paste Magazine. . Retrieved March 4, 2009.
[33] "Live Dr. Horrible Promises to be Exciting Premiere Performace" (http://www.trinitytripod.com/arts/live-dr-horrible-promises-to-be-exciting-premiere-performace-1.2174627). The Trinity Tripod. February 17, 2009. . Retrieved August 14, 2011.
[34] Hauman, Glenn (December 28, 2009). "'Dr. Horrible's Sing-Along Blog', the High School Musical" (http://www.comicmix.com/news/2009/12/28/dr-horribles-sing-along-blog-the-high-school-musical/). ComicMix.com. . Retrieved May 29, 2010.
[35] "Five College Calendar of Events: Dr. Horrible's Sing-Along-Blog" (http://calendar.fivecolleges.edu/FiveCol/calendrome.cgi?span=event&ID=303479&state_values=/). FiveColleges.edu. . Retrieved May 29, 2010.
[36] "Wesleyan Production of Dr. Horrible's Singalong Blog" (http://wesleying.org/2010/02/09/dr-horribles-singalong-blog-showing/). Wesleyan.org. February 9, 2010. . Retrieved May 29, 2010.
[37] "Dr Horrible at Cult Classic Theatre" (http://www.cultclassic.org/#!__dr-horrible/). .
[38] "BWW Reviews: DR. HORRIBLE'S SING-ALONG BLOG from Balagan at ACT" (http://seattle.broadwayworld.com/article/BWW_Reviews_DR_HORRIBLES_SINGALONG_BLOG_from_Balagan_at_ACT_20110130). Broadway World. January 30, 2011. . Retrieved August 14, 2011.
[39] "Dr. Horrible's Sing-Along Blog" (http://www.king5.com/new-day-northwest/Dr-Horribles-Sing-Along-Blog-114666024.html). King5.com. January 26, 2011. . Retrieved August 14, 2011.
[40] Smith, Matt. Halligan, Manus, ed (October 2010). *The Player* (October 2010 ed.). Trinity Publications. p. 6.
[41] "2009 Winners" (http://www.streamys.org/winners/2009-winners/). The Streamy Awards. . Retrieved August 14, 2011.
[42] "'Buffy' Creator Snags Emmy For 'Horrible' Idea" (http://www.npr.org/templates/story/story.php?storyId=112983657&ps=cprs). NPR. September 20, 2009. . Retrieved September 21, 2009.
[43] "2009 Emmy Nominations: Outstanding Special Class – Short-format Live-Action Entertainment Programs" (http://www.emmys.com/nominations/2009?tid=73). Academy of Television Arts & Sciences. . Retrieved October 14, 2010.
[44] Stelter, Brian (September 20, 2009). "Live Blog: 'Mad Men' and '30 Rock' Repeat" (http://artsbeat.blogs.nytimes.com/2009/09/20/emmy-award-countdown/?hp). *New York Times*. . Retrieved September 21, 2009.
[45] "2009 Nominees for Constellation Awards for Canadian SF Film and Television" (http://sfscope.com/2009/04/2009-nominees-for-constellatio.html). http://sfscope.com. April 8, 2009. . Retrieved October 16, 2011.
[46] Topel, Fred (April 15, 2009). "Joss & Co. reveal plans for a Dr. Horrible sequel: Maybe a movie?" (http://blastr.com/2009/04/joss-co-reveal-plans-for.php). Sci Fi Wire. . Retrieved April 19, 2009.
[47] "Nathan Fillion Talks CASTLE, DOLLHOUSE & DR. HORRIBLE" (http://thetvaddict.com/2009/05/11/nathan-fillion-talks-castle-dollhouse-dr-horrible/). The TV Addict. May 11, 2009. . Retrieved June 26, 2010.
[48] Powers, Marisa (April 3, 2010). "Dr. Horrible News – Directly From Zack & Jed" (http://www.whedonopolis.com/article.php?story=20100403171418153). Whedonopolis. . Retrieved September 18, 2010.
[49] Itzkoff, Dave (April 18, 2011). "Once More, With Feeling: Joss Whedon Revisits 'Dr. Horrible's Sing-Along Blog'" (http://artsbeat.blogs.nytimes.com/2011/04/18/once-more-with-feeling-joss-whedon-revisits-dr-horribles-sing-along-blog/). *The New York Times*. Arts Beat. . Retrieved June 5, 2011.
[50] Oswald, Brad (January 19, 2010). "Some truly wonderful, absolutely Horrible news" (http://www.winnipegfreepress.com/opinion/blogs/oswald/Some-truly-wonderful-absolutely-Horrible-news-82068467.html). Winnipeg Free Press. . Retrieved June 26, 2010.

External links

- Official website (http://www.drhorrible.com/)
- *Dr. Horrible's Sing-Along Blog* (http://www.imdb.com/title/tt1227926/) at the Internet Movie Database
- *Commentary! The Musical* (http://www.imdb.com/title/tt1378218/) at the Internet Movie Database
- *Dr. Horrible's Sing-Along Blog* (http://www.tv.com/show/75926/summary.html) at TV.com

James Gunn's PG Porn

James Gunn's PG Porn	
Format	Humor
	Satire
Created by	James Gunn
	Brian Gunn
	Sean Gunn
Developed by	James Gunn
	Brian Gunn
	Sean Gunn
Theme music composer	Tyler Bates
Country of origin	United States
Language(s)	English
No. of series	1
No. of episodes	8
Production	
Executive producer(s)	James Gunn
Producer(s)	Stephen Blackehart
	Peter Safran
Editor(s)	Peter Alton
Location(s)	Los Angeles, California
Running time	2.5 to 5 min.
Broadcast	
Original channel	Spike.com
Original run	October 8, 2008 – July 23, 2009
Chronology	
Related shows	*Du Hard ou du Cochon*
External links	
Website [1]	

James Gunn's PG Porn is a web series created by brothers James Gunn, Brian Gunn, and Sean Gunn. It consists of a series of pornography spoofs, with a humorous event occurring just before the supposed commencement of pornographic sexual acts. Each episode pairs a mainstream actor with a pornographic actress or model. The tagline is, *"For people who love everything about Porn...except the sex."*

The initial web episode premiered on Spike.com and received over a million hits in a week, and was featured on Entertainment Weekly's *The Must List*.[2] Spike subsequently picked up the series for an additional 11 episodes.[3]

The project has, however, not been without controversy. An article on the Huffington Post condemned the first episode for glorifying violence against women.[4]

According to Gunn, they developed the idea in the early 2000s (decade), before short-term Internet-based sketch comedies became popular. Stephen Blackehart of The Good Boys Productions produced the show with Jake Zim and Peter Safran of Safran Digital Group (SDG) for Spike.com.[5]

Episodes

All episodes are directed by James, and have a score by Tyler Bates.[6]

Episode 1: Nailing Your Wife
- Release date: October 8, 2008
- Writer: Brian Gunn
- Starring: Nathan Fillion as Chris, Aria Giovanni as Amber Grimes

Episode 2: Peanus
- Release date: December 18, 2008
- Writer: James Gunn
- Starring: Michael Rosenbaum as Charlie Braun, Belladonna as Lucy, Tiffany Shepis as Sally, Mackenzie Firgens as Violet, Sean Gunn as Peppermint Patty, Elisa Eliot as Marcy, James Gunn as Linus, Stephen Blackehart as Pig-Pen, Lee Kirk as Schroeder, Dr. Wesley Von Spears as Snoupy

Episode 3: A Very Peanus Christmas
- Release date: December 22, 2008
- Writer: James Gunn
- Starring: Michael Rosenbaum as Charlie Braun, Belladonna as Lucy, Tiffany Shepis as Sally, Mackenzie Firgens as Violet, Sean Gunn as Peppermint Patty, Elisa Eliot as Marcy, James Gunn as Linus, Stephen Blackehart as Pig-Pen, Lee Kirk as Schroeder, Michael Q. Schmidt as Charlie's Mom, Dr. Wesley Von Spears as Snoupy

Episode 4: Roadside Ass-istance
- Release date: January 26, 2009
- Writer: James Gunn
- Starring: James Gunn as Lance the Mechanic, Sasha Grey as Tricia Scrotey

Episode 5: Squeal Happy Whores

Notes: This video is not hosted on Spike.com. In James Gunn's words this was "Because the head of Spike Network FREAKED OUT on the, uh, raunchiness of the content and pulled it down." The video is available on James Gunn's website.[7]

- Release date: February 17, 2009
- Writer: James Gunn, Terra Naomi
- Songs: Terra Naomi
- Starring: Jenna Haze as herself, Joe Fria as Joey Bone, Peter Alton as Cameraman

Episode 6: Helpful Bus
- Release date: March 17, 2009
- Writer: James Gunn
- Starring: Sean Gunn as Jason, Bree Olson as Pretty Trashy, Craig Robinson as Havana Bob, Peter Alton as Cameraman, Mikaela Hoover as Julie, Marie Luv as Slutty Girl #1, Sarah Agor as Slutty Girl #2, Stephen Blackehart as Guido, Brian Gunn as Guy

Episode 7: High Poon
- Release date: April 22, 2009
- Writer: Brian Gunn
- Starring: Alan Tudyk, Belladonna, James Gunn, Ted Stryker

Episode 8: Genital Hospital
- Release date: July 23, 2009
- Writer: Brian Gunn
- Starring: Sean Gunn as Bill Scrotey, Belladonna as Dr. Poonwater

References
[1] http://www.spike.com/hub/pgporn
[2] "The Must List: What's Hot for the Week of Oct. 5, 2008" (http://www.ew.com/ew/gallery/0,,20230875,00.html). Entertainment Weekly. 2008-10-05. . Retrieved 2009-01-03.
[3] "Spike.com likes its 'Porn' PG" (http://www.hollywoodreporter.com/hr/content_display/news/e3ifb7c0deaad627f7cc9b6f74f520c662b). The Hollywood Reporter. 2008-09-19. . Retrieved 2009-01-03.
[4] "Huffington Post Blog Condemning PG-PORN | JamesGunn.com - Official Website for James Gunn" (http://www.jamesgunn.com/huffington-post-blog-condemning-pg-porn). JamesGunn.com. 2008-10-14. . Retrieved 2009-11-05.
[5] Nellie, Andreeva; Matthew Belloni, Jay A. Fernandez, Carolyn Giardina, Gregg Goldstein, Borys Kit, Kimberly Nordyke, Ray Richmond, Leslie Simmons, Andrew Wallenstein, David Ward and Steven Zeitchik. (2008-11-05). "Next Gen 2008: New Media" (http://www.webcitation.org/5c8ugsdoW). *The Hollywood Reporter*. Archived from the original (http://www.hollywoodreporter.com/hr/content_display/news/e3i988131294131bdd87eaff893fc071b00) on 2008-11-05. . Retrieved 2008-11-07.
[6] Eric Goldman (2008-09-22). "Lex Luthor and Malcolm Reynolds Make Porn - Rosenbaum and Fillion appear in a surprising new webseries." (http://tv.ign.com/articles/912/912168p1.html). IGN. . Retrieved 2009-01-04.
[7] "SQUEAL HAPPY WHORES...NOT on Spike.com! | JamesGunn.com - Official Website for James Gunn" (http://www.jamesgunn.com/squeal-happy-whores-not-on-spikecom). JamesGunn.com. 2009-02-19. . Retrieved 2009-11-05.

External links
- Safran Digital Group - Projects (http://www.safrandigital.com/projects.php)
- James Gunn's PG Porn (http://www.spike.com/hub/pgporn) at Spike.com
- James Gunn's PG Porn: Peanus (http://tv.ign.com/objects/142/14282753.html) at IGN
- *James Gunn's PG Porn* (http://www.imdb.com/title/tt1297123/) at the Internet Movie Database

Wonder Woman (film)

Wonder Woman	
Film poster	
Directed by	Lauren Montgomery[1]
Produced by	Bruce Timm Gregory Noveck Bobbie Page Sam Register Sander Schwartz
Written by	Gail Simone Michael Jelenic
Starring	Keri Russell Nathan Fillion
Music by	Christopher Drake
Studio	Warner Bros. Animation Warner Premiere DC Comics
Distributed by	Warner Home Video
Release date(s)	March 3, 2009[2]
Running time	75 minutes
Language	English Spanish Dutch
Box office	$6,898,033[3]

Wonder Woman is a 2009 direct-to-video animated film focusing on the superheroine Wonder Woman. The plot of the film is loosely based on George Pérez' reboot of the character, specifically the "Gods and Mortals" arc that started the character's second volume in 1987.[4] It is the fourth in the line of DC Universe Animated Original Movies released by Warner Premiere and Warner Bros. Animation.

The film is directed by Lauren Montgomery, who directed the second act of *Superman: Doomsday* and did storyboard work for *Justice League: The New Frontier*, and written by Gail Simone and Michael Jelenic. As with all previous releases in this line of films, it is produced by acclaimed DC Comics animation veteran Bruce Timm.[5]

Plot

Centuries ago, the Amazons, a proud and fierce race of warrior women, led by Queen Hippolyta (voiced by Virginia Madsen), battled Ares (Alfred Molina), the God of War, and his army. During the battle, Hippolyta beheaded her son, Thrax (Jason Miller), whom Ares forcibly conceived with her, and then defeated the God of War himself. Zeus (David McCallum), however, prevented her from killing Ares. Instead, Hera (Marg Helgenberger) bound his powers with magic bracers so that he was deprived of his ability to draw power from the aura of violence and death he could instigate, and only another god could release him. In compensation, the Amazons were granted the island of Themyscira, where they could be eternally youthful and isolated from Man in the course of their duty of holding Ares prisoner for all eternity. Later, Hippolyta was granted a daughter, Princess Diana (Keri Russell), whom she shaped from the sand of the sea shore and gave life with her own blood.

Over a millennium later, an American fighter pilot, Steve Trevor (Nathan Fillion), is shot down and crash-lands on the island, where he soon runs afoul of the Amazon population, including the war-like and aggressive Artemis (Rosario Dawson). Steve and Diana meet and fight, and she defeats him, taking him to the Amazons. Hippolyta decides he should be returned home. Diana volunteers, but is assigned to guard Ares's cell instead since her mother argues that she has not enough experience in dealing with the dangers of the outside world. Diana defies her mother and, her face hidden by a helmet and her guard duty covered by her bookish but kind-hearted Amazon sister Alexa (Tara Strong), wins the right to take Trevor back to his home.

In the meantime, the Amazon Persephone (Vicki Lewis), who has fallen in love with Ares, releases him, both killing Alexa in the process. With the additional task of capturing Ares, Diana brings Trevor to New York City, where he volunteers to help. An investigation uncovers a pattern of violence created by Ares presence that will lead to him given time, and the pair go out to a bar while they wait. After some heavy drinking, Trevor makes a pass at Diana. They argue outside, but are attacked first by thugs and then the demigod Deimos. Deimos kills himself to prevent being interrogated, but Diana and Steve find a clue on his body that leads them to a secret Greek temple guarded by the worshipers of Ares.

Once there, Diana attempts to subdue Ares, but he summons harpies that threaten to kill her, prompting Trevor to save her instead of stopping Ares. Meanwhile, Ares performs a sacrifice to open a gate to the Underworld, where he persuades his uncle, Hades, to remove the gauntlets. Later, Diana regains consciousness and is furious that Trevor saved her rather than stop Ares. Trevor argues against her abuse with his own criticism of the Amazons' self-imposed isolation and their generalizations about men, and reveals how much he cares about her.

Ares and his army attack Washington, DC. Trevor and Diana arrive to battle Ares and are soon joined by the Amazons. While Ares manages even to summon the Amazons long dead from the Underworld to fight their own sisters, his scheme is stopped by Alexa, a member of the undead host, who reveals to Artemis a chant which nullifies Ares's control over them. The undead then turn on Ares but are destroyed by his powers; in memory of Alexa, Artemis later takes up the hobby of reading. Hippolyta faces Persephone in combat and kills her, but with her dying breath, Persephone makes the queen realize that in shutting the Amazons away from the world of men, she has denied them the chance to live as women.

Meanwhile, the President, influenced by Ares's power, orders a nuclear missile against Themyscira. This act of supreme aggression increases Ares's power, but Trevor takes the invisible jet and shoots down the missile just before it hits the island. Finally, after a brutal beating at Ares's hands, Diana finally outwits and kills him. Subsequently, Ares is condemned to the underworld to attend Hades as a slave, alongside his son.

Later on Themyscira, Hippolyta realizes that Diana misses both the outside world and Trevor, and to make her happy again, she charges her daughter to become a diplomat for the Amazons. Diana accepts and returns to the world of men, where she enjoys the company of Trevor and assumes the secret identity of Diana Prince. However, their relationship comes with the understanding of her larger duties, such as when Diana sees The Cheetah robbing a museum and she excuses herself to stop the supervillainess as Wonder Woman.

Cast

- Keri Russell[6] as Princess Diana of Themyscira / Diana Prince / Wonder Woman
- Nathan Fillion[7] as Steve Trevor
- Alfred Molina[8] as Ares
- Rosario Dawson[8] as Artemis
- Marg Helgenberger[9] as Hera
- Oliver Platt[10] as Hades
- Virginia Madsen[8] as Hippolyta
- Skye Arens as Little Girl
- John DiMaggio as Deimos / Homeless Man
- Julianne Grossman as Etta Candy
- Vicki Lewis[10] as Persephone
- David McCallum[11] as Zeus
- Jason Miller as Thrax / Gang Leader
- Rick Overton as Slick / The President of the United States of America
- Andrea Romano as President's Adviser
- Tara Strong as Alexa
- Bruce Timm as Attacker

Production

The film was originally advertised as having a storyline involving the Greek god Ares escaping Paradise Island in order to capture and control a mystic item called the Hand of Rage. He would then use the Hand of Rage to bring about World War III. This storyline was later dropped.

The film's casting director, Andrea Romano, explained that Keri Russell's casting as Wonder Woman was partly inspired by Romano seeing Russell's performance in the film *Waitress*.[12]

According to producer Bruce Timm, during post-production, many action scenes had to be edited after the first cut of the film received an R rating from the MPAA.[13]

Soundtrack

Wonder Woman (Soundtrack from the DC Universe Animated Original Movie)[14]	
Film score (Digital download) by Christopher Drake	
Released	February 23, 2010
Label	New Line Records

1. "The Battle / Origins"
2. "Sparring"
3. "Ares Imprisoned"
4. "Dog Fight, Part I"
5. "Dog Fight, Part II"
6. "Crash Landing"
7. "Manhunt"
8. "Let The Games Begin"
9. "Persephone's Betrayal"

10. "Bracelets and Arrows"
11. "Computer Room"
12. "Alley Thugs"
13. "Deimos"
14. "At The Gates Of Tartarus"
15. "Cept Hemo Laudus"
16. "Hades"
17. "Ospedale and Ares Rally"
18. "DC Battle"
19. "Ares' End"
20. "She Misses Him"
21. "A New Nemesis"
22. "*Wonder Woman* End Titles"

Promotion

DC Comics gave out promotional light-up tiaras to those who attended the premiere of the film at WonderCon 2009.[15]

Upon the DVD release of the film, DC Comics arranged for several promotional packaging concepts to be released through different vendors. Working together with Mattel, they created a miniature action figure of the animated Wonder Woman that was packaged together with the 2-disc DVD sets sold through Best Buy's stores. Images of the animated Wonder Woman were made into sheets of temporary tattoos and packaged with the single disc DVD of the film that were sold exclusively through Kmart's stores. FYE and Suncoast retail stores sold pre-orders of the DVD with a promotional film poster containing a printed autograph of the film's director Lauren Montgomery. The two-disc special edition DVDs sold at Target stores included bonus Wonder Woman centric episodes from the *Justice League* animated series and its spin-off *Justice League Unlimited*, two shows produced by Bruce Timm. Borders Book Stores offered an exclusive "Making of *Wonder Woman*" booklet featuring storyboards and character designs. Finally, a lenticular cover was created for the DVD cover depicting Wonder Woman shifting her position, sold exclusively through Wal-Mart stores.

Reception

From its previews at WonderCon and New York Comic Con to its DVD release *Wonder Woman* received mostly positive reviews and has an 86% freshness rating at Rotten Tomatoes, based on 7 reviews.[16] Harry Knowles gave a positive review of *Wonder Woman* on his website Ain't It Cool News. Knowles enthusiastically lauded director Montgomery and the surprising brutality of the action scenes.[17] Jim Vejvoda of IGN praised the film's humor, action, and vocal performances, singling out the "perfectly cast" Fillion.[18] Jordan Hoffman of UGO.com gave a positive review, commenting on the film's great dialogue and the mature use of post-feminist themes in relation to perceived chauvinism.[19] Reviewing the film for Comic Book Resources, Josh Wigler gave a positive review, but criticized the unexplained inclusion of Diana's invisible plane.[20] An explanation was left out as Timm and Montgomery felt it was too convoluted and merely a pseudo-scientific explanation. The World's Finest cited a few inconsistencies but said overall it was "easily the best DC Universe Animated Original Movie title to date."[21]

The level of violence in the film - both Wonder Woman and Steve Trevor are shown killing human adversaries in several sequences, and several beheadings in battle also occur - garnered some criticism. Chris Mautner, reviewing the film for Comic Book Resources, remarked, "It is just me or does it seem more than a bit...unnecessary?"[22]

According to The-Numbers.com, *Wonder Woman* ranked #5 in DVD sales from its release of March 3 to March 8, 2009. From the total units of 106,342, it made $2,040,703 in sales.[23]

Novelization

An adaptation of the film, entitled simply *Wonder Woman*, was published in January 2009 by Pocket Star Books, an imprint of Simon & Schuster (ISBN 978-1-4165-9873-2). Written by S.D. Perry and Britta Dennison, the book follows the film's plot faithfully, but it omits some of the incidental violence (Wonder Woman and Steve Trevor killing guards, for example) featured in the film.

References

[1] "World's Finest" (http://www.worldsfinestonline.com/news.php?action=fullnews&id=104). Worldsfinestonline.com. 2008-03-26. . Retrieved 2011-01-30.

[2] "Newsarama article" (http://www.newsarama.com/tv/110818-WW-DVD.html). Newsarama article. . Retrieved 2011-01-30.

[3] "Wonder Woman 2009 - DVD Sales -" (http://www.the-numbers.com/movies/2009/0WW09-DVD.php). *The Numbers*. Nash Information Service. . Retrieved 2011-03-31.

[4] DC Comics promotional document published by Newsarama (http://www.newsarama.com/movies/DCanimated/WWmovie.html)

[5] "The World's Finest - DC Universe - Wonder Woman" (http://www.worldsfinestonline.com/WF/dcuam/wonderwoman/). Worldsfinestonline.com. . Retrieved 2011-01-30.

[6] "Keri Russell To Voice Wonder Woman For Dvd Feature - Newsarama" (http://forum.newsarama.com/showthread.php?t=143151). Forum.newsarama.com. 2008-01-14. . Retrieved 2011-01-30.

[7] "The World's Finest" (http://www.worldsfinestonline.com/news.php?action=fullnews&id=49). Worldsfinestonline.com. 2008-02-05. . Retrieved 2011-01-30.

[8] Harvey, James (August 5, 2008). ""Wonder Woman" Animated Trailer, Official Synopsis And Cast List" (http://www.worldsfinestonline.com/news.php?action=fullnews&id=224). *www.worldsfinestonline.com* (The World's Finest). . Retrieved February 2, 2009.

[9] "Wonder Woman:David Mccallum And Marg Helgenberger" (http://www.comicscontinuum.com/stories/0812/17/wonderwoman.htm). Comics Continuum. 2008-12-18. . Retrieved 2011-01-30.

[10] "SDCC '08 - DC Animation Panel" (http://www.newsarama.com/tv/080726-comiccon-dc-animated.html). Newsarama.com. . Retrieved 2011-01-30.

[11] "The World's Finest" (http://www.worldsfinestonline.com/news.php?action=fullnews&id=224). Worldsfinestonline.com. 2008-08-05. . Retrieved 2011-01-30.

[12] McLean, Tom (July 27, 2008). "SDCC '08 - DC Animation Panel" (http://www.newsarama.com/tv/080726-comiccon-dc-animated.html). Newsarama. . Retrieved 5 June 2010.

[13] Denmead, Ken (March 3, 2009). "Wonder Woman Comes To Animated Life" (http://www.wired.com/geekdad/2009/03/wonder-woman-br/). *Wired*. . Retrieved 30 June 2010.

[14] "The World's Finest" (http://www.worldsfinestonline.com/news.php/news.php?action=fullnews&id=659). Worldsfinestonline.com. . Retrieved 2011-01-30.

[15] "DC Comics Giveaway at WonderCon" (http://manga.about.com/od/conventionphotogallerie1/ig/WonderCon-2009-Gallery/WC-2009---DC-Comics.htm). About.com. . Retrieved June 30, 2010.

[16] "Wonder Woman (2009)" (http://www.rottentomatoes.com/m/1206448-wonder_woman/). Rotten Tomatoes. . Retrieved November 27, 2009.

[17] "Wonder Woman Review: Harry says that the new animated WONDER WOMAN is a wonder! - Ain't It Cool News" (http://www.aintitcool.com/node/39939). Aintitcool.com. . Retrieved 2011-01-30.

[18] Vejvoda, Jim. "NYCC 09: *Wonder Woman* Review" (http://dvd.ign.com/articles/951/951936p1.html) IGN. Retrieved on March 18, 2009.

[19] Hoffman, Jordan (2009-02-08). "Wonder Woman Review - UGO Movie Blog" (http://movieblog.ugo.com/index.php/movieblog/more/wonder_woman_review/). Movieblog.ugo.com. . Retrieved 2011-01-30.

[20] Wigler, Josh. NYCC REVIEW: "Wonder Woman" (http://www.comicbookresources.com/?id=19926&page=article) Comic Book Resources. Retrieved on March 18, 2009.

[21] The World's Finest "Wonder Woman" Reviews (http://www.worldsfinestonline.com/WF/dcuam/wonderwoman/reviews/film.php)

[22] Bloody Amazons Ahoy! (http://robot6.comicbookresources.com/2009/03/a-review-of-the-new-wonder-woman-animated-movie/), Robot 6: Comic Book Resources, March 12, 2009. Retrieved July 30, 2009.

[23] "DVD Sales Chart - Week Ending Jan 16, 2011" (http://www.the-numbers.com/dvd/charts/weekly/thisweek.php). The-numbers.com. . Retrieved 2011-01-30.

External links

- Official website (http://warnervideo.com/wonderwomanmovie/)
- *Wonder Woman* (http://www.imdb.com/title/tt1186373/) at the Internet Movie Database
- *Wonder Woman* (http://www.worldsfinestonline.com/WF/dcuam/wonderwoman/) at The World's Finest

Castle (TV series)

Castle	
Genre	- Police procedural - Comedy-drama
Created by	Andrew W. Marlowe
Starring	- Nathan Fillion - Stana Katic - Susan Sullivan - Molly C. Quinn - Jon Huertas - Tamala Jones - Seamus Dever - Penny Johnson Jerald - Ruben Santiago-Hudson
Country of origin	United States
Language(s)	English
No. of seasons	4
No. of episodes	67 (List of episodes)
Production	
Executive producer(s)	- Andrew W. Marlowe - Rob Bowman - Barry Schindel
Location(s)	- Los Angeles - New York City
Camera setup	Single camera
Running time	43 minutes
Production company(s)	- ABC Studios - Beacon Pictures - Experimental Pictures
Broadcast	
Original channel	ABC
Picture format	480i (SDTV) 720p (HDTV)
Original run	March 9, 2009 – present
External links	
Website [1]	

Castle is an American comedy-drama television series, which premiered on ABC on March 9, 2009. The series is produced by Beacon Pictures and ABC Studios. On January 10, 2011, *Castle* was renewed for a fourth season.[2] Season four premiered on September 19, 2011.[3]

Premise

Castle follows Nathan Fillion as Richard Castle, a famous mystery novelist who has killed off his main character in his book series and has writer's block. He is brought in by the NYPD for questioning regarding a copy-cat murder based on one of his novels. He is intrigued by this new window into crime and murder, and uses his connections to charm his way into shadowing the captivating Detective Kate Beckett, played by Stana Katic. Castle decides to use Beckett as the model for the main character of his next book series starring "Nikki Heat". Beckett, an avid reader of Castle's books, initially disapproves of having Castle shadow her on her cases, but later warms up and recognizes Castle as a useful resource in her team's investigations.

Cast

Main Cast

- Nathan Fillion as Richard Edgar "Rick" Castle – Castle is a best-selling mystery writer. Born Richard Alexander Rodgers, he adopted the middle name Edgar in honor of Edgar Allan Poe. Castle was plagued with writer's block after killing off his popular lead character, Derrick Storm, whom he no longer found inspiring. He then found himself involved in the case of a copy-cat killer recreating murder scenes from his novels, investigated by NYPD Detective Kate Beckett. Castle discovers a new source of inspiration in her and soon begins shadowing her investigations, affording him the opportunity to use his knowledge and skills to help solve murders. Rick told Kate that he had fallen in love with her but she claimed she didn't remember anything from the shooting.[4]
- Stana Katic as Detective Kate Beckett – Beckett, a homicide detective with the NYPD, is a first-class investigator who has gained a reputation for being intrigued by unusual cases. She joined the force after her mother was murdered in an unsolved case.[5] After meeting Beckett, Castle is inspired to begin a new series of novels about a female NYPD detective named Nikki Heat, clearly based on Beckett. Kate remembered that Rick told her he loved her but hasn't said anything.
- Jon Huertas as Detective Javier Esposito – Esposito works in the homicide division as part of Beckett's team. He is always ready with a sardonic comment to keep Beckett on her toes and enjoys the way Castle riles her up. He and Kevin Ryan are close friends, even though they constantly argue about obscure facts.[6]
- Seamus Dever as Detective Kevin Ryan – Ryan also works as part of Beckett's team. He and Esposito regularly tease Beckett, but they are also protective of her and ultimately treat her like one of the guys.[7] The character was a late addition to the show as the original presentation pilot was only 37 minutes long.[8] Ryan is recently engaged to Jenny O'Malley.
- Tamala Jones as Dr. Lanie Parish – Parish, a medical examiner with an upbeat outlook, is also a friend of Beckett's, one of the few people Beckett can talk to easily and without reservation. Parish notices the personal connection between Beckett and Castle and urges her to act on it.[9] In the third season, Lanie and Esposito began a relationship they believed was secret, though every other main character was aware of it.
- Ruben Santiago-Hudson as Captain Roy Montgomery (Season 1–3) – Montgomery, Beckett's boss, appreciates her determination and diligence but maintains a close watch to make sure the investigations go smoothly. He is amused by how much Castle annoys Beckett but also appreciates how effectively the two work together. He is killed after staging a trap to capture a hired killer involved in the conspiracy that killed Beckett's mother.[10]
- Molly Quinn as Alexis Castle – Alexis, Castle's teenage daughter by his first wife Meredith, is unusually intelligent for her age, and is often more mature and responsible than her father. She is very bright and enjoys school. A running gag in the series has her begging Castle to force her to study and do her homework instead of 'fun' activities like parties and overnight trips. Her social and interpersonal issues often parallel some aspect of the case Castle and Beckett are investigating, and Castle sometimes asks her opinion on a killer's motivation.[11]
- Susan Sullivan as Martha Rodgers – Rodgers, an actress on and off Broadway, is Castle's mother and lives with him and Alexis. She helps her son through the difficulties of raising a teenage girl (even one as mature as Alexis)

but also has an active social life of her own. She lives with Castle partly because a previous husband absconded with all her savings.[12]
- Penny Johnson Jerald as Captain Victoria Gates (Season 4) – Captain Montgomery's replacement. Formerly with Internal Affairs, Captain Gates (known to some as "Iron Gates") is more interested in career advancement, and takes a dimmer view than her predecessor of the Beckett-Castle dynamic.[13]

Recurring Characters

- Arye Gross as Dr. Sidney Perlmutter – A medical examiner who assists on some of Beckett's cases.
- Juliana Dever as Jenny O'Malley – Ryan's fiancee.
- Michael Trucco as Detective Tom Demming – A handsome robbery detective with whom Beckett briefly becomes involved.
- Monet Mazur as Gina Cowell – Castle's publisher and second ex-wife.
- Victor Webster as Dr. Josh Davidson – Beckett's mysterious motorcycle-riding, cardiac surgeon ex-boyfriend.
- Ken Baumann as Ashley – Alexis' steady boyfriend throughout season 3. Alexis recently broke up with Ashley after her father and grandmother were involved in a hostage situation.
- Michael Dorn as Dr. Carver Burke – Beckett's psychiatrist (season 4).

Real-life writers Stephen J. Cannell, James Patterson, Dennis Lehane, and Michael Connelly appear as themselves during periodic games of poker at Castle's apartment. Typically, they discuss Castle and Beckett's current case and tease Castle about his involvement with Beckett. On September 30, 2010 author Stephen J. Cannell died in real life. The characters keep an empty chair at the poker table in his honor, stating they will do so for a year.

Broadcast history

Castle premiered as a mid-season replacement on ABC on March 9, 2009. ABC renewed *Castle* for a second season with an initial order of 13 episodes; ABC later extended the order to 22, then 24 episodes.[14] [15] The second season premiered on Monday, September 21, 2009.[16] In March 2010, ABC renewed *Castle* for a third, 22 episode season, which began on September 20, 2010.[17] On November 11, 2010, ABC extended the episode order to 24.[18] On January 10, 2011, ABC announced *Castle* had been renewed for a fourth season for 22 episodes.[19] The season four premiere aired on Monday, September 19, 2011 at 10PM on ABC. On December 8, 2011, ABC ordered an additional episode bringing season 4 up to 23 episodes.[20]

US Nielsen ratings

Season	Episodes	Premiere	Finale	Rank	Viewers (million)
1	10	March 9, 2009	May 11, 2009	#35[21]	10.32[21]
2	24	September 21, 2009	May 17, 2010	#30[22]	10.25[22]
3	24	September 20, 2010	May 16, 2011[23]	#30[24]	11.44[25]
4	23[26]	September 19, 2011	May 2012	N/A	N/A

The Season 2 episode "Boom!" (the finale of a two-part episode featuring Dana Delany) not only attracted the highest audience of the show's run (14.5 million viewers), but was the highest rated show on ABC in its time slot in 14 years.[17]

DVD releases

DVD Name	Region 1 release date	Region 2 release date	Region 4 release date	Ep #	Discs	Additional information
Season 1	September 22, 2009[27]	May 6, 2010 (German)[28] November 21, 2011 (UK - English)[29]	March 10, 2010[30]	10	3	Misdemeanors: Bloopers & Outtakes, Whodunit: The Genesis of Castle, Castle's Godfather, exclusive audio commentaries and Write-Along with Nathan Fillion
Season 2	September 21, 2010[31]	March 24, 2011 (German)[32]	December 1, 2010[33]	24	5	ABC Starter Kit, On Set with Seamus and Jon, On Location with Nathan, Manhattan's Most Unusual Murders, Misdemeanors: Bloopers & Outtakes, deleted scenes and music videos
Season 3	September 20, 2011[34]	TBA	October 12, 2011[35]	24	5	Deleted Scenes And Bloopers, Murder They Wrote, CASTLE Goes Hollywood, Murder Board 101, Cast And Crew Commentary, Music Video -- "Get On The Floor"

Syndication

In June 2011, TNT acquired exclusive cable rights from Disney-ABC Domestic Television to air the first two seasons of *Castle* beginning in the summer of 2012.[36] In advance of the series' fourth season, TNT broadcast an eight-hour marathon of episodes on September 15, 2011, including five from season 3.[37]

Tie-in works

In the series, Castle writes a novel titled *Heat Wave*. As a tie-in, ABC has released that novel as a real book (ISBN 978-1-4013-2382-0) with "Richard Castle" as the author. It is entirely in character from the dedication to the acknowledgments, although the latter references the principal cast and the show's creators by name.[38] ABC released the first half of the novel in weekly increments on their website.[39] The complete novel was published in September 2009 as a hardcover, debuting at #26 on the *New York Times* Best Seller list.[40] In its fourth week on the list, *Heat Wave* broke into the top 10 at #6.[41] *Heat Wave* was released in paperback (ISBN 978-1-4013-1040-0) on July 27, 2010 and debuted at #34 on the *New York Times* bestseller Paperback Mass-Market list.[42]

Naked Heat (ISBN 978-1-4013-2402-5), the sequel to *Heat Wave*, was released on September 28, 2010.[43] *Naked Heat* debuted at #7 on the New York Times Best Seller list.[44] As they did with *Heat Wave*, ABC released a series of the early chapters online as a promotional tool.[45]

A third novel, titled *Heat Rises* (ISBN 978-1-4013-2443-8), was released on September 20, 2011.[46] It debuted at #1 on the *New York Times* bestseller list on October 9, 2011 [47] [48].

The season three finale introduced a graphic novel based on Castle's previous novel character, Derrick Storm. *Castle: Richard Castle's Deadly Storm* was published by Marvel Comics on September 28, 2011.[49] It debuted at #3 on the *New York Times* bestseller list on October 16, 2011 [50].

References

[1] http://abc.go.com/primetime/castle/index?pn=index
[2] "'Modern Family,' 'Grey's Anatomy,' 'Castle,' get early pickups; so do 3 other shows" (http://blog.zap2it.com/frominsidethebox/2011/01/modern-family-greys-anatomy-castle-get-early-pickups-so-do-3-other-shows.html). Zap2It. . Retrieved January 10, 2011.
[3] "Episode Listings for Castle at The Futon Critic - *thefutoncritic.com*" (http://www.thefutoncritic.com/showatch/castle/listings). . Retrieved 21 September 2011.
[4] "ABC.com – Castle – Bios : Richard Castle" (http://abc.go.com/shows/castle/bio/richard-castle/179200). ABC. . Retrieved July 12, 2009.
[5] "ABC.com – Castle – Bios : Kate Beckett" (http://abc.go.com/shows/castle/bio/kate-beckett/179201). ABC. . Retrieved July 12, 2009.
[6] "ABC.com – Castle – Bios : Javier Esposito" (http://abc.go.com/shows/castle/bio/javier-esposito/179206). ABC. . Retrieved July 12, 2009.
[7] "ABC.com – Castle – Bios : Kevin Ryan" (http://abc.go.com/shows/castle/bio/kevin-ryan/179207). ABC. . Retrieved July 12, 2009.
[8] DVD commentary to "Flowers for Your Grave"
[9] "ABC.com – Castle – Bios : Lanie Parish" (http://abc.go.com/shows/castle/bio/lanie-parish/179205). ABC. . Retrieved July 12, 2009.
[10] "ABC.com – Castle – Bios : Roy Montgomery" (http://abc.go.com/shows/castle/bio/roy-montgomery/179204). ABC. . Retrieved July 12, 2009.
[11] "ABC.com – Castle – Bios : Alexis Castle" (http://abc.go.com/shows/castle/bio/alexis-castle/179203). ABC. . Retrieved July 12, 2009.
[12] "ABC.com – Castle – Bios : Martha Rodgers" (http://abc.go.com/shows/castle/bio/martha-rodgers/179202). ABC. . Retrieved July 12, 2009.
[13] Bryant, Adam (July 13, 2011). "*Castle* Exclusive: Meet Castle and Beckett's New Captain!" (http://www.tvguide.com/News/Castle-New-Captain-Penny-Johnson-1035235.aspx). *TVGuide.com*. . Retrieved July 13, 2011.
[14] Schneider, Michael (October 20, 2009). "ABC gives full-season order to 'Castle'" (http://www.variety.com/article/VR1118010177.html?categoryid=14&cs=1&ref=bd_tv). *Variety*. . Retrieved December 2, 2009.
[15] Littleton, Cynthia (May 15, 2009). "ABC's pilot pickup spree" (http://www.variety.com/article/VR1118003771.html?categoryid=14&cs=1). *Variety*. .
[16] Mitovich, Matt (June 9, 2009). "ABC Announces Fall Premiere Dates for 19 Shows" (http://www.tvguide.com/News/FallTV-ABC-Premieres-1006734.aspx). *TVGuide.com*. . Retrieved June 9, 2009.
[17] Ausiello, Michael (March 30, 2010). "ABC renews 'Castle'" (http://ausiellofiles.ew.com/2010/03/30/abc-renews-castle/). *EW.com*. .
[18] "zap2it.com" (http://tvbythenumbers.zap2it.com/2010/11/11/abc-orders-two-more-episodes-of-castle/71807/). .
[19] "ABC and ABC Family renew Pretty Little Liars, Castle, Secret Life and more" (http://www.monstersandcritics.com/smallscreen/news/article_1610769.php/ABC-and-ABC-Family-renew-Pretty-Little-Liars-Castle-Secret-Life-and-more). .
[20] http://insidetv.ew.com/2011/12/08/castle-scoop-abc-orders-additional-episode-exclusive/
[21] "ABC Medianet – Daily Press Release" (http://www.abcmedianet.com/web/dnr/dispDNR.aspx?id=052709_07). *ABC Medianet*. May 27, 2009. . Retrieved July 12, 2009.
[22] Gorman, Bill (June 16, 2010). "Final 2009–10 Broadcast Primetime Show Average Viewership" (http://tvbythenumbers.com/2010/06/16/final-2009-10-broadcast-primetime-show-average-viewership/54336). *TV by the Numbers*. . Retrieved June 18, 2010.
[23] ABC Finale Dates (http://www.tvguide.com/News/ABC-Finale-Dates-1030990.aspx). Retrieved March 22, 2011.
[24] Gorman, Bill. "2010-11 Season Broadcast Primetime Show Averages" (http://tvbythenumbers.zap2it.com/2011/06/01/2010-11-season-broadcast-primetime-show-viewership-averages/94407/). TV by the Numbers. . Retrieved 5 September 2011.
[25] http://tvbythenumbers.zap2it.com/2011/06/01/2010-11-season-broadcast-primetime-show-viewership-averages/94407/
[26] http://tvbythenumbers.zap2it.com/2011/12/08/abc-orders-one-additional-episode-of-castle-bringing-season-total-to-23/113226/
[27] Lambert, David (March 13, 2009). "Castle – The Newly-Debuted (This Week!) Nathan Fillion Series Gets a DVD Release Date **UPDATE: Artwork, Extras**" (http://www.tvshowsondvd.com/news/Castle-Season-1/11487). *TVShowsOnDVD.com*. . Retrieved December 2, 2009.
[28] "Castle - Die komplette erste Staffel (3 Discs)" (http://www.amazon.de/dp/B00377ISA2/). *Amazon.de*. . Retrieved May 7, 2010.
[29] "Castle - Season 1 [DVD (http://www.amazon.co.uk/gp/product/B005MNP6J0/)]". *Amazon.co.uk*. . Retrieved November 4, 2011.
[30] "Castle S01" (http://www.jbhifionline.com.au/dvd/dvd-genres/horror-thriller/castle-season-1/479657). Jbhifionline.com.au. . Retrieved 2010-06-03.
[31] "Castle: ABC TV Series starring Nathan Fillion & Stana Katic » Store" (http://castletv.net/store). Castletv.net. . Retrieved May 24, 2010.
[32] {{cite weblurl=http://www.amazon.de/dp/B004EHVMNY
[33] "Castle - The Complete 2nd Season (6 Disc Set) @ EzyDVD" (http://www.ezydvd.com.au/item.zml/816266). Ezydvd.com.au. . Retrieved 2010-10-24.
[34] "Castle: The Complete Third Season: Nathan Fillion, Stana Katic" (http://www.amazon.com/dp/B003L77FYS). Amazon.com. . Retrieved May 23, 2011.
[35] "Castle - The Complete 3rd Season (6 Disc Set)" (http://www.ezydvd.com.au/DVD/castle-the-complete-3rd-season-6-disc-set/dp/820941). .
[36] "TNT Acquires Hit Crime Drama "Castle"" (http://www.thefutoncritic.com/news/2011/06/08/tnt-acquires-hit-crime-drama-castle-243113/20110608tnt01/). *The Futon Critic*. June 8, 2011. .

[37] Gorman, Bill (September 12, 2011). "TNT to Present Marathon of 'Castle' Episodes as Hit Crime-Drama Gears Up to Launch Fourth Season on ABC" (http://tvbythenumbers.zap2it.com/2011/09/12/tnt-to-present-marathon-of-castle-episodes-as-hit-crime-drama-gears-up-to-launch-fourth-season-on-abc/103316/). *TV by the Numbers*. .
[38] Hibberd, James (June 30, 2009). "'Castle' book to promote series" (http://www.hollywoodreporter.com/hr/content_display/news/e3i1a1890f91e4cda9a7f03fbb964d64313). *The Hollywood Reporter*. . Retrieved January 6, 2010.
[39] "ABC.com – Castle – Castle Novel" (http://abc.go.com/shows/castle/castle-novel). ABC. . Retrieved December 2, 2009.
[40] Cowles, Gregory (October 9, 2009). "Hardcover Fiction – List – NYTimes.com" (http://www.nytimes.com/2009/10/18/books/bestseller/besthardfiction.html). *The New York Times*. . Retrieved December 2, 2009.
[41] Schuessler, Jennifer (October 30, 2009). "Hardcover Fiction – List – NYTimes.com" (http://www.nytimes.com/2009/11/08/books/bestseller/besthardfiction.html). *The New York Times*. . Retrieved December 2, 2009.
[42] http://www.nytimes.com/2010/08/15/books/bestseller/bestpapermassfiction.html NY Times Bestseller Paperback Mass-Market #34
[43] Ausiello, Michael (March 17, 2010). "'Castle' scoop: Romance for Castle and Beckett? | Ausiello | EW.com" (http://ausiellofiles.ew.com/2010/03/17/castle-scoop-romance-castle-and-beckett/). Ausiellofiles.ew.com. . Retrieved May 24, 2010.
[44] Schuessler, Jennifer. "Hardcover" (http://www.nytimes.com/2010/10/17/books/bestseller/besthardfiction.html). *The New York Times*. .
[45] "ABC.com – Castle – Naked Heat" (http://abc.go.com/shows/castle/naked-heat). Abc.go.com. . Retrieved May 24, 2010.
[46] http://www.tvguide.com/News/Castle-ABC-Website-1031695.aspx
[47] Schuessler, Jennifer. "Print & E-Books" (http://www.nytimes.com/best-sellers-books/2011-10-09/hardcover-fiction/list.html). *The New York Times*. .
[48] http://tv.yahoo.com/news/castle-heat-rises-york-times-best-seller-195200005.html
[49] http://www.majorspoilers.com/castle-television-show-gets-graphic-novel-treatment
[50] Schuessler, Jennifer. "Print & E-Books" (http://www.nytimes.com/best-sellers-books/2011-10-16/hardcover-graphic-books/list.html). *The New York Times*. .

External links

- Official website (http://abc.go.com/primetime/castle/index?pn=index)
- *Castle* (http://www.imdb.com/title/tt1219024/) at the Internet Movie Database
- *Castle* (http://www.tv.com/show/75394/summary.html) at TV.com

Green Lantern: Emerald Knights

Green Lantern: Emerald Knights	
Cover of the U.S. Blu-ray	
Directed by	Christopher Berkeley Lauren Montgomery Jay Oliva
Produced by	Bruce Timm
Written by	Eddie Berganza Alan Burnett Todd Casey Dave Gibbons Michael Green Marc Guggenheim Geoff Johns Peter Tomasi
Starring	Nathan Fillion Elisabeth Moss Jason Isaacs Kelly Hu Roddy Piper Arnold Vosloo
Music by	Christopher Drake
Studio	Warner Bros. Animation Warner Premiere DC Comics
Distributed by	Warner Home Video
Release date(s)	June 8, 2011
Running time	84 minutes
Language	English

Green Lantern: Emerald Knights,[1] [2] is an animated film that tells various stories featuring members of Green Lantern Corps, including Abin Sur, Laira, Kilowog, and Mogo[3] [4] [5] It was released on June 7, 2011.[6] While not a direct sequel to *First Flight*, the film uses the same character designs and includes a cameo by Ch'p, who had a speaking role in the previous film.

It is the eleventh film released under the DC Universe Animated Original Movies banner. It is also the second DC Animated Movie following *Batman: Gotham Knight* to feature an anthology format. Though unlike *Batman: Gotham Knight,* it features a single, uniform animation style and an overall linking story.

Plot

The sun of the Green Lantern homeworld, Oa, is becoming a gateway for Krona, an evil anti-matter alien tyrant that once sought to destroy all life. As precaution the Guardians of the Universe decide to evacuate Oa of all valuables, such as the Central Battery. While in line to charge their rings before the Battery is taken away, Green Lantern Corps rookie Arisia Rrab converses with Hal Jordan and expresses her selfdoubts as the newest Green Lantern. In response, Hal tells her the story of the first Green Lantern:

The First Lantern

Avra, a scribe to the Guardians, is chosen by one of the first four power rings despite having no skill as a warrior. Avra and the other three original Green Lanterns are sent to stop a nation of warring aliens. One of the four Lanterns is killed and, with defeat at hand, Avra uses his willpower and imagination as a writer to continue the battle. He creates the first construct from his ring, a sword, that is used to decimate the alien war crafts. Taking Avra's lead the other two Lanterns also create shapes from their power rings to win the fight. Thanks to Avra the war is won and the power to shape constructs from the power rings is discovered. Avra rises in prestige among the growing Green Lantern Corps, and after his death his ring is passed down until it eventually becomes Abin Sur's and then Hal Jordan's.

Back in line at the Central Battery, Hal and Arisia meet Kilowog, the head trainer of the Green Lantern Corps. He antagonizes Arisia as a rookie and reminds her that she still has boot camp. Hal tells Arisia not to fear Kilowog and relates the story of Kilowog's own trainer.

Kilowog

Sgt. Deegan trains a rookie Kilowog and others by removing their power rings and putting them in deadly settings. Kilowog confronts Deegan and accuses him of a reckless training method and having no value for the lives of his trainees. Sgt. Deegan is then called to act with his recruits when a nearby planet comes under attack. Deegan purposefully drops Kilowog's ring before departing with the other recruits. In the battle Sgt. Deegan orders the rookies to protect the refugees as he deals with the invaders. As Kilowog catches up, Sgt. Deegan is mortally wounded. Kilowog destroys the army and goes to Deegan's side. Deegan tells Kilowog he never would have let his rookies die and that he did what was best for their training. He passes superiority to Kilowog who then takes up completing the mission.

Hal and Arisia arrive at a border patrol of the sun and await Krona's return. Arisia meets a Lantern named Laira and Hal shares her story:

Laira

Once a princess, Laira is sent on her first solo mission to her homeworld to deal with charges that her people are attacking other nations unprovoked. Standing in her way, Laira quickly defeats her father's mistress and her belittling brother. But when she faces her father she is saddened to learn that the recent war crimes were his own decision. He has been driven into rage by the loss of honor that Laira's ring chose her and not him. Laira is ultimately able to defeat her father who admits she has truly earned her adulthood. He then commits ritual suicide to maintain his honor.

Back at the border patrol of Oa's sun, every Lantern has been called to await Krona's return. The only absent Lantern noted is Mogo. Hal explains who Mogo is and why he is not present:

Mogo Doesn't Socialize

Bolphunga the Unrelenting seeks to fight and destroy all the most powerful warriors in the universe and is told he will never defeat the Green Lantern Mogo. Bolphunga's computer contains no information on Mogo but tracks his whereabouts to a mysterious green planet. There Bolphunga spends weeks tracking Mogo's power signatures but never finds the elusive Lantern. Bolphunga sets explosives all over the planet to flush Mogo out but is horrified when the planet extinguishes all the bombs and Mogo is revealed to be the entire planet.

At Oa's sun Hal and Arisia are attacked by Krona's Shadow Demons and rescued by Sinestro. Sinestro then speaks of the prophecy that Oa will be destroyed and relates a story of Abin Sur and the Lantern view on destiny:

Abin Sur

Hal Jordan's predecessor Abin Sur fights Atrocitus, an alien criminal speaking dark prophecies. Abin Sur is assisted by Sinestro in capturing the alien. Sinestro and Abin Sur then have a conversation relating to the warnings that Atrocitus spoke and Sinestro insists that he does not believe in destiny. Parting ways, Abin Sur takes the criminal to a prison planet where Atrocitus again speaks on Abin Sur's imminent death. He also warns Abin that Sinestro will rise against the Green Lantern Corps and create his own lantern corps built on the power of fear. Abin Sur however refuses to believe his friend would betray his Green Lantern duties.

Emerald Knights

Krona finally arrives from the Oa Sun. All the Green Lanterns fight swarms of Shadow Demons as Krona, an enormous figure, rises from the sun. Many Green Lanterns are killed and all others fall back. It is Arisia who devises a plan: if Krona is made of anti-matter then an equal or greater amount of matter will destroy him on contact. The Green Lanterns fall behind the planet Oa and push it at Krona. Krona uses Shadow Demons to push back and the Corps finds itself stymied while taking casualties. However, Mogo the Living Planet arrives and uses its own mass and Lantern Power to assist his comrades. Oa and Krona are forced into the sun and both are annihilated. The prophecy of Oa's destruction is fulfilled, but Krona is destroyed and the Corps is saved.

Mogo volunteers to be the Corps' temporary base as they build a new Oa. Arisia is honored with an official entry into the Book of Oa for her heroic ingenuity, although she still has to report for Kilowog's training.

Cast

- Nathan Fillion as Hal Jordan
- Jason Isaacs as Sinestro
- Elisabeth Moss as Arisia Rrab[7]
- Henry Rollins as Kilowog[8]
- Arnold Vosloo as Abin Sur
- Kelly Hu as Laira
- Tony Amendola as Kentor, Appa Ali Apsa *(uncredited)*
- Steven Blum as Kloba Vud, Palaqua *(uncredited)*, Ranakar *(uncredited)*, G'Hu *(uncredited)*, Additional Voices
- Grey DeLisle as Ree'Yu, Ardakian Trawl *(uncredited)*, Boodikka *(uncredited)*
- Michael Jackson as Ganthet
- Peter Jessop as Salaak
- David Kaufman as Rubyn
- Sunil Malhotra as Bolphunga's Ship
- Roddy Piper as Bolphunga
- Andrea Romano as Abin Sur's Ring, Deegan's Ring *(uncredited)*
- Jane Singer as Wachet

- James Arnold Taylor as Tomar-Re
- Bruce Thomas as Atrocitus
- Mitchell Whitfield as Avra
- Wade Williams as Deegan
- Gwendoline Yeo as Blu
- Bruce Timm as Galius Zed *(uncredited)*

Reception

The movie has received a mostly mixed to positive reception.[9] [10] [11] [12] [13]

References

[1] Harvey, James (May 28, 2010). ""Green Lantern" Animated Series Set For November 2011, Animated Feature June 2011" (http://www.worldsfinestonline.com/news.php/news.php?action=fullnews&id=759). worldsfinestonline.com. . Retrieved June 7, 2010.

[2] Harvey, James (June 28, 2010). "Teletoon Airing "Batman: Gotham Knight" July 2010, Upcoming Releases Update" (http://worldsfinestonline.com/news.php?action=fullnews&id=781). worldsfinestonline.com. . Retrieved June 28, 2010.

[3] Harris, Jeffrey (August 2, 2010). "SDCC2010: "Batman Under The Red Hood" Roundtables Pt 2: Timm, Greenwood, & Romano" (http://www.toonzone.net/news/articles/34609/sdcc2010--batman-under-the-red-hood-roundtables-pt-2-timm-greenwood-amp-romano). toonzone.net. . Retrieved August 2, 2010.

[4] Patches, Matt (2010-09-23). "Creators of the DC Animated U Talk Superman/Batman: Apocalypse" (http://www.ugo.com/movies/obscure-characters-and-the-future-of-dc-animated). UGO Networks. . Retrieved 2010-10-04.

[5] EdGross (October 14, 2010). "EXCLUSIVE INTERVIEW: "Green Lantern: Emerald Knights" DVD Preview" (http://comicbookmovie.com/fansites/scifimediazone/news/?a=23928). comicbookmovie.com. . Retrieved October 14, 2010.

[6] Jett (July 28, 2010). "BATMAN: YEAR ONE Release Date" (http://www.batman-on-film.com/batmovienews.html). batman-on-film.com. . Retrieved July 29, 2010.

[7] "GREEN LANTERN: EMERALD KNIGHTS" BLU-RAY, DVD DETAILS REVEALED" (http://www.comicbookresources.com/?page=article&id=31605). *Comic Book Resources*. . Retrieved 2011-06-11.

[8] "HENRY ROLLINS DISCUSSES KILOWOG & "GREEN LANTERN: EMERALD KNIGHTS"" (http://www.comicbookresources.com/?page=article&id=32390). *Comic Book Resources*. . Retrieved 2011-06-11.

[9] "WC 11: Green Lantern: Emerald Knights Review" (http://uk.movies.ign.com/articles/115/1159205p1.html). *IGN*. . Retrieved 2011-06-11.

[10] "Review: GREEN LANTERN: EMERALD KNIGHTS For Fans New & Old" (http://www.newsarama.com/film/green-lantern-emerald-knights-review-110404.html). *Newsarama*. . Retrieved 2011-06-11.

[11] "Green Lantern: Emerald Knights (Blu-ray)" (http://www.dvdtalk.com/reviews/48816/green-lantern-emerald-knights/). *DVD Talk*. . Retrieved 2011-06-11.

[12] "WC 11: Green Lantern: Emerald Knights Review" (http://uk.movies.ign.com/articles/115/1159205p1.html). *IGN*. . Retrieved 2011-06-11.

[13] "Zadzooks: Green Lantern: Emerald Knights (Blu-ray)" (http://www.washingtontimes.com/news/2011/jun/6/zadzooks-green-lantern-emerald-knights-blu-ray/). *Washington Times*. . Retrieved 2011-06-11.

External links

- Official website (http://warnervideo.com/greenlanternemeraldknights/)
- *Green Lantern: Emerald Knights* (http://www.imdb.com/title/tt1683043/) at the Internet Movie Database

Article Sources and Contributors

Nathan Fillion *Source*: http://en.wikipedia.org/w/index.php?oldid=465095924 *Contributors*: 97198, AHeKgoT, AdamDeanHall, Agentmoose, Ajshm, Aleal, AlistairMcMillan, All Hallow's Wraith, Alliswellbless, Alyssa kat13, Angelic Wraith, AniMate, AnonymousAnimus, Arlenek, Aspects, Auhsor, Aurigas, Bacteria, Batman tas, Bbb23, Bearcat, Bencey, Bib, Bkonrad, Blackmesa010, Bob rulz, Bonás, Bovineboy2008, Brilang, Butterboy, Calliopejen1, CambridgeBayWeather, Camilo Sanchez, Carmaker1, CatherineMunro, Causa sui, Chetedawg, Chicken Wing, Chrislk02, Chronolegion, Ckatz, Cladeal832, CloudKade11, Cokeandpoprocks, Cometstyles, Cornucopia, Courcelles, CovenantD, Cryptic, Cubs Fan, Cuchullain, Cyde, D6, DGuey, DMacks, DameRolyat, Dancter, Darren Lee, Dayv, Dbart, Deathregis, Dethomas, Dexter72, Dhyancraig, Diannaa, Dizagaox, Djbj16, Dominic Hardstaff, Dravecky, Drmargi, ERcheck, EVula, Ebyabe, Edenc1, Eggman64, Ellimleeuk, Emoberon, Erianna, EurekaLott, Extremegirl, Favonian, Fightindaman, Fireflier17, Fourthords, Fratrep, FrickFrack, G.-M. Cupertino, Garion96, Gary King, Gettingitrightthefirsttime, GijsvdL, Gmr2048, Gnrlotto, Goer2u4, Gordon.engel, Grendelkhan, HGArvedui, Hanacy, Haymaker, Headhunter66689, HelloAnnyong, Hirtf, Hitman984, Hourick, Hqb, HrZ, Icarus4586, Icseaturtles, ImGz, ImMAW, IndulgentReader, Inferno, Lord of Penguins, Irishguy, JQF, Jack Merridew, Jason.cinema, JayKeaton, Jaydec, Jclemens, Jeandré du Toit, Jeffq, JerryLewisOverdrive, Jimmyloram, Jkelly, Jldawg67, JohnnyPolo24, Joseph A. Spadaro, Josh Rumage, JoshuaZ, Jpfagerback, Jsled, Kanonkas, Kc12286, Kendal Ozzel, King Zebu, Kitkalil, Knownalias, Kross, Kryptonian250, Kuralyov, Kwamikagami, Kwlow, Kyle Nin, Kyle1278, L Kensington, LoganLesnarMarvel, Logical Fuzz, Lokicarbis, Lpshikhar, LtNOWIS, LtPowers, Lyuokdea, Magioladitis, MalGal, Marc87, Marcus Brute, MarkSutton, MarkTBSc, Marta Maria Casetti, Martarius, Maximusjam, Mayumashu, Mblumber, Medianyc, Mendaliv, Meryl20, Mike Castle, MikeWazowski, Million Moments, Miss Tickle, Mr. Chicago, Mr.Fennoy75, MultipleTom, Mushroom, Mxb design, Mystar, Nerrolken, Nightscream, OGoncho, Obi-WanKenobi-2005, Orangepenguino, Orayzio, Otto4711, Otus, Pejorative.majeure, Phil Boswell, PhilHibbs, Philip Stevens, Pinkfloydfan, Plange, Pm83335n, Pozyton, President David Palmer, Psider123, QuasyBoy, R.A Huston, RJASE1, RadicalBender, Radicalbunny, Raistlinsdaughter, Rcsey, RevDeath, Rich Farmbrough, Richard75, RickK, Ritto Revolto, Rjwilmsi, Rms125a@hotmail.com, Robert K S, Ronark, Ronny corral, Rossrs, Royaljared, Rusted AutoParts, Ryschauer, SMcCandlish, Saiarcot895, Salamurai, Salocin, Sammayel, Sande003, Satinandsteel, Sensorium, Sgeureka, Siberian Husky, SidP, Singing Cone, Sketchmoose, Skudo900630, SkyWalker, SoWhy, Soapfan06, Spidey104, Spiria, Splamo, Starbuck-2, Steam5, Steve, Suedars, TAnthony, Tahutton, Tassedethe, Tesseran, Tetulun, The Man in Question, TheMoot, TheoClarke, Thivierr, Thuktun, Thumperward, Tigris666, Tinton5, Tonster, Transcendentalstate, Trivialist, Tromaintern, UltimatePyro, Valistar, Vengefulantelope, Vulturell, Warreed, Wayfarer1706, Wikipelli, Wildhartlivie, Willboston, XPANMANX, XSG, Xeworlebi, Xfpisher, Xjaymanx, Xornok, Xyzzyva, ZJohnson94, Zappa2496, Zimba94, Zora, Zzyzx11, 390 anonymous edits

Saving Private Ryan *Source*: http://en.wikipedia.org/w/index.php?oldid=467089590 *Contributors*: (aeropagitica), -Majestic-, 131.128.197.xxx, 293.xx.xxx.xx, 2help, 5 albert square, 62.103.245.xxx, 95j, A8UDI, Aa35te, Ablebaker2, Ace Oliveira, Across.The.Synapse, Acroterion, Adamzanzie, Adraeus, After Midnight, Ajshm, Ajw382, Alakazam, Alansohn, Albany NY, Alexbuirds, Alientraveller, AlistairMcMillan, AliveFreeHappy, Allium, AmadorG, Ameliorate!, Analoguedragon, Andonic, Andrejj, Andres, Andrew c, Andrewericoleman, Andrij Kursetsky, Andrzejbanas, Angela, Angelic Wraith, Angr, AnmaFinotera, Anonymous Dissident, Anonymous anonymous, Antandrus, AntiVan, AnyGuy, Aqua byte, Arbero, Aristus, Arminius, Arnomane, Arthuralee, Asclepius, Asdfdsasdf, Ashadeofgrey, Ashley Pomeroy, Assassin3577, Asurbanipal, AtTheAbyss, Atlant, Attilios, Attywab, Aurigas, Axem Titanium, Ayrton Prost, B4hand, BD2412, Badanagram, Bahar101, Banana!, BarkeeperLF, Barneca, Barticus88, Bartonhall, Batmanand, Beamo superemeo, Before My Ken, BehemothCat, Bento00, Berean Hunter, Bgmax2, Bibliomaniac15, Big Bird, Bigar, Bihco, Bill shannon, Bipul07, Blank1, Bobo192, Boisemedia, Bomber-Pilot, Bongle, Bongwarrior, Boo1210, Bopo, BostonRed, Bovineboy2008, Braden 0.0, Bradeos Graphon, Brainhell, Brainscar, Brandmeister (old), Brian Crawford, Brianptorres, Bromagon, Brozozo, Bryan Derksen, BryanG, Bstrathie, Btphelps, Buckboard, Bucketsofg, Burning phoneix, Bydand, ByeByeBaby, C.Fred, CU4ever, CVA, CWenger, Cacaheaddds, Cacophony, Caerwine, Calor, Can't sleep, clown will eat me, Cantthinkofausername, Capt Jim, CaptHawkeye, Cardboardtown, Carlo V. Sexron, Carlosguitar, Carruthers, Catgut, Caue.cm.rego, Cburnett, Cdtsuperman, CelticJobber, Centrx, CharleMagne, Charleca, Charlottenc, Charmed fanatic, Chaser, Chensiyuan, Chepereira, Chickenscanskate, Chigurgh, Chitomcgee, Chris 42, Chris the speller, ChrisDilke, Civilization fan 833, Cjpuffin, Ckatz, Clarityfiend, Cliff smith, Cmdrjameson, Cocktailsrus, ColinHunt, Colonies Chris, Comar4, Comelloyellow, Cometstyles, Conchuir, Connor9909, Conversion script, CoolKatt number 99999, Cop 663, CoppBob, Courcelles, Cpo335, Cracker017, Crazy Boris with a red beard, CrazyRob926, Crockspot, Crohnie, Crserrano, Cubs Fan, Cueball8384, Cunningham, Curps, Cy431, DIEXEL, DJ Clayworth, DMacks, DMorpheus, DaMan15, DaMeanHippo, DaRk StRiDeR, Dagmik, Dan3k5, Daniel Lawrence, DarkRain616, Darklilac, Darkness2005, DarthBinky, Daveswagon, David Gerard, Dawley, Dawnseeker2000, Deadlyops, Deathbunny, Deathstar79, Decept404, Deleteme42, DeltaForceGuy89, Denisarona, Desertsky85451, Dfgarcia, Diderot, Dirkbb, Discospinster, Djpetti01, Dlloyd, Dlohcierekim, Dmaas, Dodgerblue777, Dominik92, Donmike10, DougsTech, Dr. Blofeld, Dudesleeper, Durova, Dutzi, DwightKingsbury, Dysepsion, Dysprosia, EEMIV, ETO Buff, Edlitz36, Edward, Edward321, EdwardZhao, Elfguy, Emmc5, Emsi69, Epaaj, Epbr123, Erik, Evanreyes, Evans1982, Evilgidgit, FGA-66C, FMAFan1990, Falcon8765, Faradn, FatGrover, Feureau, Fieldday-sunday, FlashHawk4, FlieGerFaUstMe262, Flippin zacary, Fltyingpig, Forest Garner, Forever Dusk, Fourthords, FrankRizzo2006, Freakmighty, Fredrick day, Freependulum, Freshh, From-cary, FrozenPurpleCube, FunPod3K, Funky Monkey, Gaius Cornelius, Gamaliel, Garion96, Garrisonroo, Gary King, Garyzx, Gatamayo, GlassCobra, Gogo Dodo, Golbez, Goldranger 50, Gourra, Goustien, Gplpark92, GraemeLeggett, GrahamBould, Gran2, Grande101, Grandpafootsoldier, Granpuff, Gregory.murphy1, Grizzwald, Gsp, Gunnafan, Hadal, Hairy Dude, Hammersfan, Haploidavey, Harryh, HawkMcCain, Hdresden, Hencetalk, HerkusMonte, Hestemand, Hildenja, Hotstuff29, Human4321, Hut 8.5, Hyliad, I'mMe!!, I-2-d2, Iamlondon, Ianblair23, Icebox482000, Igordebraga, Ilovepie316, Ilse@, Imacphee, Imroy, Ionesco, Iridescent, Irishguy, Isaokato, Izno, J Milburn, J.delanoy, JJski, JTBX, JaGa, Jackfork, Jambornik, JamesBWatson, Jameswheeler7406, Janarius, Japo, Jay-W, Jblcn1042, Jbobj, Jc-S0CO, Jchungkana, Jclemens, Jdan m, Jdcooper, Jedi Davideus, Jedi94, Jeff58, Jessemv, Jgoulden, Jimbreed, Jimfbleak, Jj137, Jmackaerospace, Jmlk17, Jndrline, Joe Fluba, JoeShlatbonk, JohnInDC, Johnc69, Johnnydc, Johnyguro, Jonathan.s.kt, Jonpat123, Jordanp, Josephwash, Joshdboz, Judas Mc'bees, Junesix, Jzummak, KConWiki, KPH2293, Kaiser matias, Kaisershatner, Katana Geldar, Kaysov, Kbdank71, Kbh3rd, Kbolino, Kcallu, Kellana, Kelvingreen, Ken keisel, Keron Cyst, Kevin W., Kevinbi2004, Khoikhoi, Kidlittle, Killingthedream, Killiondude, King88, Kingpin13, Kinneyboy90, KirbyMaster14, Kitch, Kizor, Kjammer, KnowledgeOfSelf, Koavf, Kollision, Kookyunii, Koveras, Koyaanis Qatsi, KrakatoaKatie, Kross, Kubigula, Kurt Leyman, Kusma, Kyubi, L Kensington, LCpl, LGagnon, LLcopp, LaManoTom, Lafferty15, Laggard, Lama21, LaptopGun, Laraspal00, Laurinavicius, Laxmstr25, Leighblackall, Lepeu1999, Liarhahahaha, LibLord, Liberal2006, Lights, LittleOldMe, Lockesdonkey, LogCox, Logan, LoganP, Londonclanger, Longterm, Lord Hawk, Lord Pistachio, Lord of the Ping, Loul, Lradrama, LtNOWIS, Lugnuts, Lukasz Lukomski, LukeSearle, Lupin, Lupo, M.nelson, M3tal H3ad, MBK004, MCMiller, MER-C, MPerel, Macca7174, MachoCarioca, Magioladitis, Magnet For Knowledge, Malatesta, Malcolm, Mancune2001, Mansmokingacigar, MapleLeaf, Maralia, Mark Shaw, Marshalapplewhite, Marvelvsdc, Masao, Massimo Macconi, Matariel, Materialscientist, Mathx314, Matt von Furrie, Matte89, Maverick9711, Mayooresan, Mboverload, Mdob, Mdraus93, MeltBanana, Mentatus, Mentifisto, Mentisock, Merovingian, Mervyn, Michael Dorosh, Mieciu K, MikeFTM, Mikedelsol, Mikieminnow, MileyDavidA, Millahnna, Miller473, Minaker, Mipchunk, Mojoismog, Monky1209090, Mono, Moshe Constantine Hassan Al-Silverburg, Mpt600, Mr. Lefty, MrAtoz, Mrfridays, Mrwojo, Mufka, Muhaimin azfar08, Musical Linguist, Mysdaao, Mzajac, N3me$i$, NHRHS2010, NJZombie, NWill, Nad42daN, NailPuppy, Nakon, Namazukage7, Nareek, Native truth, NawlinWiki, Neddyseagoon, Nehrams2020, Neptune's Ivory, Netsnipe, Neutrality, NewEnglandYankee, Nibuod, Nicholas Matson, Nick Cooper, Nick Number, Nicke Lilltroll, Nicknackrussian, Nielswik, Nightcrawlerdcl, Niteshift36, No Guru, Nolat, Norrello, NoseNuggets, NotMuchToSay, Notheruser, Notreallydavid, NpaK13, Nthep, Nymf, Obriensg1, OhFive, OldSkoolGeek, Oldag07, OldakQuill, Oliphaunt, Olivier, Ollyrandywalter, Ommnomnomgulp, Onikas, Ontario54, Optakeover, Orange Suede Sofa, Orbicle, Orca1 9904, Orpheus, OtherDave, OverlordQ, Owen, PDTantisocial, PPGMD, Paat, Pasachoff, Patrick, Peanut4, Pelladon, Pete.Hurd, Peter Clarke, Peter Isotalo, Phbasketball6, Philip Trueman, Pianoman320, Pill, Pinkadelica, Plasma Twa 2, Pluma, Pol430, Polluxian, Polylerus, Pomegranate, Preaky, Prestonmcconkie, PrinceCharming, Profoss, Pt, Puddhe, Pukepwnage, Quadalpha, R'n'B, RHB, RandomP, Ranma9617, RaseaC, RattleandHum, Ratzinger81, Raven4x4x, RaviPedia, Rayato, RazorICE, Razorflame, Razr95, Rdancer, Rdunn, Reaper3281, RedWolf, Redsoxiscool, Remi0o, RepublicanJacobite, ResurgamII, Rettetast, RicJac, Rich Farmbrough, Rich w thagreatest, RickK, Rillian, RiseAbove, Riyazusman, Rjanag, Rjwilmsi, Rockopete, Rocky2k, Roger Davies, Rokaszil, Rollinsk, Rossami, Rsm99833, Rui0, Rusted AutoParts, Rustfam, Rustoleum2k, Ryan666jhjdf, RyanCross, Ryansca, SCB '92, SCARECROW, SFC9394, SGGH, ST47, Salamurai, Sam Hocevar, Sanbuster, SarekOfVulcan, Satans offspring, Scanlan, Scarian, Sceptre, Scetoaux, Sciurinæ, Seaphoto, Seph Vellius, Sf, Shadowjams, Shawn D., Shell Kinney, Shirulashem, Shuuvuia, Sillypig, Silverhorse, SirNuke, Sjc, Sjyglm, Skatblac0, Skudrafan1, SkyWalker, Slakr, Sleeming88, Slightsmile, SmartGuy, Smcmanus, Smoth 007, Solicitr, SousaFan88, SpartanPhalanx8588, Spitfire19, Splash, Spork4beans, Springerjkreb, Squirrelfisher, St. Hubert, StAnselm, Stealth2525, Steam5, Steve, Storytellershrink, Sum0, SuperFlash101, Superbeecat, Supernumerary, Supertouch, Sus scrofa, Sven Erixon, Sverdrup, Swatjester, Sxc beamo, Syst3mfailur3, Szumyk, TAnthony, TCY, Tamblyn, Tanet, Tangotango, Tarquin, Taruru, Tassedethe, Tdi7457, Tearing down the wall, Techman224, Techno Prisoners, Tempshill, The Halo, The JPS, The JPTaxEvader, The Rambling Man, The Thing That Should Not Be, TheFarix, TheKillerAngel, TheLastAmigo, TheRanger, TheRealFennShysa, TheSarge13, TheXenomorph1, Theda, Thehelpfulone, Thepangelinanpost, Therunner24, Thingg, Thismightbezach, Thricecube, Tiddly Tom, Tide rolls, Tigary, Tiger Trek, Tim0907, Tiptoety, Tobias K., Tobzhooli, Tomdobb, Tommio88, Tommot22, Tommy2010, Tommyt, Tommywommy117, Tony1, Tool2Die4, Torchwoodwho, Torstein, Touchstone Pictures, Tpolerocks, Tracy2214, Trans4mers, Trebizond, Tresckow, Treybien, Triwbe, Trombosis, Trumpet marietta 45750, Trusilver, Tubby123456789, Turing, Tuspm, Typhoon966, UDScott, Ulfus, Ultimus, Unknown Unknowns, Unregistered.coward, Uvaduck, Vahistoryfan, Vanished 6551232, Vazquezlax, Vbatz, Vchimpanzee, VenomousConcept, Versus22, VeseX, Vesperholly, ViperSnake151, WHPratt, Waggers, Wareware, Wayne317, Wesbo, Who, WikiDon, WikipedianMarlith, Wikipelli, Will2k, William Avery, Williamstrother, Winterheart, Wolcott, Wollydolly1, Woohookitty, Wuhwuzdat, Wwcsa, XIntellectualxShinobix, Xavcam, Xenophrenic, Xezbeth, Xinoph, XodoX, Y2kcrazyjoker4, YUL89YYZ, Yamamoto Ichiro, Yekrats, YellowMonkey, Ylee, Yoenit, Yojimbo501, Zchenyu, Zephyrus67, Zoid62, Пrate, А. Погодин, ماني, अभय नातू, 2261 anonymous edits

Blast from the Past (film) *Source*: http://en.wikipedia.org/w/index.php?oldid=465557909 *Contributors*: A man alone, AbsoluteGleek92, AdBo, AdventHorizon, Alakazam, Alansohn, AnmaFinotera, Azumanga1, Barticus88, CALR, CSPS785, CalendarWatcher, Cayla, CelticJobber, Commander Keane, Czolgolz, Daniel Olsen, David Gerard, Debresser, Discospinster, Erik, Evans1982, Everyking, Fishhead2100, Florian Huber, Fourthords, Francis Ocoma, Groovenstein, Gurch, Gurdy, Hotwiki, Isecore, ItsTheClimb17, J 1982, Jeff Muscato, Jessegimbel, Jetpackfireman, Jkelly, Jnelson09, Kingstowngalway, Kmwmtd, Kreia, Kvsh5, L Kensington, Levineps, LoneStarWriter82, Lots42, Lugnuts, MGPCoe, MJBurrage, Mallanox, Mark5677, Mervyn, Mike Dillon, Mulad, NebraskaDontAsk, Nehrams2020, Nihiltres, PC78, Paul A, Philip Trueman, PhilyG, Polisher of Cobwebs, Power level (Dragon Ball), PrimeHunter, Psychonaut, RicardoC, Ridge Runner, RobHar, SMG055, Shining.Star, Skapur, Skier Dude, Some guy, Sonic Shadow, Str1977, Teemeah, The JPS, The Wordsmith, TheMovieBuff, Tide rolls, Tommyt, Treybien, ValenShephard, Wikieditor06, Will Beback Auto, Wjl2, Zimbabweed, Zpb52, 87 anonymous edits

Dracula 2000 *Source*: http://en.wikipedia.org/w/index.php?oldid=465955586 *Contributors*: 19jduryea, 66richardson, AN(Ger), AdamDeanHall, Aelfgar, Aericanwizard, Alejandro Manrique Hernandez Reinoso, Allixpeeke, Andrzejbanas, Ard27, Aspects, Aurast, Bbarringer, Bignole, Bovineboy2008, Bubba uk, BucsWeb, Caden, Can't sleep, clown will eat me, Canonblack, Chris G, Chris1219, Clemmy, Codenamecuckoo, Commander Shepard, Crouchbk, Ctznkne, Cube lurker, D.c.camero, Darena mipt, David Gerard, DeadEyeArrow, Doniago, Eeekster, EvilCouch,

Fantasmal, Fish and karate, Flowan, FrankRizzo2006, GhostFace1234, Guat6, Handrem, ImagineLies, Intractable, Irishguy, Irishtyme, JYi, John of Reading, Johnlongbond, Jonathunder, Kbdank71, Kuralyov, Leather Tuscadero, Lijorijo, Logan, MarnetteD, Martarius, Martinsizon, MegX, Motor, N432138, NekoDaemon, NeoBatfreak, Nightscream, Okki, OneHappyHusky, PC78, Paul A, Plasticspork, Polisher of Cobwebs, Ridge87701, RiverPhoenixgirl, Riverstepstonegirl, Rray, Satanael, Scarlett8188, Serein (renamed because of SUL), Shannernanner, ShelfSkewed, SidP, Speedway, Steakface44, Str1977, Sugar Bear, Thiseye, Tim!, TimVickers, Undead penguin, Useight, Ward3001, Warreed, Wigllzz, Woohookitty, Zahir13, Zero sharp, Zombie433, Zxcqweasd500, 170 anonymous edits

Outing Riley *Source*: http://en.wikipedia.org/w/index.php?oldid=387819715 *Contributors*: DAW0001, Fratrep, Gawaxay, Hrdinský, Jauerback, Jim10701, Nield, Nobody of Consequence, ObsessiveJoBroDisorder, SatyrTN, Somercet, Thirdover4, Werldwayd, 6 anonymous edits

Serenity (film) *Source*: http://en.wikipedia.org/w/index.php?oldid=464579178 *Contributors*: -b, 09aidepikiw, 23skidoo, 88wolfmaster, AHSports, AaronY, Adambutt, Ajshm, Aled D, Alerante, AlexanderKaras, Alexwcovington, Alientraveller, AlistairMcMillan, Allixpeeke, Alsd2, Amargo Scribe, Ameliorate!, Amorpheous, Anarchist42, Andrzejbanas, AnmaFinotera, Antandrus, Apoc2400, Arcayne, Arctic.gnome, Are1981, Argav, ArielGonzalez, Arite, Aruthra, Asatruer, Azazello, Azertus, BCSWowbagger, Bac261, Bacteria, Balder19, Barnas, Bastin, Bastun, Bckomedy, Bdj, Bensin, Beryllium, Bigtimepeace, BilCat, Bkonrad, Bleeisme, Blues-harp, Bobblewik, Bovineboy2008, Braedley, Brandeks, Brian Kendig, Bruce IV, Bryan H Bell, Btphelps, Bumbumbumbbjb, C-squared, CR85747, Cairn m, Calabraxthis, Canterbury Tail, Capricornus152, Cartoon Boy, Cbrown1023, Ceejayoz, Cfrydj, Chicagorob1, Chiok, ChrisCork, Chrisdicknson, Chubbles, Cinefile81, Ckatz, Claire angel, Cokeandpoprocks, Colonies Chris, Comp Ninja, ContiAWB, Corporal Tunnel, CosineKitty, Cpt schnookums, Crash Underride, Crevaner, Croctotheface, CronoDroid, Cruizh, Cuahl, Cyberstar, DJ Clayworth, DOSGuy, Dalf, Dan100, DanaJohnson, Daniel J. Leivick, Danntm, DannyZ, Dante Alighieri, DarkMasterBob, Diannaa, Dibol, Discofever, Discospinster, Djungelurban, Dmacw6, Dmron, DocWatson42, DoctorWho42, DogFog, Doktor Waterhouse, Doniago, Dorftrottel, Dpeifer, Dravecky, Dreadstar, Drewboy64, Drmaik, Drovethrughosts, DrumIntellect, E Pluribus Anthony, EEMIV, EVula, EasyTarget, Eban, Edemaine, Edlin2, Elcapitane, Eric TF Bat, Erik, Essjay, Etatoby, EurekaLott, Everwyck, Evil Monkey, Ewlyahoocom, Ex-machina, Fabulous Creature, Firsfron, Fishies Plaice, Fishmammal, Fishyghost, FlieGerFaUstMe262, Fnlayson, Fourthords, Fractalchez, Fram, FrenchIsAwesome, Friday, Ft1, Gadget850, GagHalfrunt, Gaius Cornelius, Gargaj, Garion96, Gary King, Gateman1997, GeeJo, GeneralDuke, Geoduck, Gertlex, Gheorghe Zamfir, Gin and Tonic, Gnrlotto, Gwilym, H3llbringer, HMFS, Hammersfan, Hang Li Po, Harryboyles, Heliocentric, Hellmitre, Herandar, Highonbread, Hohomonkey, Hqb, Hydragon, Hyju, Hyperflux, Hypnometal, IAmTheCoinMan, IanCheesman, Ikusawa, IllaZilla, Imacphee, InShaneee, IndigoStarblaster, Ingdale, Inversetime, Irishguy, J.delanoy, JBK405, JQF, Jack Merridew, Jake11, JamesMLane, Janggeom, Jason.cinema, Jayzner97, Jc-S0CO, Jcburns, Jcec1, Jclemens, Jdmxrain, Jeandré du Toit, Jediknightkarl, Jeff G., Jeffq, Jkp1187, Jnestorius, Jodamn, Joey-das-WBF, John Eager, Jonxwood, Joshfist, JoshuaZ, Josiah Rowe, Jrockley, Jtrost, Julesong, Just H, Justdevin, Jwy, Kaare, Kalaong, Kawnhr, Kayman1uk, Kd4nuh, Keith Gow, Kendal Ozzel, Khaosworks, Kidlittle, Killing Vector, Kindall, Kingdom2, Kintetsubuffalo, Kirk Hilliard, Kirstie 2001, Klapouchy, Koavf, Kobayashis, Kobol, Koweja, Krinndnz, Kuralyov, Kusma, Kwamikagami, Kylion, La hapalo, LadyofShalott, Lanky, Lavareef, LazLong, Lethargy, Lg16spears, Lhuntkenora, Liberal Classic, Ligulem, Lizzzs, Lonelymiesarchie, LordAmeth, Lovellama, Lovepush, Luk, Maestro1ca, Mairi, Mallanox, MamaGeek, Manuel Anastácio, Marblespire, Marcan, Marcus Brute, MarnetteD, Martarius, MasterGreenLantern, Matharvest, Matt72986, Mc4932, Mclay19, Mechamaniac, MegX, Meneth, Merry3, Mhking, Mhudson3, Mifter, Mike ballard, MikeWazowski, MilesVorkosigan, Millahnna, Miraculouschaos, Mitsukai, Mmarsh, Mp, Mr. Billion, Mrniceguy101, Msa1701, MuZemike, Mutley, MwNNrules, My76Strat, N5iln, NE2, Naaman Brown, Nabbia, Nalvage, Nanded, Nedward, Netoholic, Neutralaccounting, Never Mystic, Neveresa, Nique1287, NoPetrol, NotAnonymous0, Notovny, OGoncho, Ohsoh, OldRight, Orenburg1, Oscarthecat, P-Chan, PC78, PRRfan, Panifis, Paperweight, Patrick, Paul A, Pchov, Peace Inside, Pentasyllabic, Peppage, Peterdjones, Phantomsteve, Phil Boswell, PhilHibbs, Philip Stevens, Philip Trueman, Pie4all88, Planetneutral, Plange, PokeHomsar, Polymathic Darko, Ponder, Poulsen, Protious, QDE-can, Qutezuce, Qwyrxian, R. fiend, RA0808, RJHall, Radaar, RadicalBender, RandomCritic, Ray andrew, Raymar2k, RaymondYee, Rd232, RedWolfX, Reverieuk, Revontuli, Richard75, Rick Block, Righttovanish1, Rillian, Ripberger, Rje, Rjwilmsi, Rmbyoung, RoToRa, Roadmr, Robertvan1, Robin Chen, RoyBatty42, RoyBoy, Royalguard11, Runa27, Rusted AutoParts, Rypcord, SCARECROW, SECProto, SMcCandlish, Saberwyn, Salocin, Sammayel, SarekOfVulcan, SchaefDizzle, Scottcurrier, ScudLee, Scumbag, Seasleepy, Secret Squïrrel, Sepmix, Serenity1984, Seth Ilys, Shadowoftime, Shelog, Shsilver, Silver Edge, Simon12, SimonCrowley, Sinistrum, Siroxo, Sjd0218, Sketchmoose, Skomorokh, Sky Attacker, SloppyNick, Smijes08, Sockatume, Spellmaster, SpencerCollins, Splamo, SpringheelJack, St.daniel, Stephenb, Steve, SteveSims, Stevedegrace, Stile4aly, Stilgar135, Str1977, Subsolar, SudoGhost, Super Steve, Svakhine, TACD, TAnthony, TKD, Tamfang, Tamlyn, Tarkas, Tavilis, Teancum, Technicaltechy, Tennismittens, TexMurphy, Th1rt3en, The Arbiter, The Epopt, The Filmaker, The Goog, The Rambling Man, The Stealth Ranger, The Thing That Should Not Be, The Wookieepedian, TheBoch, TheChief, TheHerbalGerbil, TheKanadian10, Theadept, Theaveng, Thonil, ThunderPeel2001, Tide rolls, Tigermave, TodayIAmAClown, Tony1, TotalTommyTerror, Tronno, TruthCrusader, Tstrobaugh, Tyler3777, Ubergenius, Uglinessman, Underneath-it-All, UtherSRG, VPeric, Valdezlopez, Vanished user 03, Varlaam, Vclaw, VerasGunn, Verloren, VioletRook, Viriditas, Websurfer246, Wecats, Welsh, Whedonite, Wikiborg, Wikifried, WikiuserNI, Willardlard, Wisekwai, Wynler, XAgonyxScenex, Xeno, Xeworlebi, Xornok, Yamla, Year 2144, Ynhockey, Yuefairchild, Yworo, ZAROVE, ZH Evers, ZeroJanvier, Zomic13, Zythe, 843 anonymous edits

Slither (2006 film) *Source*: http://en.wikipedia.org/w/index.php?oldid=465786165 *Contributors*: *drew, 100110100, After Midnight, Alansohn, Andrzejbanas, AnmaFinotera, Ary29, Audiorevolver, Bacteria, Beached Oil Tanker, Bib, Big Smooth, Bignole, Bijackefloms, Bind them, Bobo192, Bonejack, Bongomanrae, Bovineboy2008, Boxofficemojo, Bryan Derksen, Bryan H Bell, Buldożer, CIS, Calair, Can't sleep, clown will eat me, Capricorn42, Captain Crawdad, Cat's Tuxedo, Cbrown1023, Chris the speller, Cigammagicwizard, Cireshoe, Claytonian, Cuchullain, CyberGhostface, Cyberion8, D6, DaveJB, David Gerard, DenCA, Destron Commander, Deyyaz, Discospinster, Dissonancetheory, Dogah, Drparrot, Ebertroeperarchivist, Elroy2, Emilynemeth2, Erik, Esanchez7587, Fearedhallmonitor, Feudonym, Frasor, GIR, Gabe Friedman, Games Junn, Gbrandt, Geoff B, Gnrlotto, GoneAwayNowAndRetired, GrahamHardy, Greenorangepeeler, GroovySandwich, Guerillafilm, H3llbringer, Hashmi, Usman, HeartOfGold, HelloAnnyong, Horkana, IKR1, Icerbung, Icseaturtles, Imafilmbuff, JDspeeder1, JQF, Jamesbanesmith, Jaydec, Jeandré du Toit, Jeffrey O. Gustafson, Jezreelver, Jlechem, Jogers, John254, JohnMFG, Jojhutton, Joltman, Jon186, Joylock, Jumping cheese, KingKroopa, Kubrick, Kung Fu Man, Kuralyov, Kwlow, L Kensington, Lassie90210, Lilylemony, Lokicarols, Lurker, Ilifa, Mad Max, Magichands, Malcontented, Mallanox, Maokart444, MarnetteD, Martarius, Master Deusoma, Mat wang, Mattbr, Megapixie, Michaeltoobin, Micropsia, Midnightdreary, Millahnna, MisterHand, Mng777, MrDrak, Nehrams2020, Nixeagle, Nscheffey, Nymf, ONEder Boy, ONUnicorn, Obamination08, Ogabadaga, Okki, Otolemur crassicaudatus, P-Chan, PacificBoy, Parable1991, Phil Boswell, Puffin, Purplepamgroupie, Qutezuce, Rich Farmbrough, Rjwilmsi, SD6-Agent, Saxifrage, Sensorium, ShakataGaNai, Shtove, Silent101, SirNuke, SkaTroma, Slippered sleep, Soundsodd, SpNeo, SpiffSupreme, Steve, Stu-Rat, Sugar Bear, TKD, Tangotango, Tbliss558, Teen ape, TemporalFlux, TheAxeGrinder, TheValentineBros, Theiiird, Tide rolls, ToobinMichael, Trlovejoy, Tromaintern, Typhoon966, Vianello, WhatGuy, Woohookitty, XX55XX, Xsmasher, Yaris678, Yournamecouldbehere, Zombie433, 440 anonymous edits

Trucker (film) *Source*: http://en.wikipedia.org/w/index.php?oldid=443717044 *Contributors*: Benatfleshofthestars, Bjones, BlueStar, CKBrown1000, CommonsDelinker, Cryptic C62, Foobarnix, Gianmazcour, Goer2u4, Indyfilmz, Ironholds, John K, KathrynLybarger, Kidhendrix, MeganDFoxFans, Montereymedia, RottenPotato, Salamurai, Treybien, 18 anonymous edits

Waitress (film) *Source*: http://en.wikipedia.org/w/index.php?oldid=466998911 *Contributors*: AceTygra, Aelfthrytha, Alichat, Andrzejbanas, Andygx, Baa, Bearboir, Belovedfreak, Boccobrock, Bokim, Bovineboy2008, Britmax, Broadwaygal, BuckwikiPDa535, CanadianLinuxUser, David Gerard, David Rush, Dr Roots, Dyontz, Easchiff, Ellen84, Elroy2, Erechtheus, Erik, Erik9, Euphrosyne, Extraspeak, Falcon9x5, Fschoenm, Garion96, Gimmetrow, HDCase, HangingCurve, Hillsboro, Icseaturtles, IndulgentReader, InfamousPrince, JYi, Jmlk17, John, Katalaveno, Korg, L'Aquatique, LuisGomez111, Melty girl, Merfles, Million Moments, Mitchell k dwyer, MovieMadness, Mr.Z-man.sock, Nashleyj, Ndkl, Nightscream, Pixelface, Pokemon Buffy Titan, Pomte, Quentin X, RDBury, Richard Arthur Norton (1958-), Rilbiz, Ritto Revolto, Rje, RoadDogXVIII, Robmccal, Rpfree, Salamurai, Seeadam, Shining.Star, Sketchmoose, Skibz777, Smyd286, Ssilvers, Swaq, Trevor MacInnis, Treybien, Trivialist, UnitedStatesian, Vagary, Voortle, WOSlinker, WereSpielChequers, Western John, Wool Mintons, ÀrdRuadh21, 112 anonymous edits

White Noise: The Light *Source*: http://en.wikipedia.org/w/index.php?oldid=463568946 *Contributors*: 31stCenturyMatt, Academic Challenger, Acid A, Adrian 1001, Andrzejbanas, Aussiepete, BPRD, Bahar101, Bender235, Black Mesa, Bovineboy2008, Chris the speller, D.brodale, David Gerard, Davidhorman, Djungelurban, Dogaru Florin, Elizabennet, Empty2005, Enter Movie, FMAFan1990, Famguy3, FrankRizzo2006, Frungi, Iicatsii, InfamousPrince, Jonesy702, Jonnyhiboy, Jrandazzofilms, Jupiter61, Legendotphoenix, Liquidluck, Lots42, Master Deusoma, Mbusby075, Mikecraig, Nehrams2020, Patrick, Pimpjoe esb, Renegade Replicant, SLWatson, Southsloper, Squalk25, The JPS, TheMovieFan, Tim!, Tony Sidaway, Trogga, Vcelloho, Wikipeterproject, X02, Xezbeth, Zengrrl, Zombie433, Zu Ninja, 101 anonymous edits

Super (2010 American film) *Source*: http://en.wikipedia.org/w/index.php?oldid=466225588 *Contributors*: AbsoluteGleek92, Agnosticraccoon, Ashley Pomeroy, Atomicscissors, Barsoomian, Belovedfreak, Bencey, Bodiusm, Bovineboy2008, Bunnyhop11, CartoonDiablo, Charlr6, Chrism, CyberGhostface, D.c.camero, DOHC Holiday, DingoateMyBabyyy, Drmies, Drzero, Erik, Faded, FromtheWordsofBR, Games Junn, Hellboy42, Himmelsk, Huntster, Hyliad, InfamousPrince, IrishStephen, JamesBWatson, Jeff G., JordoCo, JustAGal, Kendal Ozzel, LeftClicker, LetMeLogIn, Millahnna, Movingiron, Muboshgu, NBbeauty, NJZombie, Nikthestoned, Nymf, Portableops, SarnXero, Seaphoto, Sgeureka, Shining.Star, SuperSonicSandi, Timekillerj, Treybien, Triesault, TriiipleThreat, Tyevco10, VernoWhitney, Wikipelli, Woohookitty, 232 anonymous edits

Much Ado About Nothing (2012 film) *Source*: http://en.wikipedia.org/w/index.php?oldid=463598209 *Contributors*: AnonymousAnimus, Jonkerz, Josiah Rowe, ZodKneelsFirst, 10 anonymous edits

Two Guys and a Girl *Source*: http://en.wikipedia.org/w/index.php?oldid=464066710 *Contributors*: After Midnight, Algabal, Alpha Quadrant, AmigaBob, Angr, Arny, Auric, AussieLegend, BLGM5, Bluerasberry, Bobblewik, BornonJune8, BostonRed, Bovineboy2008, Brim, Broo, Bruce Hall, Chris the speller, Colonies Chris, Comicist, CommonsDelinker, Crash Underride, Curps, DabMachine, Darksun, David Jordan, Denisarona, Drpickem, Dspradau, ESkog, Emokid, Erianna, Gdgourou, Gen0cide, GlassOnions123, Gridlock Joe, Gtrmp, Guyfriday, Havarhen, Hyperman585, IndulgentReader, Insanite, It's-is-not-a-genitive, JPX7, JSteele48, Jaydec, Jeff Muscato, Jeffq, Jnk, Joel7687, John of Reading, Ken Gallager, Kendroche, KirrVlad, Lapis, LilHelpa, Lisa, Lordwow, Lpwallaby, Madhero88, Markoff Chaney, Meelar, Michaelbeckham, Mild Bill Hiccup, Mitchell-16, Monte krista, Mrschimpf, Mundaneman, Music2611, NellieBly, Nitroblu, NoNameNoFacex, Noles1984, PMDrive1061, Pinkadelica, Pladask, Polylerus, Postcard Cathy, PyroOnFire, QuasyBoy, Raman1991, RaseaC, RickDE, Ricky81682, Robert Moore, Rotring, Rvb strongbad, SQGibbon, Sam Hocevar, SanderB, SidP, Skysmurf, Slipperyweasel, SpeakFree, Stefan Kruithof, Stusutcliffe, TMC1982, The JPS, The Yeti, Thivierr, Timc, TomCat4680, Topbanana, Triwbe, Viking97, WesleyDodds, WikHead, Woohookitty, Xeworlebi, Yanks4Life23519, Zoicon5, Δ, 192 anonymous edits

Star Crossed (The Outer Limits) *Source*: http://en.wikipedia.org/w/index.php?oldid=442424674 *Contributors*: Alensha, Anthony Appleyard, Fratrep, Krasss, Rick570, Thinking of England, Warreed, Yazah, 5 anonymous edits

Firefly (TV series) *Source*: http://en.wikipedia.org/w/index.php?oldid=466788757 *Contributors*: -b, 0555, 23skidoo, 88wolfmaster, =Chica=, A 3rd, AaronSw, Abbabash, Abcdefghif2, Abel29a, Abrech, Absconded Northerner, AbsolutDan, Adambutt, Adashiel, Addit, AdultSwim, Aeuoah, Ajd, Akriloth2160, Alai, Alataristarion, Aliaspy, AlistairMcMillan, AllanManangan, Allwham, Alsd2, Alucard (Dr.), Amberrock, Amren, Anajana, Anarchist42, Anastrophe, Ancientanubis, Angelic Wraith, AnmaFinotera, Anville, Apostrophe, Arbero, Arcadian, Arcayne, Arctic.gnome, Arcturus, Are1981, Art LaPella, Ary29, Arzachel, Asatruer, Aseld, Ashmoo, Askelton, Astrocog, Attic Owl, AussieBoy, Axem Titanium, B3t, BD2412, Bacteria, Baf, Bakilas, BalthCat, Barkingdoc, Barnas, Barsoomian, Battle Ape, BaylorBoy, Bboessen, Bckomedy, Bdesham, Beetstra, Bender235, Bensin, Beryllium, Bigcurrens, BilCat, Billiedoux, Binx, Bistromathics, Bkehoe, Bkonrad, BlaiseFEgan, Bloodlikefire, Blue.Sun, BobTheMad, Bobblewik, Bobby D. Bryant, Bobfos, Bomollyok, Bonecrushah, Boomshadow, Bovineboy2008, Bovineone, BoydyB, Bozoid, BradBeattie, Bradders1227, Bradroenfeldt, Brandeks, Brandt Luke Zorn, Brian Kendig, Brian0918, Brighterorange, Brokawlol, Bryan Derksen, Bsu0a7, C777, CABridges, CIS, Calair, Calebliu, Canterbury Tail, Carioca, Casey.B.Bassett, CatherineMunro, Catskul, CaveatLector, Ceklov001, Centrx, Chairboy, Chaotic Mind, Charliewinchester, Cheeser1, Chef brian, ChirpingPenguin, Chocolateboy, Chronolegion, ChunkySoup, Ciphergoth, Citizenjamesford, Ckatz, Clemwang, Cliff smith, CmdrClow, Cokeandpoprocks, Conti, CoolKatt number 99999, Corporal Tunnel, Country Wife, Cpt ricard, Cpt schnookums, Crash Underride, Crevaner, Cryptic, Cuchullain, Curps, Custardninja, Cybercobra, Cyberia23, Cyde, Cyrus XIII, D4, DGG, DOSGuy, DT42, Dalf, Damiantgordon, Dan D. Ric, Dan100, Danbarnesdavies, Danntm, Dante Alighieri, Darguz Parsilvan, Dark Shikari, Darkfrog24, Darrenhf, Darrenhusted, David Gerard, Davidswelt, Davidwr, Davodd, Dbfirs, Dcljr, Ddeschw, DeadEyeArrow, Deckiller, DennisChu22, Design, Desmay, Dhartung, DigitalMedievalist, Digresser, Diiscool, Dikbrown, Dinoidentitycrisis, Djheini, Djungelurban, Dkriegls, Dlohcierekim's sock, DocWatson42, Docu, Doktor Waterhouse, Doppelgangland, Doubleshiny, Dr31, DrDisco, DrKiernan, Drat, Drbogdan, Drewboy64, Drewhamilton, Drgruney, DroEsperanto, Droll Sobriquet, Drovethrughosts, Dru of Id, Drunkenpeter99, Dugo, Dugwiki, Dwarven Shindig, Długosz, E Pluribus Anthony, EVula, EagleOne, Eaolson, Ebmonkey2, Edgefan23, Edgepedia, Edlin2, Edward, El benito, Elizabeyth, Eluchil, Elykyllek, Emainiac, Enonymous Cowerd, Espresso Addict, Essexmutant, Ethanalex, EurekaLott, EvanProdromou, Evil Egg, FHGJ, Failureboy1, Falcorian, Fang Aili, Fastily, Fayenatic london, Feelingscarfy, Felimrules, Ficksquoose, FinalDeity, Finn-Zoltan, FireflyBlues, Firsfron, FishPhileo, Five Cougars, FlatFoot1911, Fnlayson, Fourthords, Foxmuldr, Fred J, Fredrik, Free Bear, FrostyBytes, GDallimore, GIR, Gaius Cornelius, Gateman1997, Gavin the Chosen, GeeJo, GeneralDuke, GentlemanGhost, Get It, Ghola8, Gingermint, Gnrlotto, God of Pie, Goddessloki, GoldenTorc, Golgofrinchian, Gomm, Gosolowe, Gothwalk, Grafen, Grauw, Gridlock Joe, Gridwire, Ground Zero, Grunt, Gtrmp, Gudlyf, Guest9999, Gwernol, Gyrobo, Gzkn, HDCase, Hadal, Hairy Dude, Hammersfan, HappyInGeneral, HarryHenryGebel, Hazel-Jia, Hestemand, HexaChord, Hiding, Highguy, Hipocrite, Hires an editor, Hjaggs, Hjsss, Honeydew, Horkana, Horovits, Hourick, Howcheng, Hq3473, Hqb, Huffo35, Human.v2.0, Hux, Hydragon, Hyperflux, IAmTheCoinMan, IanCheesman, Iansk, Ideogram, IllaZilla, Illyria05, ImMAW, IndigoStarblaster, Indrian, Iuhkjhk87y678, J.delanoy, JBK405, JDspeeder1, JGStew, JQF, Jack Cain, Jack Merridew, JackWilliams, Jackalsclaw, Jacobn71, Jacoplane, JaffaCakeLover, JakeVortex, James Foster, Janggeom, Jaxler, Jay32183, Jc-S0CO, Jclemens, Jdmxrain, Jeandré du Toit, JeffW, Jeffq, Jeffrywith1e, Jmrowland, Joe Beaudoin Jr., John Doe or Jane Doe, John Eager, John of Reading, Johnmarkh, Jomasecu, Jonathan Hall, Joshfriel, Josiah Rowe, Josquius, Jprince610, Jtrost, Judgesurreal777, Justinpwilsonadvocate, KJK::Hyperion, Kalimac, Kaosium, Karenn421, Kbachelder, KeithTyler, Kelly, Kendal Ozzel, KenoSarawa, Khalidkhoso, Khanartist, Khaosworks, Kierano, Kierant, Kingdom2, Klow, KnowledgeOfSelf, Koavf, Kollision, Koweja, Kozuch, Kross, Ktrip2gs, Kuralyov, Kyle1278, Kypsos, Kyven, LPHeadstrong, Lady Aleena, Lamontacranston, LarryMac, Lavenderbunny, LazLong, Lcatgoddess, Lee J Haywood, Legotech, LeinadSpoon, Lhuntkenora, LiamUK, Liftarn, Lightmouse, LineOfBlackCars, Linkofazeroth, LittleSmall, Lobo91011, Lochaber, Lockesdonkey, Logan, Lord Bodak, Lordparadise, Lovepush, Lquilter, Lucia lennon, MJBurrage, MONDARIZ, MStraw, MZMcBride, Mac417, Madhatter9max, Magic Pickle, Makkir, Maratanos, Marchije, Marcus Brute, Mareino, Mark Richards, MarnetteD, Marnfxix, Martin Kozák, Mathewsyriac, MattManic7325, Matthew, Mav, Mbdostillio, Mccojr02, Mclay1, Mdotley, Mdwh, Meesham, Melensdad, Menchi, Meph552, Mercifull, Metahacker, Mhacdebhandia, Michael Devore, Michaelas10, Mike Peel, MikeWazowski, Mikekearn, Mikker, Millahnna, Mirrorscotty, Mirv, MisterAngus, MisterHand, Mitth'raw'nuruodo, Mjquinn id, Mlnovaaa, Mobilesworking, Mohawkjohn, Monkofbob, Monobi, Moskevap, Mr. Billion, MrWhipple, Mrfridays, Myrik, MysticalGenesis, N5iln, Naaman Brown, Nalvage, Namebrand, Nar Matteru, Nathan, Nedward, Neelix, Neil Hunt, Neilrieck, Neoncow, Netoholic, NeuronExMachina, Nev9600, Next Paige, Nfitz, Nicholasink, Nightscream, Nikai, Nikteacher, Nique1287, Nirvana888, Nivenus, Noclevername, NonNobisSolum, Norablindsided, Nskillen, Nyckname, OGRastamon, OGoncho, OMGsplosion, Ocrasaroon, Oknazevad, Onikage725, Ophois, Orangemike, Oscarthecat, Otto4711, PDH, Palnu, Partim, Pascal666, Patrick, Paul A, PaulHammond, Pax:Vobiscum, Paxomen, Peace Inside, Pentasyllabic, Percy Snoodle, Peregrine Fisher, Peruvianllama, Pete4winds, Piano non troppo, Pie4all88, Piloki, Pinkadelica, Piotrus, Pix22, Plange, Plasticup, Plastikspork, Plonk420, Pm guy1987, Pretzels, Prezcole, Prietoquilmes, Pss223, Purple Paint, Pádraic MacUidhir, QuasyBoy, Quickbeam, R. F. Layer, RJASE1, RSido, Rack88, RadicalBender, Radicaladz, Rafaelgr, Ragesoss, Rahnkrammer, RainbowWerewolf, RalfiParpa, Random Tangent, Rapier Shade, Rbcsouza, RedWordSmith, Redlazer, Redux, Reedy, Reflex Reaction, Rehevkor, Rei, Revolution Firefly, Rich Farmbrough, Richard Myers, Richard75, Ricimer, Rihk, Rjanag, Rjwilmsi, Rlquall, Rmfitzgerald50, Rmky87, Robert Brockway, RobertG, Roman Babylon, Rorschach, Rossumcapek, RoyBatty42, RoyBoy, Rpkrawczyk, Rsweens, Runa27, Runtime, Rydra Wong, Rypcord, SFBayHome, SMcCandlish, Saberwyn, Salocin, Sammayel, Samsamcat, Samuel Blanning, Sandoz, Sanguinity, SarekOfVulcan, Saudade7, Scarecroe, SchuminWeb, Scoro, Sempai, Senchang, Sendthistopeej, Sepmix, Seraphis, Serein (renamed because of SUL), Seth Ilys, Sethie, Sfeldon, Sgv 6618, Shamanchill, Shanshu, SharkD, SharmintheShaman, Shaui BlackBear, ShelfSkewed, Shsilver, SidP, SilkTork, Simon Dodd, SimonP, SkeezerPumba, Sketchmoose, Skomorokh, Skudo900630, Slackergate5, Slapyvard, Slipperyweasel, Smash, Smijes08, Snowolfd4, Sonicsociety, Sophia, Spikey, Splamo, Staecker, Stanselmdoc, Staxringold, SteedMiranda, Steel Spider, Steinsky, Steve, SteveW, Stilgar135, Stolee, Str1977, Stupidnut, SudoGhost, Surfeited, SydneyMcbeal, Sylocat, SynergyBlades, TJ Spyke, Tainted Conformity, Tales, Tamfang, Tapests, Tarotcards, Tarquin, Tassedethe, Teancum, Tec2030, Tetulun, TexMurphy, Th1rt3en, That Guy, From That Show!, The Cake is a Lie, The Epopt, The Singing Badger, The Wookieepedian, The savage mind, TheBlueRift, TheChrisRoss, TheDJ, TheIncredibleEdibleOompaLoompa, TheOtherSiguy, TheRealFennShysa, TheTVGuy, TheTripleEight, Thecinimod, Thingg, Thinking of England, Thiseye, Thismightbezach, Thorkuhn, Three ways round, Thumperward, Tide rolls, Tiger Khan, Tiotomas, Tirwhan, Tom-, Tom-b, Tony Fox, Tony1, Tony619, TonyTheTiger, Tpbradbury, TraderJack, TransUtopian, Transcendentalstate, Trasel, Treisijs, Trekkie4christ, Trendline, TrinityRocks, Tryion42, Trysha, Tuvas, Twinsdude, Tyler3777, TyrS, Ubergenius, Uncle Milty, UnicornTapestry, Unimath, Unschool, Used2Cook, Usman Farooq, UtherSRG, VBGFscJUn3, Vanished User 0001, Varlaam, Veinor, VernoWhitney, Versus22, Vocaro, Vusys, Wachholder, Wapcaplet, Waveformula, Wayfarer1706, Webturtle0, Weyes, White whirlwind, Why Not A Duck, Wig wam man, Wilfried Elmenreich, Witw, Wknight94, Woohookitty, WormNut, Wwoods, Wwwwolf, Wynler, X-Tractor, Xanzzibar, Xeno, Xeworlebi, Xjaymanx, Xodmoe, Xornok, Yp54321, Ye Olde Luke, Ylai, Yonatan, Yooden, ZachsMind, Zakssmallshlong, Zandperl, Zanimum, Zardok, Zenoseiya, Zipacna1, ZoAn, Zombie Hunter Smurf, Zsinj, Zybthranger, Zythe, ^demon, 1264 anonymous edits

Buffy the Vampire Slayer (TV series) *Source*: http://en.wikipedia.org/w/index.php?oldid=466191249 *Contributors*: $yD!, 07jhone, 10turneal, 172.177.158.xxx, 1bulma1, 23skidoo, ABCxyz, ABeckman, Aaronrbenson, Aarontay, Abbabash, Abu badali, AdamBMorgan, Addicted2books, Addshore, Addyfe, AdultSwim, Agiseb, Agustinaldo, Ahmed adeeb, Aitias, Alecsdaniel, Alientraveller, AlistairMcMillan, Allen Holt, Ally dewar?, Allycat, Almaster0, Altsarc, Ams80, Amxitsa, Anabananas27, Anacin, Andelman, Andicandi679, Andrei Cvhdsee Brazil, Andrew Kanaber, Andrew Levine, Andrewpmk, Andrudis, Andymease, Angel33311, AngelOfSadness, Angelus007, Angr, AnmaFinotera, Annesummers, AnonEMouse, AnonymousBroccoli, Ant4buffy, Ant4real, Antaeus Feldspar, Aphrodite88, Apollo Gilgamesh, Arbero, ArgentiumOutlaw, ArglebargleIV, Arjay, Arpad13, Arteitle, Artemis-Arethusa, Artemisboy, Arwel Parry, Astrotrain, Atif.t2, Atomician, Attilios, AuburnPilot, Aumakua, Aurigas, Austin316ejd, Avador, AxelBoldt, Axem Titanium, Azucar, BOARshevik, Babyboy2588, Bac261, Bacteria, Bannapple, Barkingdoc, Barsoomian, Baylink, BeachBrains, Bearcat, Beardo, Bearingbreaker92, Beatdown, Before My Ken, Belovedfreak, Ben King, Beste, Betterworld, Bignole, Bill william compton, Billiedoux, BinaryTed, Binthemix, Binx, Birtitia, Bloodloss, BlueAzure, Blueboy77, Bluemask, Bnwwf91, Bob rulz, Bobo192, Boffy Layer, Bonadea, Bongwarrior, Bonk926, Bovineboy2008, Brad, BradBeattie, BradPatrick, Bradley0110, Bradnbrad, Brandeks, BrendelSignature, Brian0918, BrianAT, Brighterorange, Brion VIBBER, Britmax, Brother William, Brunky, Bryan Derksen, Bssc81, Buchanan-Hermit, Buffycharmed90210, Buffyfan2011, Buffyfan882, Buffyverse, ButterflygirlUK, C777, CFan, Caitlinvm, CajunGypsy, Caknuck, CambridgeBayWeather, Can't sleep, clown will eat me, Cancilla, CandiceWalsh, Canterbury Tail, Captainamerica666, Carey Evans, Carinemily, Carioca, Carsonmcmillan, Casliber, Catchpole, Causa sui, Cburnett, Cdc, Cedrus-Libani, Centrx, Cfailde, Chanlord, Chaos5023, Chaosmical, ChessPlayer, Chigurgh, ChirpingPenguin, Chlamydia, Chocolateboy, ChrisCThomas, ChrisGriswold, Chrisj8910, Cirt, Ciscocosta, Ckatz, Clarityfiend, Classicfilms, CobraWiki, Coffeemusiclife, Coleh-Anya, Colethazor, Colorvision, Cometstyles, Cominoverdahill2, Conti, Conversion script, Copy of a copy cat, Cordless Larry, Corporal Tunnel, Corrupt one, Corti, Corystanish, CottrellS, Courcelles, Courtnificus, Cpt schnookums, Crjeong, Croctotheface, CrossHouses, Cryptic, Ctrl build, Cubs Fan, Curlybob1234, Curps, Cxz111, Cybercobra, DCincarnate, DJGrieve, DSatz, Da Joe, DabMachine, Daemen, DanDud88, Danbarnesdavies, Danger, Danielofficial, Danielradcliffelover, Danski14, Dapang, Darigan, DarkFalls, Darrenhusted, DarshaAssant, Darthnice, DasBooch, Dave Rave, David Newton, Davodd, Dbenbenn, Deckiller, Decoy, Dekio, Deor, DerHexer, Destron Commander, Dharmabum420, Dirac1933, Discospinster, Djungelurban, Dkidwell, Dleav, Dmlandfair, Doc W, DocWatson42, Doczilla, Dodgethis, Dogru144, Doinkies, Don Sample, Doppelgangland, Dorftrottel, Dounia, Download, DrBat, DragonQ, DragonflySixtyseven, Dragunova, Drills, Droman, Drovethrughosts, Drunkenpeter99, Druthulhu, Dsmdgold, DuaneThomas, Dugwiki, Dyslexic agnostic, ER-HP-11, ESkog, Eaglesfreak, Ebyabe, Ecb282, Echobeats, Echuck215, Ed Jefferson, Ed g2s, Eje211, ElKevbo, Elcue13, Eliazar, Elockid, Eloquence, Elwood00, Emavix, EnemyOfTheState, Epitome of beauty, Erolos, Essexmutant, EurekaLott, Evanescence rok, Evercat, Everyoneandeveryone, FF2010, FaithLehaneTheVampireSlayer, FallenAngelII, Falltilllfy, Farside6, Feestverp, Feliperijo, Fences and windows, Ferdiaob, FergieFan101, Fester unclef, Figureskatingfan, Firsfron, Fish and karate, Flewis, Flyer22, FordPrefect42, Fortdj33, Forteana, Fortyfloz, Fox, FrednFaith, FreeKresge, Friend of facts, Frostlion, Frymaster, Funnyhat, Fvw, GHe, GLKeeney, GSYH, Gaius Cornelius, Gandalfe, Garda40, Garion96, Gary D Robson, Gekkie, GeneralCheese, GeneralDuke, Geni, Ghandir, Gimmetrow, Ginadina1, Giom211, GirrlyGUrl, Gisele teresinha, Glassedphase, Gleconte1, Glenn6502, Gmanuk2007, Goldenroad, Gonzalo84, GraemeMcRae, Graham87, Greswik, Greybeard, Ground Zero, Guido MTY, Gurch, Gwernol, HGraphite, HalfShadow, Halliwell3, Hammer Raccoon, Hanaichi, Hanzo 88, Harmonica, Harryboyles, Hatsuharu 001, Hazelflag, Hbent, Headstrong neiva, Henrygb, Hermanturdle, HexaChord, HiEv, Hiddekel, Hippychick94, HornetMike, Howdybob, Hoytloosen, Hqb, HumbleBob, Hurleygirley, Hyacinth, Hydragon, Hyliad, Iglew, Igoldste, Ijon, Illyria05, Iluvashleyt, Imaboofygirl, Imjusthappy, InShaneee, Indon, Intheroom, Invincible Ninja, IrisWings, Irishguy, Islandstyles1, J Greb, J Milburn, J.delanoy, J52y, JAltman752, JHunterJ, JJH1992, JNW, JOGDH, JQF, JaGa, Jab1981, Jac16888, Jackel, Jacobshaven3, Jam95, JamesAM, Jamminjj, Jay Firestorm, Jay32183, Jayunderscorezero, Jbetteridge, Jclemens, Jeandré du Toit, Jeffgordon24, Jeffq, Jeltz, Jenlight, Jennavecia, Jeremymiles, Jessie.halbert, Jestus 13, Jfwg22, Jharpinger, Jhenderson777, Jhinman, Jillpilldilldill, Jim Douglas, Jim15936, Jim856796, Jimmyflowers, Jinxmchue, Jkelly, Jkittrell94, Jlhron, Jmacgrath, JoFerg, Joe Wallace, Joe-b, Joeyconnick, John Abbe, John254, JohnElder, JohnWhitlock, Johnnyblue387, Jomasecu, Jon Harald Søby, JopeMoro, JoshuaZ, JosieAmadeo, Joxernolan, Jpack8, Jsc83, Jte503, Jthmspreeodeath, JuJube, Julianortega, Juppiter, Jwolfe, Jwoodger, JzG, K.Nevelsteen, KGasso, Kaivaal, Kal-El, Kanamekun, Kapslock, Karen Johnson, Kaylalvc, Kcmajerski, Kendal Ozzel, Kesac, Kevin, Khanartist, Khaosjr, Khaosworks, Kinabrew, Kinaro, Kingboyk, Kingdom2, Kinitawowi, Kinkyturnip, Kirsten319, Kjaergaard, Kmweber, Knaudt, Koavf, Kollen, Koweja, Kreachure, Kslain, Kuru, Kweeket, Kwjones49, Kylu, Kyros, LCCFD, LFaraone, LL290368, LSD, La Pianista, Lady Aleena, Laefer, Lagoulue, Laszlo Panaflex, LazLong, Lcarscad, Le Messor, Lee Daniel Crocker, Leeborkman, Leflyman, Lefty on campus, Leigha926, Lemmey, Leonardo2505, Liftarn, Lightdarkness, Lightmouse, Lil Flip246, LindsayH, Ling.Nut, Little Willow, LizSnell, Lofote, Lokicarbis, Loopylizard333, Loxx, Luckykitty89, Luke4545, Lullakai, Luminum, M C Y 1008, MER-C, MJBurrage, MK8, Mackensen, Mad Max, Maelwys, MagicPath111, Magnius, Magnus Manske, Majin Gojira, Makgraf, Malcolm Farmer, Marek69, Markeer, Markell2010, Marti noxon rules, Martin Villafuerte, MastCell, Master Deusoma, Matariel, Matthew, Matthewmayer, Mav, Mbdostillio, Mboverload, Mcdoh1902, Mdwh, Mechasheherezada, Medleystudios72, Meelar, Megan elisabeth, Megan1967, MegasXLRFanX85, Melongrower, Mendors, Mephistophelian, MercyClaremont, Meweight, Mfu254, Mgaved, Michael Devore, Michael Keenan, Michaelas10, MikeWazowski, Mild Bill Hiccup, Millahnna, Miranche, Miremare, MisfitToys, MisterAngus,

Mistycreed-01, Mlaffs, Momojeng, Moncrief, Moni3, Montrealais, Moonriddengirl, Morgands1, Morven, Mosesroth, MosheZadka, Mothling, MrHen, MrJeff, Mrja84, Muchness, Musical Linguist, Musicpvm, Mwanner, Myosotis Scorpioides, Mythopoeic, Mythumbie, NP Chilla, Naddy, Naimah, Nakon, Nalvage, Naniwako, Nate Speed, Navalmagic, Negamary, NeilEvans, NellieBly, Nemissimo, NeoBatfreak, Neptunekh2, Nessyrenay, Netizen, Netoholic, Newt, Nights1stStar, Nightscream, Nik42, Nirame, NoisyJinx, Novangelis, NrDg, NuclearWarfare, Nymf, NymphadoraTonks, OLTL2002, Oddblob, Oded.yunger, Ohnoitsjamie, Ohsoh, Ojeffery, Old Soldier, OldEmpire, Oldwindybear, Oliver Pereira, Omnitrix17, Onlychild13, OompaHumpa, Orange Goblin, Orangemike, Orcatherelentless, Oscarthecat, Ostentatious, Otto4711, Ouishoebean, OverlordQ, OwenBlacker, PHDrillSergeant, PTSE, Pacific Coast Highway, Pacific1982, Painlord2k, Pak21, Palinode, Patronum02, Paul A, Paul730, Pax:Vobiscum, Paxomen, Pdb781, Peace454, Pearle, Pejhman, Pepsican, Percy Snoodle, Peregrine Fisher, Perisher1, Persian Poet Gal, Phil Boswell, Philosofool, Philwelch, Phorteetoo, Piano non troppo, Pigman, Pimpdice, Pinkadelica, Plange, Plastikspork, Plenk, Pne, Polymorp, Pop culture addict, Possum, Postdlf, Powergirl, Powqei, Pretty Green, Profoss, ProtoBuster, Proximawest, Prsgoddess187, Pseudovector, Pub14, Quadell, R.E. Freak, RG2, RGCorris, RJASE1, RL0919, RW Dutton, RWFanMS, Radaar, Raichu, RalfiParpa, Rama's Arrow, Randywilliams1975, Raven4x4x, RayvnEQ, Razzor3k, Rd232, Reactiontime, Reaper Eternal, Red Alien, RedWolf, Redeagle688, Redsignal, Redvers, Regemet, Reign of Toads, ReinforcedReinforcements, Reisio, Remco47, Renamename, Retodon8, RevRagnarok, Revmachine21, Rhindle The Red, Rhobite, Ribbons687, Rich Farmbrough, RickK, Ricky540, Ripper01234, Rishoutfield, Riverbend, Rjanag, Rjwilmsi, Rmky87, Robbie Mac, Robbiemasters89, Robert Moore, RobertG, Rockingmule, Rocksteadyvybes, Ronhjones, Roo72, Rorschach88, Rosie and her bro pippin, Rossami, Rrius, Ruehlman, Runa27, Russell29, RussellMcKenzie, Ryulong, ST47, Saberwyn, Sadisticality, Sagefoole, Saifai, Salamurai, Sam Weber, Sarah, Sarillorn, Satchfan, SatyrTN, Satyrical lyrics, Saudade7, Saulisagenius, Scarecroe, Scarlet Lioness, Sceptre, SchfiftyThree, Schmiffy94, SchuminWeb, Sciurinæ, ScottyQuick, ScreenRighter, Scubbo, Scubster, Sdedeo, SeanWillard, Seaptown, Seatum, Seb Patrick, SexyBlondKid, Sfeldon, Shadowolf, Shanshu, She-who-must-not-be-named, ShelfSkewed, Shikinluv, Shimblue, Shizane, Shmuel, SiegfreidZ, Silarnon, Silver Edge, SiobhanHansa, Siradia, Six words, Sjscott80, Sky Captain, SkyWalker, Slaniel, Slanoue, Slowking Man, Slowmover, Smartjoe299, Smash, Smijes08, Sn0wflake, Sobnambulist, Son of lucas, Sonicwav, Sophadam, Sopranosmob781, Spanish lullaby, Speedway, Speedygonzalez44, Spellcast, SpencerJW, Spiritroomforsquares, Spolky, Spunking, Square87, Ss112, StAnselm, Stargirl345, Stephen, Stephenb, Stonesoup99, Suduser85, Sunray, Supernathan, Supperidiot, Susvolans, Svick, SycamoreCanyon, SydneyMcbeal, TAnthony, TabiCaroe, Tagishsimon, Tambourineman, Tamfang, Tapests, Tarwater, Tassedethe, Tbhotch, TeaDrinker, TeaganMago, Teers, Template namespace initialisation script, Tentu, Terrirodriguez, Tesseran, Texhnolyze, Thanos Lives, Tharpdevenport, Thatha, The Bearded One, The Cool Kat, The Fellowship of the Troll, The Fiddly Leprechaun, The Man in Question, The Real One Returns, The Singing Badger, The Utahraptor, The Wookieepedian, The wub, TheJackalFiles, TheLeopard, TheMaster, TheRealFennShysa, Thedemonhog, Themarcuscreature, Thenonnymouse, Thiseye, Thomas81, Thort2007, Three in the morning, Thumperward, Tide rolls, Tiewashere, TimBentley, Timo, Tjkphilosofe, Tntnnbltn, Tom harrison, Tom3112, TomPreuss, Tomandlu, Tombomp, Tony Sidaway, Tony1, TonyTheTiger, Topher1078, Tranquileye, Transcendentalstate, Treybien, Trimalchio, Triona, Triple J, Triviumrocker, Troynoles, Troyopula, Trödel, Ts jem, Tschel, Tsunamipanda05, Typhoon966, TyrS, UkPaolo, Ultraviolet scissor flame, Unconditionaloptimism, Unyoyega, Urbanempire, Utcursch, UtherSRG, Uucp, Valen8or, Vampireeat, Vampirolog, Vashti, Velibos, Vespertine27, Violetriga, VivianDarkbloom, Vote for jon, WJBscribe, WPjcm, Wackycavegirl, Wapcaplet, Washburnmav, Wavelength, Weinfelden, When.pancakes.fly, Wiccanways, Wikignome0530, Wikipelli, Will Pittenger, Winhunter, Wmahan, Woamaria, Wockstar, Wolf Deunan, Woodshed, Wordbuilder, WriterHound, Wsiegmund, Wwesean, Wwoods, X-xmanda123x-x, X201, XPeeple, XSuperAmyx, XXxMadDogGxXx, Xanucia, Xaosflux, Xardion, Xeworlebi, Xiner, Xinoph, Xtifr, Xxhippiekatxx, YOMHER, Yamamoto Ichiro, Yamara, Yjwong, Z-vap, Zanimum, Zeppocity, Zigger, Zoe, Zone46, Zonkman, Zythe, 212, Δ, ماني, 1885 anonymous edits

Miss Match *Source*: http://en.wikipedia.org/w/index.php?oldid=442125911 *Contributors*: 97198, AndrewHowse, BD2412, Bearcat, Bensin, Bovineboy2008, Carioca, Ceyockey, CoolKatt number 99999, Count Ringworm, Da-rb, Dollvalley, Domino2097, Dugwiki, Edinborgarstefan, Gidonb, Gottago, Hadal, Igiffin, Ilion2, Isotope23, JaGa, JamesAM, Jeffrake, Kman543210, Kâlî, LarRan, Lollomonkey1, MakeRocketGoNow, Matthew, NeilCrosby, Newpeeps, Pegship, Penguinwithin, Ppoi307, R'n'B, Rafaelsilba, SD6-Agent, SidP, SnapSnap, Superfreaky56, TAnthony, TMC1982, Tedder, TobyHung1234, TonyTheTiger, Toon05, TubularWorld, Warreed, WereSpielChequers, Woohookitty, YUL89YYZ, 63 anonymous edits

I Do (Lost) *Source*: http://en.wikipedia.org/w/index.php?oldid=464617875 *Contributors*: 97198, Abu-Dun, After Midnight, Animé Dan, Arasaka, Asyndeton, BenF1, Bennetton, Brazilianboy93, Butterboy, Cake and Biscuits, Cesarm, Charleca, ChazBeckett, Chensiyuan, Chris Stoj, Cooldude3240, Couchpotato1, Crazyman50000, David Gerard, DocNox, Dreamingchelx, Einbierbitte, Elb2000, Elonka, EpcotTL, Epinheiro, Everyoneandeveryone, Funkadillo, Geofth, Gmac360, Hede2000, Ifrit, Igordebraga, Ilampsurvivor5, Jack O'Lantern, Jackieboy87, Jaespinoza, Jeff schiller, Jimmy Bing, Jogers, Josiah Rowe, Jtrost, JustPhil, Kc12286, Kiraismyname, Ludde23, Lukegruenhagen, Lutton, Lynx13371989, Magioladitis, MarkSutton, Matthead, Matthew, Mild Bill Hiccup, Minderbinder, MindlessXD, Mistafeesh, Mthteh, Muhaidib, MusiKk, N73713, Necrothesp, Nerrolken, Nightscream, Noozgroop, PKtm, Patstuart, Pemilligan, Phoenix Song, Pnkrockr, Puppet125, RMHED, RattleandHum, Riana, Rich Farmbrough, Richard D. LeCour, Riverbend, Ruby2010, SadanYagci, Sceptre, SergeantBolt, Sfufan2005, ShadowUltra, Shikinluv, ShizuokaSensei, SigmaEpsilon, Slipperyweasel, T smitts, ThatPeskyCommoner, The Rambling Man, The monkeyhate, The x house, Thecheesykid, Tiggerjay, Tim!, Tone, Tree of Sephiroth, VaGuy1973, Waziferezueus, Zellin, Zzuuzz, 146 anonymous edits

Drive (TV series) *Source*: http://en.wikipedia.org/w/index.php?oldid=460131739 *Contributors*: A Man In Black, Alliterator, Alpha5099, Anarchist42, Anlome, Auntof6, Avenger1000, Axem Titanium, Ayudante, BaconLover, Bakilas, Bearcat, Bensin, Bigcurrens, Blueracer6, Bovineboy2008, Bovineone, CIS, CIreland, Carthaginienses, ChazBeckett, Chris Bulgin, Ckatz, Clintong, DL77, DTwirler, DWP17, Dancter, Danigro89, Debresser, Deliriousandlost, DenimForce2.0, Desmond Hobson, Divsilver, Doeville, Dreftymac, Drovethrughosts, Edward Hyena, Embryomystic, EoGuy, Error47, FLJuJitsu, Fourthords, Franko1212, GargoyleMT, Gipperfish, Guat6, HeelTaker, Hotwiki, Icantbeliveijoindwiki, Icseaturtles, Illyria05, IronGargoyle, IrrTJMc, Jappa88, Jason.cinema, JayDuck, Jgbell, Jiam123, Jtrost, Ken Gallager, Keyser Söze, King Bee, Kintetsubuffalo, Kippymon, Kirkoconnell, Kurtthegreat, Kâlî, Ladida, MADCastro2012, Mandarax, Matthew, Metropolitan90, Muchness, Nalvage, Napnet, Nightscream, Ohconfucius, Oren0, Otto4711, Pafcu, PatrikR, Paul A, Phil Boswell, Phil Urich, Phil56, Pookpook282, Ppntori, Ppoi307, Fspdcmobayf2, Qoddosh, QuasyBoy, Radaar, Readymade, Redl@nds597198, Renegade Replicant, Ribald, Ridingstar, RuM, Salocin, Shimmera, SidP, Silver Edge, Simsyboy, Sodaplayer, Solidedges, Sportsnut, Stismail, TMC1982, TTN, Teknomage, The Lake Effect, Thestorm115, Tjic, TonyTheTiger, Transcendentalstate, Tripwheel, TrisJ, Tronno, UnitedStatesian, Wael Mogherbi, Woohookitty, Wordbuilder, Xeworlebi, Xinoph, Xornok, Yankeesrj12, Zackandmax, Zzglenm, 337 anonymous edits

Robot Chicken *Source*: http://en.wikipedia.org/w/index.php?oldid=467141634 *Contributors*: 041744, 150omega, 17Drew, 21655, 2D, 5 albert square, A Man In Black, A Nobody, A p3rson, A635882, A895, AMCKen, Aaron5436, Abb615, Abby 94, Abc518, Abcqwerty, Abeg92, Academic Challenger, Acalamari, Acroterion, Adamshuck, Adel Hosny, Afkatk, Aitias, Akendall, Alanhwiki, Alansohn, AllGloryToTheHypnotoad, AllTeam, Allah Gold, Amatulic, AndrewHowse, Andrewpmk, Andrewrost3241981, Andyjsmith, Anger22, Angrynight, Anonymous Cow, Aodonnell, Apparition11, Archanamiya, Archer3, Arden, Aresmo, Arknascar44, ArmadilloFromHell, Arxiloxos, Asanchez1572, Asdcaszx, AshTFrankFurter2, Astronautics, Athaler, Atomsmasher86, Autocracy, Avant Guard, Awwill, B jojo s, BITB, Bacteria, BakerBaker, Bart133, Barticus88, Bbarringer, Bearcat, Beeblebrox5000, Before My Ken, BenFrantzDale, Bentogoa, Bihco, Billycuts, Black Kat, Blackskyshining, Blueboy24, Bluesonicno1, Bobo192, Bonanza 228, Bongwarrior, Bovineboy2008, Brandeks, Brandon5485, Brequinda, BrianGriffin-FG, Brideshead, Bruce Marlin, Bryn161718, Bsadowski1, Bubbabobdingdong, Burn N Flare, Burnside65, Butmonkey3, C6541, CF84, CIreland, CTZMSC3, CWY2190, Cactus.man, Calaschysm, Caleson, Calmer Waters, Calvin 1998, Calvinballing, Camw, Can't sleep, clown will eat me, Canley, CapitalLetterBeginning, Cburnett, Celsio, Ceyockey, Chacha82, Chachilongbow, ChaosNil, Chaztheweird, Chelydramat, Chenchaoyi, ChesterG, Cheststory, Childhoodtrauma, Chitoboy, Chocl8215, Chrislk02, Chuck sample, Chukpeev, Citicat, Ckatz, Cleanmateroomba, Comicbook30, Conny, Coppertwig, Cordless Larry, Courcelles, CovertAffairs22, CptnFeelings, Cracker017, Cracklepappy, CrazyChemGuy, Crazymandude, Crazysane, Cremepuff222, Cryingnoise, CyberSkull, Cyborgrooster, CzarB, Czolgolz, DARTH SIDIOUS 2, DFTBAustin, DMacks, DTwirler, DanDare, DanGer JuLeS, Danigro89, Danrivera, Danspalding, Danucciguzman, Daredevil1284, DarkRunaway, Darkplinkoid, Dartpaw86, Dave420, Davemadoch, David Gerard, Davidthe wierdo, Dcoetzee, Dcseven, DeadEyeArrow, Debresser, Defender miz, Der kenner, DerHexer, Derek wp11, Desno, Deuxhero, Dex1337, Dhp1080, DiScOrD tHe LuNaTiC, DiamondMonster, Didsomesaybananas?*goesbananas*, Digicaveman, Dina, Discospinster, Djej1, Djerito, Dkaufman1, Doc Strange, Docta247, Doikhoikin, Domvio, Donaldo1997, Donmccullen, Doodoobutter, DorkBerger61, DougGold, Douglasr007, Dp76764, Draccon136, DragonLord1975, DragosteaDinTei, Drmies, Druss666uk, Duz, Dvavasour, Dxco, Dycedarg, DynSkeet, EEMIV, ESkog, Eaolson, Ebyabe, Ed g2s, EdGl, Eddie Guerrero 1967-2005, Edgarde, Edward321, Elijya, EoGuy, Epbr123, Erck, EricErik, EricField, Eridani, Esanchez7587, Esn, Ethridge3, Evans-t, Evil Monkey, Excirial, Extransit, Faithlessphil, Falcon8765, Falcon9x5, Family Guy Guy, Farazparsa, Farosdaughter, Feldmanpr, Fhb3, Figure, Fiquem, Firedemon727, Fishhead2100, Flami72, FlareNUKE, Flubeca, Flyguy649, Forteblast, Fourthhorseman, Fractyl, Frontside, Full Shunyata, Furrykef, Fuzheado, GOB, Gaius Cornelius, Gambit32, Gamefreeak202, GatorBucGuy, GawdHatesNoobs, Gdo01, Gettingitrightthefirsttime, Gilliam, Gizmoboy123, Gjd001, Glacialinferno, Glen, Glenn L, Gogo Dodo, Gondomwing, Gpomeroy95, GraemeL, Grandmasterka, Grapesoda22, GreenRunner0, Gregfitzy, Guitarboy1179, Guitarherofan, Gzkn, H.sanat, Hairy Dude, HalfShadow, HamburgerRadio, HandThatFeeds, Harej, Harmonica, Hasek is the best, Hazzaslipknot56, Henryodell, Hermitage, Historylesson4nerds, Honeyflake, Hoponpop69, Husky, Huysman, Hyperhippy92, IAmRodyle, IDALGHAMTFPD, IainP, Ibanez RYM, Ihateaustin122, Ike9898, Imaginationac, Imdeanlabouty, Imhungry, ImperatorExercitus, IndulgentReader, InfamousPrince, Information006, InverseHypercube, Iokerapid, Irishguy, Isaac Witte, J'onn J'onzz, J.delanoy, JDDJS, JDspeeder1, JForget, JKPrivett, JNighthawk, JQF, Jackal Killer, JackalsIII, Jackol, Jacob5539, Jacoplane, Jagged, James McNally, JamesBWatson, Jameshmarshall, Jane-21, Jarl of Torvaldsland, Jasmeet 181, Jason.cinema, Jaylethal2008, Jbl1975, Jeanology, Jeff G., Jeff Silvers, Jerem43, Jesusisntracist, Jfiling, Jj98, Jkbena612, JoeHillen, JoeSmack, John20939, JohnTheCrow, JohnnyChicago, Jokeful Guy, Joltman, Jorophose, Josegmol, Json777, Juan Balboa, Juliancolton, Jusdafax, Just H, JustSomeRandomGuy32, Justvideo, K6plqr915nsd, KKIPPES, KMFDM Fan, KafeEman, Kaiser matias, Karam89, Kblahetka, Keaton, Keelsy Blystone, Keeperstud18, Keeves, Keithcurtis, Kenneth Hardeman, Kerrylionberry, Khanearl, Kicking222, Kid1412, King Shadeed, Kinu, KnightofNEE, KnowerofEverything, Koavf, Konczewski, Korikitsune0, KramarDanIkabu, Kusma, Kâlî, L Kensington, LF, LOL, LastMutant, LeaveSleaves, LedgendGamer, Lee Davis, Legionaireb, Leszek Jańczuk, Lietk12, Life of Riley, Lightdarkness, Little Mountain 5, Livvy13, Llort, Lochaber, Logan, LoganTheGeshrat, Londonsista, Lone Wolf21000, Lonelygstar, Looper5920, LuigiFan11, Luna Santin, M.mockan, MBisanz, MC10, MGlosenger, Macslacker, Mad mage 29, Magister Mathematicae, Majorclanger, Malber, Malice1987, Marasmusine, Marcg106, Marcus Brute, Marcus190, Mario777Zelda, Mario9285, Marioman12, Mark Lungo, MarkMarek, MarkSutton, Markeer, Martarius, Martin451, Master Bigode, Mathewignash, Mattjblythe, Mazu tsai, Mbinebri, Mboverload, Mbrstooge, Mcpusc, Mduser63, Meeples, MegastarLV, Merotoker1, Mgarvin9, Mike hayes, Mikecron, Mikeo, MikeyMouse10, Milonica, Minna Sora no Shita, MissusDe, Mistress Puff, Mm824, Montayxx1, Mr Bound, Mr. Vernon, MrOllie, Mrfeek, Mrschimpf, Mschel, Mullibok, Mushroom, Musicalmelodygirl, Myrrander, N.Flen, NAHID, Nate Speed, Naveregnide, NawlinWiki, Ncasci, Nciszdabest, Nehrams2020, Nemalki, Neo-scorpio, Neoforma, Nerrawllehctim, Nessinessa, Net 91, New Age Retro Hippie, Newton2, Nihiltres, Nikolaj Christensen, NintendoFan11, Noformation, NorthernThunder, Notaverygoodidea, NuclearWarfare, Nymf, Oatmeal batman, Obi-Wannabe Kenobi, Oda Mari, Officiallyover, OhYouDidn'tKnow, OlEnglish, Oobopshark, Oopxxp, Ost316, Otheus, Otto4711, OverlordQ, P. Skiddy, PHDrillSergeant, Pacific Coast Highway, Parallaxed, Paulralph, PeaceNT, Pennyforth, Perezsteven19, Pezwookiee, Phantomsteve, Philip Trueman, Phlegm Rooster, Phydend, Pi is yummy, Pikawil, Pinkadelica, Pistolwhip66, Plinkit, Pnkrockr, Poindexter Propellerhead, Pol430, Polarbearmania, Potiscool, PrettyMuchBryce, Professor Chaos, PsychoJosh, Puceron, Pulpculture, Pyfan, Quadratic, QuasyBoy, Quintote, Quoth, R.E. Freak, RJASE1, RJaguar3, RVDDP2501, Radarmight, RadicalBender, Raldonscale25, RaseaC, RealTNAFan, Rebochan, Redskull619, Res2216firestar, RevRagnarok, RevRaven, Rhindle The Red, Rich Farmbrough, Richard D. LeCour, Richmeister, RickoniX, Rj kwah, Rlk89, Rlloyd3,

Rod Munch, Ronhjones, Rrburke, Rror, Rsm99833, Rtkat3, Rutherfordjigsaw, Ryu Ematsu, Ryulong, Ryuukuro, SNS, Salamurai, Sales2007, SalvadorRodriguez, Sam Korn, Sammmttt, Sapph, SatCam, Satori Son, Savage1666, SaveYourself87, Sbpat21, Scanlan, ScorpSt, Seb nl, Seb96, Seishirou Sakurazuka, Sennap, Ser Amantio di Nicolao, Seymour nimblefarm, ShigityShank, Shin-Goji, Shoeofdeath, ShootinPutin109, Shot dog, Siawase, SigPig, Sinkhan, Sir Osis of Liver, Skaraoke, Skybunny, Slippered sleep, Slof, Sm8900, SmartGuy, Snaxe920, Snotplinkoid, Snowyguy10, SoSaysChappy, Sophus Bie, Sottolacqua, Souris2005, Spartan-James, Speciate, SpikeSpiegelLovesEdward, Splarka, Spongebobsqpants, Sputnikcccp, Ss112, StarScream1007, Starblind, Stardust8212, Starwars404, Starwind Amada, Static3d, StealthMantis, Steam5, Storm Rider, Strawmd, Sugar Bear, SunCreator, Superior1, Supersmashballs123, Sushix1, Sweepybum, Sweetness46, T smitts, TDK, TJDay, TJRC, TK Heffer, Tae1988, TaintedMustard, Tao of tyler, Tassedethe, Tayquan, Teles, TenPoundHammer, Tgunn2, ThaddeusJP, The Angriest Man Alive, The Cunctator, The Moose, The Rogue Penguin, The Thing That Should Not Be, The stuart, The wub, TheSimpsonsRocks, TheValentineBros, Theeyefulltower, Themasterofwiki, Thesis4Eva, Thestorm042, Thewbacca1989, Thingg, Thue, ThuranX, Thyking, Tide rolls, Tim1357, Tiptoety, Tongeman555, Tony Myers, TracyLinkEdnaVelmaPenny, TrafficHaze, Tregoweth, Treybien, Trogga, Tropical Cyclone Gato, Trunkalunk, Tsuite, Tumble, Twinsday, Ubergeekguy, Ukexpat, Ultraviolet scissor flame, UnqstnableTruth, VEO15, Varlaam, Veinor, ViCorp, VideoMasher3000, ViktorZ, Viridis, VsevolodKrolikov, WCityMike, WDavis1911, WLU, Waggers, WarthogDemon, WatchAndObserve, Waywardhorizons, Wearefree, Whateley23, Whatfg, Wiki alf, Wikideric, Wilhelm Screamer, William Avery, Willking1979, Willy, your mate, Wilt, Wknight94, Wl219, Worm That Turned, Wrightaway, Wrjones18, X omega, Xanzzibar, Xasz, Xcentaur, Xenophrenic, Yamamoto Ichiro, Yettie0711, Ymp11, Yonskii, Your Next Kid, Yourgayloversteve, Z10x, ZJP, ZX81, Zack11492, Zackg323, Zander 93, Zidane4028, Zoe, Zone46, 2110 anonymous edits

List of *Desperate Housewives* characters *Source*: http://en.wikipedia.org/w/index.php?oldid=466494306 *Contributors*: 01lander, 97198, AJR, ARaleksandr, Adam061, AdamDeanHall, Akcvtt, Alan16, Alex250P, Alexisfan07, Allstarecho, Alyssa kat13, Andeefrye, Antonrojo, Arch dude, Arjoccolenty, ArkansasTraveler, Atif.t2, Augustus the Pony, Avoided, Ayse796842, BD2412, BYMAstudent, Bac261, Backstab13, Bas2804, Batmanand, Benn knight, Betreibungsverfahren, Bill2006, Billcosby, Billy Baker, Black Falcon, Bmfred, Bobo192, Boyfriend, Bratsche, Brown Shoes22, Bunny-chan, BurienBomber, CMWrestlemaniaPunkCharlie, CanadianCaesar, CapitalR, Captain-n00dle, CarbonCopy, Carlson288, Ccacsmss, Chadoz, Cheater1908, Chris the speller, ChrisCork, Closedmouth, Cmdrjameson, Commander Keane, CommonsDelinker, Cosmo.vnz, Courcelles, Craigy144, CrazyLegsKC, Cuahl, Cvhcsee, Cymru.lass, Cyzor, D.M.N., DabMachine, Dale Arnett, Dan777, DanMan22, Darreyl102, David Gerard, Davykid15, Ddawn23, Depressio1992, Desertsunrise84, Desperate101, Dev920, Dhadsb, Dhmom, DignityWithLove, Dindo94, Djistus, Dmlandfair, Dr.Luke.sc, DrBat, Dureo, Dyslexic agnostic, E-Kartoffel, EEMM1991, ESkog, Echuck215, Eclecticology, Edenc1, Edgegrrl, Elliethomson, Emersoni, EoGuy, Ettattetta, Euchiasmus, Evil Monkey, Fairfieldfencer, Ferpow, Finny1987, Firestorm566, For An Angel, Fortunato luigi, Gaius Cornelius, Germano pt, Grunny, GuinanTheCat, Gurch, GusF, Hadseys, Hallihalli, Hammersoft, Hebrides, Hollerama, Hypernick1980, Iamstrong, Ian Pitchford, Ifthisisaustin, Ike1000, Ilion2, Infinare, Iridescent, Irradescent45, Jack Cox, JayKeaton, Jbl1975, Jcsrauch, Jeffrey Mall, Jenica, Jermister3, John4272, Judo112, Jujubean55, JzG, KAMiKAZOW, Katieh5584, Kevyn82, Kimera757, Kitty16700, Koavf, Konczewski, Krrishmanhattan, Krushia, Kuru, Leflyman, Leonard^Bloom, Lightmouse, LilHelpa, Lindum, Lindzanne, Lipmingarolnick, Little Mountain 5, Liveweak, Longhair, Lord Opeth, LostHavoc, Love me 33, M-le-mot-dit, M42380, MER-C, Magioladitis, Maltmomma, Mandarax, Marcika, Matthew, Megfrey, Menasim, Michellekerchal, Michu1945, Midnight Critter, Mike R, Mikecron, Mild Bill Hiccup, Mms001, Moldy orange, Mosteiros, Movieguru2006, Mrsoffisa, Muhaidib, Mushroom, Myintermail, Mysic Slayer, NWill, NawlinWiki, Nemo24, Nil Einne, Noneofyourbusiness, Novice7, Ohcl, Omernos, OnTheCusp, OrangutanCurse, Originalsinner, Pacian, Pairadox, Patrickmgaddis, Pearle, Peterdjones, PigFlu Oink, Pjär80, Pmiize, Preston975, Princessbabyblue, PzzSchool, PzzSchoolRedux, PzzSchoolRules, Quentonamos, R'n'B, RHodnett, RSJThompson, Rah Baby, Rapsodie, Renaboss, Renaissancee, Repicanto, Retired username, Rettetast, Revan46, RhysandMe, Ridernyc, Rjwilmsi, Roadrunner3000, Robofish, Rockfang, Ron535251, RubyP, Rudi argento, ST47, Sam1012233, Scarce, Scoottscoott, ScottSteiner, SeanMack, Sfufan2005, Sherool, Sicaruma, Siemgi, Sillygostly, SirR2009, SkyWalker, Small5th, Sonic Shadow, Sparhelda, Steven Handoko, StoneOttL, Stormwhisper, Superannuated, Surtsicna, SusanLarson, TJRC, TRBP, Tabletop, The Giant Puffin, The Man in Question, The dark lord trombonator, Theshibboleth, Tiger888, Timeineurope, TimothyJacobson, Tombadevil, Tony Sidaway, Trampikey, Treskay21, Tsr neiva, TunaStreet, TutterMouse, Tvfanatic04, Tyghrufj, Tylerkarnes, Ulric1313, Urania3, Utahredrock, Vchimpanzee, VeiledAbyss, Venez111, Vontafeijos, WJBscribe, Wadems, Walsh221, We hope, WhisperToMe, Wiki Raja, Willsayshey, Wintonian, Wisterialaner19238, Xaphnir, Xiao-Mei27, Xoxwikixo, Yamla, Yellowstone County Girl, Yoursvivek, Zoltarpanaflex, Zythe, Δ, 1606 anonymous edits

Dr. Horrible's Sing-Along Blog *Source*: http://en.wikipedia.org/w/index.php?oldid=466980715 *Contributors*: (Turnip), -5-, A s williams, Advertisingman, Alliterator, Amdillae, Andropod, Angeldeb82, Aslam nathoo, Auntof6, Awakeandalive1, AySz88, Banyan, Baranjka, BassBone, Bearcat, Beef Dripping, Ben-Bopper, Benjiboi, Benstrider, Bighooley, BillC, Billbowery, Blowdart, Boomshadow, Bovineboy2008, Bradybd, Brandeks, Briansince1988, BrightStars1212, Bringa, Bucklehead, CABridges, CR85747, Calliopejen1, Cast, Catobleman, ChowRiit, Chunky Rice, CommonsDelinker, Conuly, Copysan, CraigB, Cyzor, DCEdwards1966, Daikiki, Dan337, Danbarnesdavies, Darkfrog24, Darrenhusted, Davidkevin, DeFaultRyan, Deafgeek, Diannaa, Discospinster, Dispenser, Djungelurban, Doniago, Dotvision, Dracothejuggler, Drat, Dravecky, Drbreznjev, Dreyesbo, Drmfreek, Drovethrughosts, Dubious Irony, EEMIV, EVula, Edward321, Eeekster, Einstein runner, Elendubs, Empath, Emperor, Emurphy42, Erik, Erp Erpington, EurekaLott, Explosionsnevermakeasound, F9gj329239j2j923gj, Fandraltastic, Flibolimay, Forteblast, Fourthords, Fratrep, Friendofwashoe, Frietjes, Frostie Jack, Fuddle, Gazongola, George Harrison 1963, Germayfa, GingyDude, Goer2u4, Gonzalo84, Goochelaar, Googleaseerch, Gordon Ecker, GrammarNSpellChecker, Hanzo66, Hbent, Hewinsj, Horselover Frost, Howcheng, Hqb, I'm Fixed Now, I Ran a Test!, Ice Cold Beer, Ilkali, Intothewoods29, IstvanWolf, Itai, Iuhkjhk87y678, JQF, JSagor1, JaffaCakeLover, Jarneaud, Jasonbres, Jc-S0CO, Jeandré du Toit, Jeffreymcmanus, Jherico, Jivecat, Joey-das-WBF, John of Reading, Josiah Rowe, Kanonkas, Kendal Ozzel, Kevinschmall, Kgagne, Kimberly dare, Kingdom2, Kitsunegami, Kizor, Koavf, Korbnep, Kotiwalo, Larry V, Lawikitejana, LeilaniLad, Lifesashow, Lightmouse, Loggie, LogicalFalafalcy, Looololllllololo, Lordalius, MCW07, Madcwa, Maratanos, Marblespire, Marcus Brute, Master Deusoma, Masterblooregard, MattGiuca, McGeddon, MearsMan, Meelar, MegaSloth, Mernen, MidgleyC, Millahnna, Mitchdynamite, Moncrief, Morda898, Mote, MrWhipple, MulRedux, Nalvage, Nearly famous writer, Nezu Chiza, Nights1stStar, NoseNuggets, Notacupcakebaker, Nothingofwater, NurseryRhyme, ObeseCactusFry, OldestManOnMySpace, Ost316, OtterSmith, Otto4711, Ouroan, Peabody80, PeeJay2K3, Personman, Philip Trueman, Pirkbubble, Ppoi307, Prestonmcconkie, Primal Zed, Prisonermonkeys, Psiphiorg, Q11, Qwerty Binary, RS Ren, Radicalbunny, RanmaSaotome, Rehevkor, RheingoldRiver, RiverRubicon, Rjwilmsi, Rlue, Robert K S, Ronhjones, Rror, Rushmore cadet, Salocin, Sammi.mcclain, ScribeX, Senator2029, Sephiroth BCR, Sergay, Sethant, ShadowlessClick, ShaleZero, Shmuel, Shsilver, Silverfish, Singingwolfboy, Siradia, Smiling Kevin, SnoKoneManiac, Sophieness01, Speer320, Spencer, SpikeJones, Stargirl7, Statalyzer, Steve, T-rex, Tamfang, Tanetris, The Doctor666, The Filmaker, The Man in Question, The Person Who Is Strange, The soapboxer, TheListUpdater, TheRealFennShysa, Thelb4, Thewriter006, ThunderPeel2001, Tiptoety, Tnxman307, Tom, Trivialist, TrumpetBflat, Ubernostrum, Ukexpat, Unless 68, Ursus Lapideus, Useight, Usobe, Uucp, Vegaswikian1, Vivarey, Warreed, WebMoose, Whedonite, WhiteDragon, Wolfdog, Wool Mintons, X77, Xeno, Xeworlebi, Xyzyxx, Yksin, Yuefairchild, Yukichigai, Zeke pbuh, Zero1328, Zorlin, Zwede, Zybthranger, Zythe, ÀrdRuadh21, 573 anonymous edits

James Gunn's PG Porn *Source*: http://en.wikipedia.org/w/index.php?oldid=466214909 *Contributors*: Blackehart, Carbidfischer, DMCer, Ezra802, Franko1212, Games Junn, HelloAnnyong, Hmains, Kuralyov, Legitimus, Mateinsixtynine, Muncadunc, Nightscream, Quitedeny, Searcher 1990, Thumperward, WikiKiwi, Yappy2bhere, 39 anonymous edits

Wonder Woman (film) *Source*: http://en.wikipedia.org/w/index.php?oldid=460363969 *Contributors*: -5-, Alansohn, Anabate, AnmaFinotera, Artemisboy, Cbing01, Chickenmonkey, CmdrClow, Cornprone, CzechOut, Dc20willsave, Dravecky, Drhorner, Dwanyewest, Emperor, Erik, Firestorm566, GoingBatty, Gripweed, Harrygorilla, J Greb, James IV, Jamesbanesmith, Kaijucole, Kchishol1970, Kollision, Leoni2, Letsgetgoing, Marcus Brute, Mike Castle, Millahnna, Mr.Grave, Mtminchi08, Nehrams2020, NeoBatfreak, Nightscream, Otto4711, Postdlf, Rich Farmbrough, Rjwilmsi, Rob.bastholm, Rtkat3, Scarecroe, Sesshomaru, Sir Cash, SkerrycruU2, Skier Dude, SkyWalker, SoWhy, TMC1982, ThuranX, Tinton5, WikHead, Wws1fan, Zero no Kamen, 153 anonymous edits

Castle (TV series) *Source*: http://en.wikipedia.org/w/index.php?oldid=466831289 *Contributors*: 1989 Rosie, AceNZ, Adacus12, AdamDeanHall, Adys, Alliicciiaaa, Allstarecho, Amy.hannahjones, Andrewlp1991, Andy M. Wang, AngelGraves13, Anime miz, AnonMoos, Aspects, Avythe, Badapro, Bailums810, Batman tas, Bbb23, Ben Ben, Ben76266, BilCat, Birkoff1, Bovineboy2008, Bradley0110, Bubbleoui, CaptainMorgan, Chris Chittleborough, Ckatz, CliffC, Cnorthfield2000, Colinj, Comicbook30, Coral Bay, Corinnethenerd, CovertAffairs22, Craig t moore, Cubs Fan, Cwgreece, D'oh!, D82, DC Fan 5, Dancter, Darkfrog24, Darrenhusted, Deliriousandlost, Djln, Dkchacha, DocWatson42, Dravecky, Drbreznjev, Drilnoth, Drmargi, Dsimms63, EDavidd, EZio, Ejfetters, EnDaLeCoMpLeX, Erianna, Erud, Evans1982, Ewshannon, Ezzkmo, Falcon8765, Fan70, Fetchcomms, Flapjack727, Fourthords, FrenchIsAwesome, FromtheWordsofBR, Goodacre, GordyHowell, Happy5214, Heracles31, Horkana, HrZ, ICM and proud, IanCleverly, JCDenton2052, JDamanWP, JQF, Jack Merridew, Jak86, Jakub Vrána, JamesMLane, Jarrod Baniqued, JavierMC, Jc-S0CO, JediRogue, Jerems45, Jerzy, Jjj055, JobSmee, Joepontello, Jollyroger666, JordoCo, KalliopePL, Karunyans, Kbdank71, Kedawa, Keycoke, Khalismatic, Khaosworks, Knownalias, Kuru, Kutulu, Kyle Nin, Lapis, Lazyvee, Ldubs48, Liam74656, Logical Fuzz, Londo06, Lore87, Loyolagrad, MJBurrage, MacMog, Madchester, Madcwa, Magioladitis, Mariahg8, MarvelMarble, Master Deusoma, Millahnna, Mnaumanm, Moosiy, MorrieD, Mr. Chicago, MrDolomite, Mrinvader, Musikmaker1024, Nachoha, NarSakSasLee, Nev9600, Nickyyavellian, Night Fight, Nithya.14, Obi-WanKenobi-2005, PFrisbie, Panagiotis82, Pat Berry, PeRiDoTs13, Pedro João, Pejorative.majeure, PenguinPenguinPenguin, Philip Trueman, PietrotheSecond, Pizzamaniac09, Plamenpr, Postdlf, QuasyBoy, Quitesometime, RP459, Ravenswing, Richardm9, Ricky81682, Rjwilmsi, Robksnyder, Ron whisky, Rontrigger, RoyalPains11, Rrius, Ruchirmehta89, Rusted AutoParts, S11-73-3-33, SMcCandlish, SQGibbon, Saberwyn, Salamurai, Sandraa95, Satama, Sea Island Circle, Sergay, Serienfan2010, Shads2, ShakataGaNai, ShaleZero, ShaunMcNamee, Shawn15151515, Shinoda.manu, SigKauffman, Sjones23, Sketchmoose, Sky Captain, SoWhy, Spitfire, Sppy1, Sue Kastle, Surat123, Swinglifeawayjb, Tetulun, The Letter J, The Man in Question, TheRedPenOfDoom, Therealdavo2, Thinker001, Tommyjgrimshaw, Tomrtn, Tony1, TonyTheTiger, Tonyfuchs1019, Torritorri, Tubesurfer, URunICon, V2Blast, Valistar, Varlaam, VioletShadow, Vtorok, Warreed, Warregubbi, Wasbeer, Websurfer246, Wfaulk, Wiethoofd, Xavier J, Xeworlebi, Xfpisher, Ylee, Zakaie, Zythe, Σ, Του Δημήτρη, 589 anonymous edits

Green Lantern: Emerald Knights *Source*: http://en.wikipedia.org/w/index.php?oldid=459068217 *Contributors*: -5-, CalmCalamity, Danleary25, Darklionheart728, Drgyen, Dwanyewest, GoingBatty, Gyozilla, Hellboy42, Kchishol1970, Maddox, Omeganian, OscarFercho, Peppage, Polisher of Cobwebs, R'n'B, Rtkat3, Sochwa, Super Steve, TriiipleThreat, 26 anonymous edits

Image Sources, Licenses and Contributors

File:Nathan Fillion at Serenity premiere 1.jpg *Source*: http://en.wikipedia.org/w/index.php?title=File:Nathan_Fillion_at_Serenity_premiere_1.jpg *License*: Creative Commons Attribution 2.0 *Contributors*: Flickr user RavenU

File:Star full.svg *Source*: http://en.wikipedia.org/w/index.php?title=File:Star_full.svg *License*: Public Domain *Contributors*: User:Conti from the original images by User:RedHotHeat

File:Star empty.svg *Source*: http://en.wikipedia.org/w/index.php?title=File:Star_empty.svg *License*: Creative Commons Attribution-Sharealike 2.5 *Contributors*: User:Conti from the original images by User:RedHotHeat

File:Star half.svg *Source*: http://en.wikipedia.org/w/index.php?title=File:Star_half.svg *License*: Creative Commons Attribution-Sharealike 2.5 *Contributors*: User:Conti

File:Firefly cast 2005 flanvention 1.jpg *Source*: http://en.wikipedia.org/w/index.php?title=File:Firefly_cast_2005_flanvention_1.jpg *License*: Creative Commons Attribution 2.0 *Contributors*: Flickr user RavenU

File:Joss Whedon premiere.jpg *Source*: http://en.wikipedia.org/w/index.php?title=File:Joss_Whedon_premiere.jpg *License*: Creative Commons Attribution-Sharealike 2.0 *Contributors*: Jo Anslow

File:Leary, Busch, Limon, Strong, Lenk on panel.jpg *Source*: http://en.wikipedia.org/w/index.php?title=File:Leary,_Busch,_Limon,_Strong,_Lenk_on_panel.jpg *License*: Creative Commons Attribution 2.0 *Contributors*: Flickr user RavenU

File:Anthony Stewart Head and Nicholas Brendon Aug 2004.jpg *Source*: http://en.wikipedia.org/w/index.php?title=File:Anthony_Stewart_Head_and_Nicholas_Brendon_Aug_2004.jpg *License*: Creative Commons Attribution 2.0 *Contributors*: Flickr user RavenU

File:Nathan_Fillion_at_Serenity_premiere_1.jpg *Source*: http://en.wikipedia.org/w/index.php?title=File:Nathan_Fillion_at_Serenity_premiere_1.jpg *License*: Creative Commons Attribution 2.0 *Contributors*: Flickr user RavenU

Image:Dr Horribles Singalong Blog cast.jpg *Source*: http://en.wikipedia.org/w/index.php?title=File:Dr_Horribles_Singalong_Blog_cast.jpg *License*: Creative Commons Attribution-Sharealike 2.0 *Contributors*: watchwithkristin

License

Creative Commons Attribution-Share Alike 3.0 Unported
//creativecommons.org/licenses/by-sa/3.0/

CPSIA information can be obtained at www.ICGtesting.com
Printed in the USA
LVOW092228270313

326441LV00001B/20/P